VISUAL DISPLAY TERMINALS

A manual covering
ERGONOMICS
WORKPLACE DESIGN
HEALTH AND SAFETY
TASK ORGANIZATION

A. Cakir, *Technical University of Berlin, F.R.G.*

D. J. Hart, *IFRA, F.R.G.*

T. F. M. Stewart, *University of Loughborough*

Originally published by
The Inca-Fiej Research Association, Darmstadt

A Wiley–Interscience Publication

JOHN WILEY & SONS
Chichester · New York · Brisbane · Toronto

Originally published by the Inca-Fiej Research Association 1979

Copyright © 1980 by John Wiley & Sons Ltd
All rights reserved

British Library Cataloguing in Publication Data:

Cakir, A
  Visual display terminals.
  1. Information display systems
  I. Title   II. Hart, D. J.   III. Stewart, T. F. M.
  001.6'443   TK7882.16   80–40070

ISBN 0 471 27793 2

Printed in The Federal Republic of Germany

Foreword

It is surprising, perhaps, that in spite of the vast amount of literature that has been devoted to the subject of computers, very little has been written about the people who use them and the conditions under which they are used. And yet computers have been a familiar part of the working lives of many people, in many different walks of life for many years. Even if we, ourselves, do not come into direct contact with computers at work, the contact is most certainly there in one or other aspect of our daily lives, for example in the processing of wages and salaries, bank statements, the electricity bill, travel reservations etc.

At work, a computer can help take away the tedium and monotony involved in many types of repetitive data processing job. From an occupational standpoint, this is a respectable goal and one worth striving for. But in solving one type of problem, others are created. The ability of a computer to handle large volumes of data, quickly and reliably, usually means that fewer people are required to do a given amount of work. In some cases, the problem can be offset to some extent by the fact that these same facilities also make it possible to increase the amount or extend the types of work being performed. The fact remains, however, that computers are creating an increasingly more pressing social problem as far as employment is concerned.

In the early days of computers, the popular image of the computer as a giant adding machine, capable of performing simple arithmetic computations - albeit lots of them and very quickly was not too far from the truth. The computer of today, however, is a more sophisticated machine, both in construction and in terms of programming level. Computer designers have reaped a rich reward from the development of electronics technology. The development of computer terminals has improved the possibility and efficiency of access to computers. Storage and processing capacity has become cheaper, and this, coupled with the evolution of more advanced programming software, has meant that the computer of today can seek its applications in a much broader range of industrial environments than its less sophisticated and more cumbersome predecessors.

This spreading out of the umbrella of computer applications is bringing computers into contact with occupations associated with progressively higher levels of skill. From an industrial point of view, therefore, it is not only the number of people whose employment may be affected by the use of computers that is of concern, it is also the skill categories of those affected. Nowhere, perhaps, is this more apparent than in the printing industry.

Whilst it is not the object of this book to consider the social problems of computer technology, it is against this background that any book of this kind is written. The newspaper industry is currently in the frontline of computerisation. This helps to explain why it is that the initiative for a study of this kind should come from an industry that is not generally known to be in the frontline of technical research.

To many people, the prospect of working with computers and visual display terminals is a source of anxiety. For some, these anxieties stem from the fear of job insecurity and the prospect of redundancy. For many, however, anxieties have also arisen from a fear that working with a visual display terminal - the outpost of a central computer - might pose some form of health or safety risk. Within the past two years, this has been the subject of considerable debate. And in spite of a great deal of research effort, the information which has hitherto been available has been largely uncoordinated and too sparse in many aspects to put this subject into practical perspective.

To help bridge these gaps in knowledge, the International Research Association for Newspaper Technology, IFRA, brought together two of Europe's leading authorities in the fields of man-computer interaction, computer ergonomics and human science in an attempt to analyse the ergonomic, health and safety aspects of working with VDTs. The outcome of this work is presented in this book, and it is with some pride that IFRA extends its thanks to the professors and staff of the Institut fuer Arbeitswissenschaft, University of Berlin, F.R.G., and the Department of Human Sciences, University of Loughborough in England for their guidance and unfailing efforts throughout the duration of this two-year exercise. In undertaking this investigation, the authors have sought the help of a great many people in medical centres, occupational health and safety authorities, universities, trade unions and in a wide variety of industries. Not least, the authors have also sought the help of a great many VDT and computer users. So many have contributed information and comment during this investigation that it would be impossible to credit them individually, but to these, the authors would like to express their most sincere thanks.

In dealing with a subject as broad and as complicated as this, an attempt has been made to write this book in such a way that those most concerned, i.e. the user him- or herself, can read, easily understand and apply the information that is given. It is an inescapable fact that the involvement of the people who will eventually be working with a computer system in its conception and installation is one of the best and most desirable safeguards against future dissatisfaction and complaints of discomfort. But however desirable this form of participation may be, the fact remains that neither those designing a system nor those using it can actively contribute without some fundament of knowledge. It is with this spirit in mind that this work has been undertaken, and it is with the same spirit that IFRA, and the authors of this book, sincerely hope to have contributed in some way by shedding light onto a subject that is of major concern to many computer and VDT users.

Contents

Preface

The main purpose of this report is to provide the designers, planners and users of computer systems with the most recent ergonomics knowledge relevant to the design and selection of VDTs and VDT workplaces. This knowledge has been derived from a large number of experiments and field studies conducted by the present authors and many others in recent years. Detailed references have not been given in the text because the primary aim of this report is to be useful and practical rather than academic. However, the bibliography lists the sources used and readers interested in greater detail on particular points are recommended to consult the original reports or articles.

Report Structure

This report covers five major areas. The first chapter starts with a basic description of *how a VDT works* and this is followed by a discussion of *the VDT as a systems component*. The second chapter deals with the basics of *light and vision* that is necessary if the reader is to fully appreciate the subsequent sections.

Chapter three covers the *ergonomics of VDTs* in some detail starting with displays and display legibility and ending with the ergonomics of keyboards. However, many of the ergonomic problems of working with VDTs stem more from the workplace and working environment in which they are used rather than from the equipment itself. Chapter four therefore discusses various aspects of *VDT workplaces* and covers such environmental issues as lighting, heating, air conditioning and so on.

Both chapters three and four contain considerable detail in the text. So in order to facilitate the easy use of the specific recommendations they contain, these are repeated in checklist form at the end of each chapter. The final chapter reviews the various issues raised in the earlier chapters in terms of their effects on the operator's health.

The report ends with a series of appendices which support the text in the five principal chapters. These present the main checklist, a glossary and bibliography, and a description of an eye test procedure for VDT operators.

How to Read the Report

The report has been written in such a way that each chapter can be regarded as more or less complete. As a result, there is a certain degree of overlap between chapters to ensure that any reader who is referring only to one chapter does not overlook important or relevant material in other sections. However one theme which emerges from the report is that there are many interacting factors involved in the design, selection and implementation of VDTs and VDT based systems. It is important to keep in mind, therefore, that interpreting the recommendations which are made in this report may involve considerable skill and compromise in specific applications. Indeed, in order to make the best use of the report, it is first necessary to consider the role of ergonomics in the design process.

The ergonomist has two main objectives when designing equipment, workplaces or working environments. The first is to ensure the well-being and safety of the operator at work, the second is to make the best use of his or her skills and abilities.

When the first objective is ignored or overlooked, the penalties may be high for both the individual and employer. Unsafe, dangerous and uncomfortable work should not only be avoided on humanitarian grounds but is increasingly being restricted by legislation in several countries.

The results of ignoring the second objective, however, are usually less dramatic although they may well be as costly in the longer term. Failure to design in such a way that the skills, abilities and other characteristics of the operator are adequately matched results in excessive errors, delays and other decrements in job performance. This, in itself, can also have an adverse effect on operator well-being. For example, a poor match between the facilities of a computer system - in terms of both hardware and software - and the needs of the individual user can be a major source of job dissatisfaction in addition to being counterproductive.

There are nevertheless times when 'unergonomic' design may not result in any apparent decrease in task performance. In situations such as these, however, the individual may over-compensate for the non-functional or relatively unusable features of the equipment by expending more mental or physical effort. This effort is not without cost and can also result in problems for the individual or his employer in the longer term. Performance measures such as speed or error rate, therefore, need to be supplemented with some measures of effort or strain in order to satisfactorily evaluate equipment or workplaces.

Ergonomic Requirements for VDTs

It follows from the above that the primary ergonomic requirements for a VDT is that it should perform all of the functions required of it. Whether or not these requirements are met not only depends on the design of the equipment and of the workplace, but also on the characteristics of the user(s) and of the tasks they wish to perform.

There is therefore no single 'ergonomic' VDT. Different user and task combinations generate their own specific requirements.

In the newspaper industry, there are a number of applications which may be relatively similar in different newspapers and which could, therefore, give rise to common requirements, e.g. for an editing or page make-up terminal. The exact ergonomic requirements of such a terminal will, however, depend on the detailed nature of the user's task. For this reason, this study on the human aspects of working with VDTs has placed great emphasis on the analysis of the various types of VDT task. It is hoped that specific detailed ergonomic requirements may eventually be established for the various types of VDT use. In the meantime, however, there are a number of general requirements which can be laid down and these form the basis of this report.

The relative importance of some of these requirements depends, of course, upon the user's task so that care should be taken in interpreting the recommendations which are presented in the master checklist. The 'best' answer is not always as obvious as it might seem.

Where general recommendations apply, the preferred answer is indicated in the master checklist. In many cases, however, the preferred answer will depend on the specific task in question so that only those involved with the planning of the system and the users themselves can decide which is the preferred answer. For example, although illegible characters are undesirable for any task, this may not always be a critical factor, e.g. when reading the display screen is only an infrequent checking activity. If, on the other hand, reading the display is the predominant task activity, e.g. proofreading, good display legibility is an essential attribute of the VDT. In addition, not all facilities are necessary or even useful for all types of VDT task, so the VDT with the greatest number of facilities is certainly not the most obvious choice for any given task.

A second problem with such a checklist is that there are a wide range of individual differences among people in their psychological as well as their physical characteristics. There are many situations in which it makes sense to design to suit an 'average' man. Unfortunately, there are also situations where the result is that neither one end of the range nor the other receives satisfactory attention. Thus, for example, when the preferred seating height, the preferred screen format or the preferred workplace layout is indicated, this refers to the best compromise for a large proportion, typically 95%, of all users. This may be quite different from the height, format or layout that best meets the need of the individual user.

Designing for 95% of the population means that 1 person in every 20 would find it difficult or impossible to work with the equipment or at the workplace. In practice, this may be too great a proportion to ignore, especially for systems which are to be used by a large number of persons. In applying recommendations such as those contained in this report, therefore, there must remain a certain degree of flexibility. It is for this reason that, where possible, many of the recommendations are formulated in such a way as to indicate ranges of values and characteristics that will permit the user to design or have designed for him a working environment that is best matched to his or her own needs. It cannot be emphasised too strongly that it is the comfort and well-being of the real individual and not that of a 'hypothetical' average that is the primary concern of the ergonomist and of this report.

Chapter 1

VDT BASICS

Foreword

Ever since the development of the CRT display terminal a little more than a decade ago, visual display terminals or *VDTs* and the computer systems of which they are an integral part have found widespread application in graphics, text and data processing. The VDT as an input/output device permits access to and dialogue with the storage and processing capacity of a central computer. In other words, the VDT is a part of a *system* comprising a computer, terminals and other items of peripheral equipment, e.g. printers, controllers and a software package that is specifically tailored to the processing requirements of the application in question.

The key to the attractiveness of computer systems in most business applications is the rapid processing speed and large volume of data that can be handled. But in addition to the purely functional characteristics of the system, it is also necessary to consider the VDT as a piece of equipment to be used by persons with a wide range of physical characteristics, skills and individual or task-related requirements. This combination of *functional* and *human* requirements represents the ergonomic criteria which are among the most important factors to be considered in designing and specifying a computer system.

This chapter is intended to provide an introduction to the design and operational characteristics of VDTs and VDT systems and, in particular, to the role of the two main elements of the VDT - the display screen and keyboard. Much of this information provides a necessary background with which to better understand the subsequent chapters which deal with the ergonomic requirements of VDTs and VDT workplaces.

HOW A VDT WORKS

A visual display terminal or *VDT* comprises four main elements:

- a display screen
- a keyboard
- an electronics circuit pack and
- a power supply

These elements are usually housed in a metal, fibreglass or plastic housing and cooled by means of a motor-driven fan to keep the internal temperature within safe operating limits.

For most practical purposes, the user of a VDT need know little more than this in order to be able to use the VDT in his or her work. In order to determine and understand which of the design and operating features of the VDT and VDT system are important from the human point of view, however, some basic understanding is required of how a VDT works and the role that is played by the VDT as a systems component.

The following sections are intended to provide a background with which to better understand the subsequent chapters in this report which deal more specifically with the ergonomic requirements of VDT design and operation. This chapter is not intended as a comprehensive text on the complexities of VDT design[1] but rather to serve as a guide to better understanding the importance of the two main constructional elements of the VDT - the display screen and the keyboard. These are the points of human contact with the VDT itself and with the system of which the VDT is part.

THE CRT DISPLAY

The cathode ray tube or *CRT* is the basic element around which most display terminals are constructed.

A cathode ray tube is basically an evacuated glass tube with an electron 'gun' at one end and a screen which is coated with a light emitting material called a phosphor at the other.

When a high electrical voltage - usually between 12 and 15 kilovolts - is supplied to the electron gun, a stream of electrons is produced. This stream is then focussed into a narrow beam by an electronic 'lens' system, and the beam is directed to any desired position on the face of the screen by means of either an electrostatic or electromagnetic deflection arrangement located in or around the 'neck' of the tube, see Figure 1.2.

When the beam strikes the phosphor coating on the inner surface of the screen, the electrons interact with the phosphor material in such a way as to cause the grains of phosphor at each point of impact to glow. To the observer viewing the face of the screen, each point of impact appears as a bright spot of light.

The interaction between the electron beam and the screen phosphor, and the method of character generation together play a crucial role in determining the visual quality of the display. Not all applications are equally demanding in this respect but for most text processing applications the need for a high quality display is of great importance.

---

1. The subject of VDT design and operation has been dealt with in several recent publications and special mention can be made of 'Visual display units - and their application', edited by D.Grover and published by IPC Science and Technology Press Limited, London, 1976 on behalf of the British Computer Society.

(a)

(b)

Monitor   Character refresh card   Microprocessor card   System timing card   Memory card

Display console chassis   Power supplies   Circuit card chassis (Space for 7 cards)

Figure 1.1 A typical text-processing VDT showing: (a) the external view, (b) the major internal components.

There are two basic types of CRT:

- *Refreshed CRTs* in which the image must be continually refreshed in order to present a stable, flicker-free image to the operator and

- *Storage CRTs* with the ability to maintain the image on the screen without the need for continuous regeneration.

The CRTs which are used in text processing VDTs are usually of the refreshed type. They are very similar, and in many cases identical, to those used in domestic television receivers. CRTs of this type lend themselves more readily to interactive operations such as text editing and correction.

Storage tubes on the other hand are more widely used for the display of graphic information e.g. charts, line pictures, etc., because of their high level of image stability and resolution. However, VDTs of this type have hitherto been less suited for text processing applications for basically three reasons:

- more energy is required to activate the image than with refreshed CRTs,

- the display image is usually less bright than on refreshed CRT displays, and

- once the image has been written, it is usually necessary to erase the entire display if any part of the display must be altered.

In spite of these disadvantages, however, storage tube technology is progressing rapidly - particularly in providing the facility for selective erasure by means of more sophisticated software and by the use of storage mesh techniques. CRTs of this kind are particularly well suited for certain types of layout work, page make-up etc.

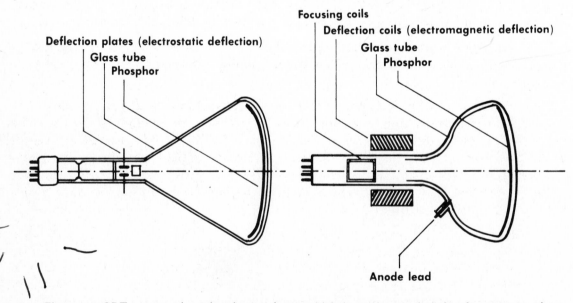

Figure 1.2 CRT construction: the electron beam which is used to 'write' the characters on the display screen is controlled by either (a) an electrostatic or (b) electromagnetic deflection system.

The following sections, however, are concerned only with refreshed types of CRT display.

Beam scanning

The scanning control circuitry sweeps the electron beam across the entire usable surface of the CRT screen in a series of regularly spaced horizontal or vertical lines called *scan lines*. The character images are then written on the face of the screen by switching the beam 'on' and 'off' as it travels through its scanning pattern.

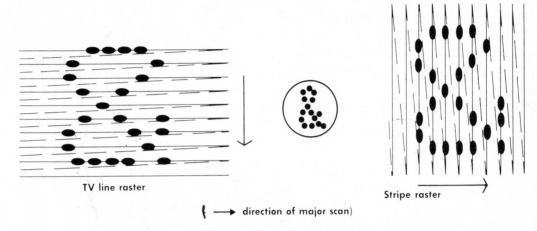

TV line raster

(⟶ direction of major scan)

Stripe raster

Figure 1.3 Building up a character by (a) horizontal or (b) vertical slicing and dot matrix assembly. (Inset: normal appearance) Ref. G.19

With few exceptions, the motion of the electron beam in text processing CRT displays follows the same type of *raster scan* that is used in conventional television receivers. For this reason, the raster scan is often referred to as a *TV raster*.

An alternative technique, but one which is used less frequently that the conventional TV-raster, is to scan the face of the CRT in a series of vertical stripes. This type of beam scanning, which is illustrated in Figure 1.3(b), is usually referred to as a *stripe raster*.

More complicated arrangements are used only in VDTs on which it is required to display different character sizes or on which graphic information is to be displayed together with text.

The number of scan lines is one of the factors that determines the resolution of the display. Generally speaking, the more scan lines which are available, the finer the resolution of the character shapes. CRTs designed for the U.S.A. use 525 scan lines across the tube whereas 600 lines are used in European CRTs. It should be noted, however, that the number of lines is constant, regardless of the size of the CRT. Thus the lines on a 24 inch (60,96 cm) tube, for example, are spaced twice as far apart as the lines on a 12 inch (30,48 cm) tube.

The characteristics of the phosphor and the resolution of the character shapes together determine the time required to display a single line of text. This, and the number of character lines on the display, then governs the time required to generate a full display. In the case of large capacity displays, this poses a problem to the VDT designer because it becomes increasingly more difficult to maintain an adequate refresh rate without sacrificing display resolution.

To help overcome this problem, VDT manufacturers can modify the conventional TV raster scan in one of two ways, i.e. by *interlaced raster scanning* or by *skipping*, see Figure 1.4.

When interlaced raster scanning is used, alternate lines only are refreshed in each pass. To the observer, this produces the visual effect of a faster refresh rate than is actually the case.

The skipping technique is based on a different principle. In this case the true refresh rate is maintained by scanning only along those lines which determine the vertical extent of the character images. Using this technique, the scan is advanced or 'skipped' to successive blocks of lines which make up succeeding character rows.

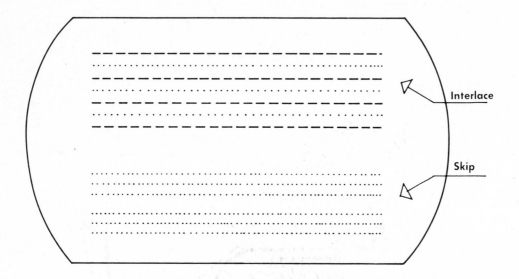

Figure 1.4 (a) 'Interlace' and (b) 'skip' techniques of preventing screen flicker. With interlaced raster scanning alternate lines are refreshed on consecutive fields. Using the skip technique only those lines which determine the vertical extent of the character image are refreshed. Ref G.19

Distortion control

The beam which writes the image on the face of the CRT is focussed and deflected so that its horizontal and vertical strokes form a circular arc. The 'focal point' of the writing beam is then at a fixed radius from the point of deflection. Since the surface of the screen is relatively flat, however, the focal plane of the writing beam is not the same as the plane of the display screen, see Figure 1.5. In fact, the two planes intersect, with the result that if no corrections were applied, the image shapes would appear fuzzy and distorted everywhere on the display screen except at those points where the focal plane of the beam and the plane of the display screen coincide.

In the case of a 110° CRT, the distance from the point of deflection to the corners of the screen is about 40% greater than the distance from the source to the centre of the display. For a 90° CRT, the difference is only about 10%, see Figure 1.6.

The different radii of curvature of the focal plane of the beam and the CRT screen also gives rise to other types of distortion that must be corrected to produce a good image.

For example, without corrective circuitry, a line drawn across the face of the screen would appear to bow in an arc, the effect being greatest along the edges of the screen. This type of distortion is known as *pin-cushion* or *barrel distortion*. Similarly, the curvature of the screen can produce an optical effect whereby the character images in the centre of the screen appear to be larger than those at the edges. This type of distortion is termed *cigar distortion*.

To overcome these types of distortion, the motion of the electron beam must be suitably modified and the writing area of the display must be centered so as to avoid writing the characters too close to the edges of the screen.

Generally speaking, these types of distortion increase and become more difficult to control as the length of the CRT decreases. The use of a longer CRT, i.e. with a smaller angle of deflection of the writing beam, makes it easier to correct against image distortion, but at the same time increases the depth of the terminal.

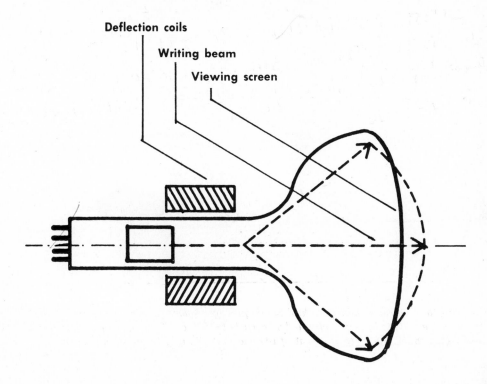

Figure 1.5 Because the phosphor surface of the CRT is relatively flat and the focal point of the writing beam is at a fixed radius from the point of deflection, the character images tend to become defocussed as the beam sweeps across the screen.

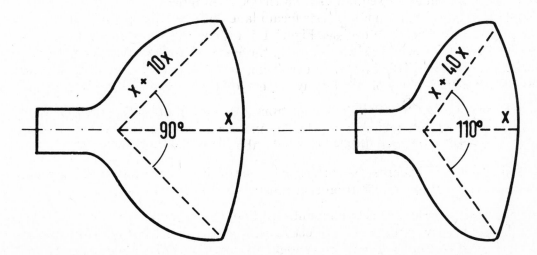

Figure 1.6 Distortion caused by defocussing of the writing beam is less marked in the case of (a) a $90°$ CRT to (b) a $110°$ CRT because of the relatively smaller distance from the source to the centre of the screen. Ref. R.18

The phosphor

The light-emitting coating which is applied on the inside surface of the CRT screen is called the *phosphor*. These types of material are crystalline compounds - usually sulphides or fluorides - which fluoresce when struck by a beam of electrons and phosphoresce when the excitation is removed.

By convention, screen phosphors are designated by a 'P' number, e.g. P4, P11, and there are many phosphor types which are available to the VDT designer, although their suitability for specific applications varies. In the case of alphanumeric displays, the most important factors which govern the choice of the phosphor are:

- the *grain* of the phosphor
- the light emitting *efficiency* of the phosphor
- the colour or *chromaticity* of the emitted light, and
- the decay rate or *persistence* of the phosphor

Grain

The visual quality of the character images in the display depends primarily on the resolution of the individual dots or strokes which depict the shape of the characters. This resolution depends on the particle size or *grain* of the phosphor coating. In addition, the dot spacing, the width of each character image and hence the number of characters that can be displayed in each line is directly proportional to the dot size.

To produce a sharp and well-defined image, the dots must be equally small, round and sharp, i.e. free from blurring, and this requires the use of a phosphor with a fine, uniform grain. Too coarse a grain produces a less well-defined or fuzzy image and increases the risk of dot overlap and elongation during scanning.

Phosphor efficiency

Not all of the electron beam energy is converted into light energy by the phosphor. In fact, the light emitting *efficiency* of the phosphor seldom exceeds about 20%, see Figure 1.7, the remaining energy being converted into heat.

The excess heat energy must be dissipated as effectively as possible in order to prevent local overheating or *burn* of the phosphor.

The *burn resistance* of the phosphor is an important phosphor characteristic because this has a significant effect on the operational life of the CRT. For this reason, all phosphors which are used in text processing VDTs fall into the 'highly burn resistant' or 'moderately burn resistant' categories.

Phosphor	Light output (lm/W)	Phosphor efficiency (%)
P1	520	6
P4	285	
P7	230 .. 285 .. 370	
P11	140	21
P31	425 .. 350	
P39	515	

Figure 1.7 Luminous efficiency and light emission for some typical phosphors. By courtesy of JEDEC and Telefunken.

Colour

The colour of the light which is emitted by the phosphor is another important consideration when selecting the screen phosphor.

Phosphor	Colour	λ_{max} (nm)	Coordinates in the CIE colour triangle	
			x	y
P1	Yellowish-green	525	0.218	0.712
P4	White	460/560	0.270	0.300
P7	Yellowish-green	555	0.357	0.537
	Violet-blue	440	0.151	0.032
P11	Blue	460	0.139	0.148
P31	Green	520	0.193 . . 0.226	0.420 . . 0.528
P39	Yellowish-green	520	0.223	0.698

Figure 1.8 Wavelengths of maximum luminous radiation and colour positions of some typical CRT phosphors. By courtesy of JEDEC and Telefunken.

The apparent colour of the display is the result of the effect of the eye in integrating the various wavelengths of light generated by the phosphor. These colours are never pure, and the *chromaticity* of several commonly-used VDT phosphors are shown in the CIE colour triangle in Figure 1.9.

There are two important considerations when selecting a colour for a CRT display image:

- ease of focus
- the ability of the display to provide colour contrast

Under certain conditions, the colour sensitivity of the eye should also be considered, particularly when the display is to be used under low levels of ambient lighting. In most office applications, however, such very low lighting levels are rarely encountered and the ability of the operator to focus easily is of greater importance.

Nevertheless, the normal light-adapted eye is most sensitive to the light in the green part of the spectrum with a slight shift towards the blue end of the spectrum as the overall level of illumination diminishes, e.g. at night or in a darkened room.

For this reason, it is often recommended that the colour of the characters on the display should preferably fall in the green-yellow part of the spectrum. In practice, however, the consideration of colour is secondary to the need for adequate contrast and display clarity to ensure ease of readability. For this reason, the choice of colour is more a matter of personal preference than of scientific decree.

Persistence, refresh rate

As soon as a character is projected onto the CRT screen, it begins to fade at a rate which depends on the *persistence* of the screen phosphor. In order to keep the image visible on the screen, it must be continually regenerated or refreshed. If the image is not refreshed sufficiently frequently, the display will appear to blink or 'flicker' and this is not only distracting, it can impose a strain on the eyes of the operator.

The *refresh rate* of a CRT phosphor is the frequency with which each point on the surface of the CRT is re-illuminated by the electron beam as it sweeps through the raster. The rate at which it is necessary to refresh the display in order to avoid perception of the flicker depends upon the persistence of the phosphor, i.e. how long it remains illuminated after the electron beam has excited it.

The persistence of CRT phosphors falls into three categories, i.e. short, medium and long persistence. Although the distinctions are to some extent arbitrary, persistence can be described in terms of the *time constant* of the phosphor which is the time required for the luminous intensity to drop to about 1/e or 37% of its initial value. For short

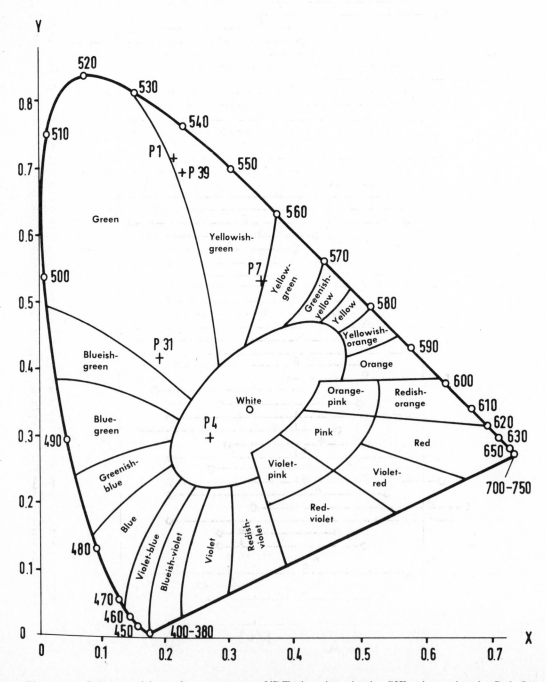

Figure 1.9 Colour positions of some common VDT phosphors in the CIE colour triangle. Ref. C.2

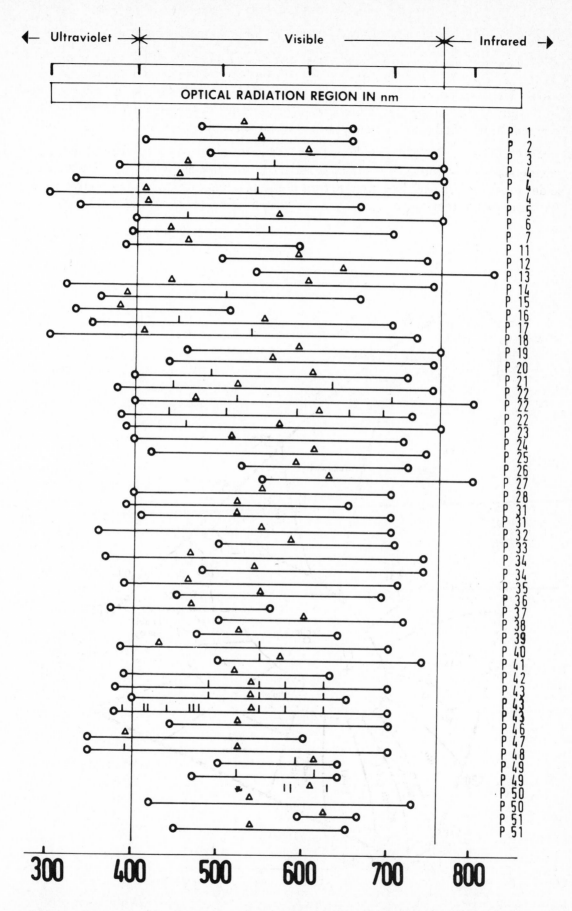

Figure 1.10 Estimated spectral energy distribution characteristics of CRT phosphors. Ref. M.31

persistence phosphors, the period of phosphorescence usually does not exceed about 1 millisecond. Medium persistence phosphors do not phosphoresce for more than about 2 seconds whilst long persistence phosphors may phosphoresce for several minutes.

Provided that the display presents a static image - as in the case of alphanumeric VDTs - use is generally made of short to medium persistence phosphors. Television receivers, on the other hand, use only short persistence phosphors since the motion of the image on the screen would otherwise result in blurring.

In principle, there are three ways of ensuring that the image is flicker-free:

- by coating the screen with a long persistence phosphor and using a low refresh rate
- by using a short or medium persistence phosphor and relying on a high refresh rate - of the order 50-60 Hz
- by making use of an interlaced or skipped raster, usually in combination with a medium persistence phosphor.

The persistences of the screen phosphors which are most commonly used in text processing VDTs are summarised in Figure 1.11.

The persistence values refer to the time required for an image to decay to a given fraction of its initial light intensity. The 10% and 1% levels are often selected for reference purposes, with the former taken as the minimum discernable brightness in high ambient lighting and the latter as the approximate limit in dimly lit surroundings.

In considering the relative merits of short and long persistence phosphors there is, however, another factor which should be borne in mind. In order to produce the same average character brightness, short persistence phosphors must be energised to a higher peak brightness than long persistence phosphors. Consequently, the light intensity varies over a much wider range with the result that whilst these types of phosphor can give a sharp and stable image, the image tends to appear less sharp than is the case when long persistence phosphors are used.

For reasons such as these, higher refresh rates using short to medium persistence phosphors are normally used in text processing CRTs, and the refresh memory is synchronised with the mains frequency - 50 Hz in Europe, 60 Hz in the U.S.A.

Phsophor	Chromaticity		Persistence	
	Fluorescence	Phosphorescence	10% (s)	1% (s)
P1	Yellowish-green	Yellowish-green	24×10^{-3}	
P4	White	White	22×10^{-3} 60×10^{-3}	150×10^{-3} 470×10^{-3}
P7	Violet-blue	Yellowish-green	$46 .. 60 \times 10^{-6}$ $0,4 .. 3$	300×10^{-6} 3
P11	Blue	Blue	$35 .. 50 \times 10^{-6}$	
P31	Green	Green	35×10^{-6}	250×10^{-6}
P39	Yellowish-green	Yellowish-green	150×10^{-3}	

Figure 1.11 Persistence and chromaticity of some screen phosphors commonly used in text-processing VDTs. By courtesy of JEDEC and Telefunken.

Character generation

For alphanumeric displays, there are basically four methods by which the character images can be generated on the screen:

> •*facsimile generation* in which a master 'copy' of the character set is scanned by a scanning raster to produce information which can be simultaneously copied - or 'facsimiled' - on the screen by the display raster.
>
> •*stroke generation* in which the shape of the character is formed by a series of connected line segments or 'strokes'.
>
> •*lissajous generation* in which the shape of the individual characters is built up by inter-connected segments of electronically-generated curves known as lissajous curves, and
>
> •*dot matrix generation* in which the shape of the character image is defined by an appropriate series of dots in a given rectangular pattern.

Facsimile generation

Prior to the development of the electronic data store which permits storage of the character shape information in digital form, the technique of facsimile generation was widely used in visual display equipment. Using this technique, the character shapes were stored in analogue form on a mask which was built into a cathode ray tube. Once a character was selected at the keyboard, the character set mask was scanned by the 'reading beam" and the output was used to control the movement of the "writing beam" in the display screen cathode ray tube.

Stroke generation

Using the technique of stroke generation, the character shapes are composed of sequences of straight-line segments or 'strokes'.

The individual character stroke coordinates are digitally stored in the character generator logic together with an appropriate beam intensity control signal. The character image is formed on the display screen by a succession of horizontal, vertical and diagonal movements of the electron beam. Usually, only the required number and sequence of strokes for any given character image are addressed in which case the beam intensity signal is kept at a fixed value, although this is not necessarily the case. It is also possible to sequence through all of the possible stroke movements, intensifying only those which are required. In this case, the electron beam is switched 'on' and 'off' as directed by the character shape and beam intensity information in the data store.

Each character image occupies a rectangle or cell, the size of which is determined by the height and width of the character. Some degree of character rounding at the corners can be achieved with the help of integrators in the beam deflection circuitry. To achieve a uniform character brightness, the intensity of the electron beam is usually increased for longer strokes. In addition, the application of a 'jitter' signal can be used to increase the character line width to improve character legibility.

Lissajous generation

In Lissajous generation, the character shapes are composed of sequences of curved and straight-line segments which are synthesised electronically. As in the case of stroke generation, the start and end coordinates of all the strokes for each character are digitally stored in the character generator logic. This information also controls the switching of the electron beam 'on' and 'off' as the image is traced on the display.

A somewhat simpler version of Lissajous generation can be obtained by combining straight-line segments with circular quadrants.

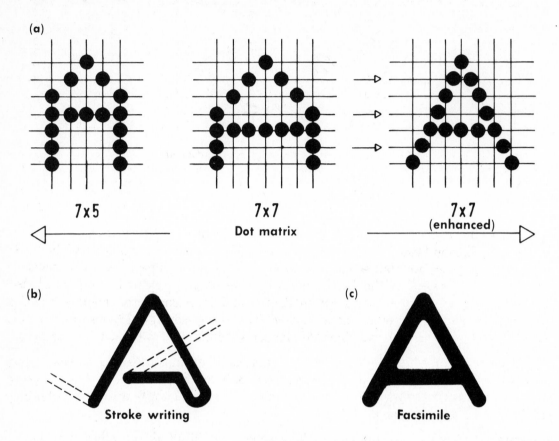

Figure 1.12 The character images are usually built up (a) by a series of dots in a so-called dot matrix, (b) by a series of strokes or (c) by a facsimile representation of the character. Ref. G.19

Dot matrix generation

Dot matrix character generation is the technique which is most commonly used for text processing VDTs using the raster scanning principle.

By this method, the required dot positions for each character are stored in a *dot matrix memory* which is incorporated in the refresh store and coupled to the scanning system of the CRT. Depending upon which character is selected at the keyboard, the required dot information is retrieved from the refresh store and is used to control the brightness of the electron beam. The sequence of dots thus generated builds up the character shape on the screen.

Each character is defined by a selected set of dots from a rectangular matrix of dots as the electron beam scans through its raster pattern. The resolution of the matrix is defined by the number of horizontal and vertical dots (in that order) which determine the maximum possible horizontal and vertical extents of the character image, e.g. 5 x 7, 7 x 9 etc.

In general a 5 x 7 matrix is adequate for displaying capital letters and numerals but is usually considered to be the bare minimum requirement for combined upper and lower case displays. The reason for this becomes apparent when lower case letters with descenders are reproduced in the display, see Figure 1.13.

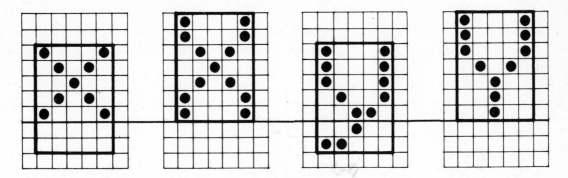

Figure 1.13 Upper and lower case Xs and Ys displayed in a 5 x 7 dot matrix. The total area occupied on the screen by each character is actually 7 positions wide by 10 deep, but the character design must be confined to the 5 x 7 area indicated by the heavy box. Note that the lower case character is displaced two positions below the base line.

The basic character image may still be contained in the 5 x 7 matrix, but in order to maintain a common base line, the matrix must be displaced two lines below the baseline in order to accommodate the descender. This, in effect, creates a 5 x 9 matrix of which the upper seven or the lower seven can be used for capitals and lower case descenders respectively. Allowing for inter-line and inter-character spacing, the cell within which the character image is formed is actually seven positions wide by ten positions deep even though the character image is confined to the basic 5 x 7 matrix.

To provide for a more efficient use of the raster and to avoid confusion between certain numerals, upper case and lower case letters, e.g. B, 8, m, w, preference is usually given to more dense dot matrices and matrix densities of 7 x 9 and above are most commonly used in text editing displays.

To further improve the shape and hence the readability of the characters in the matrix, various techniques have been devised for *enhancing* the character images, see Figure 1.14.

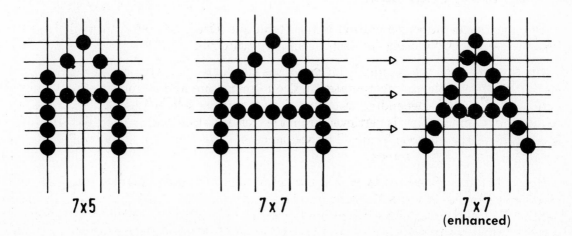

7x5   7 x 7   7 x 7
                                     (enhanced)

Figure 1.14 The appearance of the character images can be improved by displacing some of the horizontal dots in the matrix by a distance equal to half of the dot separation. This is called half-shift character enhancement. Ref. G.19

A commonly-used technique is the so-called *half-shift* enhancement or character rounding, the effect of which is to horizontally displace some of the dots in the matrix through a distance equal to half the dot separation either to the right or left as required. The effect is most noticeable in the shape of capital letters and numerals which take on a more natural proportion. Other, equally simple and inexpensive techniques include dot stretching or elongation.

Generally speaking, character definition improves as the density of the dot matrix increases, but until recently, preference for the 5 x 7 matrix was governed by economic necessity to conserve the amount of capacity required to store the dot information for each character image. Only recently have the costs of data storage come down to a level where the use of more dense character matrices is economically viable.

THE KEYBOARD

The keyboard of a text processing VDT usually comprises three, and sometimes four, groups or *sets* of keys, see Figure 1.15:

- the *alphanumeric* or main keyset,
- the *function keyset* including the shift, lock and editing function keys,
- a *cursor control keyset* including the tab and space bar, and
- perhaps an *auxiliary numeric keyset*.

In addition, a series of *indicator lights* is often mounted on the keyboard. These lights are used to indicate the operational status of the terminal, e.g. ON/OFF, SEND/RECEIVE. These lights and other controls may also be situated alongside the display screen.

Figure 1.15 A typical complex VDT keyboard layout. By courtesy of Atex.

The alphanumeric keyset

The *alphanumeric keyset* provides the means for entering text and numerical data, and the basic layout and function of this keyset is usually identical to the familiar typewriter layout, see Figure 1.16.

The basic set comprises 26 upper and lower case characters, 10 numerals and a number of special symbols, e.g. &,!,?,% etc.

Minor differences, both in the number of character and symbol keys and in the layout of the main keyset may be necessary depending upon

- the occurrence of accented letters (the English language is one of the few European languages that has no accented characters in its alphabet),
- national preferences for the siting of certain letters in the keyset, e.g. the QWERTZ layout which is used in the German-speaking countries and the AWERTY layout used in France,
- provision for a special arrangement or duplication of the numeric keypad, usually for applications which involve large volumes of numerical data entry, and
- provision for particular application-related symbols.

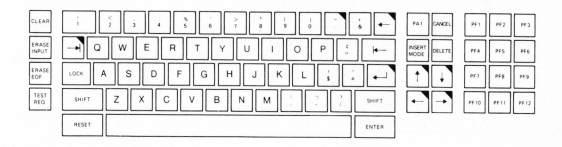

Figure 1.16 The QWERTY alphanumeric keyboard. By courtesy of IBM.

Auxiliary numeric keyset

For certain types of application, particularly those requiring rapid entry of large amounts of purely numerical information, a separate or *auxiliary* numeric keypad is provided in addition to the numeric keys in the central alphanumeric block. Where such

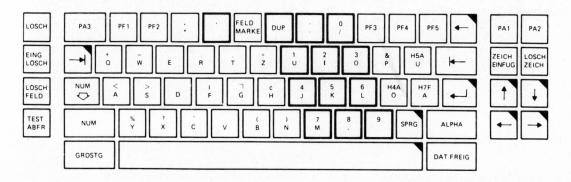

Figure 1.17 The QWERTZ layout used in German-speaking countries (without function keys). In this particular layout the numeric keys are incorporated within the alpha keyset. By courtesy of IBM.

a facility is provided, the keys are generally laid out in an adding machine cluster which is usually located to the right of the main keyset, see Figure 1.18.

In the simplest arrangement, the numeric pad operates in precisely the same way as the numeric keys in the main alphanumeric keyset except that it is not affected by the shift keys.

Figure 1.18 A VDT keyboard with an auxiliary numeric keypad with the keys arranged in adding machine layout. By courtesy of Chromos.

In more sophisticated terminals, on the other hand, functions can also be assigned to some or all of the auxilliary numeric keys, see Figure 1.19. Depending upon the intelligence of the terminal, these functions may represent assigned editing functions, e.g. insert, delete, search, or user assignable functions, e.g. for multiple character sets which at a single keystroke can be called to the display or transmitted.

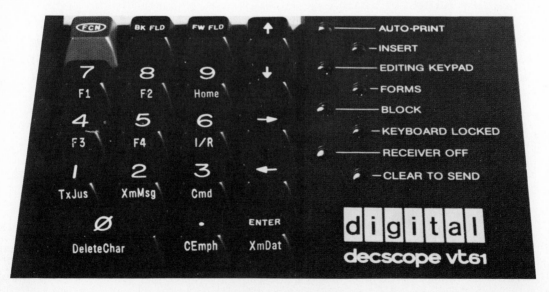

Figure 1.19 In more sophisticated terminals the auxiliary numeric keypad can be used to provide special functions accessed by a shift key. By courtesy of DEC.

Function keyset

The function keys provide for four types of command:

- operating or mode commands, e.g. shift, tab, lock, scroll, etc., that enable the operator to change from one mode of entry or command to another, e.g. lower case to upper case shift, special function access etc.,

- editing commands, e.g. insert, delete, etc., some of which may be hardwired into the terminal and some of which may be user programmable,

- communication and typesetting commands, e.g. SEND, PRINT, etc., which establish a link between the VDT and the central processor, the terminal controller or some other output device such as a line printer, and

- user programmable instructions which may be accessed via the function keyset or an auxiliary numeric keypad in combination with a shift or super-shift command. These keys generate character codes that are identified by the user's own programme. In their simplest form these keys can be used to enter blocks of frequently recurring characters, e.g. names, thereby reducing the number of required keystrokes. If more sophisticated programmes are used, the special function keys can be used to perform more complex editing functions e.g. search/replace.

Cursor control keys

The *cursor* is a position indicator and is displayed on the screen as a special symbol, usually as an underline marker or block, which might also blink so as to easily attract the attention of the operator. The cursor control keys are usually located in a separate block which is usually positioned on one side of the main keyset.

The basic cursor controls include:

MOVE -   separate keys are provided to direct the movement of the cursor to the left, right, up, down, to the beginning of the first line (home top) or the beginning of the bottom line (home bottom).

TAB -   moves the cursor to the desired tab stop

RETURN -   which moves the cursor to the first character position on the next line

LINE FEED -   which moves the cursor to the same position on the next line.

From the keystroke to the screen

The sets of displayable characters i.e. the alphanumeric and special symbol sets, are stored in coded form in the character generator logic. In order that the system can respond by displaying the correct symbol on command from the keyboard, each key must be connected with the character generator logic and the signal which is transmitted from the keystroke must be compatible with the display coding in the character store, see Figure 1.20.

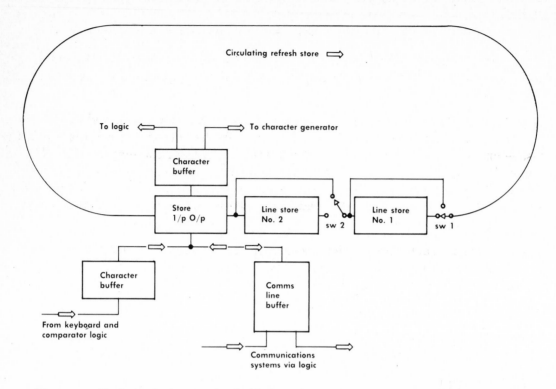

Figure 1.20 Typical refresh store showing logic and control characteristics. Ref. G.19

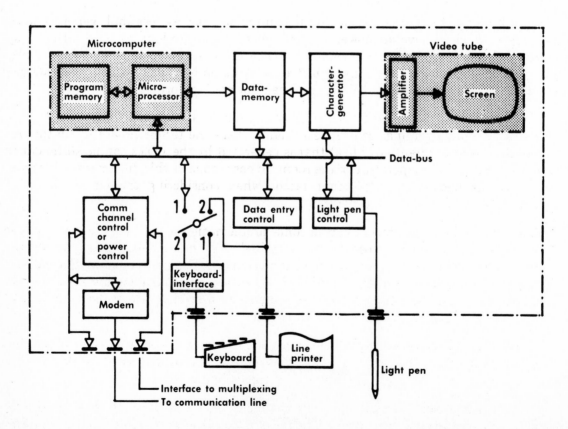

Figure 1.21 Schematic block diagram of a typical VDT showing the principal stages between the keystroke and the display of information on the screen.

Most text editing and composition VDTs are designed according to one of the two internationally standardised data codes, the ASCII or ISO 7-bit code or the EBCDIC 8-bit code. The ISO code has a total of 128 combinations of which 32 are reserved for control codes. The 8-bit EBCDIC code has 256 combinations.

The *control* codes differ from the display symbol codes in that they are (usually) non-displayable and are used to identify certain basic command functions e.g. new line, shift and tab instructions.

In most text editing applications, the message is preceded and followed by a series of 'head and tail' codes which may be used to identify the author, the destination of the message and to provide indicators for the 'start' and 'end' of the message. In addition, some of the control codes, e.g. the 'new line' instructions, will be hidden in the body of the text. These codes have to be recognised, interpreted and acted upon and, depending upon the code, a 'decision' has to be made as to whether or not the code in question must be stored with the text.

For this reason, each signal which is generated at the keyboard first passes through a *comparator* which instructs the character generator as to whether the incoming command is a character or control code.

OTHER CONSIDERATIONS

VDT cooling

Like all items of electrical or electronic equipment, display terminals generate heat. Depending upon the overall power requirements of the terminal, i.e. the cathode ray tube and the control circuitry, the amount of heat that is generated by a VDT is usually in the range 100-400 Watts. This compares with ca 35-50 Watts from a conventional electric typewriter and ca 100 Watts from each person at work.

This quantity of heat is sufficient to raise the temperature inside the cabinet of the terminal. In multi-terminal centres, especially where the terminals are in continuous operation, the total quantity of heat that is generated by the VDTs can be sufficient to noticeably raise the temperature of the room. In cases such as this, heat generation from the terminals becomes a significant factor when considering the air conditioning requirements of the terminal centre.

This type of heat generation can become problematic for two reasons. Firstly, the temperature environment close to the terminal may become less pleasant for the operator even if the overall room temperature is not significantly increased. Secondly, if the internal temperature of the terminal is increased without adequate provision for removing the heat, the temperature may increase to a level at which the reliability of some of the electronics components is threatened.

To overcome these types of problem, most VDTs are equipped with a fan to provide air circulation within the terminal cabinet which is also provided with ventilation slits to permit the free flow of air into and out of the cabinet.

From the users' point of view, adequate cooling of the terminal is of course a desirable feature. But if cooling is provided by means of a fan, it is worthwhile bearing in mind some of the noise and air flow problems which have arisen in practice. These problems are considered in more detail in a later section.

Voltage stability

The stability of the electrical power supply is an important factor as regards the security of both the computer, the terminals and other items of equipment in the system, and the information which is stored within the system.

Mains power supply, i.e. power taken directly from the national supply grid, is not as constant as is commonly supposed. This is particularly true in areas with a concentration of heavy industry and where the loading on the mains grid is both high and likely to change significantly throughout the day and night. Variations in loading at the central power station result in 'slow' changes in the supply voltage, and voltage fluctuations within ± 10% of the nominal rated mains voltage are not uncommon.

In addition to slow variations of supply voltage, more spontaneous types of voltage fluctuation can occur whenever large and high power consuming items of equipment such as motors, generators, lifts, air conditioning systems, etc., are switched on and off. These surges of power demand and release on the supply line can cause sudden and large voltage peaks or drops although usually of very short duration. Most items of equipment in a computer system are so designed that power surges and slow changes of supply voltage and frequency can be tolerated but there are limits beyond which the possibility that the system may be adversely affected can no longer be ignored. At the functional level, the most obvious consequence of unstable voltage supply is shut-down of the system due to the activation of the central or local fuses. But in some cases, this may not be sufficient protection against damage to some of the more sensitive electrical components in which case re-start may not be possible without some form of maintenance effort. In any case, repeated fluctuations of supply voltage over a prolonged period may shorten the life of certain components thus reducing the overall availability of the system and increasing the maintenance requirement.

At the operational level, instability of the power supply can also affect the storage and display of information in the system. Voltage overloads, for example, can have the effect of erasing or modifying the information which is held in storage or which is displayed on the VDT screens. Less drastic, but to the operator nonetheless disturbing effects can also occur with respect to the display screen. Short duration power surges, e.g. when the air conditioning system is switched on and off, may cause the information on the display to 'jump'. In addition, if the supply voltage is consistently below the nominal voltage rating of the VDT, the signal strength may be insufficient to ensure a static image. In this case, the image might appear to oscillate or 'jitter'. This is usually visible to the operator who might, albeit incorrectly, attribute the effect to flicker caused by the refreshing of the image.

It is usually recommended that the power supply to a computer system is dedicated in the sense that the system power supply should not be shared by other items of equipment or systems, particularly if they have a high and variable power requirement.

Uninterruptable power supplies

For the most part, the user of a computer system has little or no possibility to control the causes of instability in the power supply to the system. So, depending upon the actual condition of the local mains supply, and the likelihood and consequences of system errors due to voltage instability, it may be necessary to consider the installation of a power stabilizing system.

One solution is the installation of an *uninterruptable power supply* or *UPS*. In a typical UPS installation, the mains power is first converted to a d.c. signal which is used to drive a solid state a.c. generator, the output from which is very much more uniform, usually within ± 0,5%, than the original supply voltage.

There are three basic types of UPS, i.e static, rotary and hybrid types. A static UPS incorporates an inverter which generates a.c. power to the system from a d.c. line which is supplied by the rectifier charger and batteries. The batteries are floated on the d.c. line so that, if the input power is disrupted, the inverter will continue to provide power for the system for a period which depends upon the capacity of the batteries. If a reserve generator is provided, the required capacity of the batteries would, of course, be reduced.

The decision to provide a UPS when installing a system is essentially an economic one in which the costs of system malfunction, part replacement, maintenance and downtime due to power supply instability must be weighed against the capital and running costs of the UPS. The results of such a calculation will inevitably vary from one application to another but, as a general rule, if system malfunction may have critical consequences, provision of a UPS is recommended.

Implosion safeguards

Because the VDT operator sits in close proximity to the VDT, it is usual to provide some form of protection for the viewer in the event of CRT breakage. Under normal office circumstances, the risks of such a failure are slight but in some working environments where VDTs have been introduced, e.g. factory floor environments, the risks of damage and breakage may be higher.

The CRTs which are used in VDT equipment are usually of the so-called *rim guard* type with a metal band - the rim band - stretched under tension around the edges of the CRT face. This helps to hold the broken pieces of the tube together during failure. Additional protection may be provided by an implosion shield to safeguard against flying fragments from the rear of the tube.

RADIATION

The utility of the VDT screen as a means for information display depends upon the radiation of visible light which is generated by the interaction between the electron beam and the screen phosphor. Depending upon the spectral characteristics of the phosphor, however, other forms of radiant energy may be generated as a by-product of this interaction. In addition, the physical processes which are involved in the interaction between the electron beam and the phosphor material can also lead to the generation of x-radiation. Finally, some of the components and electronic circuits within the VDT can generate radio frequency types of radiation.

The generation of one or several forms of secondary electromagnetic radiation is an inevitable consequence of the application of CRT technology to VDT design. It is also one that has lead to the establishment of stringent safety regulations with which the designers of CRT and electronics equipment in general must comply.

To the individual user, however, the idea that the VDT might be a source of radiation can be a cause of anxiety. We are all aware that exposure to certain forms of radiation may be harmful but that the senses generally give no warning that the harm is being done. For this reason, the types of radiation which might be looked for in a VDT are reviewed in this section.

Radio frequency (RF) radiation

The radio frequency band extends from a few Hz to about 10^9 Hz with wavelengths between many kilometers and about 0,3 m. The higher frequency part of the band is used for radio and television broadcasting.

The field strength of RF radiation can be described and measured in terms of the strength of the electric and magnetic fields induced by the radiation. The likelihood that this type of radiation is emitted from a VDT depends upon the operating characteristics of the electronic components and circuits, particularly oscillator circuits. RF radiation may be emitted at particular frequencies depending on the oscillator characteristics of the component or circuit from which the RF is generated. In practice, however, the field strengths of this type of radiation are likely to be very small and confined to the immediate vicinity of the source. This has been confirmed by the results of RF field strength measurements using several types of text processing VDT in which neither the electric nor magnetic field strength components could be detected.

Microwave radiation

The microwave region of the spectrum ranges from about 10^9 to 3×10^{11} Hz with wavelengths ranging from about 30 cm to 1 mm.

There are no known sources of microwave radiation in a VDT or television receiver.

Infrared radiation

The infrared region extends from approximately 3×10^{11} Hz to about 4×10^{14} Hz. The full IR bandwidth is usually subdivided into four regions in relation to their proximity to the visible radiation band. Thus the *near IR band* is closest to the visible light band and extends from ca 780 to 3000 nm. The *intermediate IR band* extends from ca 3000 to 6000 nm, the *far IR band* from 6000 to 15 000 nm and the *extreme IR band* from 15 000 nm to 1 mm.

The screen phosphor in a VDT fluoresces when excited by the electron beam and, depending upon the emission spectrum of the phosphor, it is possible that some quantities of infrared radiation may be generated in the near IR band, see Figure 1.10. Very few screen phosphors do in fact overlap into the IR region and measurements made in the U.K. have confirmed the absence of detectable IR radiation in the range 400 nm to 1400 mm, i.e. including that part of the near IR band that is closest to the visible radiation emission spectrum of the phosphors. This has also been confirmed by the results of a recent investigation undertaken by the NIOSH in the U.S.A.

Ultraviolet radiation

The ultraviolet region of the spectrum extends from about 8×10^{14} Hz to approximately 3×10^{17} Hz.

Some quantity of ultraviolet radiation may be generated by the phosphor depending upon its emission spectrum, see Figure 1.10, but it is unlikely that UV would pass through the screen glass due to the trapping properties of the glass constituents. For example a small quantity, e.g. 0,08 to 0,1% of ferrous oxide, Fe_2O_3, would trap all UV below about 250 nm. Measurements of UV emission from VDTs and television receivers made in England, Sweden and the U.S. have shown that emission of UV radiation in the range 200 to 400 nm is usually undetectable. Measurements made recently by the NIOSH in the U.S.A. on three types of terminal used in newspaper production showed that the UV radiation in the range 200 to 400 nm varied between 0,5 to 2×10^{-9} W/cm^2. This can be compared to the occupational exposure standard of 1×10^{-3} W/cm^2.

X-radiation

An x-ray is produced whenever the field of electrons surrounding the nucleus of an atom of matter is disturbed to such an extent that at least one of the nuclear electrons is caused to migrate from a lower to a higher energy state and back again. One way of creating a disturbance of this kind is to 'fire' another particle, say a free electron, at the atom so that it interferes with the nuclear electrons.

The type of radiation which is generated in this way is often called *induced radiation*. In the most extreme, but at the same time most unlikely, case that one of the nuclear electrons is actually knocked off the atom, the result is a strong *ionisation*, and a correspondingly high x-ray energy emission. This represents the upper limit on the energy of x-radiation.

In most cases, however, the interaction between the bombarding electron and the nuclear electrons results only in temporary adjustments of electron energy level causing x-ray emissions of lower energy. This means that if the atoms of a material are bombarded by a stream of electrons - which occurs for example in any type of thermionic valve such as the CRT in a television receiver or a display unit - the x-radiation which is generated is characterised, not by a single energy level, but by a spectrum of energies with a well defined upper limit.

Because of the extremely short duration of these types of electron interactions, x-rays are characterised by their very short wavelengths which are typically about 10 000 times shorter than the wavelengths of visible light, i.e. from about 0,25 to $1,0 \times 10^{-8}$ cm.

To better describe distances at these very small scales, wavelengths of radiation are often measured in terms of a unit known as the Angstrom Unit (A.U.) rather than the meter. 1 A.U.=10^{-10} meter. In terms of this unit, visible light extends from 4000 to 7000 A.U. Wavelengths of the different spectral colours in A.U. are approximately 4000-4500 (violet) through 5700-5900 (yellow) to 6300-7500 (red).

Knowing the wavelength of a given photon or package of radiation, the radiation energy can be calculated. It is this, which in practice determines the precautions that should be taken in the design of vacuum components such as thermionic valves and CRTs to safeguard against the escape of x-rays to the outside of the device.

Background radiation

Man is, and always has been exposed to a number of radiations of natural origin and the intensity of these *background radiations* helps to provide a scale with which to compare the intensity of radiation from artificial sources.

To measure radiation dosage, scientists commonly use a unit called the *rad* which represents the quantity of energy dissipated per gram of matter. 1 rad=100 ergs/gram. In addition, a unit called the *rem* is used to represent the amount of energy absorbed with correction for the biological effects of the different kinds of radiation. In the specific case of exposure to x-radiation, the most commonly used unit of dosage is the *roentgen*, and for x-radiation 1 rad=1,07 roentgens, and 1 rad=1 rem.

With the exception of some geographical regions which are locally rich in deposits of radioactive minerals such as uranium and thorium, the total dose of background radiation to which the population as a whole is exposed usually varies between 0,1 and 0,3 roentgens/year, i.e. about 0,01 to 0,03 milliroentgens/hour (mR/h).

Occupational exposure to x-radiation

For reasons of personal safety, it is legally required that any working place in which an individual might be occupationally exposed to a high level of radiation intensity must be designated as a 'restricted area' and that the employer shall take adequate steps to ensure that access to such working areas is strictly controlled. Based on the current regulations throughout Europe and the United States, this is normally taken to apply to any working area in which the average levels of radiation are likely to exceed 1,25 to 1,5 R/year or between 0,65 and 0,75 mR/h depending upon specific local requirements and definitions of the working year. Persons who are employed in high radiation environments such as these are also required to be classified with the local medical authorities, provided with radiation monitoring or 'film' badges and kept under regular medical supervision.

In those cases where, due to the nature of the work, certain parts of the body are likely to be particularly prone to radiation exposure, permissable doses of radiation to the different parts of the body and its organs are prescribed. According to the U.S. Department of Labour regulations relating to employees working in a restricted area, for example, the permissable doses are as follows:

Permissable radiation dose Rem/Calender quarter	Comment
1,25	Whole body, head and trunk, lenses of eyes, gonads, blood forming organs
7,5	Skin of whole body
18,75	Hands, forearms, feet, ankles

Figure 1.22 Permissable doses of x-radiation according to U.S. Department of Labour regulations.

Where these levels apply, the use of radiation monitoring equipment is required for any person likely to be exposed to 25% of these dose levels, and no employee under the age of 18 years may be exposed to more than 10% of these levels. Under normal circumstances, however, an employer may permit an individual working in a restricted area to receive doses to the whole body which are higher than these levels provided that the cumulative dose does not exceed 5(N-18) rems, where N is the person's age in years at his last birthday. Similar regulations are also prescribed by the European health and safety authorities.

Where regulations are prescribed in terms of an allowable radiation dose per calendar quarter, this is normally taken to refer to any three-month period of thirteen consecutive working weeks, although the U.S. regulations also make provision for a minimum calender quarter comprising twelve consecutive weeks.

By either definition, and presuming a five-day, fourty-hour working week, the regulations throughout Europe and the United States correspond to a permissable exposure of about 2,5 mR/h to the eyes, i.e. ca 125 times greater than the normal background level.

From the point of view of equipment design, it is required that the manufacturers of any form of high intensity radiation generating equipment must demonstrate that adequate steps have been taken to safeguard the health of the personnel operating the equipment and of persons who may be required to service or test the equipment. This requirement is not mandatory, however, for most types of equipment in which low intensity or soft x-rays can be generated as a by-product of the normal mode of operation. Throughout Europe and the United States it is the responsibility of the equipment manufacturer to ensure and, if necessary, to demonstrate that adequate shielding is provided to safeguard against radiation emission at a level greater than 0,5 mR/h at any point located a distance of 5 centimetres from the surface of the equipment. This level is about 25 times greater than the typical levels of background radiation, and applies to all forms of domestic or industrial display equipment which incorporates a cathode ray tube and other types of electronic valve for rectification or voltage regulation.

X-ray sources in VDTs

The most commonplace types of electrical component in which x-rays can be generated are power vacuum tubes in which a flow of electrons from the cathode to the anode is stimulated by a high voltage. Basically, any thermionic type valve or similar device which operates with an anode voltage greater than about 5 kilovolts may produce x-radiation.

In a VDT, the largest and most obvious device of this kind is the cathode ray tube. In the case of text processing types of visual display terminals, the operating potential or *anode voltage* is usually about the same or less than that used in conventional monochrome television receivers, i.e. between ca 12 and 20 kV. This voltage is the most important factor governing the intensity of x-radiation within the CRT.

Outside of the normal working conditions of the CRT, however, and particularly if the anode voltage exceeds the maximum voltage rating of the tube, x-radiation can occur through the neck of the tube. This occurs as the result of a high voltage breakdown or current leakage at the electron gun. The radiation thus induced is independent of the beam current and tube manufacturers are required to specify the maximum voltage difference for which it is assured that the x-radiation through the neck of the tube will not exceed 0,5 mR/h.

Finally, since the x-radiation absorption characteristics of the anode contact in the tube differ from those of the surrounding glass, additional shielding is provided to safeguard against x-radiation leakage through this contact.

Based on national regulations concerning exposure to x-radiation and on the codes of practice which have been established within the electronics industries, CRT manufacturers are required to indicate the voltage ratings for their CRTs which correspond to the maximum levels of x-radiation which can be anticipated when the CRT is in use. This has resulted in stringent controls as regards the choice of glassware from which CRT bulbs are manufactured, tube ratings and testing methods.

The x-ray emission characteristics of CRTs can be described in several ways but the two basic methods which have been adopted by the JEDEC in the United States are particularly illustrative and simple to understand.

JEDEC X-radiation limit curve

For a given tube, the exposure rate[1] measured in mR/h is determined by the combination of anode voltage and beam current when the CRT is in operation. If the exposure rate is plotted graphically against the anode voltage for a given beam current, the result is a diagram of the type shown in Figure 1.23. The exposure rates from all CRTs follow this same basic form but their exact positions in the diagram vary according to the absorption characteristics of the bulb glass.

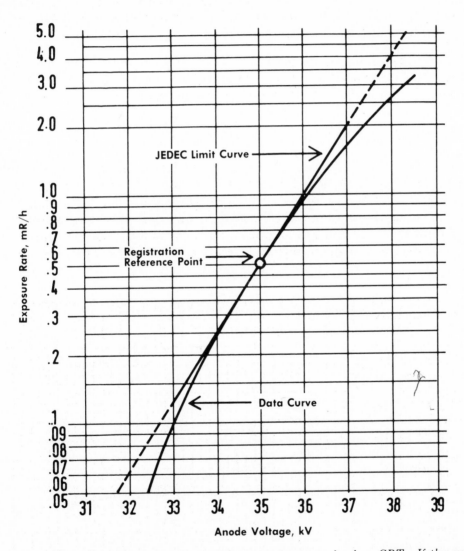

Figure 1.23 The radiation emission curve for monochrome and colour CRTs. If the curve for a typical CRT is known, the exposure rate in mR/h can be determined for a particular anode voltage, enabling voltage ratings for the CRT to be fixed. Ref. J.3

1. Measured values of x-ray emission from a CRT are conveniently described in terms of the 'exposure rate' in milliroentgens/hour,(mR/h).In other words, the emission of x-radiation is described in terms of the rate at which an object located at a specified distance from the point of maximum emission is exposed to the emitted radiation.

The shape of this diagram shows hows rapidly the exposure rate increases with increasing anode voltage; the exposure rate is typically proportional to the twentieth power of the anode voltage.

Diagrams such as these are used to determine the voltage ratings for a given CRT, and this is done by locating a *registration reference point* on the diagram which corresponds to a pre-determined exposure rate. Since an exposure rate of 0,5 mR/h is the commonly accepted legal limit for exposure to x-radiation, this value is often used as the designers guide in selecting the CRT bulb glasses. It is also the value which has been adopted in defining the reference voltages of CRTs for television receivers and display units.

Having located the reference point corresponding to an exposure rate of 0,5 mR/h on the x-radiation curve which is supplied from the tube manufacturer, a straight line is drawn tangent to the curve at that point, and this line is termed the *limit curve*. These limit curves correspond to a constant beam current of 300 microamperes in the case of colour television tubes and 250 microamperes for monochrome tubes.

These limit lines are used to define the voltage ratings for the CRT and since the limit line is drawn tangent to the data curve, these ratings are conservative for voltage levels which are both higher and less than the reference voltage.

The JEDEC Isoexposure rate limit curve

The so-called *isoexposure curve* is another useful way of representing the x-radiation characteristics of a CRT. In this form of presentation, the anode voltage is plotted against the beam current for a predetermined and constant value of the exposure rate. This results in a diagram similar to that shown in Figure 1.24. The main advantage with this type of diagram is that all combinations of anode voltage and beam current which fall outside the curve will result in excessive x-radiation exposure whilst all

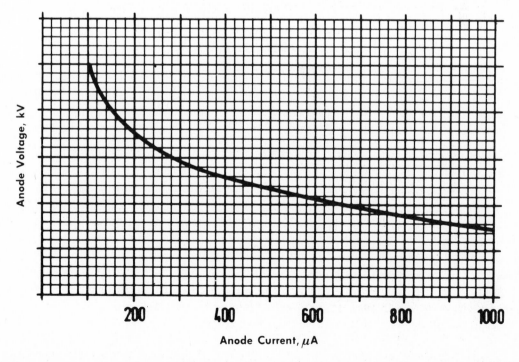

Figure 1.24 Shape of the radiation isoexposure curve corresponding to known combinations of the CRT anode voltage and beam current. This enables combinations of anode voltage and beam current which will result in excessive x-radiation to be determined. Ref. J.3

combinations of anode voltage and beam current which fall within the boundaries of the curve will ensure that the exposure rate is less than or equal to the prescribed value. For the reasons mentioned earlier, an exposure rate of 0,5 mR/h is usually selected as the basis for drawing this type of diagram which is calculated from the measured x-radiation curve. For monochrome CRTs, the curve is constructed within a voltage interval of ±2 kV about the reference voltage defined earlier. In the case of colour CRT receivers, the current span extends from 50 to 2000 microamperes.

Valve components in the HV power supply

Prior to the development of solid state technology, the designers of electronic power circuitry were forced to rely on the use of vacuum devices to perform the necessary control functions in the high voltage supplies to cathode ray tubes in display units and domestic television receivers. Today, this situation has changed. Improvements in the reliability of solid state components coupled with their compactness are the major factors which explain why solid state devices have replaced vacuum components in modern types of display equipment.

Nevertheless, some older types of display equipment still incorporate valves for voltage rectification and regulation. During the earlier development of computer and other items of equipment such as video displays, it was found that under some circumstances devices such as these could become emitters of x-radiation. In most cases this type of emission tended to become problematic due to the deterioration of the valve electrodes with age. But observations such as these prompted valve manufacturers and circuit designers to develop better means for shielding this type of stray emission with the result that glasses with greatly improved absorption properties came into general use, and metal screens were provided as a means for shielding the entire valve assembley.

In modern types of terminal equipment the high voltage power supply circuitry is almost invariably an all solid-state construction. For this type of equipment, there are no elements which could produce any form of x-radiation emission.

Effects of terminal age and malfunction

Although it is assured that under normal operating conditions the emission of x-radiation from a display unit is negligable, it is perhaps natural to wonder whether or not there is any likelihood that the radiation emission would increase due to deterioration of the terminal with age or as the result of malfunction in the equipment.

Consider firstly the cathode ray tube. Provided that the anode voltage does not exceed the rated value of the tube, the emission of x-radiation from the CRT stays within the prescribed limits. But if, for some reason, a condition develops whereby the anode voltage is increased to a level which is much greater than the rated value, the intensity of radiation would tend to increase accordingly. If such a condition should develop, the fault would normally be traced to the malfunction of one of the electronic components in the high voltage power supply, probably to one of the rectifiers, or to the high voltage transformer. For example, if a short circuit should develop in the primary windings of the transformer, the output voltage would increase significantly. If for this or some other reason the anode voltage were maintained at a level higher than the rated value, voltage breakdown would occur at the electron gun and the arcing or leakage thus caused would result in higher emission levels through the neck of the tube.

For this reason, the tube designer is required to specify the maximum voltage difference for which it is assured that the emission rates will not exceed 0,5 mR/h, and to ensure that this area is sufficiently well shielded to safeguard against higher emission levels. Although in practice there is a possibility, albeit a slight one that this type of malfunction can occur, it would almost certainly mean that the display unit as a whole would cease to operate until the fault had been corrected.

As a cathode ray tube ages, the electrodes in the gun end of the tube begin to deteriorate and stray particles begin to disperse throughout the tube in the form of a loose gas. When this happens, the tube is sometimes said to have become 'gassy'. Under normal circumstances it would take many years for this type of condition to develop, but when it does, the gas particles interfere with the display beam, eventually to such an extent that the displayed images begin to look fuzzy.

Due to the increased number of collisions between the electron beam and the gas particles, the intensity of x-radiation would be expected to decrease rather than increase.

It has already been mentioned that certain types of malfunction in the high voltage power supply circuitry can affect the anode voltage to the CRT to such an extent that the possiblity of higher radiation intensities would be increased, albeit that the terminal would almost certainly cease to function. But in some older types of display unit, i.e. those with valve rectifiers, the deterioration of the rectifier could, under some circumstances, result in higher radiation emission levels from the device. Normally, the voltage potential across the valve electrodes is very small compared with the high potential in the CRT, too small in fact to induce any significant quantities of radiation under normal operation which would not otherwise be completely absorbed by the walls of the valve. In a valve of this kind, however, the cathode emission would tend to decrease as the valve cathode deteriorates resulting in a progressively higher voltage across the electrodes. Ultimately a point would be reached where the walls of the valve could no longer absorb the radiation with the result that the exposure rates outside the valve would be increased.

With all solid-state components in the high voltage power supply, this type of problem does not occur, but even in the older designs, a deterioration of the valve functions would impair the operation of the equipment as a whole to the point where it would finally cease to operate.

X-ray absorption in CRTs

In view of the fact that the cathode ray tube is an evacuated glass bulb, the thickness of the glass walls must be sufficient to withstand the atmospheric pressure on the outer surfaces so as to avoid the risk of implosion. The final choice of wall thickness depends therefore on the mechanical strength of the glass which is selected as the manufacturing material, and on the design safety margin. Tube glass qualities are selected on the basis of both their mechanical strength and their ability to absorb x-radiation.

The rate of x-ray attenuation through an absorbing medium is directly proportional to the intensity of the incident radiation. So, if I_0 denotes the initial radiation intensity, and I_x denotes the intensity of the x-rays which have penetrated a thickness x into the absorber,

$$I_x = I_0 e^{-\mu x}$$

and the constant μ is called the *linear absorption coefficient*.

The thickness of absorber - which for the tube designer is glass - needed to reduce the initial intensity by half is termed the *half-value layer*, where;

$$X_{0,5} = \frac{ln\ 2}{\mu}$$

For most types of soft radiation, an absorber thickness of between 8 to 10 times that of the half value thickness is usually sufficient to provide virtually complete radiation absorption.

Glass is manufactured by mixing together a variety of different materials in order to produce a desired set of optical and strength characteristics. In other words, glass is a composite material, and each individual component material absorbs radiation quite independently of the other materials. But to the tube designer, it is the linear absorption coefficient of the composite glass μ_g, which describes how effective an absorber of x-rays the glass is, and what thickness would be required to absorb a given quantity of radiation.

Provided the absorption properties of the individual glass components are known, the linear absorption coefficient for the composite glass, μ_g, can be calculated with a reasonable degree of accuracy. In order to make this kind of calculation the linear absorption coefficient for a specific wavelength of radiation is defined as the product of density, ρ, and the so called *mass absorption coefficient*, ω_g, for that wavelength so that:

$$\mu_g = \rho\ \omega_g$$

In a composite such as glass, the mass absorption coefficient of the glass can be calculated by summing together the effects of the individual components such that

$$\omega_g = \sum \omega_c\ f_c$$

where f_c denotes the weight fraction of each component material.

According to the recommendations of the JEDEC in the United States, it is conventional to characterise the x-ray absorption properties of television bulb glass in terms of their linear absorption coefficients corresponding to an x-ray wavelength of 0,6 A.U. which corresponds to the theoretical limiting intensity of radiation in the x-ray spectrum for an anode potential of about 20kV.

To illustrate the relative absorbing powers of some common glass elements, the mass absorption coefficients for a variety of materials have been listed below in Figure 1.25. This table shows for example how effectively lead oxide, with its high atomic weight, absorbs x-radiation.

Consider for example, the tube of a visual display unit operating with an anode potential of 20kV. The radiated intensity in the x-radiation spectrum will reach a maximum at a wavelength of 0,93 A.U., and the radiation energy at this wavelength would be about 13,3 keV requiring a half value layer of glass of ca. 0,3 mm based on the absorption characteristics of pyrex glass. Assuming that a thickness of about 10 times the half value layer would be sufficient to completely absorb the radiation, a wall thickness of 3 mm would be required. This can be compared with wall thicknesses in the range 10 to 15 mm at the screen end of display tubes, and thicknesses of 5 to 6 mm along the tube neck, see Figure 1.26. Quite clearly, these thicknesses provide a very high margin of safety against the risk of x-radiation leakage from any surface of the tube. At the neck end of the tube, where radiation levels could be increased in the event of a high voltage breakdown, a glass with a high lead content, typically about 40% by weight, is invariably selected to provide an added measure of protection.

Material	ω_c	Material	ω_c
TiO_2	9,12	CeO_2	25,3
Al_2O_3	2,11	As_2O_3	33,2
Li_2O	0,55	Rb_2O	54,5
Na_2O	1,69	SrO	53,4
K_2O	8,45	BaO	25,1
MgO	1,92	PbO	82,9
SiO_2	2,34	Sb_2O_3	18,2
F	1,20		

Fig.1.25 Mass absorption characteristics for glass materials corresponding to radiation wavelength $\lambda = 0,6$ A.U. Ref. J.3

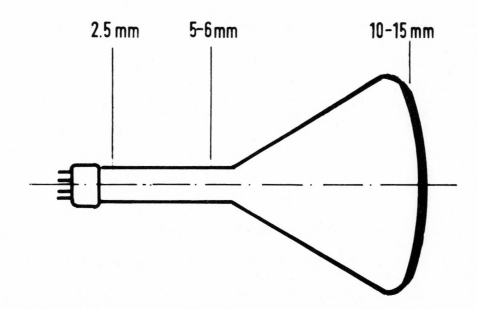

Figure 1.26 Typical glass wall thickness of cathode ray tube bulb. The lead content in the tube neck glass is typically 40%.

X-radiation measurements on VDTs

In recent years, many national occupational safety authorities and industrial associations have gathered together and analysed the results of radiation measurements which they themselves have commissioned or which have been made by individual glassware, CRT and display equipment manufacturers. Using this data, the necessary controls and test methods have been established to enable CRT manufactuers to comply with the appropriate safety standards.

Much of this data derives from measurements made on monochrome and colour television receivers but since the CRTs in visual display terminals are in many cases identical to those used in domestic television receivers, this data is also relevant in the present context.

The JEDEC has recently published a review of the radiation characteristics of CRTs manufactured in the United States. The results from these tests showed that, with very few exceptions, the reference voltage corresponding to an exposure of 0,5 mR/h [1] was greater than 20kV. Likewise, the anode voltage levels corresponding to the typical level of exposure to background radiation, i.e. about 0,02 mR/h, were also in excess of 20kV.

It is largely based on observations of this kind that it is generally concluded that an otherwise all solid-state terminal operating with an anode voltage of less than 20 kV does not produce measurable, i.e. greater than background, levels of x-radiation.

During the present investigation, a survey was conducted among the manufacturers of text processing VDTs and it was found that all existing VDTs comply with the requirements of local safety standards. Some of the results are shown in Figure 1.27.

Terminal	X-ray exposure rate (mR/h)	Anode voltage (V)	Source
IBM 3277			Philadelphia Newspapers
Ferranti 38B/1090		16 kV/100 A 16 kV/200 A 18 kV/0,8 mA	Ferranti Ltd.
Siemens 8150 Siemens 8151 Siemens 8152		10kV	Bayerisches Landesinstitut fuer Arbeitsschutz
Dymo DELTA 5000		18kV/250 A	Clinton Electronics
Harris 1100 Harris 1500 Harris 1600	<0,2		University of Florida
Atex EDIT I Atex EDIT II Atex EDIT V			Atex Inc.
Linoscreen 300			Linotye-Paul
Hendrix Edit III			Hendrix
Teleram P1800			Teleram Communication Corp.
Compugraphic Unified Composer			Compugraphic Corp.

Figure 1.27 Radiation measurements on a sample of text-processing VDTs. Note: low radiation levels such as these are difficult to measure accurately.

1. This requirement is prescribed in DHEW-42-CFR-Part 78. Similar requirements exist throughout Europe.

THE VDT AS A SYSTEMS COMPONENT

VDTs are not used in isolation. Usually they are part of a data or text processing *system*. In order to understand the human aspects of VDT design and usage, therefore, it is necessary to consider the role which is played by the terminal as a part of a system.

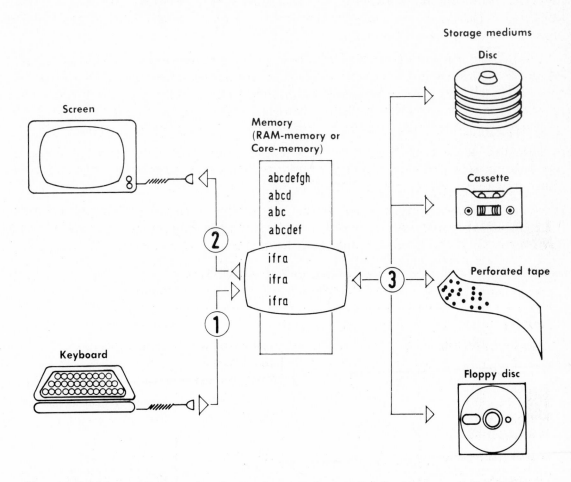

Figure 1.28 Major components of a system where text is entered, edited and stored. Ref. K.26

Regardless of the size and application of the system, the visual display terminal may provide the means for:

- entering data/text or commands into the system
- retrieving and visually inspecting the raw or processed data/text
- editing and correcting the data/text using either the internal processing capacity of the terminal or the remote capacity of the computer
- consigning the processed data to production, directly or indirectly, via the internal storage capacity of the central processor or via some form of auxiliary storage device, e.g. punch tape, magnetic tape cassette, floppy disc etc.

In most practical applications, VDT systems offer the potential advantages of fast processing speed, increased accuracy of working and better efficiency in handling large volumes of data arriving from different sources and at different times.

35

In designing a VDT system to perform a certain *task*, there are three main factors which should be initially considered:

- the operations which are *basic* to the particular task in question and which must be performed by the VDT and computer system

- *additional* operations and facilities which, whilst not basic to the task, might improve the speed or efficiency with which the task is carried out, and

- the likelihood that the requirements for or of the task in question might *change* at some future point in time, thereby necessitating a modification to the configuration of or the facilities offered by the system.

In other words, the designer must consider the basic requirements of the task, how the use of a VDT/computer system might in itself change the structure or requirements of the task and finally how these requirements might change in time.

The speed, facilities, ease-of-use and reliability of the system are the next group of factors to be considered. These depend not only on the design of the software and main items of systems hardware, e.g. the terminals, controllers, central processor etc, but also on:

- the *intelligence* of the VDTs and other parts of the system,

- the type, capacity and reliability of the systems *communications network*, i.e. the network of transmission lines and interfaces that link the terminals with the central processor or other systems components, e.g. controllers, printers etc., and

- the *configuration* of the terminals, i.e. the way in which they are linked singly or in groups to the central processor.

The intelligent terminal

Until comparatively recently, computer systems were *hardwired* in the sense that once the basic tasks were defined, the electronic circuitry in the computer was designed for those and only those tasks. Later modification, to accommodate additional operations or to cater for changes in the requirements of the task in question, required extensive modification to the circuitry, usually at great expense. For many years, this restricted the application of computer systems to the types of task, e.g. mathematical computation, in which the basic operations or algorithms were unchanging.

With the advent of semi-conductor technology, however, the costs of data storage capacity have been substantially reduced. In addition, the introduction of micro-processors has made it possible to distribute the *intelligence* throughout the system.

Initially, the trend was to increase the overall intelligence of the system by providing for a wider range of facilities within the central processor itself. This centralised intelligence offered two practical advantages:

- by increasing the intelligence of the processing unit, the intelligence available to all terminals connected with it was increased at the same time, and

- use could be made of relatively simple and less costly types of input terminal.

The main drawbacks with a completely centralised intelligence, however, are most readily appreciated by considering the consequences of a breakdown in the processing unit. In this case, failure of the central computer means that the entire system is out of operation until normal working can be restored.

To improve system reliability and at the same time reduce the communications load, the current trend is towards decentralised or *distributed intelligence*.

This has been facilitated by the development of the microprocessor which can be incorporated in the terminal itself or other elements in the system, e.g. terminal controllers, multiplexers etc., to relieve the main computer of some of the operations required by the operator.

The word 'intelligent' has therefore become a common adjective in describing the capabilities of many systems components and not least the terminal itself. Most modern alphanumeric display terminals are intelligent although to varying degrees. Basic editing tasks can usually be performed locally which means that fewer transmissions to and from the central processor are required. Furthermore, in the event of a breakdown at the central site, the internal processing and storage capacity of the terminal permits a certain amount of continued off-line working.

COMMUNICATION

Data transmission

The communications link between the terminals and the computer is usually a dedicated data transmission line. In remote applications, the communications link is usually a voice-grade transmission line, i.e. a telephone line, that can either be directly coupled between the terminal communication interface and the computer or via a *modem*.

In some terminals, the modem is built into the terminal as an integral unit in which case the terminal can be coupled directly with a telephone line. More usually, however, the modem is a separate unit.

In most portable terminals, an *acoustic coupler* is provided so that the terminal can be coupled with the central processor using a conventional telephone receiver and by dialling on a public telephone line.

Transmission mode

Communication between the terminal and the central processor is usually made by transmitting the data in either *half-duplex mode* in which case information can be transmitted in both directions but only one way at a time, or *full-duplex mode* where data can be transmitted in both directions at the same time.

Where the terminal is used purely as a remote input device, e.g. transmission from a field reporter terminal to the central processor, transmission usually takes place in one direction only, the so-called *simplex mode*.

Text processing systems can be designed to operate in either half-duplex or full-duplex mode, and even though it is seldom required to transmit data in both directions at the same time, full-duplex transmission reduces the response time. If the terminal is buffered and it is required to receive messages from the central processor or some other source whilst communication is in progress, then both the terminal and communication line must be full-duplex.

Data transmission over the communications lines can be either synchronous or asynchronous.

If the transmission is *asynchronous*, the data is transmitted in such a way that the time interval between the transmission of successive characters can vary. If the data is transmitted *synchronously*, on the other hand, the rate at which the terminal transmits the data is synchronised with the receiving rate at the computer and the time interval between each character is always constant. In this case, timing or *clocking* information accompanies the transmitted data to ensure perfect synchronisation.

Most text processing terminals are provided with local storage capacity so that transactions between the terminal and the central processor can procede by the transmission of blocks of characters or whole messages rather than by character-by-character transmission. This means that the transmission time need not depend on the variable time required to key in each character as is the case in some on-line teletype terminal systems for example - so that synchronous transmission and faster transmission rates can be used.

Transmission rate

In remote applications, the VDTs are usually linked to the computer by means of voice-grade telephone lines which restrict the speed of transmission to 4800 baud, i.e. about 500 characters/second, or less. Higher speeds, but seldom more than 9600 baud, can be used on dedicated private or leased lines.

In order to improve the efficiency of data transmission in a multi-terminal system, the network of terminals and communications lines is usually designed so as to be able to transmit as much data as possible, as quickly as possible through the least number of data lines. In these types of system, therefore, the terminals are often grouped in 'clusters', each cluster being linked to the central processing unit by a high speed, full-duplex transmission line.

Depending upon the application in question, the efficiency of data transmission within the system can be further improved by using terminals which offer the facility of *split transmission rates*, i.e. with slow speed transmission from the terminal to the central processor and high speed transmission in the reverse direction.

Address, error and parity checking

Once communication has been established between the terminal and the central processor there are basically three types of *check* that the message can be subjected to:

   • a check on the identity of the operator

   • a check for errors in the control or function codes due, for example, to the omission of an instruction at the keyboard, and

   • a check for errors in the character coding due to either interference in the communication line or faults in the transmitting (VDT) and receiving ends (central processor) of the line.

For security reasons, access to some or all of the display terminals might be restricted to certain operators, the identity of which must be made known to and approved by the central processor before communication can take place. This is usually by means of a *password* known only to the operator and the system. In some cases, the password is a keyed sequence of characters; in others the password is encoded on an *identity badge* - usually a plastic card with a magnetic stripe code - which is inserted into a badge reading device which is built into or beside the terminal.

Communication errors can be detected by a variety of methods, one of the simplest of which is the even-odd or *parity check*. In this case, an extra parity bit is inserted in every uneven character code so that each code contains an even number of digits. This type of checking procedure helps to safeguard against errors due to the pickup of spurious extra pulses or the dropping of pulses during the transmission of the data. For many applications, this type of data checking procedure is sufficient but more sophisticated error checking routines can be used to help improve the reliability of error detection.

System response time

Ideally, a text processing VDT system should respond 'instantly' to any command made at the keyboard. In practice, however, there is always a time delay or waiting time between the keying-in of a command and the receiving of the response on the screen. This waiting time is called the *system response time* and is determined by;

- the loading of the system when the request is made,
- the processing capacity of the system,
- the nature, i.e. complexity and volume of the job,
- the processing and storage capacity of the VDT, and
- transmission delays.

Loading of the system

Clearly, the more terminals in the queue for service by the central processor, the longer will be the waiting time.

During the peak hours before deadline in newspaper production, for example, the loading on the editorial and composing room system increases as the number of stories to be edited, headlined, hyphenated and justified (h & j'ed) and sent for typesetting increases. In practice, the peak loading requirement, i.e. number, frequency and volume of jobs to be processed is a prime factor to be considered in determining the processing capacity of the central processor, terminal controllers and individual terminals, the type and speed of communication network etc.

Repeated delays, due either to excessive waiting times or system breakdowns can be a major source of frustration to the individual operator.

System processing capacity

The processing capacity of the system refers to;

- the number of jobs that the system can process simultaneously,
- the speed with which each request can be serviced including the time to access the appropriate file, once the nature of the request has been identified.

39

Nature of the request

Not all text or data processing functions are equally time and storage consuming. In a text processing system, for example, commands such as the insertion or deletion of a character or block of characters clearly require less processing time and capacity than, say, the hyphenation and justification of a complete story or the retrieval of a story from a directory. In most text processing systems, simple editing functions can be executed using the processing capacity of the terminal, i.e. without having to rely on the processing capacity of the central computer and data transmission to and from the computer.

If the processing of a given job requires transaction between the terminal and the central computer, then as a general rule, the greater the volume of data to be processed or the more complicated the type of processing to be performed, the longer is the waiting time between the processing of each job in the queue.

VDT processing capacity

The internal storage capacity of a VDT usually ranges between 1000 and 10 000 characters. Larger capacities are generally made available by the use of auxiliary storage devices such as cassettes, floppy discs or, as in some types of system, by storage capacity in a dedicated controller.

At the lowest level, the internal processing power of a VDT is restricted to the functions which are hardwired into it via the keyboard. This can be extended by means of programmable logic elements. When simple editing commands can be accommodated internally, the response time is determined by the processing speed of the VDT and the screen writing speed.

Transmission delays

The rates at which the VDT can send to and receive from the central processing unit can have an effect on response times. In general sense, the transmission times can be broken down into two parts:

> • the transmission time in sending data to and from the central processing unit or from the VDT to the controller and from the controller to the CPU and vice versa, and

> • the contention time and polling overhead, i.e. the time which is lost due to the CPU having to make routine polling interrogations of all VDTs or controllers in order to stay in control of the system.

Depending upon the intelligence of the controller, the transmission rates from the VDT to the host computer and vice versa need not be identical. If the data requires a large amount of processing it is not unusual to choose VDTs in which the keyboard (transmitter) and screen (receiver) are logically separate elements. In this type of *parallel connection*, the keyboard is connected to the processor using a normal, low-speed serial interface and the display is connected by a high speed, usually 4800, 9600 baud or higher, interface. This type of time-reducing connection is sometimes called *split transmission*.

TERMINAL CONFIGURATION

On-line vs off-line

VDTs may be incorporated into a system in one of three ways; on-line, off-line and on/off-line.

If the VDT is connected *on-line* to the central computer, the VDT has immediate access to the computer if it needs it. If the VDT is used *off-line*, on the other hand, the data which is entered at the VDT is first stored on an intermediate storage medium, e.g. on paper tape, punched card, magnetic tape or floppy disc. The data can then be entered into the systems processor as and when required.

If the terminal has no built-in processing and storage capacity, its availability is determined by the availability of the systems processor. In this case, should a breakdown occur in the central computer, the terminal operator is usually required to stop working until the operation of the computer has been restored. If the terminal is provided with internal processing and data storage capacity, on the other hand, the operator is no longer dependant on the availability of the central processor. In this case, should a breakdown occur in the central processor, the terminal operator is able to continue working off-line.

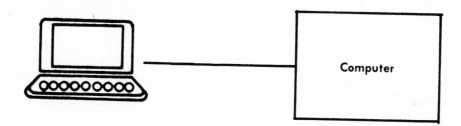

Figure 1.29 On-line terminal operation: the data entered at the VDT is transmitted directly to the computer, and the system availability is determined by the availability of the mainframe.

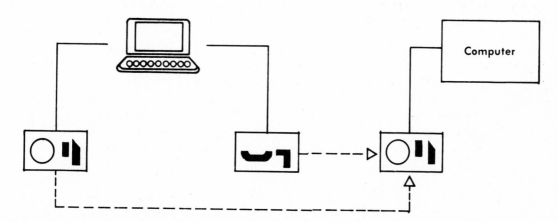

Figure 1.30 Off-line terminal operation: data entered at the VDT is stored either at the terminal or in an auxiliary store. The data is transmitted to the mainframe or output as and when required.

In many VDT systems, it may be desirable for the operator to work either on-line or off-line as desired. In this case, single terminals or terminal clusters can be interfaced either directly to the central computer or to some form of intermediate storage or output device.

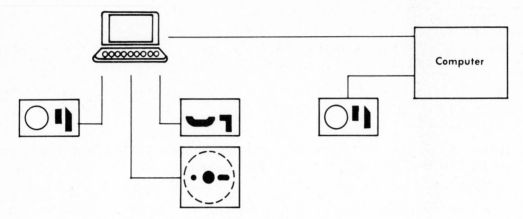

Figure 1.31 On/Off-line terminal operation: simultaneous on-line and off-line transmission.

Portable terminals

Certain requirements in news reporting, e.g. coverage of special events such as sports events and other froms of 'on-the-spot' reporting, make it desirable for the field reporter to have at his disposal a remote input terminal which, after having entered the story, can later be coupled with the central processing unit. Terminals of this kind, which are called *portable terminals*, are easy to carry and can be operated from a normal a.c. mains connection or, in some cases, from a car battery.

The contents of the memory can be transferred to a magnetic tape cassette for intermediate storage for later transmission to the central processor over a conventional telephone line using an acoustic coupler and/ or modem.

At the receiving station, the signal can be handled by any device which has been programmed to be compatible with the sending device. The signal can then be brought to a printer, paper tape punch, magnetic tape recorder, another VDT or directly into the store of the central processor.

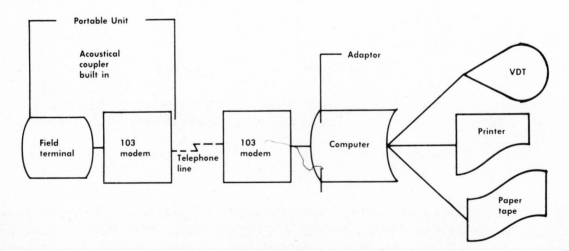

Figure 1.32 Block diagram showing a remote portable terminal communicating with a system. A terminal of this type is often used for 'on-the-spot' reporting.

42

Stand-alone terminals, terminal clusters

Depending upon the type and volume of data traffic that must be handled by the system and on the intelligence of the terminals themselves, a distinction is often drawn between *stand-alone* and *cluster* terminals. To some extent, however, the distinction is not a clear one; stand-alone terminals can also be grouped in 'clusters'.

Basically, the terms stand-alone and cluster are more aptly used to describe the configuration of the system rather than the characteristics of the terminals themselves, even though the two may be - and usually are - related.

Stand-alone or intelligent terminals can be coupled directly to the computer or, in remote applications, via a modem and telephone lines. In some systems configurations, the terminals are also connected to the main computer in groups or *clusters*.

To help reduce transmission costs, however, most of the terminals in larger, multi-terminal networks are grouped in clusters around a terminal or cluster control unit. The terminals in each cluster share a common communication line from the control unit to the central procesor. To further improve the utilisation of the line, individual stand-alone terminals can be 'dropped' or 'multi-dropped' onto the line, see Figure 1.33.

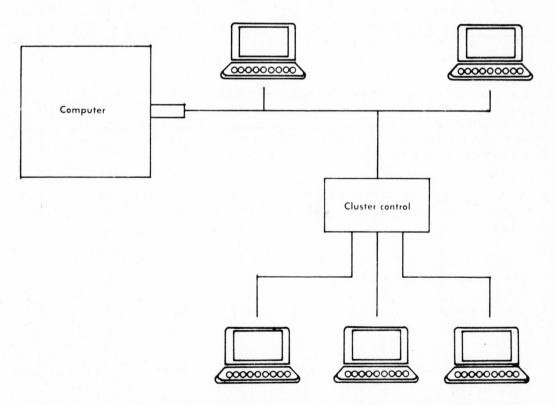

Figure 1.33 A computer system using stand-alone and clustered terminals. This often helps to reduce transmission costs. Terminals in a cluster share a common line to the central processor.

In some systems configurations, the VDTs may be connected to the central processor via an intelligent control unit, i.e. one that in addition to controlling the communication between the VDT and the main computer also incorporates processing and storage facilities. In this type of system, the central computer is relieved of some part of the systems work load, and the processing facilities of the terminals can be expanded.

Point-to-point coupling

If each terminal in the system is directly coupled to the central processor by its own, dedicated communication line, the terminal and processor are said to the coupled *point-to-point*, see Figure 1.34.

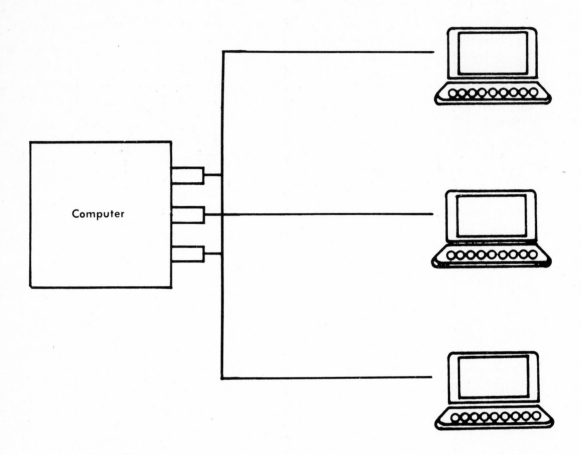

Figure 1.34 A point-to-point network. Each terminal is directly coupled to the central processor by its own dedicated line.

Provided that the number of terminals in the system is less than the number of input/output ports which can be reasonably accommodated on the computer, point-to-point coupling helps to reduce transmission delays since the terminal and processor have immediate access to one another at all times. But if the number of terminals in the system is too large to permit point-to-point coupling, a technique has to be found that will enable more than one terminal to be linked on each available data line.

This can be done by arranging the terminals in groups or clusters, so that the terminals within each cluster share a common transmission line to the computer. But regardless of whether the terminals are point-to-point linked to the computer or grouped in clusters, it is necessary to maintain some form of discipline as to the order in which each terminal cantransmit a message to or receive a message from the central processor. This can be done in one of several ways. The computer can, for example, be programmed to scan or 'poll' each terminal, inviting each in turn to transmit its data. This technique is known as *polling*, see Figure 1.35. Alternatively, the computer can be programmed to recognise an *interrupt* signal, i.e. a signal from a terminal that it is ready to transmit, in which case the computer will interrupt the work that it is then doing at a suitable point in order to deal with the request from the terminal.

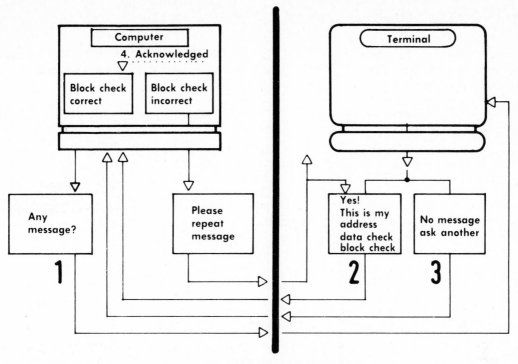

POLL FROM COMPUTER

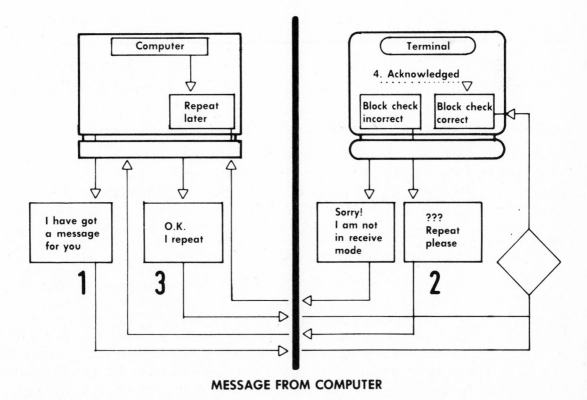

MESSAGE FROM COMPUTER

Figure 1.35 Polling. With several terminals sharing a common line to the central processor, one way of ensuring that they all receive adequate service is for the central processor to scan or poll each terminal in turn, (a) transmitting data or (b) receiving data from the terminal.

In any computer system, it is the computer and not the individual terminals which controls the communications discipline within the system. Inevitably, there is a delay in the response from the computer depending upon the number of terminals that require to transmit at the same time, the volume of each request and the speed with which the computer can process each request.

In addition, use of the polling technique requires that each terminal can distinguish the response that is intended for it. In a clustered network, this can be catered for either in the VDT software or in the software of the cluster controller. If stand-alone terminals are dropped onto the line, however, this must be accommodated within the terminal software.

In practice, deciding on the number of terminals that can share each line is a trade-off between transmission costs, and the consequence of a breakdown in the communication line and the number of terminals that would be thus affected.

Multiplexing

Multiplexing is a technique that can be used to sub-divide a common transmission line into a number of channels which provide a link between terminal clusters and the central processor or, if necessary, between the processor and each cluster controller.

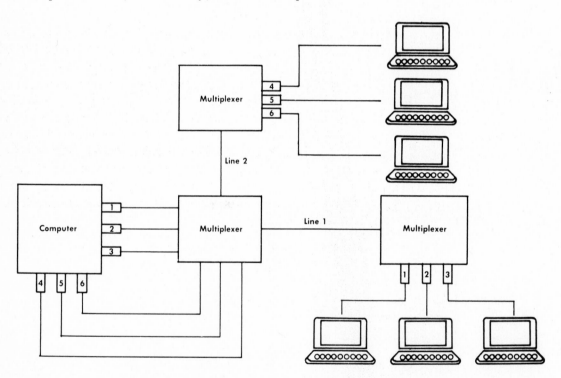

Figure 1.36 A multiplexed network. A common communication line is sub-divided into a number of channels.

Multiplexing is well suited for computer systems with a small number of available input/output channels to the computer and with a large number of terminals which are used for processing short messages or which do not require very frequent dialogue with the computer. If the terminals are used for processing large volumes of data, however, e.g. in some commercial and technical data processing applications, care should be taken in the use of multiplexing since individual response times can be rather high.

Concentration

It is rarely the case that all of the sub-channels in a multiplexed line are used to capacity at the same time. For example, intermittent keying at the keyboard - particularly smaller volumes of data - makes inefficient use of the multiplex channels. To improve the efficiency of a multiplexing facility, a device known as a *concentrator* can be used to accept the signals on several channels, add the appropriate identification data and transmit the data to the processor over a single channel.

Concentrators are usually programmed for the particular network that they are required to serve although intelligent multiplexers which can be independently programmed to meet the requirements of a network, e.g. if the configuration of the system is changed at some date, in some cases also offer additional facilities, e.g. error detection.

Acknowledgements

The authors would like to express their thanks to the many people who have contributed information for this section of the report and in particular to Mr. D. Grover of the British Computer Society for permission to draw on the material contained in the recent BCS publication 'Visual display units - and their application'.

Those sections of this chapter concerning radiation emission from VDTs are based on information which was supplied from many CRT and VDT manufacturers and from occupational health and safety authorities in Europe and in the United States. Special thanks are due, however, to Mr. J. Hassman of the Electronics Industries Association, Washington D.C., U.S.A; to Professor W. Mauderli of the University of Florida, Gainesville College of Medicine, Gainesville, Fla, U.S.A.; to Mr. H.W. Eriksen of the Liberty Mutual Insurance Co., Allentown, Pa; to Mr. E.G. Weatherley of the U.K. Health and Safety Executive, London, England; Herrn Eder of the Bayerisches Landesinstitut fur Arbeitsschutz, München, F.R.G; Herr J. Karlberg of the Statens Strålskyddsintitut, Stockholm, Sweden. Additional thanks are due to the many newspaper companies and equipment manufacturers who made available the results of radiation measurements made on their behalf.

Chapter 2

LIGHT, VISION AND THE OPTICAL CHARACTERISTICS OF VISUAL DISPLAYS

Foreword

To see, we need light. To see clearly and without undue effort, we need sufficient light, an adequate sense of vision and visual objects which are themselves clearly defined and easy to recognise.

Visual discomfort occurs as a result of the effort of trying to see. Depending upon each of these three basic attributes of 'seeing' - illumination, the individual sense of vision and the optical characteristics of the visual objects - this effort may result in unfavourable posture, excessive visual effort and other forms of behaviour which may very rapidly lead to fatigue.

In order to better understand the nature of these problems and their significance as regards the design and implementation of VDTs and VDT workplaces, this chapter is devoted to the subjects of light, vision and the optical characteristics of printed and CRT displays. Character formation and legibility are examined in relation to illumination and visual acuity, and the effects of glare and reflections are dealt with in some detail.

LIGHT AND VISION

Light is a form of radiant energy which induces a luminous sensation in the eyes. It is this luminous sensation that provides us with the sense of *vision*; in other words, to see, we need light.

Light consists of packets or *quanta* of energy, and the energy contained in each quantum is a function of frequency. The frequency components of visible light are most easily demonstrated when a beam of light is diffracted through a prism. Each frequency is diffracted through a slightly different angle so that the beam emerges from the prism as a fan of light in which all the spectral colours are visible. Each spectral colour is light of a different and characteristic frequency.

All types of so-called electromagnetic radiation are essentially the same and the physical difference between radio waves, infrared, visible light, ultraviolet and x-rays is their frequency. Only a very narrow band of these frequencies stimulates the eyes to give vision and the perception of colour.

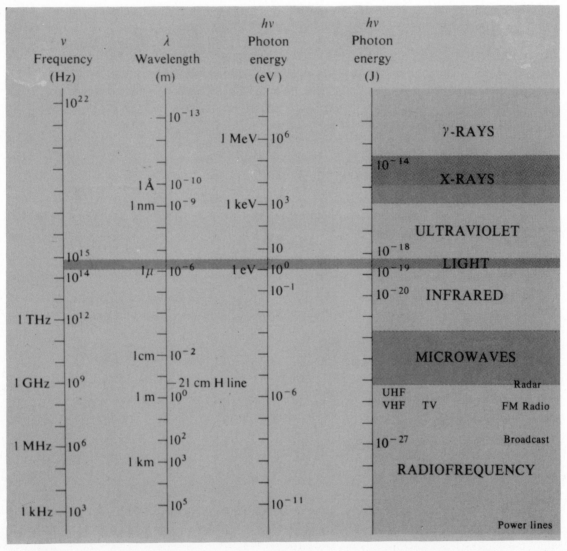

Figure 2.1 Light occupies only a narrow region of the total electromagnetic spectrum which includes radio waves, infra-red, ultra-violet and x-rays. The physical difference is purely the wavelength of the radiation. Within the octave to which the eye is sensitive, different wavelengths give different colours. Ref. G.16

The human eye and vision

The human eye is a beautifully contrived and extremely sensitive optical instrument, the main components of which are illustrated in Figure 2.2.

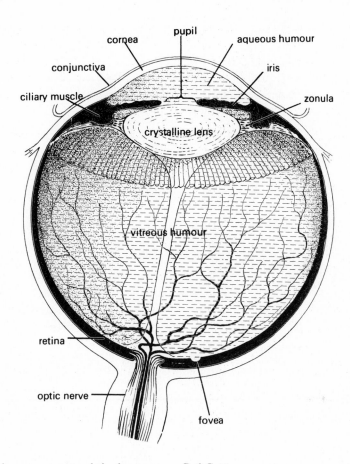

Figure 2.2 The main components of the human eye. Ref G.16

Light enters the eye through the *cornea*, is focussed by the *lens* to give a minute, inverted image which is projected onto the *retina*. Here, the patterns of light are converted into electrical pulses which are carried to the visual centres of the brain by the optic nerve.

The movement of each eyeball is controlled by six external muscles which control the orbital position of the eye and which rotate the eyeballs in order to follow moving objects or direct the eyes towards a particular visual object. In addition to the external muscles, there are also muscles within the eyeball. The *iris* is an annular muscle which forms the aperture - the *pupil* - through which light passes to the lens. The contraction of the iris reduces the aperture of the lens in bright light and also when the eyes converge to view near objects. Another muscle, the *ciliary muscle*, controls the shape and hence the focussing of the lens.

Although the lens is relatively unimportant as regards the formation of the image on the retina, it plays a vital role in the ability of the eyes to accommodate to different viewing distances. This is done by changing the shape of the lens; for near vision the tension in the membrane surrounding the lens is released by the contraction of the ciliary muscle thus allowing the lens to take on a more convex form. In this case, the reduced radius of curvature of the lens makes the lens more powerful. If the lens is incorrectly adjusted, the image may be projected on a plane which is slightly in front of or behind the retina. This results in the condition of either short sight or long sight.

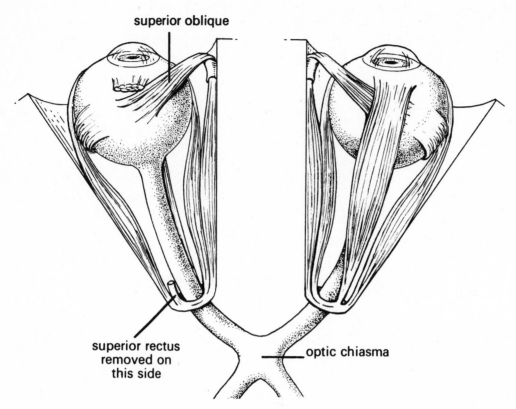

Figure 2.3 The muscles which move the eye. The position of the eyeball is maintained by six muscles which move it to direct the gaze to any position and give convergence of the two eyes for depth perception. Ref. G.16

The development of the lens in later life has important consequences from the point of view of vision and age. The lens is built up in layers from the centre which is thus the oldest part of the lens. With increasing age, and as more cells are added to the lens, the cells in the centre become more and more separated from the blood system. Thus starved of oxygen and nutrient, they die and harden so that the lens becomes progressively stiffer and eventually too stiff to permit change of shape for accommodation.

The retina is a thin fabric of blood vessels, nerve and other cells, including the light sensitive rod and cone *receptors* which convert light into electrical neural pulses. The retina is the first stage in visual sensation and an object can only be seen clearly and sharply-defined when the image that is projected onto the retina is itself clearly and sharply defined.

The retina has often been described as an 'outgrowth of the brain' and since some of the data processing for perception actually takes place within the retina, it is indeed an integral and specialised part of the brain.

The retina is equipped with two kinds of light receptor cells which are called *rod and cone* cells. Vision in daylight and the perception of colour is due to the function of the cone cells. The rods function in dim light and only permit the perception of shades of grey. Daylight vision, i.e. when the cone cells are most active, is called *photopic vision*. Dark-adapted vision using mainly the rod cells is called *scotopic vision*.

The size of the receptors and their packing density in the retina are important as regards the ability of the eye to detect and discriminate fine detail. The density of receptors is greatest in a small region called the *fovea* and the images which are projected onto this region are perceived as being 'sharp'. It is this characteristic of the retina that enables the reception of unnecessary information to be minimised. In other words, we have the ability to select a particular object in a visual field that might, and usually does, contain many other objects.

Eye movements

The eyes are in continuous, so-called *saccadic movement*, and these movements are essential to vision. Once an image has been optically stabilised on the retina, vision begins to fade after a short while, usually a matter of seconds. Part of the function of the saccadic movements of the eyes is to continually scan the image over the receptors so that they do not adapt and so cease to send the image signals to the brain.

The eyes are separated by a small distance with the result that each eye receives a somewhat different view of a given object.

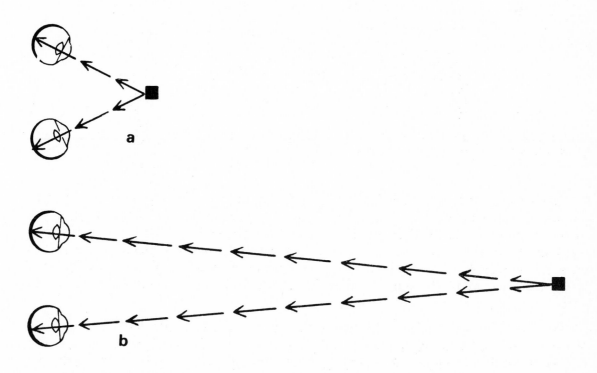

Figure 2.4 Convergence or range-finder depth perception. The eyes converge on an object we examine, the images being brought to the fovea. In (a) we see the eyes converged to a near object, in (b) to one more distant. The angle of convergence is signalled to the brain as information of distance, serving as a range-finder. Ref G.16

For objects placed not too far, say less than 50 metres, from the eyes, this enables the perception of depth by stereoscopic vision, i.e. the synthesis of two slightly different visual images into the perception of a single, solid object. When viewing objects at great distances, on the other hand, we are effectively one-eyed.

The sensitivity of the eyes to light

In the broadest sense, the term 'sensitivity' refers to the ability of the eyes, particularly the retina and visual centres of the brain, to detect and correctly interpret the light signals which enter the eye and which enable us to see brightness, colour, movement etc.

As the intensity of the light entering the eyes increases, the rate at which the receptors in the retina signal the brain also increases. With no light entering the eyes, it might be imagined that no signals are transmitted between the eyes and the brain, but in fact this is not so. There is always some signal traffic in the visual system, even when the retina is not stimulated by light. When the retina *is* stimulated by light, the brain has to decide whether the signals coming from the retina are in fact due to light entering the eyes or merely due to 'noise' in the system.

This background noise is an important characteristic of the human visual system. The eye is a very sensitive instrument but one which would be even more sensitive were it not for this noise activity. There is also some evidence to suggest that the internal noise in the visual system increases with age and may be partially responsible for the reduction in visual functions as we get older.

In a rather more specific sense, the term sensitivity is used to describe the ability of the eyes to evaluate different wavelengths of the light entering the eyes. The eye is not equally sensitive to all wavelengths although this also depends to some extent on the quantity of light entering the eye. Figure 2.5 shows how the spectral sensitivity of the eye varies according to whether the eyes are light or dark adapted, i.e. for photopic and scotopic vision.

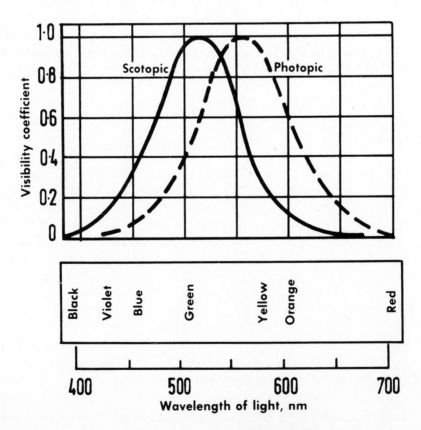

Figure 2.5 The spectral sensitivity of the dark and light adapted eye.

Within the retina, the rod and cone cells adapt at different rates and in a sense it is as if the eye has not one but two retinas.

When it is dark, the eye is more sensitive to blue than when it is light. The reverse is true as regards the sensitivity of the eyes to red. In addition, the dark-adapted eye is most sensitive to green light with a wavelength of about 525 nm. The light adapted eye is most sensitive to a more yellow/green shade with a wavelength of about 555 nm. In both cases, the sensitivity of the eyes to red, ca 650 nm, is only about 10% of the maximum sensitivity. This means that the quantity of radiation in the red region of the spectrum would have to be about 10 times greater than that in the green region in order to appear equally bright.

Adaptation

The term *adaptation* refers to the adjustment of the receiving properties of the eye in relation to the prevailing luminance conditions. There are two mechanisms which make this possible. Firstly, the pupil, as a mechanical element, can change its surface area in the younger eye in the ratio 1:16. The amount of light entering the eye can thus be changed in the same ratio. The pupil reacts very quickly and the minimum reaction time is typically ca 0,2 seconds.

The eye can, however, adapt in a ratio of $1:10^{11}$, i.e. the greatest luminance within which the eye can still work is 100 billion times greater than the lowest level. Of course, this enormous range cannot be accounted for by the reaction of the pupil alone, but is due more to the nature of the switching processes in the visual nervous system.

The properties of the eye differ considerably according to the conditions of adaptation. When the eye works in the lower luminance region, it loses its ability to discriminate between colours - at night, all cats look grey. The eye also loses its ability to accommodate to different distances. By increasing the level of luminance, all visual functions improve, colour perception increases and the ability to accommodate improves. Within the range 1 to 100 cd/m^2 [1], these changes are very important, and the effect of adaptation on the visual function is illustrated in Figure 2.6.

Age and vision

From about the age of 10 years, all visual functions are subject to deterioration although to some extent these losses are counterbalanced by the fact that with increasing experience and familiarity with a given visual object, increasingly less information is required for the purposes of recognition. Taken as a whole, however, visual ability diminishes with age and it is necessary to consider these effects in more detail and particularly to understand which visual functions are most affected and in what way.

Visual acuity

Between the ages of 20 and 60 years, the visual acuity of a normally sighted individual is reduced by about 25%. This reduction occurs progressively but the rate at which visual acuity diminishes increases with age, see Figure 2.7(a).

1. 1 cd/m^2 corresponds to a moderately well lit street at night, a black visual display screen or white paper with a 4 Lx illumination. 100 cd/m^2 corresponds to white paper at 400 Lx.

In practice, this means that careful attention has to be paid to the design of visual tasks in order to properly take into account the variations in visual abilities among individuals at work and, in particular, the somewhat lower visual abilities of older persons. In the case of most normal visual tasks, e.g. reading printed text, it is usually sufficient to raise the general level of illumination of the visual object. In practice, however, even this simple precaution is not without some difficulties since sensitivity to glare also increases with age.

Finding a means to compensate for reduced visual acuity is rather more difficult when reading the self-illuminated characters on a display screen. For example, if the luminance contrast is sufficient for an individual in the age range 20 to 30 years, a general increase in the level of illumination in the room would have the effect of reducing the contrast level. It is, however, precisely the opposite effect that should be aimed for in improving the readability of a display screen. For this reason, it is important that older as well as younger employees should be given the opportunity to test the equipment when purchasing a VDT system.

Whilst the reduction in visual acuity with age is unavoidable, it is nevertheless possible to minimise the effects of such a reduction. Figure 2.7(b) illustrates the change in visual acuity for a group of 696 persons of differing age. Some members of this group were non-spectacle wearers, some wore spectacles that were prescribed before the test and the remainder were provided with the best possible spectacle correction just prior to the test. The results from this investigation showed that, using the proper correction, it

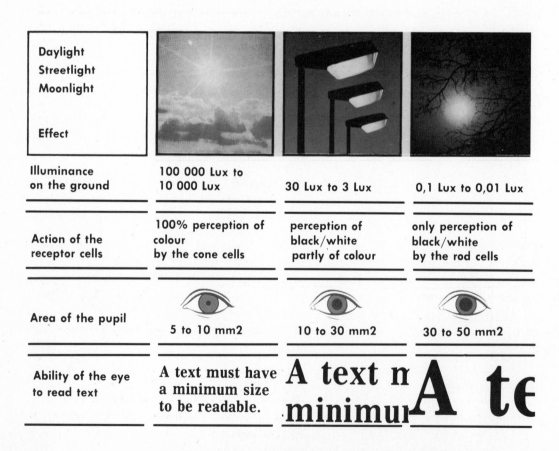

Figure 2.6 Illuminance: On a clear summer day, the illuminance of sunlight at midday is typically about 100 000 lux. The illuminance of street lighting usually falls in the range 3 to 30 lux; the illuminance of moonlight is typically 0,01 to 0,1 lux. This diagram shows the effect of these levels of illuminance on the size of the pupil and on the size of printed text required to permit reading. Ref F.9

is possible to correct for the reduction in visual acuity in the age range 60 to 69 years to a level that is somewhat higher even than for the 20 to 29 years age group with the spectacles used prior to the test!

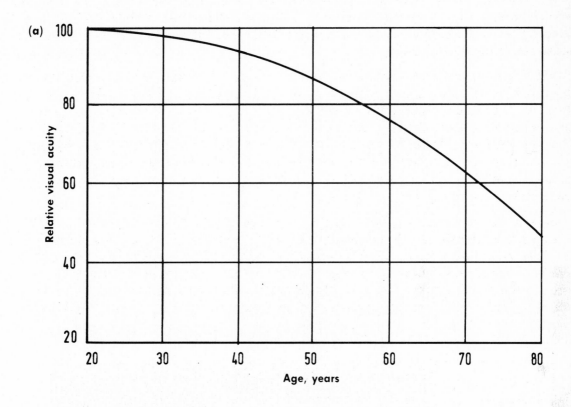

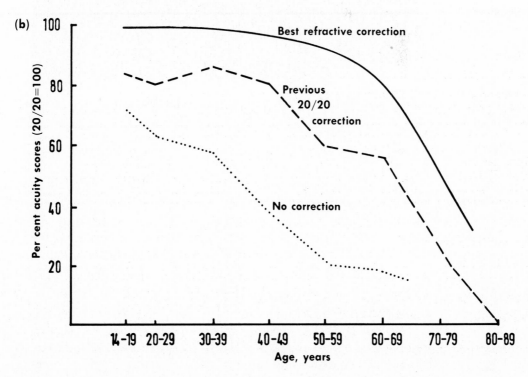

Figure 2.7 (a) The reduction of visual acuity with age, and (b) the effect of spectacle correction (1) with no correction, (2) with spectacles (but not necessarily giving optimal correction) and (3) with the best possible correction. Ref I.2

Accommodation ability

The ability of the eye to adjust or *accommodate* to different visual distances diminishes very rapidly with age, see Figure 2.8. As the diagram shows, the accommodation range decreases from 14 dioptres, i.e. equivalent to a near point of vision of about 70 mm, at the age of 5 years, to 2 dipotres corresponding to a near point of 500 mm at the age of 50 years.

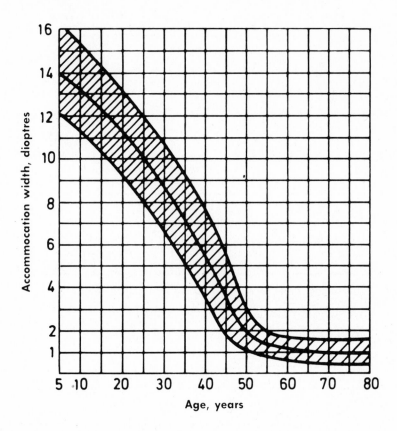

Figure 2.8 Variation in accommodation range with age. The middle curve represents the average value, the shaded area the variation for a large number of individuals. Ref H.11

The *speed of accommodation* also decreases rapidly with age and the increase in accommodation time is especially important when considering working with visual display terminals. This is because the visual distances involved are changed rapidly, typically within a time interval of less than 0,5 sec, and very often. In typical data entry tasks, it has been found that the VDT operator changes his or her viewing direction between at least three objects, the screen, the keyboard and a source document of some kind, once every 0,8 to 4 seconds. The increased accommodation time with age means that the older user must either work at a rather slower pace or accept a somewhat greater risk of error.

Because of these effects, the visual objects involved when working with VDTs should ideally be situated at roughly the same distance from the user's eyes. Furthermore, the older user should preferably carry out the type of work where accuracy rather than speed is important. Other points to bear in mind are:

- the inputting of redundant text requires less frequent changes of vision than the inputting of less redundant matter, e.g. numerical data

- proofreading and correction tasks using a VDT involve less frequent changes of visual object

- journalistic and many types of tele-sales tasks do not necessarily require the use of paper so that one of the visual objects common in most VDT tasks is omitted.

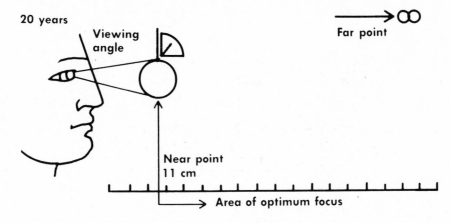

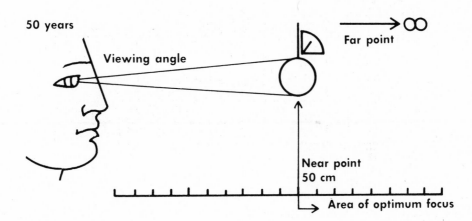

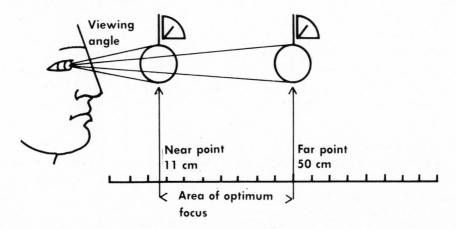

Figure 2.9 Accommodation range (the difference between the far and near points of vision) at 20 and 50 years of age with and without refractive correction.

Glare sensitivity

Sensitivity to glare also increases with age and it is not difficult to appreciate why this should be so, see Figure 2.10.

Glare is caused by the scattering of light in the eyes, and this scattered light is superimposed on the image that is projected onto the retina. As we get older, the humour of the eye becomes increasingly more opaque, an effect which increases both the light scattering effect and the loss of contrast. Tests have shown that besides the increasing opacity of the humour, other processes must also contribute to the contrast loss, e.g. changes in the colour of the eye lenses.

In trying to counterbalance the reduced visual abilities of older persons by improving their visual tasks at work, account must also be taken of their higher sensitivity to glare.

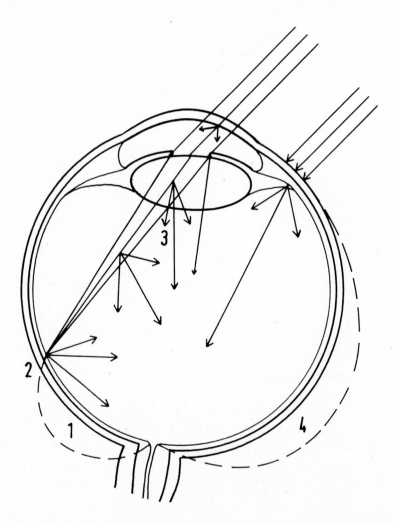

Figure 2.10 The physical cause and the physiological effect of glare. Light scattering in the retina, lens and the vitreous humour (3) reduces visual contrast. Light from the glare source impinging on part of the retina (2) reduces the sensitivity of the retina (1). A similar effect results from light impinging on the sclera (4).

Loss of contrast sensitivity

As with the other visual functions, the ability of the eye to detect very small differences in luminance also diminishes with age. Figure 2.11 shows the increase in contrast that is necessary in order to perform a given visual task. The difference between persons in the age ranges 20 to 30 years and 60 to 70 years is very great.

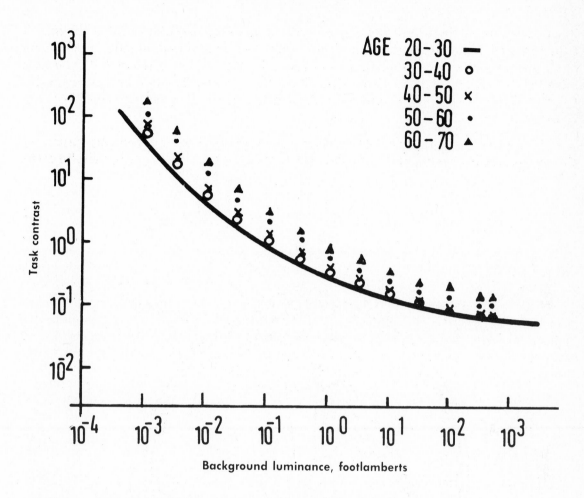

Figure 2.11 The effect of age on required task contrast for task performance. Ref I.2

The measurement of light

Since light is a form of radiant energy which induces a luminous sensation in the eye, the sensitivity of the eyes must also be taken into account in the measurement and description of light. The branch of science that is concerned with the measurement of light is called 'photometry', and some of the more important photometric quantities are described in the following sections.

Luminous flux

The term *luminous flux* is used to describe the quantity of light which is emitted from a light source per unit time and is expressed in units of lumen (lm). The luminous flux is calculated in accordance with the spectral sensitivity of the 'standard' human eye.

It is clear from this definition that the luminous flux provides no indication as to the direction of light flow and yet, as experience tells us, light sources seldom emit light uniformly in all directions. In order to describe this directional effect, additional photometric quantities are needed.

Luminance

Luminance is a measure of the intensity of light which is emitted from a light source per unit surface area normal to the direction of the light flux. In this context, the term 'light source' not only includes self-luminous sources such as lamps, but can also be any light transmitting or reflecting surface such as a wall, desktop etc.

Quantity	Symbol	Unit	Abbreviation
Luminous flux	Φ	Lumen	lm
Luminous intensity	I	Candela	cd
Illuminance	E	Lux	lx
Luminance	L	Candela/m^2	cd/m^2

Figure 2.12 Photometric quantities and units.

Luminance is a very important quantity as far as lighting and vision are concerned since it is a measure of that attribute of light which produces the sensation of brightness or *luminosity*. Since an object can radiate light in such a way that the intensity of light emission is different in different directions, the luminance also varies in different directions. In practice, therefore, the light from natural and artificial light sources in a room combine to produce a distribution of luminance rather than a constant level. This is important not only from the point of view of vision, but also with respect to the aesthetic qualities of room lighting.

Luminance is expressed in units of candela/m^2, cd/m^2, and is usually denoted by the letter 'L'.

Illuminance

Illuminance is that part of the total luminous flux that is incident on a given surface and, as such, is a measure of the quantity of light with which a given surface, e.g. a desktop, is illuminated. In practice, this depends on both the flow direction of the light and on the spatial position of the surface in relation to the light flux.

In lighting technology, illuminance is usually measured in both the horizontal and vertical planes. Those values which are normally to be found in lighting tables, standards etc., are usually the values of *horizontal illuminance*. These values are important in describing the illumination of objects, e.g. desks, which are positioned in the horizontal plane. However, the values of horizontal illuminance do not adequately describe the illumination of objects in the vertical plane, e.g. objects on storage shelves, book cases, display screens etc. In order to be able to read the images on a display screen, for example, we need light in the vertical plane.

At VDT workplaces, therefore, both the horizontal and vertical illuminances are important. A document lying on the desktop is illuminated by the *horizontal illuminance* whereas the display screen is illuminated by the *vertical illuminance*.

Illuminance is measured in units of Lux (lx) and is often denoted by the letter 'E'.

In an office which is illuminated from above, the ratio between these two quantities is usually between 0,3 and 0,5. So if, for example, the illuminance in the room is quoted to be 500 lx, the horizontal illuminance is 500 lx whilst the vertical illuminance might be somewhere in the range 150 to 250 lx.

Reflectance

The term *reflection* is used to describe the ability of a surface to 'send back' some part or all of the light that is incident upon it. If the surface is glossy, the angle between the reflected light and the surface is equal to the angle between the incident light and the surface. Objects which are reflected in this way are clearly defined, at best mirror-image like, and this type of reflection is referred to as direct or *specular reflection*.

If the surface is completely matt on the other hand, the reflected light is diffused. This type of reflection is called *diffuse reflection*.

The term *spectral reflection* refers to the ability of a surface to reflect light selectively according to wavelength. Neutral colours, white, grey or black reflect the same proportion of incident light regardless of wavelength. Coloured surfaces, on the other hand, tend to reflect light in different proportions according to wavelength.

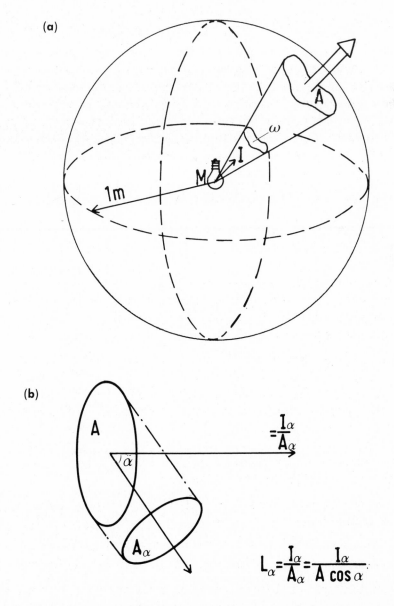

$$= \frac{I_\alpha}{A_\alpha}$$

$$L_\alpha = \frac{I_\alpha}{A_\alpha} = \frac{I_\alpha}{A \cos \alpha}$$

Figure 2.13 (a) A light source with a luminous intensity I, generates a luminous flux, Φ (b) The luminance of a given surface depends upon the angle at which the surface is viewed and the luminous intensity in this direction. Ref. O.13

The ratio between the quantities of reflected and incident light is termed *reflectance*. This is a very important surface property but insofar that reflectance is only related to the *quantities* of reflected and incident light, it is not a sufficient quantity with which to describe all of the reflection characteristics of a surface.

When light is diffusely reflected, the relationship between luminance and illuminance is as follows:

$$L \ (cd/m^2) = \rho \ \frac{E(lx)}{\pi}$$

where ρ, the reflectance may take a value between 0 and 1. As an example, the black printed text on this page has a low reflectance, less than 0,1, whilst the paper on which the text is printed has a high reflectance, greater than 0,8.

Reflectance is an overall measure of the light which is reflected from a surface. In practice, however, the most important part of the reflected light is that part which is directed towards the eye of the observer, see Figure 2.14. In viewing a perfectly matt surface, the luminance of the surface would appear to be the same regardless of the viewing direction.In other words, the surface would appear uniformly bright. In viewing a very glossy surface, on the other hand, the surface would appear to lack brightness when viewed from certain directions. In practice, these effects are very important as regards the subjective and objective evaluation of reflected glare, e.g. from keyboards, display screens etc., and loss of contrast.

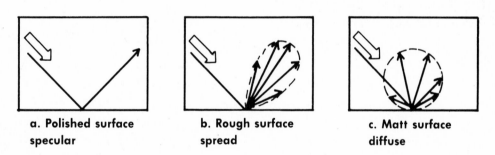

a. Polished surface
specular

b. Rough surface
spread

c. Matt surface
diffuse

Figure 2.14 The type of reflection varies with different surfaces (a) polished surface (specular), (b) rough surface (spread) and (c) matt surface (diffuse) Ref I.2

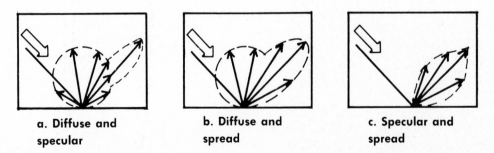

a. Diffuse and
specular

b. Diffuse and
spread

c. Specular and
spread

Figure 2.15 Examples of compound reflection: (a) diffuse and specular, (b) diffuse and spread, (c) specular and spread. These types of reflection are very important for the assessment of reflected glare e.g. from keyboards and display screens Ref I.2

Transmittance

The term *transmittance* is used to describe the ratio between the quantities of transmitted and incident light. In this sense, the transmitted light flux refers to that quantity of light which leaves a particular medium from a surface other than that on which the light was incident.

The most important light transmitting media on a VDT are the front face of the display screen and the filters which are or may be used to reduce reflections on the

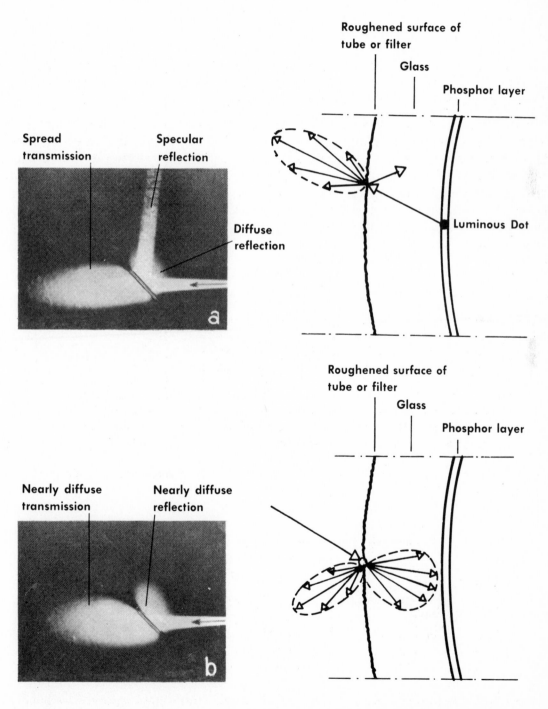

Figure 2.16 The effect of a roughened screen glass surface (a) on the light emitted from a character, (b) on the light incident on the screen surface.

65

screen. Both media should transmit the light from the characters without diffusing it. If this light is diffused, the character images look blurred.

It is also necessary, however, that the surfaces of the display screen and filters are not glossy so that specular reflections are avoided. To achieve such a condition, the surface may be roughened, e.g. by etching, and Figure 2.16 shows the effect of a rough surface on light transmission when light is incident on the smooth side of the panel and on the light emitted from the characters in the display.

These diagrams also demonstrate that the transmission and reflection characteristics of a surface are not independent. By using a surface, the reflection characteristics of which are good in the sense that specular reflections are avoided, the character images may become blurred as the transmitted light is diffused.

Absorptance

The sum of the reflectance and transmittance of a medium is always less than unity which implies that some quantity of light is lost in each transmission. If some part of the luminous flux remains within the medium, the process by which this quantity of light is retained is known as *absorption*. The retained light energy is normally converted into heat.

The sum of the reflected, transmitted and absorbed luminous fluxes must always be equal to the incident flux. In other words, the sum of the reflectance, transmittance and absorptance is always equal to 1,0.

Luminance contrast

The term *contrast* is often used to describe the perceived difference in colour or brightness or both of the objects within a particular field of vision or from one point in time to another. Whilst contrast is not, strictly speaking, a physiological quantity, it is nevertheless one of the most important photometric quantities insofar that it is related to most visual functions, e.g. visual acuity, contrast sensitivity, speed of recognition, etc.

In the objective sense, the term *luminance contrast* is used to describe the ratio between the difference in luminance of an object and its surroundings and the luminance of the surroundings or *background luminance*. Thus:

$$C = \frac{L_2 - L_1}{L_1}$$

where L_2 = luminance of the object, and

L_1 = background luminance

In calculating the contrast value, it should be noted that the formula is not symmetric since numerical values of the contrast, C, are not the same when L_2 is greater than L_1 and when the same luminance values are used but when L_2 is less than L_1.

If the luminance of the object is very much greater than the background luminance, the numerical values of contrast are large and increase rapidly. If, on the other hand, the luminance of the object is less than the background luminance, the values of C tend asymptotically to the value C = −1.

This is illustrated in the following examples:

$$L_2 = 2L_1 \ldots C = 200\% \text{ (or } +2; \text{ positive)}$$
$$L_2 = 0,5L_1 \ldots C = -50\% \text{ (or } -0,5; \text{ negative)}$$
$$L_2 = 10L_1 \ldots C = 900\% \text{ (or } +9; \text{ positive)}$$
$$L_2 = 0,1L_1 \ldots C = -90\% \text{ (or } -0,9; \text{ negative)}$$

Figure 2.17 Luminance contrast in relation to the ratio between background and visual object luminance.

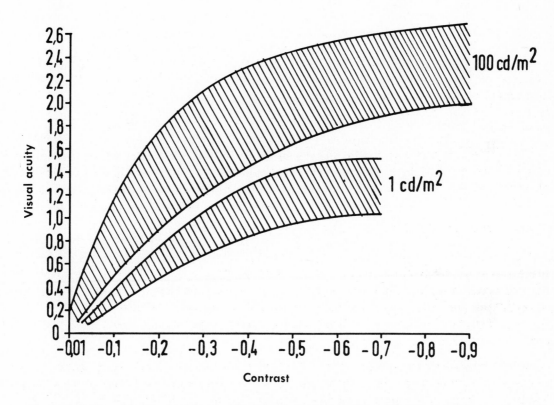

Figure 2.18 The visual acuity of normally sighted persons (25-50 years of age) at different levels of contrast and background luminance (1 and 100 cd/m²). Ref H.11.

LIGHT EMITTING vs ILLUMINATED CHARACTERS

Printed characters are made visible by virtue of the light which falls on them. The characters on a CRT display are made visible by virtue of the light which they emit. This difference is an important one.

In order to be visible, a printed character must reflect the light in a way that differs from that in which light is reflected by the surroundings. The bigger the difference in these reflection characteristics, the greater is the perceived contrast between the character and the background, and hence the more legible the character image becomes. If, in practice, it is found that legibility is unsatisfactory, the illumination can be increased. The contrast, however, remains the same.

In the case of light emitting characters, this is not so. The brightness of the character images is determined by the characteristics of the VDT. If the incident illumination is increased, the contrast is reduced.

The eye is more sensitive to small changes in contrast than small changes in brightness. But whilst minor variations in contrast may sometimes appear to reduce the legibility of the text, reading performance may not necessarily be adversely affected. Of course, this is not always the case. Under certain conditions, legibility can indeed be impaired and the various factors in this respect are considered in the following sections.

The optical characteristics of visual displays

Character luminance[1]

The *luminance* of a self-illuminated character on a VDT screen is not an exactly definable quantity and there are several reasons why this is so. In the first place, it is very difficult to obtain an exact measure of the luminance in such small fields without resorting to very complicated measuring equipment. Secondly, the luminance is not constant at all points within the boundaries of the character image.

The relationship between the luminance and legibility of printed characters can be investigated by varying the conditions under which the text is illuminated. However, it is not possible to do this on a VDT screen since the stroke intensity and also the distribution of luminance within each character shape and across each stroke changes according to the overall level of luminance. Since these changes depend very much on the method of character generation, it is necessary to devise very complicated testing procedures in order to arrive at correct and meaningful measures of character luminance. Difficult though they may be, however, these problems can be overcome. But there remain a number of other problems. For example, the size and shape of the character is important. The shape of a 5 x 7 dot matrix image with a character height of 10 mm and a dot size of 0,8 mm, for example, is less affected by changes in luminance than the same image with a height of, say, 4 or 6 mm.

For these reasons, therefore, there exists no single definition of character brightness and its distribution within each character image that is meaningful from the point of view of character recognition.

Part of the problem can be resolved by measuring the luminance at certain points within each character stroke in order to determine both the levels and distribution of luminance. The results from a series of measurements of this kind are shown in Figure 2.19.

These figures show the horizontal and vertical distributions of luminance through single dots at different positions on a relatively good CRT display. By comparing the upper and lower halves of the diagram, it can be seen that the horizontal extent of the dots is greater than the vertical extent. In other words the dots are not perfectly round but are somewhat oval in shape. Furthermore, the dots are significantly broader in the upper left hand part of the writing area than in the centre.

---

1. In everyday language, the term 'brightness' is used in a sense which differs from the more exact, scientific definition. In the case of character images on a CRT display, however, it is the *character luminance* which is normally referred to as brightness. Luminance is an extremely important - but not unique - quantity as regards the visual perception of the brightness of an object. For example, snow at night appears to be brighter than coal in daylight. By measuring the luminances, however, the reverse is in fact the case. The discrepancy is due to the fact that the impression of brightness depends not only upon the luminance of the object that we look at but also on the luminance of the environment in which the object exists. 'Brightness' therefore, is a quantity that is related to individual sensitivity whereas 'luminance' is a measurable, photometric quantity.

An additional characteristic, and one that is common to all CRT displays, is that the luminance varies over quite a wide range at different points on the display screen. In this case, the luminance was found to vary between 62 cd/m^2 in the upper left corner of the display to 73 cd/m^2 in the centre to about 24 cd/m^2 in the lower right hand corner.

Individual terminals differ greatly in this respect and the closer the boundaries of the writing area come to the edges of the CRT, the greater this variation becomes.

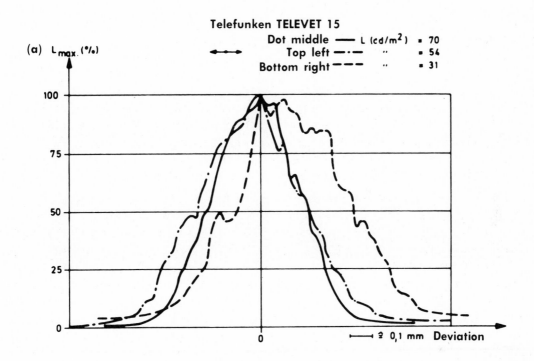

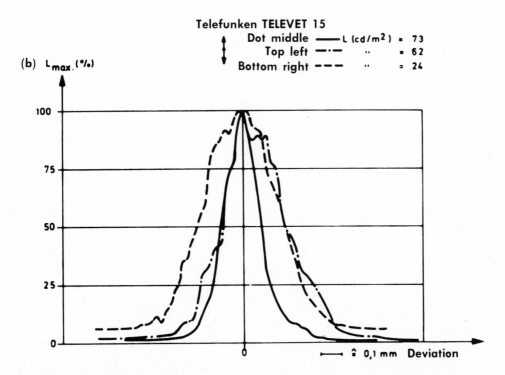

Figure 2.19 (a) Horizontal and (b) vertical luminance distributions through single dots at different positions on a relatively good CRT. Ref C.2

In Figure 2.20, the character images on two VDT displays are reproduced. On both displays, the character images are generated using the dot matrix technique. The terminals whose characters are illustrated on the right is used in practice with a luminance between 80 and 120 cd/m^2, still with readable images. The terminal on the left can produce a maximum luminance of only 30 to 40 cd/m^2 by which time the character images are blurred and no longer readable.

In this case, one could prescribe 12 and 120 cd/m^2 respectively as the maximum usable luminance levels for these two terminals.

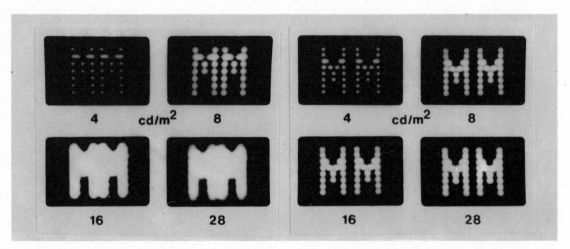

Figure 2.20 A comparison of two characters on different VDTs, with four character luminance levels.

Contrast

Knowing the values of character luminance and background luminance, the luminance contrast values can be calculated.

On most types of VDT, the background luminance and hence the contrast is determined by the quantity of incident light and the reflection properties of the screen surface.

Under normal office lighting conditions, good terminals can attain contrast values which are comparable to those which are typical of printed text. The image quality differences between the VDTs now available on the market, however, are very large indeed.

Visual acuity and readability

The importance of luminance and contrast can be most easily shown in terms of their effects on *visual acuity*. Visual acuity is a measure of the ability of the eye to discriminate between or resolve fine detail, e.g. characters or parts of a character image. It is also an important and indeed one of the best available measures for evaluating the legibility of a visual display.

The term 'visual acuity' is used here in a sense that differs somewhat from the normal usage. It is sometimes believed that this is a constant property which provides a fixed measure of the visual ability of the eye. More correctly, however, visual acuity is a quantity which depends on a number of parameters including character size, shape,

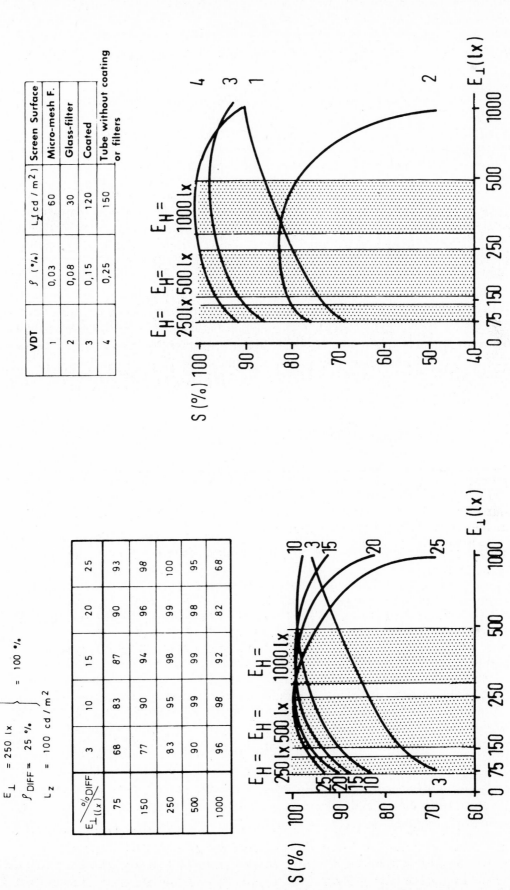

Figure 2.21 (a) Relative visual acuity in relation to the diffuse reflectance of the screen surface and illuminance. (b) The visual acuity characteristics of 4 VDTs with differing screen surface characteristics. Ref C.2

contrast, luminance, colour and so on. When the other parameters are fixed for a given display, the effects of luminance and contrast on the visual acuity of an individual observer can be determined. If the maximum acuity of a 'standard' observer is defined as 100%, then the visual acuity under different conditions can be used as a comparitive measure.

Figure 2.21[1] shows the visual acuity characteristics of four VDTs with differing surface characteristics and character luminances. In considering these diagrams, two things become readily apparent. Firstly, the two display screens without filters, screens 3 and 4, exhibit the highest character luminances and the highest levels of reflection from the surface of the screen. Secondly, these screens also exhibit the highest visual acuity under lighting conditions that are typical of those found in office environments.

To illustrate the practical significance of different values of visual acuity for two terminals, consider the following example. If a VDT operator could comfortably read a given text at a distance of 500 mm, a text with 20% poorer visual acuity would have to be placed at a distance of 430 mm. In this case, the operator would have to chose between a somewhat higher visual loading by locating the text with poorer visual acuity at the same distance, or to change his or her posture in order to ensure optimum readability. This choice is important in most VDT applications because the eyes are required to focus on the display screen, the keyboard and the text on a source document, and often in quick succession. To help overcome these problems, therefore, it is advisable to use a VDT with a higher visual acuity.

Referring back to Figure 2.21, the difference in visual acuity between terminal 1 and terminal 4 in a typical office environment with 500 lx illumination is about 25%. This corresponds to the deterioration in the visual acuity of a normally sighted person between the ages of 20 and 60 years.

From the foregoing comments, it can be seen quite clearly that the optical and photometric characteristics of visual displays are of differing but very real importance as regards both the design and use of CRT displays.

The optical characteristics of source documents

In most types of work involving the use of visual display terminals, a significant amount of the information to be processed either originates from or is presented in the form of paper copy, or both. In some cases, hardcopy is more important than the display screen for the presentation and transfer of information.

Information which is presented on hardcopy usually appears as a positive image, i.e. dark, usually black characters against a light coloured, usually white background. This ensures good optical contrast but is no guarantee for easy readability, even under normal office illumination or in daylight. Just how readable a given piece of text is depends, among other things, on the reflectivity of the unprinted paper surface and the colour and optical density of the ink. These effects are best appreciated by looking at a glossy photoprint.

The effects of reflectance are easily appreciated by looking at a glossy photoprint. Depending on the angle at which light is made to fall on a print of this kind, the image can be made to appear either as a positive or as a negative image. Somewhere in

1. These figures are derived from a luminance-contrast-acuity- formula. This is neither a sufficient nor an accurate way of describing the visual acuity characteristics of VDT type character images but it does provide a useful way of illustrating the order of magnitude of the various effects.

between, there is a certain angle at which the entire image appears to be uniformly bright and is no longer visible. This effect is illustrated in Figure 2.22.

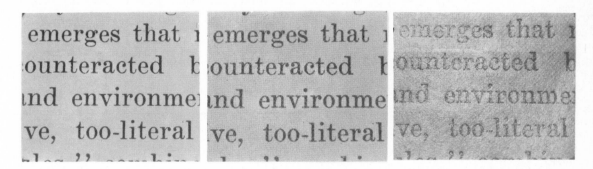

Figure 2.22 Appearance of text viewed from different angles.

The picture on the extreme left was exposed under favourable lighting conditions. The centre picture was less favourably exposed, in this case, with a lamp suspended directly over the text. Finally, the picture on the right shows the result of having illuminated the text from such a direction that the text is no longer readable. Had the lighting angle been increased still further, the text would have completely disappeared.

If a glossy paper is illuminated at an angle of less than 30°, the unprinted areas appear to be highly glossy with a corresponding angle of light reflection. If the paper is printed with a matt coloured ink, the brightness of the text is always less than that of the unprinted surface of the paper albeit that the contrast depends to a large extent on the viewing angle. If a glossy ink is used instead, there would be no apparent difference in brightness between the printed and unprinted areas.

A glossy paper printed with a glossy ink gives less contrast for most viewing angles. Such a text is most easily read under diffuse illumination, e.g. under a uniformly cloudy sky. In the working environment, however, this type of lighting is the exception rather than the rule, and neither is this type of lighting particularly desirable.

Quite clearly then, the so-called 'gloss effect' which can seriously disturb the ability to read easily and comfortably is not only a problem which is related to the use of CRT displays; it is a problem which occurs frequently in all types of visual task.

The visual quality of source documents not only depends on their contrast, but also on the brightness distribution within each character image. In Figure 2.25, several reproductions of the character 'M' are shown, beginning with the image that was produced on matt paper using a typewriter with a good carbon band.

At work, however, typewritten originals are seldom used. More usually it is the first or a lower order carbon copy that is used. These types of copy, computer print-outs, photocopies and telex copies are the most common types of source document used in VDT tasks.

Figure 2.25 shows how the character images become distorted and less readable as the result of carbon copying. In this particular example, the copies were made on white paper, a fact which for organisational reasons, is also becoming less common. Copies are more frequently being made on coloured or off-white paper such as telex, telegram paper etc. These types of paper reflect less light than white paper grades so that the contrast is usually rather less than that shown in these reproductions.

The effect which this has on the readability of the text is shown in Figure 2.26. With brighter papers, the readability of the text is progressively improved. Microfilm

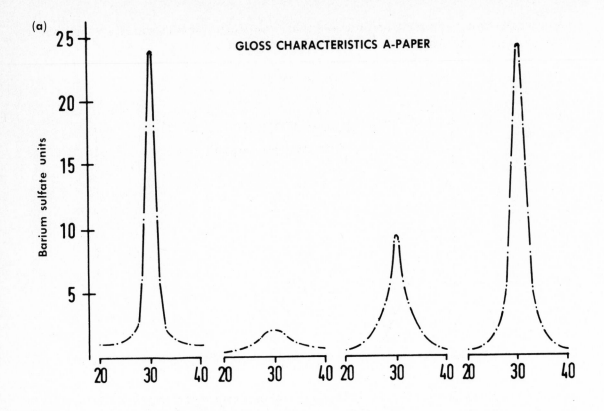

(a)

GLOSS CHARACTERISTICS A-PAPER

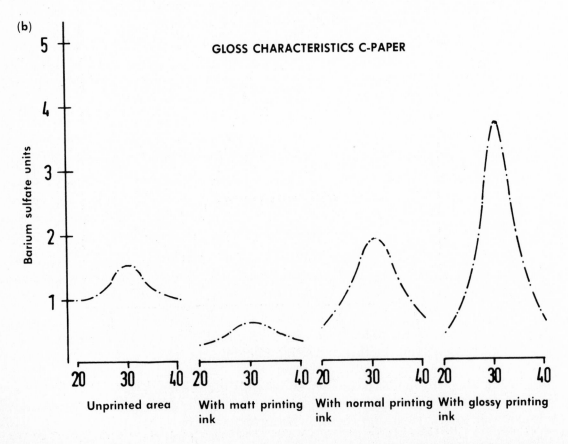

(b)

GLOSS CHARACTERISTICS C-PAPER

Unprinted area   With matt printing ink   With normal printing ink   With glossy printing ink

Figure 2.23 Reflection characteristics of paper surfaces and different printing inks (a) gloss paper, (b) moderately glossy paper. Ref. H.11

enlargements usually have an optical quality that corresponds roughly to that shown in the middle of the diagram.

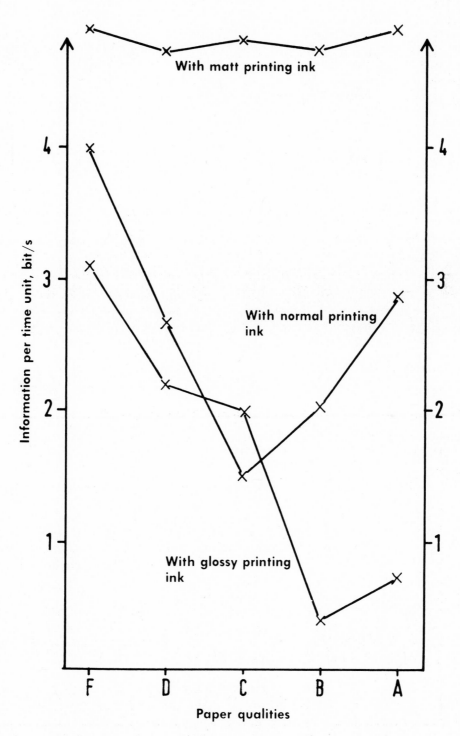

Figure 2.24 Comparison of reading performance for printed material with papers and printing inks of different gloss. Ref. H.11

Many VDT operators work with telex copy, the optical quality of which is often very much less than that of the CRT display. In cases such as this, working with the VDT may very well lead to a subjective feeling of fatigue, but due more to the poor readability of the copy than of the display screen. In very many VDT applications, telex copy is used and read more frequently than other, more legible types of copy.

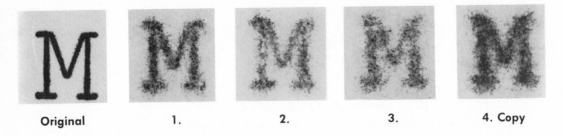

| Original | 1. | 2. | 3. | 4. Copy |

Figure 2.25 The quality of typewritten text: original typewritten character reproduction and successive carbon copies.

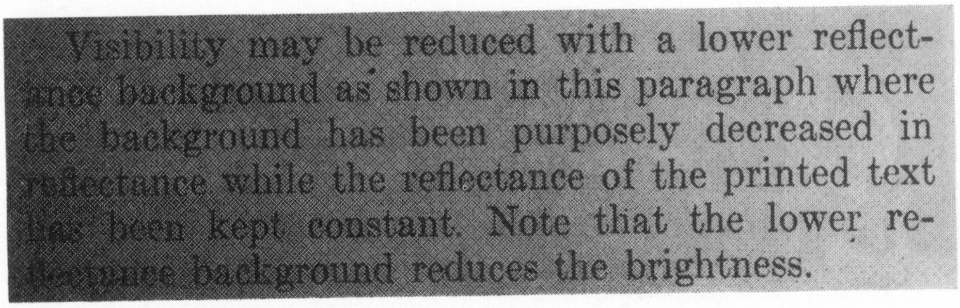

Visibility may be reduced with a lower reflect-ance background as shown in this paragraph where the background has been purposely decreased in reflectance while the reflectance of the printed text has been kept constant. Note that the lower re-flectance background reduces the brightness.

Figure 2.26 Effect of decreased paper brightness upon readability.

Subjective evaluation of the readability of source documents and CRT displays

The readability of a document may be poor for a number of physiological and psychological reasons, some of which have been considered in the foregoing sections. But are these problems merely of theoretical interest or do they have practical significance in everyday working life? In addition, how do these difficulties compare with those of reading and identifying the character images on a CRT display?

To help answer these questions, a series of laboratory tests was carried out in order to quantify the physical and photometric characteristics of the more commonly used types of source document at VDT workplaces. These data were then compared with the corresponding values for CRT displayed texts.

As a rule it was found that the quality of the text on printed copies or originals from a good and regularly cleaned typewriter was superior to that which was displayed on a VDT screen. However, it was also found that such high quality document originals are seldom encountered in practice.

If the quality of character reproduction on VDTs is compared with that on commonly-used document or 'hard-copy' sources e.g. photostat copies, many types of computer print-outs etc., then as a rule, VDT reproduction is of a superior quality.

In order to determine how VDT operators themselves judge these differences, a survey was carried out in which several pertinent questions were asked. In answer to the question:

'Does the text on the display screen look more like a typewritten
original or more like a carbon copy?'

the response was as shown in Figure 2.27. In other words, the answers showed a preference for the CRT display. Figure 2.28 shows how this same group, which comprised more than 800 VDT operators, judged the readability of their hardcopy originals.

**'Does the text on the display screen look more like
a typewritten original or more like a carbon copy?'**

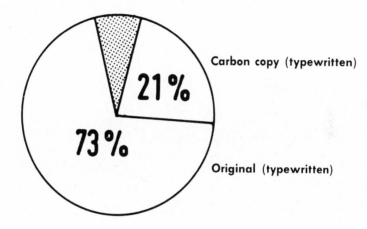

Figure 2.27 Subjective evaluation of the text on the VDT screen in relation to the quality of typewritten and carbon copy text.

'The hard copy originals are easily readable?'

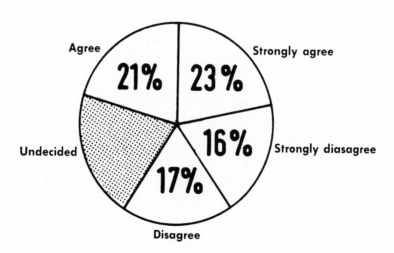

Figure 2.28 Subjective evaluation of the readability of VDT task source documents.

More people within this group judged their source documents to be 'easily readable' than 'difficult to read', 44% vs 33%, but this does not mean that character reproduction on their originals could be described as favourable. Only when the proportion of those who judge their hardcopy to be 'easily readable' exceeds about 70% could we begin to speak of good readability.

By comparison, the way in which the subjects judged their VDT displayed text is shown in Figure 2.29.

It can be seen that the majority of the subjects described the readability of the display as 'good'. A more direct comparison between the subjective judgement of the readability of source documents and CRT displayed texts is shown in Figure 2.30.

'The text on the VDT screen is easily readable?'

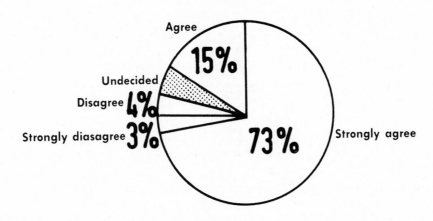

Figure 2.29 Subjective evaluation of the readability of text on the VDT screen.

'The text on the VDT screen is often more easily read than the hardcopy originals?'

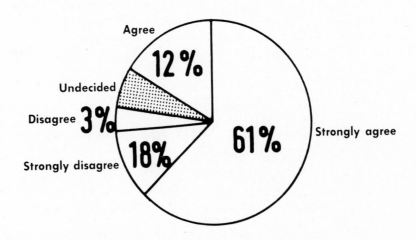

Figure 2.30 Subjective evaluation of the readability of hardcopy text and VDT text display.

But what do these figures really mean? Do they, as they seem, praise the merits of the VDT? Of course not; the VDT, like all forms of data and text presentation has its own advantages and disadvantages, most of which are discussed elsewhere in this report. What these observations do show, however, is that *when VDTs are introduced into a particular working environment, the problems which can occur must not necessarily be due to or blamed on the VDT itself!*

In all working situations where source documents are used, visual problems can arise which have little or nothing to do with the display terminal. For this reason, there may seem to be little point in striving to achieve the 'optimum VDT' when many other, and perhaps more easily modified, features of the workplace are unfavourable. In reality, of course, the goal should be to optimise all aspects of the working environment, including, but not only, the VDT.

GLARE

Glare is a visual condition that occurs when the range of luminances in the visual field is too great, e.g. when bright sources of light such as luminaires, windows or their reflected images, fall within the field of vision, with the result that the processes of visual adaptation are disturbed. Due to this effect, glare may be experienced as a source of distraction, as a source of actual visual discomfort or it may, in more extreme cases, impair vision, e.g. by reducing visual acuity.

As far as the effects of glare are concerned, therefore, there are two important consequences:

- visual discomfort and / or
- visual impairment or disability

The type of glare that results in an impairment of vision is termed *disability glare*, and the type of glare that is experienced as discomforting is referred to as *discomfort glare*. Both types of glare may, but need not necessarily, occur simultaneously, and for this reason they are usually considered separately.

Glare from interior lighting sources may often be a source of discomfort but seldom disability. When considering the design of the lighting system in VDT rooms, therefore, it is necessary to place some form of restriction on discomfort glare, i.e. by the appropriate choice, positioning and shielding of the luminaires. However, if these restrictions are too harsh, the resulting illumination may be lifeless and lacking in relief. If the task *does* require definite restrictions on discomfort glare, it may be possible to provide some relief to the appearance of the room by providing a few, locally bright areas to add lustre but without causing glare.

It is also necessary to make a further distinction as regards types of glare according to whether the glare is caused directly by the light sources - *direct glare* - or by their reflection from illuminated surfaces such as walls and desktops, *reflected glare*.

Glare increases with increasing luminance of the luminous surfaces and their size within the visual field, but decreases when the glare sources are more remote from the viewing direction or when the areas surrounding them are made brighter. This is one of the reasons why bright ceilings are normally recommended for offices.

Under some circumstances, the visual surfaces of the task may themselves be a source of discomfort glare or even disability. This is particularly true of large surfaces, e.g. glossy desktops, paper with too high luminance under the prevailing illumination etc.

Unfortunately, there is no universally accepted method for evaluating the perceived levels of glare. Different methods have been established in different countries. In the

United Kingdom, glare is calculated using the so-called BRS-Glare formula and the levels of glare are referred to in terms of a *glare index* [1]. In the U.S.A., glare is evaluated using the Guth-formula and in West Germany, the evaluation of glare is based on the use of a series of 'luminance limit curves'.

Reflected glare

The lighting conditions in a work room may still give rise to problems of glare even with the appropriate level of illumination and when adequate precautions have been taken to safeguard against direct glare, e.g. by installing glare shields on the luminaires, curtains at windows etc. In cases such as this, the problem can usually be traced to reflected glare which occurs when objects with a high luminance are reflected from smooth and glossy surfaces.

In office environments, there are many possible sources of specular reflections, including the paper which is used, particularly if it has a glossy finish such as photographic prints. In VDT workrooms, however, the display screen represents an additional source of specular reflection and one which, for the reasons explained below, makes the display screen potentially one of the most important sources of reflected glare.

Among the IES recommendations concerning glare, the following may be used as a guide in relation to the design of VDT workrooms:

> Visual tasks should preferably be so located that no bright source of light or its reflected image lies close to the line of sight. If this is not practicable, the glare source should be screened from view or its luminance reduced, or the relative positions of task, operator and source changed appropriately. In some circumstances an increase in task illuminance may be necessary.

> In an interior where more than one type of work or activity takes place, the glare index or corresponding restriction should not exceed the lowest of the limiting values for the individual occupations.

> If it is not convenient to calculate a glare index or corresponding value, or if it is not possible to suitably restrict the luminance of luminaires, e.g. according to the recommendations of the CIE, an empirical method should be used to ensure that discomfort glare is not excessive. For example, the lamp may be shielded from direct view by means of reflectors, louvres or structural features of the interior. The lamps may be enclosed in diffusing covers whose average luminance at usual angles of view is not greater than 500 cd/m^2.

1. The glare index is a series of numbers in the sequence 13, 16, 19, 22 and 25. For a given set of room and lighting conditions, the glare index can be calculated using the method described in the IES Code. If the ability to perform the task demands severe restrictions on discomfort glare, the glare index should not exceed 13. For most tasks involving the use of keyboards and the reading of text on a display screen, the glare index should not exceed 16.

SCREEN REFLECTIONS

Most CRT terminals have a large screen area - usually with a diagonal measure of 28 cm or more - with a curved glass screen surface which tends to reflect some part of the light that falls on it. In addition, VDTs are often used in brightly-lit office environments and frequently situated close to windows and other bright surfaces.

In many VDT applications, reflections on the display screen are a major source of distraction and complaints of visual discomfort at work can, in many cases, be traced back to the effects of screen reflections

The reflection characteristics of visual display screens - and other surfaces - can be described in terms of two components:

> • the *direct reflectance* which provides a measure of the luminance of the image that can be seen as directly reflected on the surface of the screen, and
>
> • the indirect or *diffuse reflectance* which provides a measure of the luminance of the screen when light falls on it.

Surface reflections which are predominantly of the direct kind, i.e. mirror-image type reflections, are sometimes referred to by the term "gloss".

These two types of reflection are not necessarily related to one another. With the appropriate choice of the surface reflectance properties of the equipment, materials, job aids and other surfaces in the working environment, visual displays can usually be partially or completely freed from disturbing reflections. In this way, VDTs can be successfully integrated into the office environment from the point of view of colour and luminance.

The disturbing effects of screen reflections

Specular reflections on the VDT screen are a major source of distraction and discomfort for basically two reasons. Firstly, this type of reflection reduces the brightness contrast of the display with the result that the displayed character images become more difficult to read. Secondly, the reflected images obscure the visual display.

In addition to these two effects, it has often been suggested that screen reflections can also be a source of glare and one which increases the likelihood of visual discomfort.

Reflection 'glare'

In office environments, the highest levels of luminance due to the room lighting usually fall in the range 5000 to 8000 cd/m^2. Since the direct reflectance of an untreated VDT screen is typically less than 4%, the luminance of the images reflected on the display screen would then be expected to fall in the range of 200 to 300 cd/m^2. This can be compared with the luminances of paper copy, desktops etc., which fall typically in the range of 150 to 250 cd/m^2. In view of the fact that paper documents and other light reflecting surfaces represent the greater part of and, in many VDT tasks e.g. text and data copy entry, the more frequently referred to parts of the visual field, screen 'glare' cannot be considered as a major factor as regards visual discomfort.

Reflections and accommodation difficulty

Reflections on the face of the VDT screen represent an additional image which is interposed between the eye of the operator and the plane on which the character images are displayed. In other words, the focal plane of the reflected images is closer to the the eyes than that on which the character images are displayed, and the consequences of this effect are shown in Figure 2.31.

Figure 2.31 shows the reflection of a light source L on the display screen B on which a character, say Z, is displayed. In order to see the character Z clearly, both eyes accommodate according to the distance between the eyes and the character, i.e. to avoid seeing a double image, the visual axis through both eyes intersect at Z. With the eyes thus accommodated, however, the reflection is seen by the left eye to be in the position L'', and by the right eye in position L'. In this way, the viewer perceives a double image of the reflection.

When this occurs, signals pass between the eyes and the brain in an attempt to bring the perceived double image into clear focus with the result that the eyes tend to re-accommodate in order to bring the points L'' and L' together. In this position, however, the character Z is now perceived as a double and unclear image and the accommodation process is repeated. In the long run, therefore, the accommodation position oscillates between the plane of the character Z and that of the reflected image L.

This type of disturbance increases as:

- the luminance of the reflected image increases
- the direct reflectance of the screen surface increases
- the form of the reflected image becomes more sharply defined
- the horizontal extent of the reflected image decreases
- the distances L' and L'' decrease, and
- the distance between $\dot Z$ and L', L'' decreases.

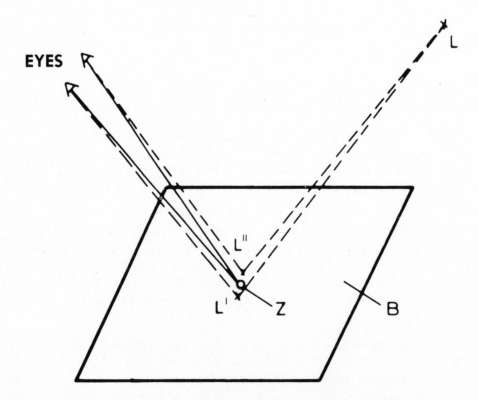

Figure 2.31 An illustration of the effects of screen reflections and the difficulty of accommodation.

In general, an unstructured source of reflections, i.e. one without a clearly defined shape, results in a more diffuse type of reflected image which is less disturbing than mirror-image type reflections. This has very important consequences in the design of VDT workrooms. Luminaires should be shielded so as to avoid their direct reflection on the display screens. Windows should be shielded by pattern-free curtains or roll blinds rather than by venetian blinds, louvres or similar types of blind that might cause a pattern of light stripes, especially on sunny days.

It has been found that neither character brightness nor colour play a particularly important role as regards the disturbing effect of reflections. The most important display feature in this respect is the uniformity of the background luminance.

As a general rule, reflections with sharp contours and high luminance should be avoided even when the contrast between the character and background luminances on the visual display is sufficient.

Contrast reduction

In the absense of reflections, the luminance contrast on the display screen can be calculated as follows:

$$C = \frac{L_z - L_U}{L_U} \times 100\%$$

If L_D is the luminance of a directly reflected image, the contrast is reduced to a value that can be calculated from:

$$C' = \frac{(L_z + L_D) - (L_U + L_D)}{L_U + L_D} \times 100\%$$

where L_z = character luminance, and

L_U = background luminance of the screen

Consider the following example. The character and background luminances on VDT displays are typically L_z 140 cd/m^2 and L_U 20 cd/m^2 respectively, giving a contrast C of 600%. With an ambient luminance of, say, 8000 cd/m^2 and a screen with a direct reflectance of 3%, the luminance of the reflected image would be L_D 240 cd/m^2 in which case the contrast is reduced to 46%!.

Due to the fact that the reflected images are not uniformly distributed over the face of the screen, the characters are, or at least appear to be, more readable in the higher contrast regions of the display than in those areas with low contrast. Most VDT operators try to overcome this problem by adjusting the character luminance to a higher level, and this is one of the reasons why character luminance control is usually regarded to be an essential feature of visual display equipment.

In practice, windows are one of the most important sources of reflections on VDT screens. On the face of things, it would seem quite easy to avoid problems of this kind by shielding the windows with curtains or blinds, but in practice, this is not always as easy as it sounds. Even on a cloudy winter day, the contrast can vary by a factor of two or more, and on a day such as this, few people would think of drawing the curtains or pulling down the blinds. To many, louvre-type blinds appear to offer a solution to this kind of problem but blinds such as these can easily give rise to a striped or otherwise patterned structure of reflections on the display screen.

One way of reducing the effects of screen reflections is to make use of a screen filter. However, the most effective and least costly way of avoiding this type of problem is to adjust the position of the terminal so that reflections are no longer visible.

Under constant artificial lighting with an illuminance of 500 lx in a room with a depth of 4 metres or more, daylight has relatively little effect on screen reflections provided that the face of the screen is at right angles to the line of the windows.

The use of screen filters

Screen filters, of one type or another, are often used by manufacturers and individual operators in an attempt to combat the problem of screen reflections and thereby to improve the visual quality of the display. It should be borne in mind, however, that it is not possible to place a filter between the eye and the visual display and thereby improve all of the characteristics that contribute to the 'quality' of the display. Whilst the use of an appropriate type of filter can be effective in reducing reflections, this is invariably accomplished at the expense of reduced character brightness and resolution.

The use of screen filters, therefore, is something that should be approached with caution. It is worth reiterating that, in most cases, screen reflections can most effectively be reduced, not by using a filter, but through the much simpler expedient of adjusting the position of the terminal. If the use of a filter is being considered, however, it is important that the operator clearly understands the characteristics of the various types of filter that are available to him.

Reflectance of the untreated CRT glass surface

The smooth glass surface of the CRT screen typically reflects about 4% of the light which falls onto it. When the surface is less smooth or dusty, this value is reduced to about 3%. This is sufficient to produce clearly visible and sharply defined reflections on the screen. Even under quite low ambient illumination, the operator is usually able to see his or her own image clearly reflected on the screen. The luminance of an untreated CRT display is usually in the range 100 to 300 cd/m^2.

When the phosphor is bonded directly onto the inner surface of the screen glass, i.e. without any intermediate filter substrate, the diffuse reflectance of the screen is typically in the range 22 to 27%, and the screen usually appears milky-grey in colour.

The untreated display has the highest character and background luminances under ambient illumination. However, some part of the incident light is transmitted through the phosphor with the result that reflections can occur within the CRT. This tends to reduce the luminance contrast on the screen.

Filter panels

In spite of the fact that there are several kinds of glass or plexiglass panels which can be installed in front of the display to provide some measure of filtering, the reason for doing so is not always very clear.

In some cases, panels of this kind are used to change the apparent colour of the display. It is not uncommon for individual VDT operators to use colour filters to produce

diff (%)	Make, Type, Manufacturer or Distributor	Colour	L(cd/m²)	L(ratio)
<5	All VDTs with micro-mesh-filter, Pol-filter ADS 3000, Nixdorf 620/38, Siemens 8161, etc. Nixdorf 8870/b	black	1-2	1:70 1:100
5-10	Pol-Filter, dark glass filter, dark coating Dietz 600/10, Omron 8025 BD, CMC, Harris 8171, Comko 2000, Alpha 128, Redactron, Ruf System 95, Ruf 90, ICL 2251, ADDS Consul 980, Teleprint M40, Variant, Data 100 Keybatch Data 100-82, CMC 103 Keystation, Interdata CRT 1200, Terminal Products, CDC 730, Tektronix 4015-1	dark grey or dark green	2-5 (150 lx) 4-8 (250 lx)	1:70-1:27 1:33-1:17
10-15	Glass filter, light coating, bonded screen Tealtronic, Bunker Ramo 9017, Bunker Ramo 9015, Hazeltine Telex System III 3807-25, SEL 3287, 3286, LCL 82, Infoton, MDS 21-20, Telex TC 277 B, CTM 900, HP 2640 A	middle grey or green	5-7 (150 lx) 8-12 (250 lx)	1:27-1:19 1:17-1:11
15-20	Light coating, bonded screen Raytheon, Teleprint VT 5700, SEL 3286	grey	7-10 (150 lx) 12-16 (250 lx)	1:19-1:14 1:11-1:8
20-27	Untreated screen, or light matt surface IBM (all models), Siemens 8150, Compudata, Consul 980, Interdat CRT 1100, Grundig DS 7240 (Triumph) Digital VT 52, Bross 10	light grey	10-13 (150 lx) 16-21 (250 lx)	1:14-1:10 1:8-1:6

Figure 2.32. Diffuse reflectance, screen luminance and screen/source document luminance ratio for several types of VDT (measured at the 1977 Hanover Fair). Ref C.2

a preferred screen colour and this raises no problems unless the terminal is to be used by several operators who might not agree as to what is and what is not a pleasing colour! The use of coloured filters to produce what is supposed to be a 'less tiring' colour, however, is a less justifiable reason for using a filter of this kind.

There is a great deal of confusion concerning colour and visual fatigue. It is often claimed, for example, that green is a suitable colour for visual displays because the spectral sensitivity of the eyes is greatest in the green part of the spectrum, and hence less tiring. Provided that the luminances and luminance contrast of the display are sufficient to ensure good readability, however, there is no evidence to suggest that any one colour is less tiring than any other.

Although colour filters are sometimes used in the belief that the resulting effect is less tiring on the eyes, these types of filter tend to have the opposite effect but for reasons quite unrelated to colour. Colour filters and most other types of glass or plastic panel usually have a smooth, glossy surface which is less uniform than the surface of the screen glass. This results in a highly reflective surface!

A further disadvantage in using filter panels is that the filter material usually absorbs between 30 and 70% of the character luminance, and the background luminance is also reduced. Taken together, filter panels reduce the legibility of the display and tend to increase the visibility of screen reflections.

Polarisation filters

The only type of panel filter which can sometimes be used to advantage is the so-called *polarisation filter* in which the incident light is polarised and later dispersed after reflection from the surface of the screen.

Polarisation filters reduce both direct and diffuse reflections but suffer the drawback that they too are usually glossy and prone to be reflective, sometimes to the extent that the images reflected by the surface of the filter may be clearer even than those on the untreated glass screen.

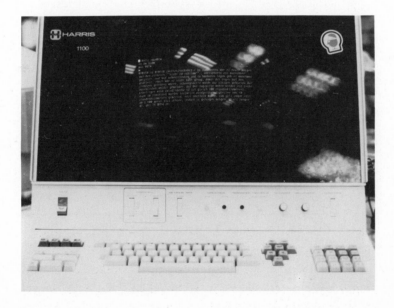

Figure 2.33 An example of reflections produced by the front surface of a polarisation filter.

Because the filter material is usually plexiglass, it is not possible to reduce specular reflections on the surface of the filter by vapour depositing an anti-reflection coating. To overcome this difficulty, however, a thin glass layer can be suitably treated and bonded to the surface of the panel.

Polarisation filters are most effective on small display surfaces, e.g. meter displays, but are not widely used for larger displays due to the practical difficulties and costs involved in overcoming the problems described above.

Micromesh filters

Meshed or *micromesh filters* placed directly onto the surface or a short distance in front of the display screen are quite often used to help reduce reflections. Filters of this kind usually give the screen a black appearance, and the mesh behaves effectively as a large number of very small tubes, the effect of which is illustrated in Figure 2.34.

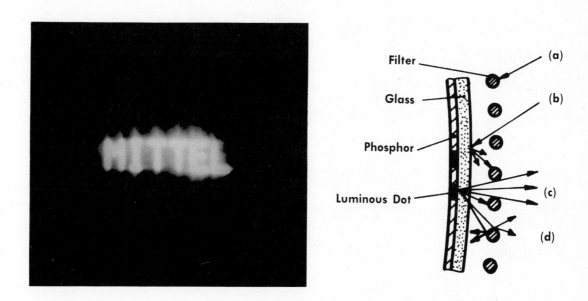

Figure 2.34 Micro-mesh filters for the prevention of screen reflections: (a) the reflectance of the surface is very low, the incident light is scattered with a diffuse reflectance typically ca. 5%, (b) that part of the incident light which passes through the filter is mainly directly reflected from the screen surface, (c) the character luminance is reduced, (d) part of the light emitted from the characters is scattered. In the case of black filter materials the scattered light has a low luminance, ca. 3-5% of the character luminance.

Micromesh filters are an effective way of reducing reflections but not without certain penalties, some of which outweigh the advantages to be gained to such an extent that their use is often of questionable value.

The main drawbacks with this type of filter are:

- depending on the coarseness of the mesh, the display is obscured by the mesh when viewed from certain oblique angles,
- some of the light passing through the mesh is scattered, and
- the characters appear less bright because some part of the light which is emitted from each character is absorbed by the filter, in some cases up to 70%.

Provided that the terminal is used by only one operator whose sitting position and the height of the display screen are adjusted to permit direct viewing, the directional readability of the display is not a problem.

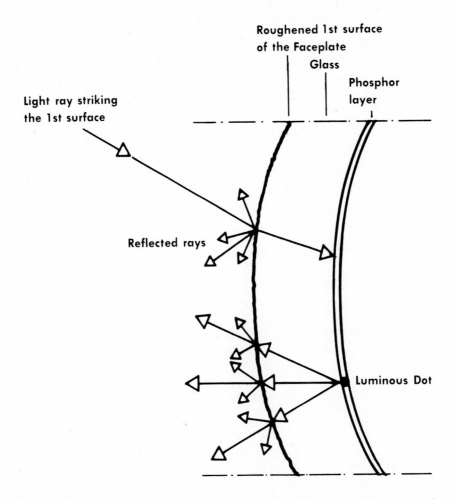

Figure 2.35 A diffusing surface used to reduce specular reflections. When light rays from outside sources strike the first surface they are scattered, the reflected image is diffused and out of focus. The same thing happens to the light rays coming from a character or point generated in the display. When the light rays from the character pass through the diffusing surface they too are diffused. Ref R.18

The effect of the filter in scattering and absorbing some of the light which passes through it depends on the coarseness of the mesh and on whether the filter is bonded to, laid on or placed at a short distance in front of the screen surface, e.g. in a frame.

If the mesh is placed *in front of but not in contact with the screen glass*, direct reflections can be almost completely avoided because the direct reflectance of the surface is reduced from about 4% to less than 1%. The diffuse reflectance is also reduced, however, from a level typically about 25% to ca 3 to 5%.

The sharpness of the displayed character images, i.e. the brightness distributions within and along the edges of each character image, is not appreciably disturbed by the use of a mesh filter provided that the mesh is free from dust and has not been distorted as a result of having been touched, e.g. by fingers, pencil points etc.

The reduction in character brightness, however, is a more serious problem. Depending upon the coarseness of the mesh, the character luminance can be reduced by between 30 and 70% due to light reflection and absorption within the mesh.

Provided that the mesh is free from dust and the screen glass is uniformly smooth, the reduction in sharpness of the character images due to light scattering in the mesh is usually less of a problem. If the glass is not smooth, however, other types of optical effects can occur, e.g. Newton rings. In addition, the character luminance is usually reduced by more than 50% and in some cases by as much as 80%.

Many of these problems can be overcome by *adhesively bonding the mesh to the glass surface*. In this case, the diffuse reflectance of the surface is seldom more than 3%. However, the effectiveness of the filter depends very much on how the mesh is bonded to the glass. It is important to use an adhesive which does not, itself, produce a glossy surface.

Micromesh filters can be used to advantage only if the ambient illuminance exceeds about 500 lx. Since the filter also helps to reduce reflections from other bright surfaces in the work room, the effectiveness of the filter may in some cases be determined by the luminance of the reflecting surfaces.

Even if micromesh filters can be effective in reducing reflections, this is inevitably realised at the expense of readability. The display contrast is often reduced to such an extent that the display looks 'flat' and may, in extreme cases, be more difficult to read than handwritten copy!

Etching the screen glass surface

Direct reflections can also be reduced by roughening the screen glass surface e.g. by etching, or by installing a roughened glass panel in front of the screen. This can be effective but there are main drawbacks.

Only the outer surface of the screen glass can be treated in this way; it is not possible to roughen the phosphor side of the glass! So, not only can the sharpness of the character

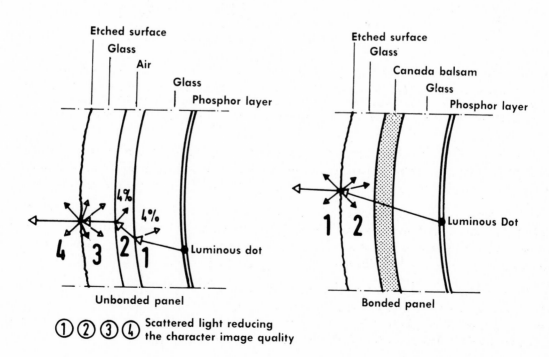

Figure 2.36 *Due to reflection from the air/glass and glass/air surfaces between an unbonded filter panel and the screen glass, light is scattered, reducing the quality of the character images. This effect is minimised by bonding the panel onto the screen glass.*

images be greatly reduced due to light scattering, but the greater the distance between the visual object - the character images in this case - and the roughened surface, the greater the light scattering effect will be. This is greater still if a roughened panel is placed in front of the display screen.

Figure 2.37 Reflections of high luminance areas on an etched screen surface.

An etched glass surface can reduce the direct reflectance from ca 4% to about 2,5 to 2% and perhaps a little less, but only at the expense of reduced image clarity. Nevertheless, the problem of light scattering might not, in itself, be so important if it were not for the additional problem of reduced character brightness. Etching the glass surface can reduce character brightness by as much as 80% and the effect may be greater still if an etched panel is placed in front of the screen glass.

The effectiveness of the etched surface in reducing reflections depends very much on how the surface is etched. The end effect can vary from a very coarse, highly diffusing surface to a fine surface finish in which case the scattering effect on the character images is very small.

If one is either unable or unwilling to directly etch the screen glass, a separate panel can be etched and then bonded to the screen glass. Providing an etched panel in front of the display without bonding does not reduce reflections and serves only to reduce the quality of the character images.

Spray-on anti-reflection coatings

The main drawback in applying spray-on coatings to the external surface of the display screen is that light is scattered as it passes through the coating. This reduces the sharpness of the character images, sometimes to so great an extent that the characters appear to be surrounded by a halo. This effect is particularly likely if the grain of the coating is too coarse and if the coating thickness is uneven.

Vapour deposited screen coatings

It is technically possible, though more costly, to overcome some of the disadvantages with spray-on filter coatings by vapour depositing a thin layer of a suitable material onto the glass surface of the screen. The main advantage with this technique is that the structure of the surface is less coarse and the resolution of the characters at a normal reading distance is not appreciably reduced.

Thin-film layers

Another method of treating the glass surface with an anti-reflection coating but without diffusing the character images is the vapour deposition of a thin-film layer with a thickness equal to one quarter the wavelength of light. This type of filter is usually referred to as a 'quarter wavelength' or $\lambda/4$ *layer*.

Using a filter of this type, the luminance of the reflected images can be reduced by a factor of about 10 without reducing the luminance of the character images. In this way, the perceived quality of the character images is greatly improved.

In spite of the obvious advantages in using this technique, the method is not without some drawbacks. One is the relatively high cost of the filter which cannot be applied directly to the screen glass but has instead to be applied to a glass panel which has then to be bonded to the screen glass. If the CRT is replaced, a new filter would be required. A second disadvantage is the sensitivity of the filter to dust and finger touch. If the filter surface is not regularly and carefully cleaned, the character images tend to look smeared. Nevertheless, the use of a $\lambda/4$ layer filter is a very effective way of reducing specular reflections.

Tube shields

It is also possible to reduce reflections on the screen by fitting a tubular type of shield around the display screen. This is not a new idea, shields of this kind have been used ever since the invention of the CRT, but their use in office environments is new.

Tube shields are often fitted as a visor on CRT oscilloscopes to avoid reflections and improve display contrast. In this type of application, however, the information content on the screen is not very great - certainly much less than on a VDT screen - and the display screen is consulted much less frequently. If a tube shield is to be fitted to a VDT, care must be taken to ensure that the shield is not fitted in such a way that the operator is required to sit in an awkward position in order to be able to read the display.

Figure 2.38 Under unfavourable lighting conditions the use of a tube shield can reduce screen reflections and enhance image contrast. However in the office environment, the use of tube shields is an extreme measure as they tend to enforce a fixed, often unfavourable working posture.

Subjective evaluation of screen filters

In examining the attitudes of VDT operators as to the effectiveness of and problems caused by the use of different types of filter, no clear correlation has been found between the surface characteristics of the display and visual discomfort. This is partly due to the fact that there are other variables which have a much more important effect in this respect. As might have been expected, however, a very clear correlation has been found between legibility and the surface characteristics of the display.

CRT displays with fine-grained anti-reflection coatings, i.e. so-called 'anti glare' displays, or with a high quality etched surface are more highly ranked by VDT operators than other types of filter both as regards their effectiveness in reducing reflections and the legibility of the display. From the point of view of efficiency in reducing reflections alone, micromesh filters have been judged to be equally effective.

Visual displays with anti-reflection coatings are effective in reducing reflections in 500 lx room lighting but are as ineffective as other types of filter if the VDT faces a window.

The subjective evaluation of untreated visual display screens has been found to depend very much on the visual environment in which the terminal is used. In using CRT displays of this kind, careful attention must be paid to the height and inclination of the display screen in relation to both the viewing angle of the operator and the position of luminaires and reflecting surfaces in the room. As a general rule, however:

> • Visual displays with anti-reflection shielding, i.e. so-called anti-glare displays are preferable to displays with untreated display screens.

Displays with glass or polarisation filters are usually less favourably judged, especially from the point of view of display legibility which, under typical office conditions, is far less than that of other types of display. For as long as the optical quality of this type of filter cannot be improved, their use cannot be recommended.

Black micromesh filters are also poorly judged by most VDT operators, again due to their effect in reducing display legibility. Only when the ambient illuminance exceeds 500 lx and the problem of reflections cannot otherwise be resolved can micromesh filters be used to advantage. This can apply to some VDT workplaces close to windows or in environments that cannot be controlled in terms of favourable illumination, e.g. shops, warehouses, booking halls etc.

Summary

Glare shielding the surface of the display screen in order to reduce the luminance of specular reflections can be satisfactorily accomplished in many ways. The simplest, least costly, and often the most effective is to adjust the position of the VDT in relation to the sources of the reflections. As far as the use of filters is concerned, each technique has its own advantages and disadvantages, the individual merits of which may vary from one application and environment to another. For this reason, it is not possible to give general recommendations as regards the use and selection of filters but in normal office environments, the various types of filter can be ranked in effectiveness as follows:

> • $\lambda/4$ thin film layer
> • etching

- polarisation filter anti-glare treatment
- micromesh filters
- polarisation filters.

If the environment is less favourable than the normal office environment, filter effectiveness may then be ranked as follows:

- micromesh filters
- etching

If the lighting conditions are extremely unfavourable, any one of these techniques may be combined with the use of a tube shield.

Chapter 3

ERGONOMIC REQUIREMENTS

FOR VDTs

Foreword

The legibility of the display and the feel and useability of the keyboard are often the most important criteria by which the individual operator himself judges the 'quality' of a VDT and the merits of working with a VDT-based system. Having examined, in the foregoing sections, the basic features of VDT design and the optical properties of visual displays, attention is now turned to the ergonomic requirements that should be considered in the design and selection of VDTs.

To ensure good readability of the *visual display*, a number of requirements should be satisfied as regards the design, formation and stability of the character images. Coding, display capacity and formatting also play a major role in determining the suitability and ease of use of a VDT in specific applications.

The VDT *keyboard* differs from the familiar typewriter keyboard in providing for additional function keys, some of which may be user-programmable, cursor control keys, multiple shifts etc. Because of these differences, neither the design nor the operation of a VDT keyboard can be directly likened to working with a typewriter. These differences not only affect the users performance, but also his or her posture at work. In this and in later sections it is shown that the characteristics of the keyboard play a major role as far as the incidence of fatigue and other forms of discomfort among VDT operators is concerned.

This section contains many specific recommendations which are intended to serve as a guide to the designers, purchasers and users of VDTs. These recommendations are summarised in the form of a checklist at the end of the chapter and again in Appendix I.

THE VISUAL DISPLAY

The *visual display* provides the operator with a means - and often the only means - for checking the content and accuracy of the information which is entered via his or her own keyboard or which is communicated to the terminal from other parts of the system, e.g. the central processor, other terminals etc. In most VDT applications, therefore, the visual display serves a vitally-important *control function* in allowing the information to be searched in order to locate specific items of information, errors etc.

The effectiveness and ease with which this can be done depends on both the *legibility* and *readability* of the display.

Poor legibility can have serious consequences on the ability of the individual operator to successfully and reliably carry out the work for which the VDT is intended. Crucial in this respect is the 'cost of error'.

At the simplest level and provided that they are not too frequent, errors are a source of inconvenience rather than cost. At a higher level, however, e.g. billing, credit checking, the consequences of errors, however infrequent, can become more serious and costly. In extreme cases, e.g. in air traffic control and many types of military application, the costs of errors can be disastrous!

Display legibility is, therefore, one of the most important criteria by which the merits of a VDT-based system are judged and by which the individual operator of a VDT himself judges the 'quality' of the VDT.

Legibility specifications

No other attribute of VDT design and display evaluation has been more intensively studied than display character formation and design. As one author put it   . . ."work on the design of alphanumerics has become almost an industry in itself".

Studies of 'legibility' usually require that one or more human subjects try to recognise letters or read words that are presented on a visual display screen. The set of letters or letter characteristics that give the best reading performance e.g. speed of recognition, freedom-from-error, is customarily said to be the most legible. The objective in studies of this kind is usually to investigate how reading performance depends upon factors such as character size and style, brightness, spacing and other geometric and photometric properties of the characters and display. It is then presumed that the results demonstrate that the 'best legibility' is given with certain values of these properties because reading time or error rate was less with these than with other values of these characteristics.

Notwithstanding the usefulness of experiments of this kind, the results should nevertheless be interpreted with some caution in devising a VDT specification. In formulating a display specification on the basis of this type of data, attention is directed away from the practical realities and differences of human performance and too much emphasis may be placed on the details of its presumed components.

It is tempting for the writer of a display specification to list the particular values of symbol and display characteristics that he believes most likely to provide good legibility. This list of values then becomes the display specification and it is presumed that the display will have 'good legibility' if the display properties meet the specified requirements.

Whilst it is both helpful and technically sensible to state ranges of values for brightness, character size etc., the list of values that is written into the display specification must necessarily be restricted to narrow ranges in order to ensure that no combination of conditions occurs, the combined effects of which would reduce 'legibility'. For this reason, the writer of the specification is then tempted to list the best known values for each characteristic with the result that the specification is made overly conservative.

A VDT specification whose sole guarantee of good legibility rests on the dependability of the listed values of display characteristics runs the risk that the prediction may not be as reliable or even as relevant as it ought to be. Human reading performance depends upon a great many variables, many of them task related, whose effects interact in a complex manner. The conversion of these data into actual human performance at work is difficult, and often impossible, to do in general terms.

It is important, therefore, that the writer of the VDT specification understands that the relationship between the generally recommended values of display characteristics and real human performance is technically not sound enough to warrant placing one's faith *entirely* in a specification of this kind.

Legibility and readability

The ability to read is a skill that most of us take for granted; what is important is the fact that we *can* read, not *how* we read. But to the display designer, an understanding of the *processes* that enable us to read is of very real and practical importance from the point of view of 'designing for readability'.

Reading is essentially a four-stage process, see Figure 3.1, and one which depends on the interaction of many geometric and photometric characteristics of individual characters, character groups and the conditions under which the characters are viewed. Reading is only effective when all four stages operate simultaneously and effectively.

Although the terms *legibility* and *readability* are often used interchangeably in everyday language to describe those attributes of visual presentation pertaining to identification and understandability, this use of terms is neither clear nor correct.

Legibility, i.e. the ability to detect and discriminate between individual characters, is an essential pre-requisite, and as such a component of readability. Similarly, readability is necessary in order to permit interpretation and understanding, i.e. readability is a component of comprehension.

	Stage	Marker	Mechanism	Basic concept
1	Detecting and	Characters	Eyesight	Legibility
2	Discriminating	and signs		
3	Transforming into meaningful units	Spacing of words	Eye movements	Readability
4	Integrating and understanding the message	Texts, graphs, tables, layout	Mental Processing	Understandability

Figure 3.1 The components of readability.

Legibility

The legibility of alphanumeric symbols is usually measured in terms of the confusion - or lack of confusion - that occurs in recognising and discriminating between individual characters in a displayed group. Given the ability to detect each character in a visual display, i.e. by sufficient size, resolution, brightness and contrast, the tendency to confuse characters is determined primarily by similarities of shape and construction. The most commonly-confused letters and numerals in visual displays are illustrated in Figure 3.2.

Mutual	One-way
O and Q	C called G
T and Y	D called B
S and 5	H called M or N
I and L	J,T called I
X and K	K called R
I and I*	2 called Z*
	B called R,S, or 8*

*The three often comprise 50% or more of the total confusions.

Figure 3.2 Commonly confused alphanumeric characters. These should be clearly distinguishable on the display screen.

Clearly, the greater the similarity between the perceived shapes of characters, the greater is the risk of confusion and error in their correct identification. It has also been found that asymmetric character shapes are less prone to mis-identification than symmetric character shapes.

In designing a visual display character set for readability, therefore, it is important that each character shape is designed in such a way that fine differences in stroke length, curvature, etc., are preserved in order to avoid similarity.

Taking dot matrix characters as an example, fineness of detail is improved by increasing the resolution of the dot matrix. Thus a 7 x 9 or 9 x 13 matrix is usually judged to be more legible than say a 5 x 7 matrix because of the ability of a fine matrix to present a more natural image to the viewer. The 5 x 7 matrix is usually regarded to be the minimum resolution from the point of view of character discrimination, especially in mixed upper and lower case displays.

The example of dot matrix generated characters also serves to highlight another important interrelationship between legibility, resolution and character size.

Based largely on familiarity with typewritten and printed matter, it is often presumed that character legibility increases in proportion to character size. But the same assumption can no longer be so rigorously applied in the evaluation of CRT generated and displayed characters and symbols. Once the resolution of each symbol, i.e. the number of dot or stroke elements, has been fixed, increasing the size of each character leads only initially to an improvement in character definition. Beyond a certain size, however, further increases in character height serve only to dissociate the individual dot or stroke elements of each character and hence disrupt the ability and the speed with which the viewer is able to correctly identify the character in question.

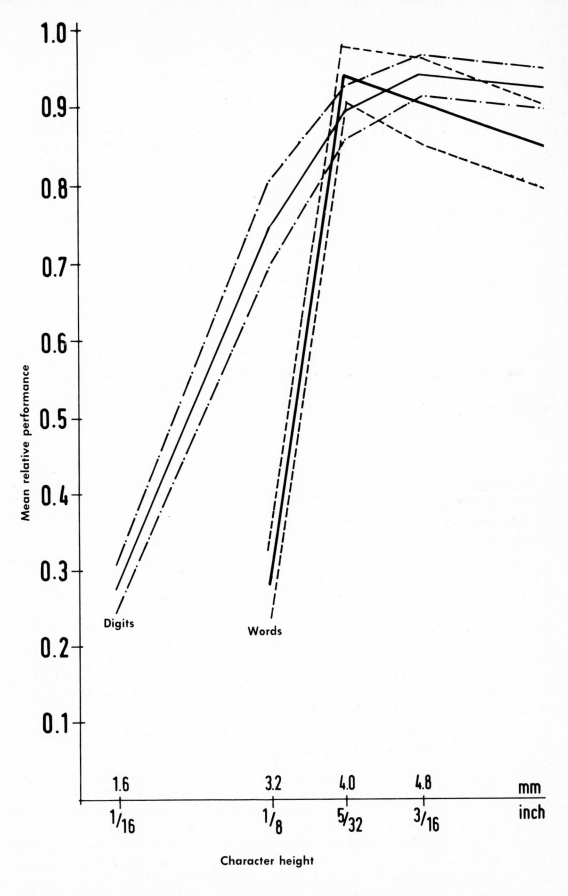

Figure 3.3 Relative performance when reading visually displayed words and digits of different character heights showing 95.5% confidence limits.

In most types of visual displays, therefore, there is in addition to the *minimum size* which is required to ensure a basic ability to detect and discriminate between similarly-shaped characters, an *optimum size*.

This effect is clearly seen in the case of dot matrix generated characters. If the character sizes are increased beyond the optimal value corresponding to the resolution of the matrix, dot size etc, the dissociation of the individual dots ceases to present a continuous image to the viewer.

The optimum character size for a given resolution also depends to some extent on the brightness of the characters. In most displays, increasing the brightness of the characters has the secondary effect of enlarging either the apparent dot size or stroke width. In the case of dot matrix characters, this effect can be used to partially compensate for the sparseness of the dots in low-resolution matrices.

Character formation

Scanning resolution

The number of raster lines within which each character matrix is formed affects the degree of refinement of the character shapes. Generally speaking, the number of raster lines per character should not be less than 10.

Character height and width

Even under poor lighting conditions, it is usually possible for the human eye to detect a weak point of light, e.g. with a brightness of about 1 cd/m^2 and subtending a viewing angle of 1′ of arc. On this basis, the minimum character size in a 5 x 7 dot matrix would be 14′ high and 10′ wide and this, from a physiological point of view, represents the minimum character size to permit identification. At a viewing distance of 50 cm, this corresponds to a character height of 2,1 mm[1].

In seeking to optimise character size, however, the ability to identify individual characters, i.e. the lower limit of perceptability, is less important than the ability to simultaneously and clearly recognise consecutive groups of characters.

Provided that the visual object is clearly in focus, it is possible for the eye to clearly recognise all objects which fall within a viewing angle of between 1° and 2° of arc. With a 1° viewing angle, a character width of 10′ or 15′, and allowing for a character spacing equal to 50% of the character width, only four or five consecutive characters could normally be clearly identified with only one fixation of the eye. So, in order to minimise the number of eye movements in reading text, restricting character width and spacing is as important as ensuring that the overall size of the characters is optimised from the point of view of legibility.

The results from an investigation in which 130 VDT operators were asked for their opinions concerning the size of the characters on the display screen, showed that 15% of the subjects were of the opinion that a character height of about 16′ of arc was to small. With a character height corresponding to 20′ of arc it might be expected that the proportion would be about 5% or less. This response compares well with other estimates of the optimum character size which is usually estimated to fall in the range 15′ to 22′, depending upon the method of character generation and resolution.

---

1. Character height (mm) 0.0003 x Arc (′) x Viewing distance (mm)

In order to maintain a natural proportion in the visual appearance of each character, the width of the cell in which the character image is generated should be between 70% and 80% of the height of the cell. This requirement, coupled with the use of an

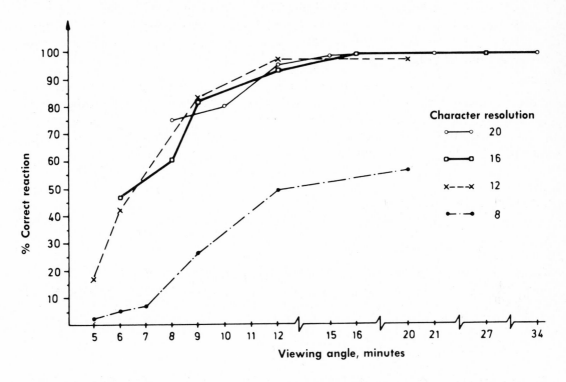

Figure 3.4 The relationship between viewing angle and the accuracy of alphanumeric character recognition for different scanning resolutions. (Presentation rate of four characters/10 sec.)

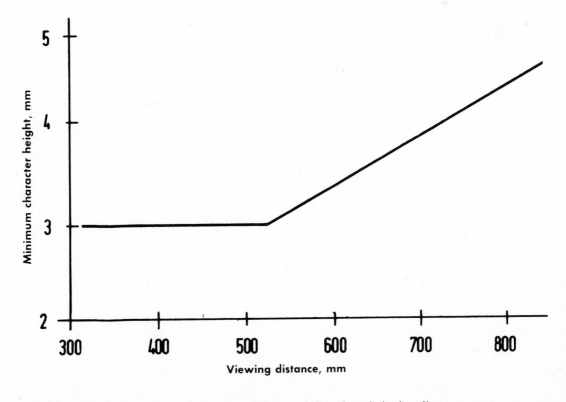

Figure 3.5 Preferred minimum character height as a function of viewing distance.

appropriate character spacing and character height, ensures the correct balance between the legibility of individual characters and the readability of consecutive characters.

Finally, it is worth emphasising that just as the character images can be too small, they can also be so large that either the clarity of the image is disturbed or the character width is increased to a level whereby reading effort, i.e. the number of eye movements, is significantly increased.

Character heights should not be less than 16′ of an arc, i.e. 2,5 mm at 50 cm viewing distance, and should preferably exceed 20′ of arc, i.e. 3,0 mm at 50 cm. Preferred minimum character heights are shown as a function of viewing distance in the following diagram.

Character widths, i.e. the width of the matrix or cell within which each character image is formed, should be between 70% and 80% of the character height.

Depending upon the method of character generation and the resolution of the character images, the size of each character should not be so great as to improve the legibility of individual characters at the expense of the readability of character groups. In the case of 5 x 7 dot matrix generated characters, the recommended maximum height is about 22′ of arc, i.e. ca 3,3 mm at a viewing distance of 50 cms.

In order to ensure clarity of each character image, the stroke width should be between 1/6 to 1/8, i.e. 12% - 17%, of the character height.

Intercharacter spacing

The intercharacter spacing, together with the width of the character matrix determines the number of the characters which can be recognised with a single fixation of the eye. It is therefore an important attribute of written, printed or displayed text, both from the point of view of readability and as regards the visual effort of reading.

In addition to the basic mode in which text is presented on the display screen, character spacing also becomes an important consideration if the text is displayed in justified form, and where the technique of line length justification involves providing additional increments of intercharacter spacing.

To ensure adequate discrimination between individual characters, the character spacing should not be less than about 20% of the character width. Likewise, to ensure good readability and to maintain the visual distinction between individual characters and words, the character spacing should not exceed about 50% of the character width.

Line spacing

The vertical spacing between lines also has a significant effect on readability. Reducing the packing and line density of the characters in the display obviously reduces the number of characters that can be displayed but at the same time increases the legibility of those that remain.

Date	Source	Generation method where specific	Character height and viewing distance or subtended angle	Character heights standardised for 711 mm (28 in.) viewing distance	Character width/height ratio	Stroke/height ratio
1956	Harris				3/4	
1959	Howell and Kraft		optimum 27′ arc minimum 16′ arc	optimum 5,6 mm minimum 3,3 mm		1/9
1965	Luxenberg and Bonness	Raster scan	minimum 10′ arc minimum number of lines 10	minimum 2,1 mm	2/3	
1966	Barmack and Sinaiko		at 28 in. minimum 0,1 minimum 0,3	minimum 2,5 mm maximum 7,6 mm		
1966	Poole		at 28 in. High brightness 0,1 - 0,2 in. Low brightness 0,15 - 0,3 in.	High brightness 2,5 - 5,1 mm Low brightness 3,8 - 7,6 mm	2/3 - 5/7	1/8 - 1/6
1967	Shurtliff		minimum 12 - 15′ arc	min. 2,5 - 3,1 mm		
1968	Cropper and Evans (Woodson and McCormick)		at 36 in. minimum 0,2 in.	minimum 4,0 mm	letters 4/5 - 1/1 numbers 3/5	1/8
1968	Gould	Raster scan	min. No. of lines 10			
1969	Hemingway and Erickson	Raster scan	min. No. of lines for symbols 8 subtending 10′ arc	minimum 2,1 mm		
1970	Giddings	Raster	at 30 in., optimum letters 5/32 in. numbers 3/16 in.	optimum 3,6 mm optimum 4,4 mm	4/5	
1970	Vartabedian	Monoscope stroke and 9 x 7 dot	optimum 0,12 - 0,16 in.	optimum 3,1 - 4,1 mm	3/4	

Figure 3.6 Character size recommendations.

An important requirement is that immediately adjacent ascenders and descenders should not overlap or intersect.

Generally speaking, interline spacing should not be less than 100% and not greater than 150% of the character height.

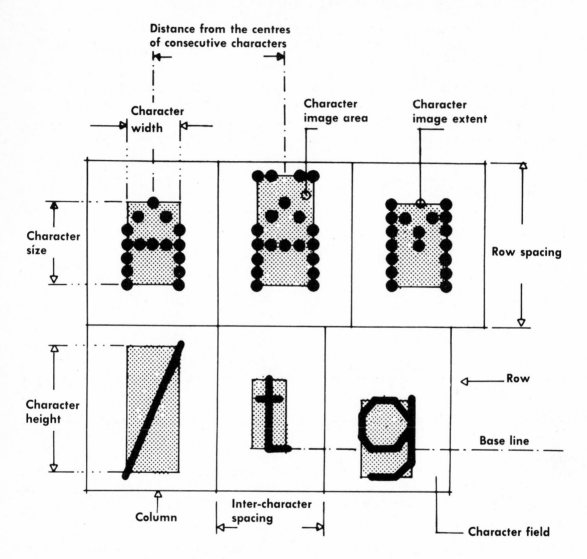

Figure 3.7 Definition of character image size and spacing parameters.

Minimum character height	15 - 20′ of arc 3,1 - 4,2 mm
Maximum character height for dot matrix 5 x 7	4, 5 mm
Width to height ratio	3/4 - 4/5
Stroke to height ratio	1/8 - 1/6
Minimum number of raster lines	10 lines

Figure 3.8 Recommended character dimensions and resolution.

Upper and lower case characters

Text which is written with both upper and lower case characters is generally easier to read than all upper case. This is primarily because the use of ascenders and descenders gives each character and word a more natural and characteristic shape so that words can be recognised as units rather than read character by character.

It is important, therefore, that descenders project below the base line of each line of text. Unfortunately, this is not permitted by all character sets which therefore tend to look strange and are somewhat more difficult to read.

Another problem arises in that in making provision for the display of ascenders and descenders, the number of dots which remain for the body of lower case characters can become unacceptably small. This is particularly true in the case of 5 x 7 dot matrix characters unless interlacing or some form of character rounding technique is used.

Display capacity

The display capacity of a VDT depends on:

- the size of the display screen, and
- the number of characters which it is possible to display simultaneously.

Screen size

The viewing area of a VDT screen is usually specified in terms of the *diagonal size*, i.e. corner-to-corner dimension of the screen or by the height and width dimensions of the viewing area.

The ratio between the height and width of the viewing area is called the *aspect ratio* of the screen, and the aspect ratio of most VDT displays in which the CRT is horizontally mounted is 3:4. For VDTs in which the CRT is vertically mounted - usually for graphic layout or 'page-view' - the height of the display is greater than the width of the viewing area. When conventional CRTs are used for these types of display, the aspect ratio is then usually 4:3 which corresponds approximately to the proportions of an A4 sheet of paper.

The most common CRT sizes for desk-top VDTs have a diagonal dimension of 12″ or 15″ (30,5 or 38 cm) although smaller, down to 9″ and 7″ in some portable remote terminals, and larger screens with a viewing area diagonal of as much as 20″ (50 cm) are used for text input and editing purposes.

It should always be borne in mind, however, that the viewing area of the screen is always somewhat less than the face area of the CRT, and different manufacturers may chose to use more or less of the available area depending upon whether the main aim is to:

- provide as large a viewing area as possible
- to minimise distortion at the edges of the screen caused by the curvature of the CRT face, or
- to achieve a particular aspect ratio.

For a 12″ (305 mm) display, the viewing area is usually about 6.75 x9″ (170 x 230 mm), and for a 15″ (381 mm) display, about 8,25 x11″ (210 x 280 mm).

Available character spaces

The principal limitations on the number of available character spaces are:

- the requirement that the individual characters shall be large enough to be easily read and scanned,
- the number of raster or scan lines with which to generate the character images, and
- the requirement that the writing speed, i.e. the scanning rate shall be compatible with a high enough refresh rate to ensure a stable or 'flicker-free' display.

For good readability, a '7-dot' character height is usually considered to be a minimum requirement and in most editing terminals, the character height is formed by 9 dots or more. So, allowing room for the interline spacing and perhaps for an underscore type of cursor or label, the number of available character lines on a 525 scan-line CRT is 24 or 25. In the case of a 600 scan-line CRT, this number is increased to about 30.

The optimum width-to-height ratio of the character is between 0,7 to 0,8. So, once the height of the character has been fixed, so too has the character width and hence the number of characters that can be displayed on each line.

The refresh rate of the CRT is usually synchronised with the mains frequency which in Europe is 50 Hz. To keep within these limits, therefore, it is seldom possible to display more than 80 characters on each line.

The display capacity of most text input and editing VDTs seldom exceeds 25 to 30 lines of text in a single column format with 80 characters per line. This corresponds approximately to the display capacity of a typewritten A4 sheet of paper.

Within certain technical limits, therefore, there is the possibility of a trade-off between character size and display capacity. Some manufacturers prefer to display somewhat less text on the screen - by reducing the number of lines or characters per line or both - in order to provide for a slightly larger character size.

Display memory, scrolling

In many practical situations, the text to be input and edited might require a greater character display capacity than the screen is able to accommodate. For this reason, editing VDTs are usually provided with internal storage capacity or *display memory* - usually between 1500 - and 19000 characters depending on the type of terminal - which can be recalled onto the display by means of a *scrolling* facility.

Most editing terminals are provided with a *roll-scroll* facility with which the movement of the text on the screen is analogous to the movement of printed copy on a tele-typewriter. As each line of text is retrieved from the store, all existing lines of text in the display move up or down by one line to make room for the new line. Correspondingly, a line of text is removed from the display unless the amount of text remaining on the screen is less than the available display capacity.

As an alternative to roll scrolling, some VDTs offer the facility of *page scrolling* or paging, which is the electronic equivalent of reading the text (calling the text from the store) page by page.

More recently, some VDT manufacturers have looked to the development of a third alternative, namely that of *pan scrolling* which is a more continuous form of roll scrolling and similar to the panning movement of the credits which follow television programmes.

For many types of text input, editing and correction application, additional character storage capacity is essential in allowing the operator to jump backwards and forwards through the text of an article, the character content of which is greater than the screen capacity. The amount of extra storage capacity required clearly depends on the task in question and in the case of news text processing, on the stage which the story has reached prior to typesetting. Generally speaking, there is little added advantage to be gained from extra storage capacity which exceeds the maximum length of job to be entered or processed. This is particularly true of text composition terminals which are used to input text from hardcopy originals.

In certain types of VDT task, the convenience with which the operator can recall and refer to parts of the stored text is an important consideration. In applications such as these, adequate display storage capacity and a scrolling facility should be provided. In some applications, however, the convenience of being able to recall parts of the text by scrolling may be less critical or important to the operator than the time it takes. In cases such as these, a short response time to enable the writing up of the next screenful of information may be more useful than a relatively slower scrolling time.

Finally, all terminals should be provided with a safeguard against 'overfilling' the display memory. In some types of terminal, problems can arise in that it is possible for the operator to enter more text than can be displayed on the screen or stored in the display memory. In this case, there is a risk that the first part of the text can be lost or overwritten unless some form of warning signal is provided, either audibly, by keyboard lock-out, or by means of a special display code to indicate that the operator is approaching or has reached the capacity of the terminal. Clearly, automatic limits should be provided to safeguard against problems of this kind.

Image stability

The stability of the image on the display screen is another of the characteristics by which the operators and would-be operators of VDTs judge the 'quality' of a VDT. Ideally, the display should be completely free of perceptible movement but in practice, the visual display may exhibit a certain degree of instability due to one or several causes.

Display instability is often referred to as 'flicker'. This is a useful way of describing the behaviour of the unstable image, the movement of which is usually perceived as a rapid blinking or flickering motion. The use of the term flicker can, however, be misleading since it is used more specifically to describe the periodic dimming and brightening of the display due to refreshing of the images in the display. This is dealt with in some detail in the following section.

In most VDTs with refreshed CRT displays, the refresh rate is synchronised with the frequency of the mains electricity supply which in Europe is 50 Hz and in the U.S.A. is 60 Hz. In a normally-working VDT it is doubtful that the apparent flicker on the screen could be attributed to this type of fluctuation, particularly if a medium persistence phosphor is used. The perception of image instability is in many cases more likely to be due to certain types of instability in the power supply to the terminal and in the synchronisation of the line scanning.

In some CRT deflection systems, the screen is split into two or more fields. This occurs, for example, with the interlaced technique of character formation. If the refresh rate is 50 Hz, then each interlaced field will be refreshed at 25 Hz with adjacent scan lines refreshed alternately. This can cause a disturbing 'jittering' effect. The perception of this type of jittering motion is closely related to visual acuity and will be detected when the motion is large enough to be resolved by the eye at the selected viewing distance. Assuming that the minimum separable acuity is about 1 minute of arc, then movement of a scan line subtending 3 minutes of arc at the eye will be detected when this motion is between half and one line width. It will be noticeable either as a blurring or as actual motion of the image. The perception of jitter is otherwise likely to be dependent on the same variables as the perception of flicker.

Swim or *drift* is a slow movement of the image without any change to the image itself. It is caused by mains interference in the d.c. supply circuitry and is reduced by careful screening and positioning of the components.

Faulty synchronisation is something that many of us are familiar with in connection with domestic television receivers. Poor synchronisation causes the picture to 'hunt', the perceived effect of which is often described as flicker. Too low a signal strength is another cause of line jitter, and this effect can occur in VDT systems with an unstabilised power supply and in which the voltage levels to the terminals are close to the lower operating limits of the VDT.

More sporadic types of image instability can also occur as the result of short term surges of power in an unstabilised power supply. For example, when the air conditioning is switched on or when the presses are started up in a printing plant, the demand on the power supply is momentarily very high and the voltage spikes which can occur at these times may cause the image to jump or hop.

It is important, therefore, that the apparent instability of the image on the display screen is not automatically attributed to 'flicker' without additional thought to other likely causes. Although the refreshing action of the CRT is a well-known attribute of VDTs, the key to improving image stability lies, in many cases, in the stabilisation of the power supply, both as regards voltage and frequency, to the VDT.

Flicker

As soon as a character is projected onto the CRT screen it begins to fade at a rate which depends on the persistence of the screen phosphor. To keep the character visible on the screen, the signal must be continually regenerated or 'refreshed'. If the signal is not refreshed sufficiently frequently, the display will appear to blink or *flicker*.

The perceptibility of screen flicker depends upon a great many factors, among the most important of which are the brightness, size and density of the display, wavelength of the light and the age of the viewer. As a general rule, the brighter, the more dense and the larger the display, the more noticeable is the flicker. But as we get older and our visual acuity diminishes, so too does our ability to detect rapidly flickering objects.

As the frequency of a flickering stimulus is increased, a point is reached where the flicker appears to cease and the individual sensations are fused into a continuous uniform sensation. This point is known as the *critical fusion frequency* or CFF.

The frequency at which fusion occurs is, however, not constant; it varies and is dependent on many different environmental and constitutional factors. From the point of view of equipment design, perhaps the most important factor influencing the perception of flicker is the screen luminance. The Ferry-Porter law states that the critical fusion frequency increases directly with the logarithm of the field luminance but is also dependent on the location and size of the stimulated retinal region, the level of adaptation of this region and the brightness of the surrounding field. The Ferry-Porter law can be plotted as shown in Figure 3.9.

For flicker to be imperceptible, therefore, the brightness of the screen must be kept reasonably low, but for legibility reasons, a certain level of contrast between the characters and the background must be maintained.

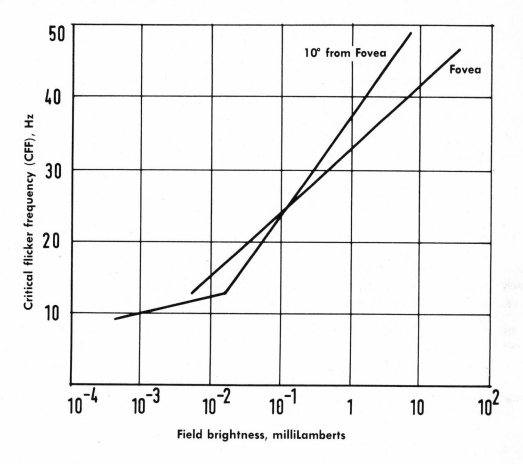

Figure 3.9 Relationship between critical fusion frequency and luminance: the Ferry-Porter law.

The refresh or regeneration rate is usually limited according to the required display bandwidth and by the need to maintain adequate resolution. In order to produce a 'flicker-free' display, ideal regeneration rates of 50 - 60 Hz have been recommended. Displays made with a refresh rate of under 20 Hz are usually very annoying to the viewer, and they are not flicker-free under about 50 Hz. It has been suggested that flicker is likely to be a problem only when the stimulation is very intense and a large area of the retina is affected.

Many manufacturers try to reduce flicker by altering the persistence of the phosphor, by changing the scan order or by filtering out the shorter component of a cascade phosphor.

To produce the same average character brightness, short persistence phosphors must be energized to a higher peak brightness than high persistence phosphors. Consequently, the instantaneous light intensity varies over a wider range when using short persistence phosphors so that higher refresh rates must be relied upon in order to avoid the perception of flicker.

A long persistence phosphor is less likely to cause flicker problems but suffers the disadvantage that the image is more likely to smear when it is scrolled up or down. It must also be borne in mind that longer persistence phosphors have a shorter life and some are quite susceptible to burning. This is a very important factor where fixed messages, e.g. system control messages, are written and remain on the screen for long periods of time. Long persistence usually means short tube life so the most popular and generally best phosphors, P4, P31 etc. are short to medium persistence phosphors.

The persistence of some common CRT display phosphors is shown in Figure 3.11 together with empirically determined critical fusion frequencies at different levels of screen luminance.

Scan order has been found to have little effect on the minimum required refresh rate except for long persistence phosphors. It has been found that pseudorandom, random

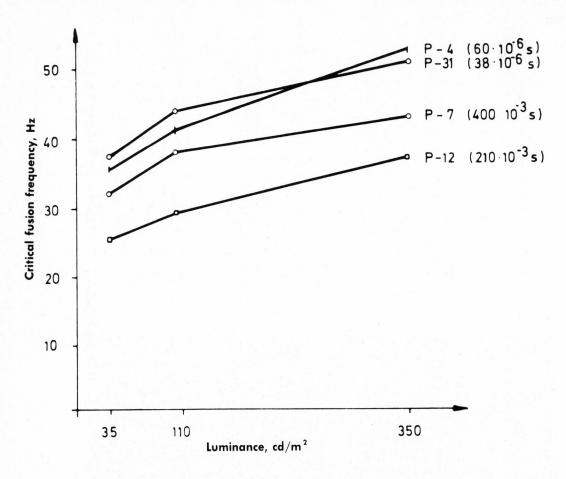

Figure 3.10 Relationship between critical fusion frequency and luminance for some CRT display phosphors (small fields, i.e. < 2°).

Phosphor	Persistence to 10%, secs.	C.F.F. small fields, Hz		
		10 ft L 34,3 cd/m²	32 ft L 109,6 cd/m²	100 ft L 342,6 cd/m²
P4	60 x 10⁻⁶	35	41	47
P7	400 x 10⁻³	32	38	43
P12	210 x 10⁻³	25	29	32
P31	38 x 10⁻⁶	37	44	51

Figure 3.11 Persistence and empirically determined flicker frequency of some common CRT display phosphors (Gould 1968).

and dot line interlace scan orders reduce the perceptibility of flicker although they do not affect the minimum required refresh rate for flickerless displays with short to medium persistence phosphors.

Display format

The basic requirement in formatting a visual display is that of ensuring that the communication between the operator and the computer is organised and structured in a form which is appropriate to the task and to the frame of reference of the operator. Crucial in this respect is the structure or sequence required in the way in which the data is to be entered into the system and displayed.

Narrative format

If the VDT is to be used solely for the purposes of entering and editing straight text matter, e.g. in journalism and reporting, the structure of the display is usually of little importance to the operator. For this reason, a basic single column or *narrative* type of format is sufficient.

However, situations frequently arise in copy editing and text composition where it is desirable to simultaneously view two versions of a story, e.g. in comparing and merging two wire versions of a story, or to inspect the effect of a given set of typographic and layout commands whilst listing and editing the commands themselves. For this type of work, split and dual screen VDTs have been introduced.

In a *split screen display*, the basic single column format can be split into a two column format in which the number of characters per column line is a little less than half of the number of characters per full screen line.

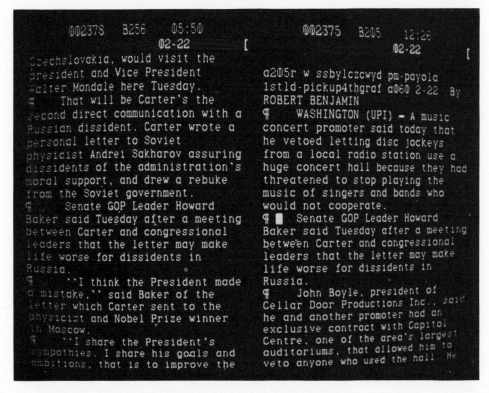

Figure 3.12 A split screen display. By courtesy of Harris.

In most cases, the two columns can be independently controlled, i.e. scrolled up or down, from the keyboard and this is a particularly useful feature in editing and merging.

For typesetting applications, *dual screen VDTs* are often used to display (a) the typographic commands for the layout of a given piece of text and (b) the visual appearance of the text according to these instructions. This type of procedure is sometimes referred to as *soft typesetting* and is widely used in text and graphics composition.

Figure 3.13 A dual screen display. By courtesy of Ferranti.

Tabular format

In most applications involving the use of VDTs, however, the structure of the display assumes a much greater importance. In cases such as these, but depending upon the task in question, preference may be given to a tabular type of format.

In the presentation of directory lists or those types of information with a high numerical content, e.g. stock market reports, sports results etc., or with a specific requirement as regards the sequence in which the information is displayed, the merits of a tabular format are self-evident.

The sequence in which information is entered into the computer system is also important in most applications in which the terminal operator is in dialogue with either the computer or a customer or both, perhaps simultaneously.

This situation arises in most types of tele-sales activity where the terminal operator has to enter data obtained from a customer. In this case, the sequence in which the information is requested from the customer not only affects the efficiency with which the data is entered into and handled by the system, it can also have an effect on the relationship between the sales operator and the customer. To illustrate the importance of sequence and formatting, the sale of classified advertisements provides a useful example.

Situations often arise in tele-ad sales where it is necessary to establish the creditworthyness of the customer before the advertising order is accepted. In a situation such as this, some degree of embarassment can be avoided by first enquiring as to the identity of the customer, e.g. 'What is your name and telephone number please?' To the customer, the question is a relevant and appropriate one and provided that the credit rating file in the system is coded by name or telephone number, enables the operator to check the rating of the customer discreetly and without risk of affront.

When satisfied, the operator can then request the information that is relevant to the production of the advertisement i.e. date(s) and issue(s) of publication, classification, desired format, lineage, account mode, box numbers etc. This information, which is sometimes called the *header* information, can be entered into the system by a form-filling technique using a special format called onto the VDT screen which provides spaces in which the appropriate header information is entered. In order to prevent more characters being inserted than the number which is permitted to define an instruction, the formats are usually protected to prevent overfilling.

Having entered the header, the ad text can then be entered via the keyboard in narrative format after which the text can be dictated back to the customer and amendments made on the screen where necessary.

First screen format in Classified Order Entry

Classified insertion		Ref No. X Z Q R		
Publication	. . . .			
Class No.	. . . .			
	Daily	**Weekly**	**Insert patt**	
Insertions	. . . .	. . . .	. . . .	
	Code	**Ins**	**Q T R S**	**Cols**
Style	. . . .	. . . .	. . . .	. . . .
Account mode	. . . .	Tel		$ . . . .
Special request	. . . .			

'Choice' screen for compositors for text correction

CORRECTION - AMENDMENTS

Classifieds	Take No.	URN . . . .
	Take Clear	Section . . . .
Features	Take No.	Section . . . .
	Take Clear	
Amendment	**UNIQUE REFERENCE**	

Figure 3.14 A typical screen format for the order entry of classified advertisements in newspaper production.

In selecting a format for an application such as this, there are several factors which should be taken into account:

Simplicity, relevance

The format should be as *simple* as possible, i.e. no more complex than is actually dictated by the needs of the task in question. Only information which is directly *relevant* to the handling of the job - by the operator and in other parts of the production process - should be displayed. It is always tempting to provide information which might be useful or is useful on some occasions. In general this only clutters the display and makes the important information less understandable. Additional information is better provided on a second display.

Sequencing

The sense and logic behind the *sequence* in which information is requested and entered into the display should derive from the nature of the task rather than convenience for the computer. This is particularly true in the case of tele-ad sales; tele-sales involves maintaining a good relationship with customers and is not simply a data entry task!

Consistency

Screen formats which are designed with a specific task in mind should be *consistent:*

a) between different displays engaged in the same task,
b) with other modes of handling the same task, and
c) with the input requirements of subsequent stages in handling the data.

For example, advertisements might enter the system through tele-ads, over the front counter or by post. Handling the information is made more efficient and less confusing if 'form-filling' involves the same or closely-similar formats.

Similarly, once the information has been entered into the system, the information content and the way in which the information is coded should be consistent with the requirements of both the typesetting and accounts departments.

Grouping, spaciousness

Grouping similar items together in a display format improves their readability and can highlight relationships between different groups of data. Grouping, and the use of blank spaces can also be used to provide *structure* in the display and aid in the recognition and identification of specific items of information.

Formatting the display is an important consideration in most VDT applications. Simply providing the operator or the system with the correct information and disregarding or paying too little heed to its presentation may prove to be a false economy! Badly or inappropriately formatted displays waste time, can be confusing and certainly cause errors to be made both in reading and in interpretation.

Advertising formats

In newspaper production, the format and typographic style of display and classified advertisements is something which varies considerably from one newspaper to another. Yet the basic problem of formatting ad layouts is common to most newspapers in that it involves selecting and cataloguing a certain number of preferred or 'standard' formats depending upon the style and format of the newspaper, and storing each layout code in the computer.

Once selected, ad formats become a special example of protected tabular formats and the same general rules apply although to a rather different degree. In this case, the ad format, i.e. height, depth, typestyle etc., must satisfy several constraints, some of them practical and related to the style and format of the newspaper, and some of them aesthetic.

One of the most important problems in computer-assisted ad formatting, therefore, is that of selecting an appropriate number of standard formats (a) to satisfy as fully as possible the number of format requirements of the advertiser and (b) to enable the typographer to come as quickly as possible to a suitable format where no particular format has been specified by the advertiser.

Display coding

The VDT operator is usually concerned with basically two types of coding:

- alphanumeric codes, e.g. for identification, instruction etc., and

- enhancement codes which relate to the mode in which the information, or selected parts of it, are discriminated in the display.

Alphanumeric codes

In order to utilise the limited data storage capacity of the computer most effectively, some types of data, particularly those concerned with identification, command and format instructions etc., are often encoded or abbreviated in some way. Generally speaking, alphanumeric codes usually fall into one of three categories:

(a) *"copy coding"*, i.e. some part of the data may be copied directly. For example, just as airline destinations are often denoted by the first three letters of the destination, e.g. FRA is the common code for Frankfurt, so the codes 'FI' and 'SE' might be used to represent the instructions FILE and SEND.

(b) *"associative coding"*, in which case the code serves as a stimulus and has associated with it some unique response, this response having been previously assigned to the code. This type of coding forms the basis of most national telephone dialling systems, e.g. '01' is the STD code for London exchanges. In VDT text processing applications, associative coding is perhaps the most widely used method for encoding typographic, user-programmed and format instructions etc.

(c) *"transformational coding"* in which a strict set of rules is applied to the data in order to derive a code. For example the identity of 'J. Smith, 133 Fletcher Street, Manchester' might be encoded as 'JS133FSM'.

With both copy and transformational coding, it is possible to derive the code for new data provided the rules are known. However, with associative codes the choice of code is usually arbitrary and has either to be learned or read off in a reference list of some kind.

Regardless of which method of coding is used, the system should, from the operators point of view, be as simple as possible to use. In other words, the user should be able to communicate with the computer in a language with which the user is, or can easily become, familiar. Likewise, the system should respond in a language which is compatible with the input coding, i.e. in a language which has some obvious significance and meaning to the operator.

Requirements such as these are important when considering the use of alphanumeric codes, both from the point of view of their ease of use and in learning. Where it is possible to use them without running the risks of ambiguity or confusion, the use of commonplace terms or easily recognised abbreviations may be preferred to more synthetic types of alphanumeric coding - human language is sometimes (but not always!) preferable to machine language.

There are nevertheless, many types of VDT application where the use of a synthetic type of coding offers certain practical advantages to the operator. This is especially true in applications where the number of codes, e.g. for addresses, formats, typestyles etc., is very large and where the use of a simple form of copy code would either be too cumbersome, or might introduce too great a margin for confusion or error. In cases such as these, there is much to be said in favour of the adoption of a unique, associative type of coding.

Nevertheless, copy and transformational codes can be used to advantage in many situations where the number of codes is relatively small as is the case for example in many data entry tasks, journalistic and reporting activities.

Consider for example a journalist who wishes to write a story into an editing system. He has first of all to let the system know that he wishes to write in a story so that the system can make the computer available to the terminal. The journalist must also let the computer know what to do with the story when it has been entered into the system, i.e. where and how the story must be filed. To begin with then, some form of 'start' and 'file' introduction is required.

From the computer's point of view, only two or three letters or digits might be required in order to uniquely define these instructions. The instruction codes in this case might suitably be 'ST' followed by the initials of the operators name or, if necessary, by an appropriate file or directory reference number.

Figure 3.15 shows how one VDT manufacturer has applied this form of copy coding to text input and editing instructions in a newspaper editorial system.

In spite of the apparent advantages in using what appears to be simple language coding, however, the question can also be raised as to whether instructions of this kind are in fact 'everyday' terms or merely another form of synthetic, albeit readily identifiable, form of coding?

Regardless of the extent to which seemingly everyday-language can be adapted to visual display coding, it can be argued that the match can never be perfect in the general sense since computer technology constrains the use of 'language' to the level of one *specific code* for each *specific instruction*. In other words, the computer does not permit the same degree of flexibility in the use of language as does normal voice communication.

Provided that the number of codes is manageably small, however, part of this problem can be overcome - but even then only a small part - by building in the possibility for a certain degree of redundancy in the way an instruction is encoded. For example, in order to open a line to the computer, the operator might be offered the facility of keying in the word 'START', even though the computer would act only on the first two characters ST, the remaining keystrokes being redundant. In this case, the risk of ambiguity is reduced, the use of the code is easy to remember and would usually aid in gaining familiarity with the use of the VDT system.

be rpe	begin
en	end
fe 12647	fetch
tr 12647,net	transfer
co 12647,adv	copy
ch 12647,13206,10731	chain
pu	punch
pr 12647	print
se	set
xt	x-take or remove
hj	hyphenate and justify
mo	move
li	list (directory)
wi pa	fetch wire service index
ge	get wire service take

Figure 3.15 An example of the use of copy coding for text input and editing.

Enhancement coding

The term *enhancement coding* refers to the use of graphical techniques, e.g. the use of brightness or colour, to enhance the visual appearance of selected parts of the information on the display screen. This type of coding helps to attract the attention of the operator to specific items of information in the display and, on a more general level, permits visual distinction between certain classes of information.

The provision of one or more enhancement coding dimensions is usually an essential attribute of the VDTs in an interactive system in which the information on the display screen is to be searched and manipulated.

There are several coding dimensions which may be provided singly or in combination for the display of alphanumeric information, but the most commonly-used techniques are brightness coding, reverse video coding, blink coding and the use of special symbols and character styles. The display of graphical information often requires the use of other and more appropriate coding dimensions, e.g. the use of colour, symbol, shape and size coding etc.

Brightness coding

One way of separating different items of information on the screen is to display each class of item at a different luminance level. This technique is known as brightness coding or *contrast enhancement*, and is widely used in the display of alphanumeric information.

The effectiveness of brightness coding and the number of brightness levels that it is practicable to use for coding purposes depends mainly on the ability of the operator to clearly detect the changes in contrast at each coding level. The optical properties of most current types of alphanumeric display are such that it is doubtful if more than two, at most three, levels of brightness can be clearly distinguished.

To ensure the effectiveness of brightness coding, it is recommended that no more than two brightness levels be used, corresponding to normal and bold appearance. If the application requires additional levels of coding, this should be provided for by introducing an additional coding dimension.

In addition, the use of higher brightness levels should not detract from the legibility of the coded data. This is a distinct possibility on most currently available displays, particularly if the 'normal' character brightness is adjusted to an initially high level.

Reverse video coding

The term *reverse video* is used to describe the technique whereby coded data is displayed as a negative image, i.e. data which is normally displayed as light characters on a dark background is displayed as dark characters on a light background. This is made possible by reversing the polarity of the electron beam so that the beam is 'on' when it would normally be 'off' and vice versa. In other words, the beam is controlled in such a way that each character image is made visible, not by generating the dot or stroke pattern of the character image in the matrix but by 'filling in' the background.

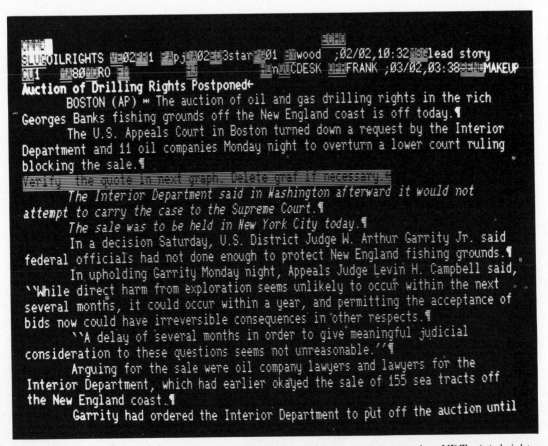

Figure 3.16 Common enhancement coding dimension on text processing VDTs (a) brightness coding (b) reverse video (c) italic style. By courtesy of Atex.

Reverse video is a very effective coding dimension and it is usually possible to display single characters, selected fields or even the entire contents of the screen in reverse video. It should be noted, however, that where a large area of the screen is displayed in reverse video, flicker is more likely to be perceived.

Blink coding

Blink or *intermittency coding* attracts the attention of the operator to particular items of information by blinking the character or field that represents the relevant data. To be effective, the blink rate should be such that the operator can search for and locate the coded data as quickly as possible. If the blink rate is too low, the blink action may not be immediately obvious to the operator, particularly if only a small part of the display e.g. a single character, is thus coded. If the blink rate is too high, on the other hand, the blink action may again be imperceptible. There is, therefore, an optimum blink rate which minimises the time required to search and locate the coded data, and it has been found that the optimum blink rate is in the range 3 to 5 Hz.

It is technically possible to employ more than one blink rate in order to increase the number of coding levels but this is of questionable value. Firstly, the frequency range within which blink coding is most effective is a narrow one and it is doubtful if the provision of more than two blink rates would help to reduce search time. Secondly, and perhaps of more practical significance, the simultaneous blinking of different parts of the display at different rates, particularly if several small fields are involved, may confuse the appearance of the display and hinder, rather than aid, the interpretation of the coded data.

A further disadvantage with blink coding is that the blink action may be a source of annoyance to the operator. For this reason, blink coding is more appropriate for small fields and means should be provided for suppressing the blink action once the coded data has been located and is being attended to.

Symbol and style coding

The use of special symbols is used extensively as a coding dimension on many types of graphic display but is less commonly used on alphanumeric displays. If symbols are provided, they should be easy to distinguish and in the case of graphic displays, they should, if possible, have a high level of association with the objects they represent. In both graphic and alphanumeric displays, symbols which already serve some purpose in the display should not be used additionally for coding purposes. In addition, the symbols which are used for coding should be distinct from one another to avoid the risk of error in interpretation.

Two commonly-used coding symbols on alphanumeric text processing displays are the underscore (a̲) and strike through (a̶) symbols. The use of the underscore as a coding dimension prohibits the use of the underscore as the cursor symbol.

The ability to display different character styles also provides a useful means for coding parts of an alphanumeric display, and the italic or *cursive* style is suitable for this purpose.

Multiple coding dimensions

In considering the effectiveness of enhancement coding, the coding requirements of the application in question should be viewed in relation to the number, type and levels of coding dimensions that it is possible for the operator to distinguish between.

119

Enhancement coding should be an aid to the operator and neither a hindrance nor a source of confusion or annoyance.

In most applications involving the use of alphanumeric displays, it is generally preferable to provide several coding dimensions which may be used singly or in combination rather than too many levels of a single dimension. The use of combination coding, e.g. reverse video/blink, bold/underscore, extends the number of available coding levels without sacrificing the efficiency of any single dimension due to the difficulty or inability to discriminate between levels.

Edit trail

Very few data processing applications require more than a few levels of enhancement coding but the simultaneous use of several coding dimensions can be a very useful aid in certain text applications. Consider as an example the evolution of a "story" that is written into a system by a journalist or reporter. In progressing from the original to the printed version of the story, a number of editing changes are likely to be made, possibly by several persons - including the journalist himself - and on several different occasions. To the editor and very often to the journalist concerned, it is useful to have a record of the editing history of a particular article in order to see what changes have been made, when, by whom and with what effect as regards the size or content of the article in question. This can be accomplished by using a technique that is often referred to as an *edit trail* whereby the original version of an article can be displayed showing all changes that have been made to the original content, e.g. error corrections, deletions, additions, block moves etc. This is made possible by using several coding dimensions the most commonly used of which are strike-through, reverse video, contrast enhancement and underscoring.

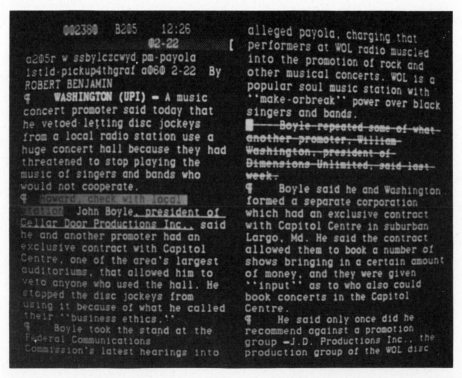

Figure 3.17 The 'edit trail' facility; this multiple use of enhancement coding permits the display of the original text as well as the editing changes during the evolution of the text. By courtesy of **Harris.**

Other coding dimensions

The use of *colour* as a coding dimension is possible only on CRT displays with the facility for multicolour display. It is an effective means of visual coding and one which enhances contrast and the ability to discriminate between different classes of objects. It is, however, a costly and technically complex method, and the brightness of coloured CRT displays is usually less good than that of monochromatic CRT displays.

In considering the merits of colour coding, it should also be borne in mind that quite a high proportion, ca 8%, of the male population is colour blind. It has also been found that peripheral colour vision varies greatly from one individual to another.

Notwithstanding these difficulties, however, coloured CRT displays are well-suited for many types of graphical display where the ability to rapidly and clearly distinguish between various items is a prime criterion.

Size coding, i.e. the ability to display an object at different size levels, is a useful technique for encoding a limited amount of graphical information but beyond three different sizes, interpretation errors may become unacceptably frequent due to the inability to clearly distinguish between the coding levels.

Other methods of coding which may be useful in graphic displays and computer generated drawings include *motion, focus, distortion* and *line orientation* on the display surface. In several applications involving the representation of three dimensional bodies, the use of lines to represent the three axes and their orientation can provide a useful depth cue.

Cursors

The *cursor* is an important feature of an alphanumeric CRT display because it indicates the position on the screen to which the operator's attention should be directed. The basic function of the cursor is to indicate the position in the display where the next character will appear. In this role, the cursor is analogous to the carriage position on a typewriter.

As a more general position indicator, however, the cursor may be used to indicate the location of specific items of information in the display or the position at which one or a group of characters is to be inserted or deleted, or where a command is to be given.

Several types of cursor are used on alphanumeric displays, the most common of which being the underscore, box, block and other special symbol type cursors. In addition, the cursor symbol may blink or it may be static, i.e. non-blinking. However, the type of cursor that is best suited for an alphanumeric CRT display depends very much on how the terminal is used. There are some types of display, e.g. those used in non-interactive, retrieval-only systems, in which there is no special need for a cursor. In interactive systems, on the other hand, the cursor is an essential display feature and one that may have a significant effect on operator performance and particularly the search and move times involved in editing the displayed information.

The general qualities required of a cursor are that:

- the cursor should be easy to locate at any random position in the display,
- the cursor should be easily tracked as it is moved through the display,

- the cursor should not interfere with the reading of the symbol that it marks,
- the cursor should not be so distracting as to impair the searching of the display for information unrelated to the cursor,
- the cursor should not be represented by a graphic technique or symbol that is used for some other purpose in the display.

Depending upon their effect on the symbols they mark, cursors can be divided into three categories, i.e. superimposing, replacing or enhancing cursors. *Superimposing cursors* do not alter the appearance of the symbol, e.g. a box drawn around the symbol. A *replacing cursor* is one that actually replaces the marked symbol by a special graphic symbol, e.g. a cross, thus obliterating the original symbol. To overcome the problem of obliteration, the cursor symbol can be alternated with the marked character. An *enhancing cursor* is one that applies some form of graphic attribute to the marked character, e.g. by intensifying its brightness or by displaying the character in a reverse video block.

In order to aid in the detection of the cursor, the cursor symbol is usually made to blink. It has been found that both cursor form and blink rate have a significant effect on search time and on the subjective evaluation of the effectiveness of the cursor. It has been found that a blink rate between 3 and 5 Hz minimises both search and tracking times, although a facility for suppressing the cursor blink should be provided to prevent annoyance either when the display is not in use or when, having located the position at which a change is to be made, the change is being attended to.

Generally speaking, box and block type cursors with a 3 Hz blink rate are to be preferred. The use of underscore cursors may not be permitted if the underscore symbol serves another function in the display.

THE KEYBOARD

The purpose of this section is to consider the basic processes of operating a keyboard or *keyboarding* and to discuss the factors which affect keying speed and accuracy and the design characteristics of keyboards.

Typing and keyboarding

Keyboarding is a complex psychomotor process in which the movement of the hands and fingers is activated and controlled by motor *command signals* from the brain. These signals can be generated in response to either the creative generation (writing) or visual recognition (read/writing) of word sequences. Once this process has been started, *response signals* are continually fed back to the brain and these signals are used to control the actions of the operator.

Keyboarding actions are controlled by three basic types of feedback:

- kinesthetic feedback, i.e. by the sensation of touch, position and movement,
- auditory feedback, and
- visual feedback

All three forms of feedback inform the brain that the command signals have been acted upon and all, but to varying degrees, assist in the self-detection of errors. Feedback, therefore, is important for accurate and rapid keying.

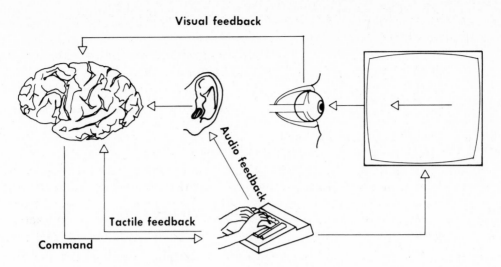

Figure 3.18 An illustration of the basic types of feedback in keyboard entry using a VDT.

Keyboarding has been studied in some detail by manufacturers of typewriters and computer equipment and the main elements in the keyboarding process can be described as shown in Figure 3.19.

At each stage in the process, a checking element may be required or introduced, depending on the operators' confidence that the correct operation has been effected. The introduction of checking elements may reduce keying speed whereas their omission may result in errors, especially if the keyboard or task places demands on particular parts of the process. For example, the use of a difficult-to-read source document may result in smaller blocks of text being stored in the short term memory of the operator, with more time being spent in reading and checking.

Keying speed may also be affected when the operator is creating a text rather than transcribing source copy. In this case, the user's short term memory may be required both for creating and for keying. Typically, creative keyboarding is slower and more error prone than typing from source copy.

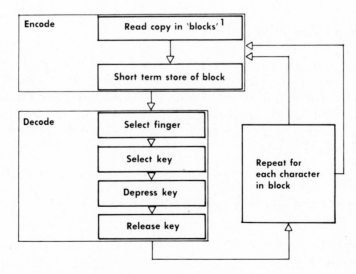

Figure 3.19 The main elements in the keyboarding process.

1.The term *block* is used here in the technical sense to describe any group of characters or digits which represents a meaningful block of information to the operator.

A second major factor which affects keying speed and accuracy is the meaningfulness, orderliness and clarity of the source material to the operator. Various experiments have shown that experienced keyboard users can key meaningful material, e.g. straight text, significantly faster and more accurately than coded matter. Familiarity with the text is also important. Thus relatively more typing errors occur when keying the less frequently occurring letters of the alphabet although this may also be partly due to aiming errors by hitting adjacent keys.

Keyboarding *errors* usually fall into one of four categories:

- Substitution errors = where a wrong character is put in place of a correct one.
- Omissive errors = where data is lost during keying.
- Transposition errors = where characters are keyed in reverse order.
- Insertion errors = where additional keystrokes are inserted.

Any of the above-mentioned types of error can occur when keyboarding text, numerical data or even command instructions. Another type of error which can occur arises when a wrong command is keyed. For example, if an operator has keyed in a command but is unsure as to whether or not the system has responded to the command he or she may be tempted to repeat the instruction. This type of error may be influenced to some extent by the design of the keyboard.

Feedback plays an important role in the self-detection of errors. Typically 70% of all errors in keying tasks are self-detected and thence may be self-corrected. However, the efficiency of self-detection and correction may be adversely affected if the operator is working under pressure.

Visual feedback of the keyed material has been found to aid the detection of errors for unskilled or novice operators, but has little effect on skilled keying performance. In addition, skilled i.e. faster typists tend to make fewer errors.

Generally speaking, skilled operators do not need to see what they have typed but they do need to make visual reference to the keyboard and to see their own keyboarding movements.

Key and keyboard design

There are a number of parameters of the keyboard and of the individual keys which affect the feel and useability of the keyboard. These include:

- the shape and profile of the key tops
- keyboard profile
- keyboard thickness
- the dimensions of the keys
- size and coding of the key legends
- key force and travel
- tactile feedback
- key-roll characteristics
- security safeguards
- colour and reflection characteristics of the key and keyboard surfaces.

Key shapes and profiles

The keytop serves both as the target for the key-pressing action and for the display of the character, number or function legend. The shape of the keytop must, therefore, satisfy several ergonomic requirements:

- aid the accurate location of the user's finger
- minimise reflections
- provide a suitable surface for the key legends
- prevent the accumulation of dirt, dust, moisture etc. on the surface, or from falling into the mechanism
- be neither sharp nor uncomfortable to press.

The shape (b), in Figure 3.20 best satisfies the above criteria and is generally to be recommended.

1 - Reflective part of the keytop

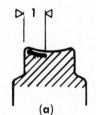 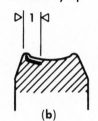  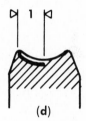

(a) (b) (c) (d)

Figure 3.20 Keytop profiles illustrating the point of light reflection with unfavourable illumination. Keytop surfaces should be matt finished in order to minimise reflection. Generally speaking, shape (b) is to be preferred.

There has been considerable variation in key shapes used by manufacturers over the years but relatively little systematic research has been carried out to investigate the practical significance of the various materials and shapes. Most VDT keyboards, however, use moulded plastic key tops.

The surface of the keytops should be given a matt finish both to reduce specular reflections and also to provide a non-slip target. However, care must be taken to avoid excessive roughening of the surface as this leads to a more rapid accumulation of dust and grime which may obscure the key legends and which is also aesthetically and perhaps hygienically unpleasant.

The relative merits of circular and square keytops are unclear, although there is some evidence to suggest that the size of the keytops is a critical factor as far as keying performance and error rates are concerned. Since square tops provide a bigger target area for a given spacing between key centres they are generally regarded to be more suitable.

Keyboard profile

The profile of the keyboard may be stepped, sloped or dished, see Figure 3.21

When the keyboard profile is dished, the profile curvature of the keytops in each of the four rows must be slightly different to ensure that the overall dish shape is maintained. This arrangement is reported to improve the keying rate for skilled operators and, when combined with slightly deeper depressions in the home row keys, to 'instil a sense of confidence in the operator'.

Both the profile and angle of the keyboard are important from the point of view of the position and motion of the hands and fingers while keying. To minimise the physiological loading in the hands and to ensure good keying performance, the profile angle of the keyboard should be between 5 and 15°.

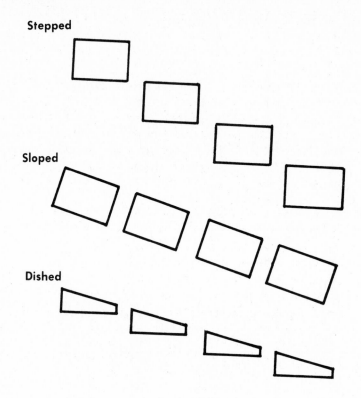

Figure 3.21 Three of the most common keyboard profiles.

Keyboard thickness

The operation of a keyboard requires a specific working posture. Even when the task in question requires only a relatively small number of keyboard entries, the operator will usually try to adjust, for example, the seating height in order to ensure an optimum position of the arms. The most favourable arm position would be achieved if it were possible to rest the keyboard directly on the thighs, the keyboard having as small a thickness as possible and ideally having zero thickness.

In practice, of course, this is not possible, but every millimeter that can be spared in keeping the thickness of the keyboard to a minimum helps to reduce the postural loading on the user by ensuring the correct working level, the beneficial effects of which are two-fold:

> • the static loading in the arms and shoulder muscles is reduced, and
>
> • the viewing distance between the eyes and the documents resting on the desktop in the event that a document holder is not provided, or used, is reduced.

The question of keyboard thickness and height is dealt with in greater detail in Chapter 4 'Ergonomic Requirements of VDT Workplaces', but it is desirable that the thickness of the keyboard, i.e. the distance from the base of the keyboard to the home row of keys, should not exceed about 30 mm.

Key Dimensions

The size of the keytop is to some extent the result of a compromise between providing a large enough target area and surface for the legend on the one hand, and keeping the overall size of the keyboard down to a manageable size on the other. Although there have been several studies of the significance of key size, it is largely by design convention and evolution that most typewriter and VDT keys have acceptable dimensions. A square keytop size of 12-15 mm with an intercentre spacing of 18-20 mm is recommended.

Key legends, size and coding

Using key tops of this size, a maximum of two legends may be printed on the top surface. Since the keys are expected to be durable, two-shot moulding is recommended. Using this technique, the legends are moulded directly into the key top during manufacture. Although tooling costs are higher than with other techniques, the resulting keytop is extremely resistant to wear.

There is no clear evidence concerning the optimum size of key legends but since the keyboard should be ideally at the same viewing distance as the VDT screen, the legends should not be smaller than the minimum acceptable character size i.e. 3 mm.

Where the users are relatively skilled in keying, the legends serve primarily to identify infrequently used keys or functions. For users less skilled in keying or unfamiliar with the keyboard, all key legends are important since a major proportion of the time is spent looking at the keyboard. The key legends need therefore to be as explicit and easy to understand as possible. Generally, simple abbreviations are adequate although in some cases it may be preferable to modify the name of a full command or function rather than attempt to squeeze a long code onto the keytop.

The labelling of function keys should generally use abbreviations or codes except when standard symbols exist. Cursor controls for example can use arrow symbols very effectively when the keys are arranged so as to correspond to the cursor movement. Generally it is unwise to label editing functions purely with symbols since there may be and often are several conflicting and equally plausible explanations for their meanings. It is also more difficult for users to remember symbolic labels. A sensible abbreviation of a meaningful function is easily remembered.

Consistency and simplicity in labelling aids identification and allows the user to more rapidly search and locate the desired key. The practice of varying the size of the legend from key to key to fill the available space only adds inconsistency and confuses the user both in searching and in using the keys. Where possible, the main alpha legends should be as large as possible, clear and uniform in size regardless of whether other characters are available on other shifts or not.

Multishift keyboards and the provision of user-programmable keys have obvious advantages in VDT tasks involving the frequent repetition of long names or phrases. If the user can simply press a single function key, instead of keying e.g. 'highly desirable residence', considerable savings in time and error can be made.

However, the way in which such facilities can best be used is not clear. Very few users can remember more than a few such functions and it is difficult to imagine how meaningful abbreviations could be written onto the appropriate keytops. In practice, most VDT operators refer to look-up lists of one kind or another when they wish to use functions of this kind. This may well be the best solution and one which certainly seems preferable to cluttering the keytops and hence making all legends unreadable.

It is also worth pointing out that the use of look-up lists of this kind is often an extremely efficient way of providing users with appropriate *aides memoire* and this practice should certainly not be resisted in the interests of the 'paperless office'. In any event, individual users will probably adopt such measures for themselves if they feel it necessary and it is generally more satisfactory if management encourages rather than hinders any process which the users themselves feel to be of value and help to them.

Key force and travel

Early typewriter keyboards were purely mechanical in construction and it was necessary for the operator to exert considerable pressure in order to operate each key effectively. The introduction of electromechanical and more recently electronic keyboards has greatly improved operator performance by reducing the physical effort required and hence delaying the onset of fatigue during keyboarding. Neither are modern keyboards subject to most of the design constraints imposed on key positioning, travel and other key parameters in mechanical keyboards. Potentially at least, this allows for greater flexibility in keyboard design and particularly for better taking into account individual task and user requirements. However, this flexibility does not seem to have been fully exploited.

Author	Date	Diameter		Displacement		Load	
		min. mm	max. mm	min. mm	max. mm	min. g	max. g
Grisez (experimentally derived)	1959	(22,5 mm used)		4 optimum (min. used)		200 optimum (min. used)	
Deininger (subjectively derived)	1960	13 optimum		3 optimum		99 optimum	
Wallis	1960	13	-	3	-	227	1361
Dreyfuss	1960	10	25	6	25	113	1361
Morgan	1963	13	-	3	38	284	1134
Kellerman	1963	12	-	-	-	250	1100
Woodson	1964	6	13	3	6	284	1134
Murrell	1965	13	-	6	25	199	850
Damon	1966	13	25	2 (optimum 3	19 6)	284	1134

Figure 3.22 Comparitive table of pushbutton recommendations.

Mechanical keyboards did, however, incorporate some good features from the users' point of view and it is important that these should be retained in modern designs. One such feature was the mechanical interlock which prevented two keys being struck together. This is further considered in the section dealing with 'security safeguards'. Another desirable feature was that the 'feel' of the key during its travel bore a direct relationship to the output process. There was considerable tactile and audible feedback to the operator to indicate that a keystroke had been successful. With light-action keyboards, on the other hand, the feel of the key may not always be a sufficiently reliable indicator that the keystroke has been actioned. In addition, the design of some mechanical keyboards provided the operator with the facility of adjusting force/displacement characteristics of the keys to suit their own style or even degree of fatigue.

Most research in this area has shown that there is a fairly wide range of acceptable key force/displacement characteristics, see Figure 3.23.

Force required for key displacement	**0,25 - 1,5 N**
Key displacement (travel)	**0,8 - 8 mm**

Figure 3.23 Recommended key characteristics.

Tactile feedback

The nature of the feedback to the operator to indicate that the keystroke has been successfully actioned appears to be an extremely important keyboard characteristic although the exact requirements vary according to individual levels of keyboarding skill.

Relatively infrequent or unskilled keying is both faster and more accurate if tactile feedback is provided. Figure 3.24 shows how tactile feedback provided by a collapsing spring or a similar snap-action mechanism, gives the key a positive feel which helps the operator to avoid missed or multiple key-strokes through uncertainty or as the result of 'teasing' the key.

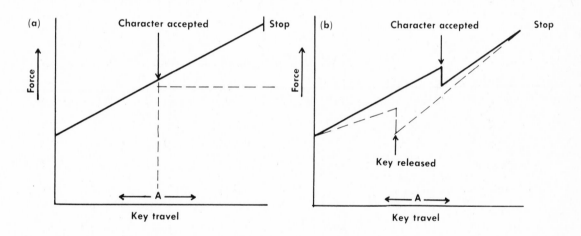

Figure 3.24 Key force/displacement characteristics (a) without and (b) with tactile feedback.

Tactile feedback seems to be less important for skilled operators although some degree of feel may still be necessary to aid the self detection of keying errors. However, too positive a snap-action may actually increase errors among experienced operators.

Some audible feedback or 'click' to indicate successful operation can also help to reduce undetected errors for both skilled and unskilled operators, mainly by aiding in the self-detection of omitted and duplicate keystrokes. The results from one investigation showed that the undetected error rate may be reduced by a factor of between 2 and 3 when an audible feedback signal is provided.

Security safeguards

There are a number of keyboard characteristics which can help to minimise inadvertant key operation or other miskeying problems.

One of the most important features of this kind is that of *key roll-over*. When keying at high speed, the user may produce bursts of key strokes with very short interkeying times, typically 20 to 30 ms. This often results in more than one key being in the depressed state at a given time and, depending on the roll characteristics of the keyboard, may give rise to lost key strokes. Figure 3.25 illustrates the action of a keyboard with no roll-over, with two-key roll-over and n-key roll-over.

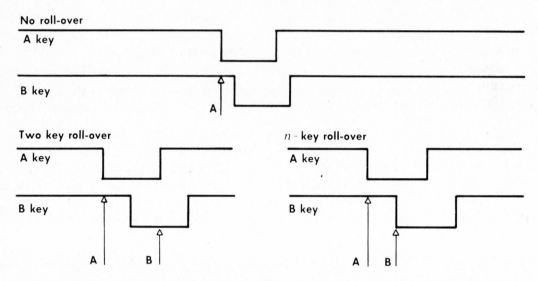

Figure 3.25 The principles of key roll-over showing the effect of the simultaneous depression of two keys when the first key is released before the second key (a) with no roll-over, (b) with 2-key roll-over and (c) with n-key roll-over.

Regardless of the number of keys which are depressed at the same time, the *n-key roll-over* keyboard is able to store all the keystrokes and generate all the characters in their correct sequence. With *no roll-over*, the second keystroke is lost completely.

The difference between these features is even more significant when the second key is released before the first. This is called *shadow-roll*. Only with n-key roll-over are the characters generated correctly.

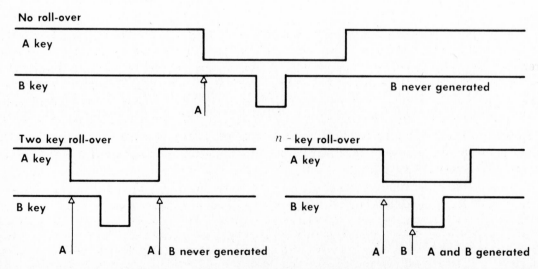

Figure 3.26 The principles of key roll-over when shadow rolling, i.e. when the second key is released before the first key, (a) with no roll-over, (b) with 2-key roll-over and (c) with n-key roll-over.

A major problem can occur when users change from a keyboard with one type of key-roll to another. Keystrokes may be lost or double characters generated, and it may be very difficult for the user to discover why. Error rates may be as much as 30% lower with n-key roll-over as compared with 2-key roll-over. Given time, the user is able to adapt his or her keying style to the different constraints but in the meantime, the difficulties of so doing may be a source of frustration.

A second type of keyboarding safeguard concerns the use of either *chord keying*, i.e. the required simultaneous depression of two or more keys, *double pressing*, i.e. the repeated action of a given key or *sequential keystroking*, i.e. the depression of two or more keys in a specific sequence to prevent the inadvertant operation of critical function or command keys. There is no direct evidence as regards which of these three approaches to safeguarding against critical errors is most effective but in many VDT applications where faulty command errors may have serious consequences, the provision of some type of safeguard is essential.

The provision of excessive safeguards, however, is usually of little practical benefit and may actually be self defeating. For example, if the system automatically questions a given command in order to determine if it really was intended, there is a danger that the operator may confirm automatically without actually checking. If some form of multiple keystroking is required, however, the accidental or inadvertant key press can more easily and consciously be rendered harmless .

In many types of VDT system, the delete or 'kill' key is one of the most important keys as far as the consequences of inadvertant operation are concerned. In applications such as these, it should be possible for the operator to 'undelete' a killed item if it is later decided that the command was inappropriate[1]. This can be a useful facility without necessarily imposing a high software overhead cost.

As a general rule, safeguarding should be restricted to genuinely important or critical functions since it adds appreciably to the time and effort involved in entering commands and this may, in some cases, disrupt the flow of input by the operator. In fact, a well-designed keyboard should have all critical command keys positioned separately from the more frequently used alpha, numeric and less critical function keys.

Key repeat

The provision of a facility to *repeat* certain characters or symbols continuously can be a very useful aid to the operator. This can be provided either by having a separate 'repeat' key which, when depressed, will repeat any other key instruction that is depressed at the same time, or by using *typamatic* keys which automatically repeat when depressed for more than a short period of time, typically about half a second. For most applications, only a few characters e.g. the underline symbol, need to be regularly repeated so that the selective use of typamatic keys may be sufficient to provide this facility without otherwise requiring the operator to use both hands for the operation of a separate repeat key.

---

1. In the case of systems designed to handle and permit the editing of large volumes of material for which the inadvertent killing of some part of the material may have serious consequences, e.g. the loss of one or more stories in a news agency or newspaper production system, the provision of a specific 'kill file' may be a worthwhile consideration. All material which is accidentally or deliberately killed may then be committed to this file for recall, if necessary, at a later stage. The frequency with which such a file is purged would normally depend on the capacity and volume of traffic in the system file. In practice, the value of such a safeguard depends on the 'cost' of error.

Colour and the reflection characteristics of keys and keyboards

The layout of the keyboard should obviously aid the user in locating the correct key, and the use of colour coding of the keys can play a major part in this. Colour can help to give a structure to the keyboard and this greatly reduces search times and search errors. The combination of coloured keytops and keys laid out in blocks imposes an order to the layout of the keyboard that is both functionally desirable and aesthetically pleasing.

In practice the reflection characteristics of keyboards are often determined more by considerations of styling than ergonomic reasoning. In many cases, the keyboard designer tacitly assumes that the keyboard will be operated by skilled typists, i.e. those with the ability to touch-type. In reality, however, this is seldom the case.

The ability to touch-type is a skill that is associated with the operation of the alphanumeric keyboard on a conventional typewriter. By comparison, however, a VDT keyboard is a more complex instrument. On the one hand, the keyboard itself is more complicated since, in addition to the main alphanumeric keyset, one or more sets of function keys are provided and perhaps also an auxilliary numeric keyset. Even the most skilled typist finds it necessary to look frequently at the keyboard when operating the function and numeric keys. Secondly, the fact that the VDT is part of a system in which the flow and manipulation of information takes place in abstract form compared with the more tangible form of paper in a typewriter, requires care in the use of the function and command keys, particularly those, the inadvertant operation of which may have serious consequences. This inevitably results in greater visual reference to the keyboard.

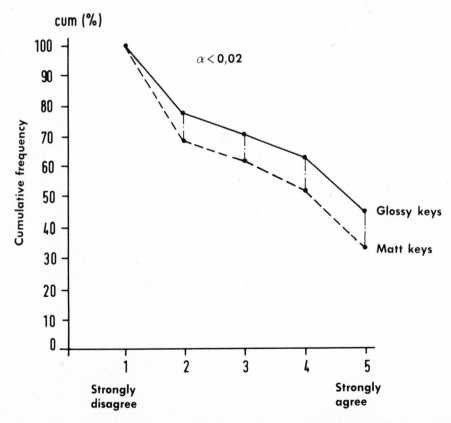

Figure 3.27 Subjective ratings of the incidence of pains in the neck when using VDTs with glossy and matt keys.

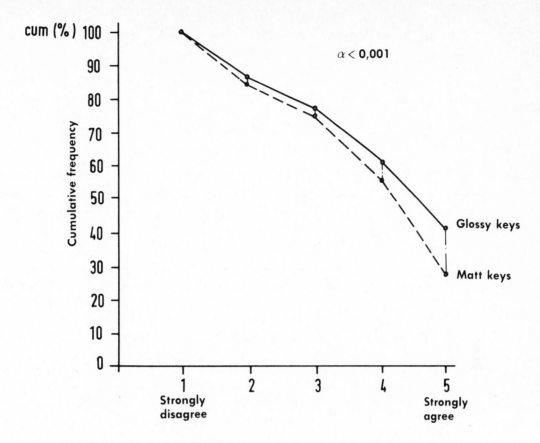

Figure 3.28 Subjective ratings of fatigue when using VDTs with glossy and matt keys.

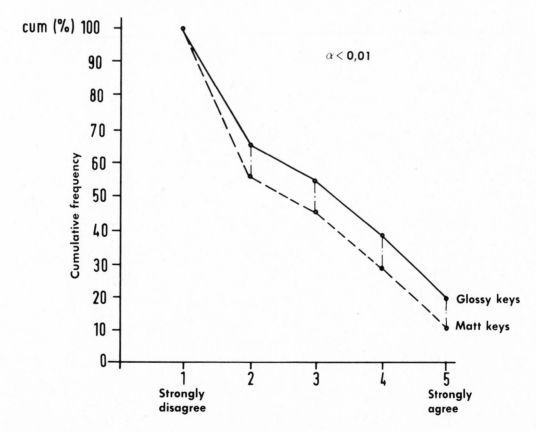

Figure 3.29 Subjective ratings of the incidence of headaches when using VDTs with glossy and matt keys.

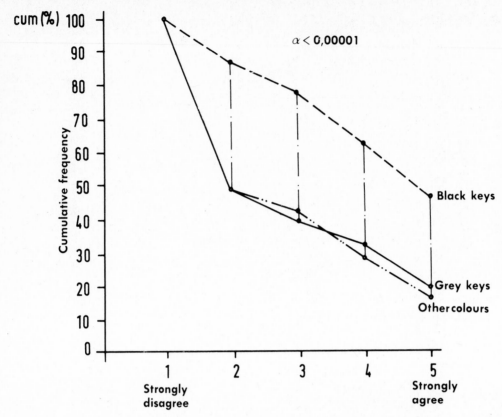

Figure 3.30 *Subjective ratings of glare from windows when using VDTs with black, grey and other key colours.*

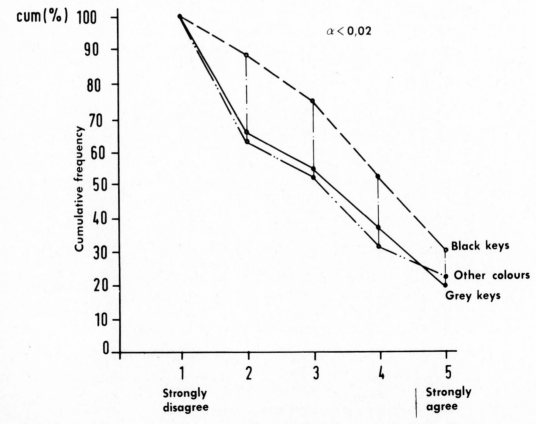

Figure 3.31 *Subjective ratings of glare from luminaires when using VDTs with black, grey and other key colours.*

134

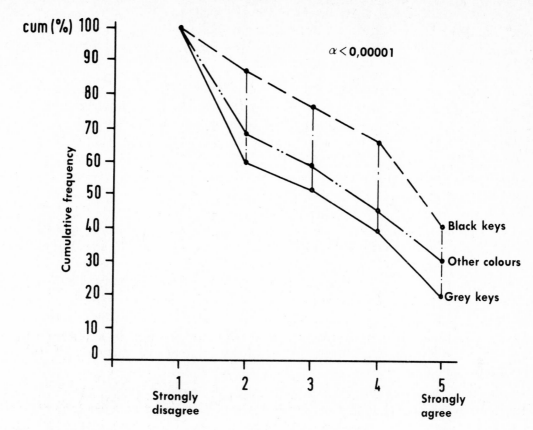

Figure 3.32 Subjective ratings of eye discomfort when using VDTs with black, grey and other key colours.

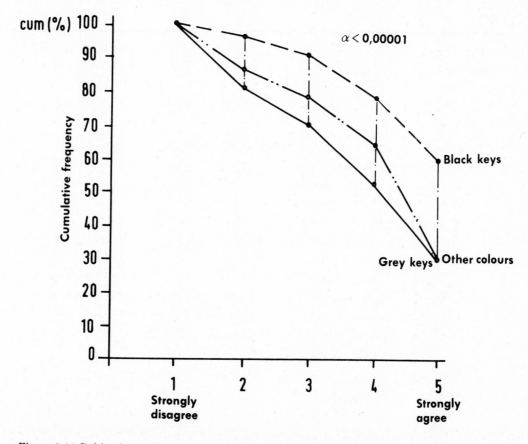

Figure 3.33 Subjective ratings of fatigue when using VDTs with black, grey and other key colours.

Keyboard layout

Alpha keys

The basic layout of the typewriter keyboard has remained essentially unchanged since its invention more than a century ago. Many of the features to be found on current VDT and typewriter keyboards are a direct result of design decisions that were necessary to overcome the purely mechanical limitations of the technology at that time. Their persistence today is largely the result of habit and custom rather than attention to sound ergonomic principles.

The QWERTY keyboard layout, with minor national variations, has become the universal keyboard layout for typewriter and terminal keyboards. But in spite of the continued preference for the QWERTY layout, the relative placings of the characters were not, as is commonly supposed, chosen for the convenience of the operator but for reasons associated with the construction of the type bar mechanism in mechanical typewriters. The keys for some of the more common letters pairs or *digrams* in the English language were well separated to help avoid clashing of the type bars. The rows were also offset to give each key a single, straight linkage to the block.

These features lead to a substantial increase in typing speed by reducing type bar clashes and also by allowing alternate hands to be used when typing some of the more common digrams.

Apart from the rudimentary considerations that were originally given to digram frequencies in the English language, however, the QWERTY arrangement is not tailored to any of the structure of any major language.

The movement and physiological loading of the hands, fingers and arms during keyboarding is necessarily related to the characteristics of the language. Of particular importance in this respect are the frequency of occurrence of individual letters and multigrams, accented letters, word-ending and word-beginning letters etc. The frequent use of capital letters in some languages, e.g. in German, requires frequent use of the shift key which results in correspondingly more frequent use of the little fingers than is necessary when typing, say, English or French language text.

The main physiological criteria that should be considered in the arrangement of a keyboard are that:

- operation of the keyboard should require as many hand changes as possible,
- the letters in the home row of keys should include those which occur most frequently in the language,
- there should be a roughly even distribution of load between the right and left hands but with slight emphasis on the right hand,
- the distribution of load on the key rows should give emphasis to the home row, then to the top and bottom rows in that order,
- the least use should be made of the ring and little fingers, i.e. the keys at the ends of each row should correspond to the least frequently occurring letters in the language,
- the number of keying sequences requiring the consecutive use of the middle/ring and ring/little fingers should be kept to a minimum,
- wide and awkward spans of the fingers on each hand should be avoided or at least kept to a minimum,

- keying should require as few jumps from the base to the top row and vice versa as possible, and

- the number of keying sequences requiring the repeated use of any one finger should be as small as possible.

In considering how these criteria might best be satisfied in arranging a keyboard, the structure of the language inevitably becomes a primary consideration. All attempts to reform the basic QWERTY-type layout have been based on letter and multigram frequencies in order to place the most frequently used keys under the stronger fingers and to concentrate more of the work load onto the right hand.

One of the criticisms that can be levelled at the QWERTY layout is that, in English language typing, about 60% of the work load is carried by the left hand which, for most of the population, is the non-preferred hand. In addition, too little typing is done of the home row, about 30%, whilst about 50% is done on the back row, see Figure 3.34. As shown in Figure 3.35, the situation is much the same in the case of German language typing.

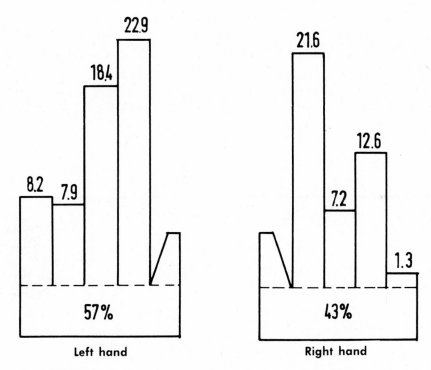

Figure 3.34 The QWERTY keyboard layout and workload distribution when typing English text. Ref. S.30

From the table of individual letter frequencies shown in Figure 3.36, it can be seen that the 10 most frequently used letters in the English language account for 73% of the overall utilisation of the alphabet. The corresponding figures for the German, Spanish and Swedish languages, for example, are 72%, 76% and 71% respectively. The six letters 'e', 'a', 'n', 'r', 's', and 'i', are among the ten most frequently used letters in each of these four languages, but only two of these letters, 'a' and 's', are included in the home row of the QWERTY keyboard.

By keeping the letters in the most common digrams well separated on the keyboard, one of the most important physiological requirements as regards keyboard layout is satisfied, i.e. that of frequent changes of hand. Figure 3.37 shows the most common digrams in the German, English and Spanish languages.

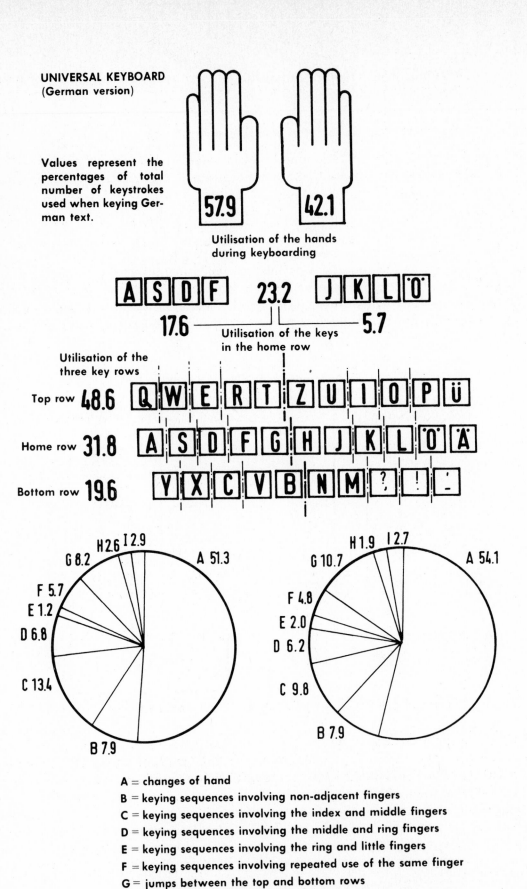

UNIVERSAL KEYBOARD
(German version)

Values represent the percentages of total number of keystrokes used when keying German text.

57.9   42.1

Utilisation of the hands during keyboarding

A S D F   23.2   J K L Ö

17.6 ——— Utilisation of the keys in the home row ——— 5.7

Utilisation of the three key rows

Top row 48.6   Q W E R T Z U I O P Ü

Home row 31.8   A S D F G H J K L Ö Ä

Bottom row 19.6   Y X C V B N M ? ! -

H 2.6 I 2.9
G 8.2   A 51.3
F 5.7
E 1.2
D 6.8

C 13.4

B 7.9

H 1.9 I 2.7
G 10.7   A 54.1
F 4.8
E 2.0
D 6.2

C 9.8

B 7.9

A = changes of hand
B = keying sequences involving non-adjacent fingers
C = keying sequences involving the index and middle fingers
D = keying sequences involving the middle and ring fingers
E = keying sequences involving the ring and little fingers
F = keying sequences involving repeated use of the same finger
G = jumps between the top and bottom rows
H = keying sequences requiring broad stretch of the finger span
I = double key strokes

Figure 3.35 The QWERTZ keyboard layout and workload distribution when typing German text.
Ref. M.17

	English			German			Spanish			Swedish	
		%	$\sum$%		%	$\sum$%		%	$\sum$%		%	$\sum$%
1	e	12,41	12,41	e	16,55	16,55	e	13,77	13,77	e	9,97	9,97
2	t	8,90	21,31	n	10,36	27,01	a	11,26	25,03	a	9,34	19,31
3	o	8,13	29,44	i	8,14	35,15	o	8,41	33,44	n	8,78	28,09
4	a	8,09	37,53	r	7,94	43,09	s	8,40	41,84	t	8,62	36,71
5	r	7,13	44,66	s	5,57	48,66	n	6,94	48,78	r	8,41	45,12
6	i	6,46	51,12	t	5,43	54,09	r	6,84	55,62	s	6,51	51,63
7	n	6,41	57,53	a	5,15	59,24	d	5,61	61,23	i	5,71	57,34
8	s	6,41	63,94	h	4,76	64,00	i	5,56	66,79	l	5,29	62,63
9	h	4,73	68,67	d	4,21	68,21	l	4,83	71,62	d	4,47	67,10
10	l	4,10	72,77	u	4,01	72,22	c	4,58	76,20	o	4,04	71,4
.				.			.			.		
.				.								
	z	0,10	100,00	y	0,03	100,00	w	0,01	100,00	q	0,01	100,00

Figure 3.36 A comparison of relative letter frequencies in four languages for typewritten text. Ref. M.17, A.7

German			English			Spanish		
en	ne	6,1 %						
er	re	5,7 %						
ei	ie	4,4 %						
						de	ed	4,0 %
			er	re	3,9 %			
						es	se	3,8 %
			th		3,5 %	en	ne	3,5 %
						re	er	3,5 %
ch		3,3 %						

Figure 3.37 The most frequent digrams in the German, English and Spanish languages. Ref. M.17

The ten most common digrams and their reverses in the German language, see Figure 3.38, represent about one-third of all digrams in the language. The first 20 digrams represent about half and the first 40 represent about two-thirds of the total.

1. en	ne	6,1 %	6,1 %	6. te	et	2,7 %	25,0 %
2. er	re	5,7 %	11,8 %	7. in	ni	2,5 %	27,5 %
3. ei	ie	4,4 %	16,2 %	8. ge	eg	2,2 %	29,7 %
4. ch		3,3 %	19,5 %	9. es	se	2,2 %	31,9 %
5. de	ed	2,8 %	22,3 %	10. un	nu	2,2 %	34,1 %

Figure 3.38 The ten most common digrams and their reverses in the German languages. Ref. M.17

Based on the combined frequencies of digrams in the German, English and Spanish languages, for example, only 17 of the 30 most frequent digrams, i.e. about 20% of the total can be keyed using alternate hands, and of these 17, very few are among the most common.

Over the years, there have been many attempts at reforming keyboard design by better tailoring the arrangement of the keys to the requirements of individual languages, i.e. to develop national keyboard layouts. In addition, several attempts have been made to develop multilingual arrangements and sometimes with considerable apparent success. Among the best known multilingual keyboard arrangements are those that were developed by Levasseur, Dvorak and Meier, and of these three keyboard designs, the Dvorak arrangment is perhaps the best known.

With the Dvorak layout, about 56% of the work load in English language typing is concentrated on the right hand and the loading on the individual fingers gives emphasis to the stronger index and middle fingers. In addition, about 70% of the typing load is given to the home row of keys, 20% to the top row and 10% to the bottom row.

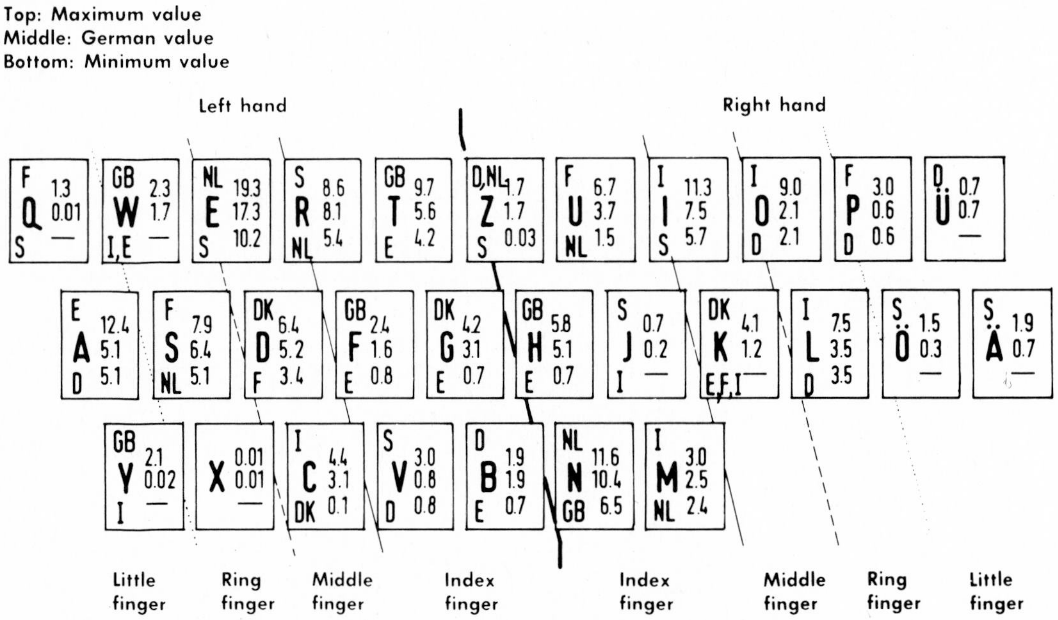

Figure 3.39 Frequency of key usage for eight languages. Ref. M.17

Based on the digram frequencies in the English, German and Spanish languages, 23 of the 30 most frequent digrams, i.e. about 40% of all digrams, require two-handed keying sequences. With the Levasseur keyboard, for example, 45% of all digrams require the use of both hands.

It has been claimed that the layout of the Dvorak keyboard reduces the amount of training time which is necessary and that among experienced operators this particular keyboard layout promotes a higher output when measured in terms of the number of words/minute. But despite several investigations to compare operator output and efficiency, these claims have never been satisfactorily substantiated.

The design and operating characteristics of the Meier keyboard are shown in Figure 3.41 which shows that the apparent deficiencies of the QWERTY layout can be overcome without sacrificing the basic desirability of a multilingual keyboard layout.

140

Quite a different approach to keyboard design, but one which was considered in some detail when keyboards started to be used by an increasingly high proportion of non-skilled typists on computer terminals, was the so-called alphabetic keyboard. On the face of things, this would seem to be quite a plausible layout and one that need not be influenced by traditional or mechanical constraints. However, various experiments have failed to show any practical benefits in using this layout which in fact only helps the user by making it easier to locate the first few and the last few letters of the alphabet. The minor advantage gained by making it easier to scan the rows of keys in order to locate a given letter is more than offset by the awkwardness of keying the most common digrams and other sequences.

Yet in spite of these and many other attempts to introduce reform into keyboard design, the QWERTY layout has survived and has become a virtual standard and it is perhaps the seemingly high costs of retraining that inhibits change.

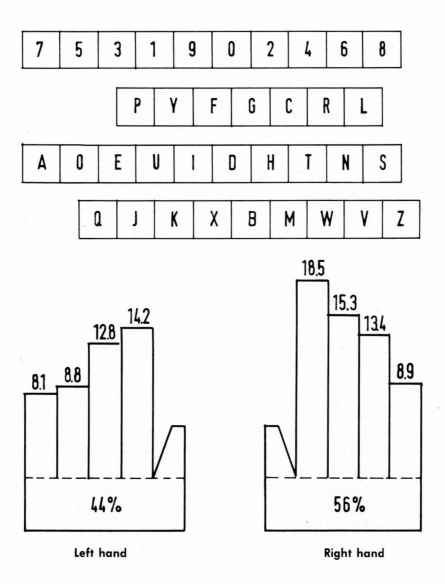

Figure 3.40 The DVORAK keyboard layout and workload distribution in typing English language text. Ref. S.30

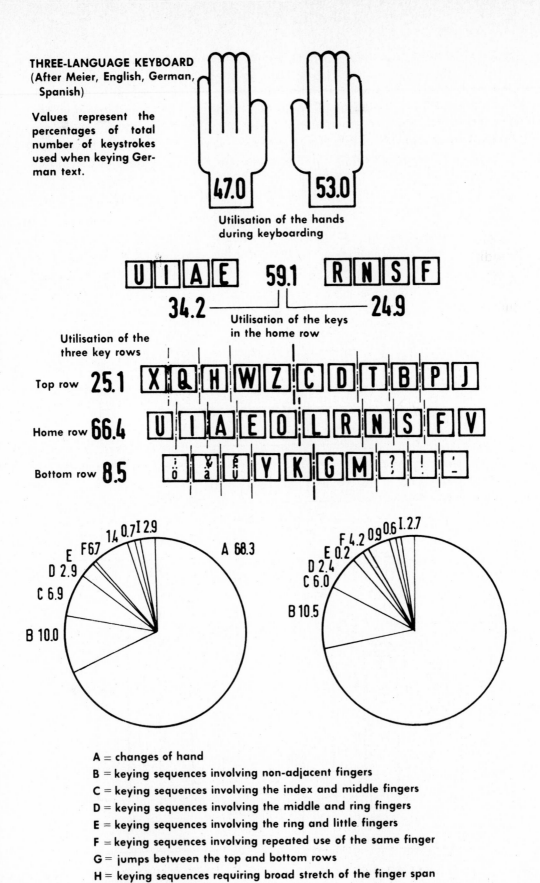

THREE-LANGUAGE KEYBOARD
(After Meier, English, German, Spanish)

Values represent the percentages of total number of keystrokes used when keying German text.

47.0 **53.0**

Utilisation of the hands during keyboarding

U I A E 59.1 R N S F
34.2 ——— 24.9

Utilisation of the keys in the home row

Utilisation of the three key rows

Top row **25.1** X Q H W Z C D T B P J

Home row **66.4** U I A E O L R N S F V

Bottom row **8.5** ö à ü Y K G M ? ! ' -

E F67 1.4 0.7 I 2.9   A 68.3
D 2.9
C 6.9
B 10.0

F 4.2 0.9 0.6 I 2.7
E 0.2
D 2.4
C 6.0
B 10.5

A = changes of hand
B = keying sequences involving non-adjacent fingers
C = keying sequences involving the index and middle fingers
D = keying sequences involving the middle and ring fingers
E = keying sequences involving the ring and little fingers
F = keying sequences involving repeated use of the same finger
G = jumps between the top and bottom rows
H = keying sequences requiring broad stretch of the finger span
I = double key strokes

Figure 3.41 The Meier keyboard arrangement and workload distribution based on the single letter and digram frequencies for the German, English and Spanish languages. Ref. M.17

Numeric keys

There is still considerable variation in the location of numeric keys on the keyboard, but the most suitable location varies from task to task. When the keyboard is used mainly for text entry, the numeric keys should be positioned along the top row of the keyboard as on a conventional typewriter keyboard.

However, when substantial quantities of numbers must also be entered, a separate numeric keypad should be provided, preferably in addition to the standard numeric keyset. This offers the advantage that block sequences of numbers can be entered single-handedly whilst mixed alphanumeric data can be typed in a conventional manner.

The layout of the keys on numeric keypads has been the subject of much debate due to the different layouts used on telephone and adding machine keypads. For most purposes, both layouts provide for more efficient use than the standard, linear numeric key arrangement, but there is certain evidence to support the claim that the telephone layout is preferable to the adding machine layout, particularly for low-skill operators.

Even setting aside purely ergonomic considerations, it is desirable that the layout of keyboard numeric pads should be compatible with telephone pads, particularly since push-button telephones are increasingly being used in conjunction with VDTs. Certainly in the longer term, the '1, 2, 3' layout should be adopted in order to avoid excessive transfer errors when both pieces of equipment - the VDT and the telephone - are used together.

On some VDT keyboards, numerics are incorporated in the main alpha keyset and are accessed using the shift key. Although this type of layout might appear suitable for applications requiring very infrequent entry of numerical data, this type of layout can lead to frequent shift errors.

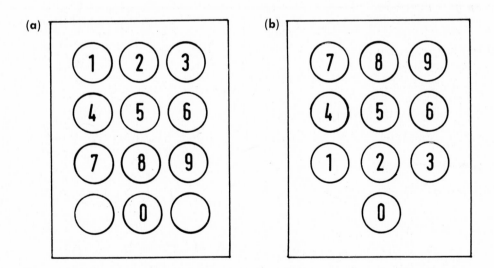

Figure 3.42 Numeric keypad layout: (a) telephone layout, (b) adding machine layout.

Function keys

As mentioned earlier, there will be an optimum number of function keys for any given type of use. If there are too few then either facilities are not available at all or they involve an excessive number of keystrokes. If there are too many, then they are not used in practice because remembering them and how they operate requires more effort than finding a longer way of doing the same thing.

The principal recommendations at present are that there should not be more function keys available than the user can easily access otherwise the excess of choice makes all of them difficult to use. There is, however, a distinction to be made between function keys which the user programs to replace long character strings, e.g. football team names, and function keys which provide commands, editing functions or other operations. In the former case the user will almost certainly refer to a look-up list and so may at times make use of a large number of such keys. However, in the latter case, only a limited number of distinct functions will actually be usable and essential in practice. Esoteric functions may appear attractive in the sales brochure but in the working situation they will not only be unused frills but may actually reduce the useability of the terminal.

It is important that the layout of the keys is such that typical operational sequences form a logical flow on the keyboard. This helps to reduce errors and to maintain the operators' keying rythm. However it is also important that the layout minimises the effect of likely errors. Overreaching frequently used keys or failing to change shift are both extremely common and should not result in critical errors. Keys with major or 'fatal' effect should be located so that inadvertant operation is unlikely.

SUMMARY OF RECOMMENDATIONS

The Display Screen

Character formation

		YES	NO
1.	Does the screen have a display capacity, i.e. number of available character spaces, that is sufficient for the task?	▶ ☐	☐
2.	If the display capacity is less than the maximum capacity required by the task, is there sufficient display memory?	▶ ☐	☐
3.	Is the display memory accessed by		
	▶ roll scrolling?	☐	☐
	▶ page scrolling?	☐	☐
	▶ pan scrolling?	☐	☐
4.	Is scrolling under keyboard control?	▶ ☐	☐
5.	Is the character set sufficient for the task?	▶ ☐	☐
6.	Is the colour of the characters in the display		
	▶ white?	☐	☐
	▶ yellow?	☐	☐
	▶ green?	☐	☐
	▶ other?	☐	☐
7.	Is the character height greater than or equal to 3 mm?	▶ ☐	☐

8. Do the character height and viewing distance ensure a visual angle of at least 16°, preferably 20°? ▶ ☐ ☐

9. If the characters are generated by dot matrix, do the individual dots merge sufficiently well so as to produce a sharp and well defined image? ▶ ☐ ☐

10. Is the resolution of the dot matrix

   ▶ 5 x 7? (acceptable) ☐ ☐

   ▶ 7 x 9 or greater? (preferred) ▶ ☐ ☐

11. Is the character width 70-80% of the upper case character height? ▶ ☐ ☐

12. Is the stroke width between 12% and 17% of the character height? ▶ ☐ ☐

13. Is the space between the characters between 20% and 50% of the character height? ▶ ☐ ☐

14. Is the row spacing between 100% and 150% of the character height? ▶ ☐ ☐

15. Does the VDT permit the display of both upper and lower case characters? ▶ ☐ ☐

16 In displaying lower case characters do descenders project below the base line of the matrix? ▶ ☐ ☐

17. Is it possible to clearly distinguish between the following characters

       X and K? ▶ ☐ ☐

       O and Q? ▶ ☐ ☐

       T and Y? ▶ ☐ ☐

       S and 5? ▶ ☐ ☐

       I and L? ▶ ☐ ☐

       U and V? ▶ ☐ ☐

       I and 1? ▶ ☐ ☐

18. Is it possible to clearly distinguish between the number "0" and the letter "O" (it should be noted that the letter Ø is included in several Nordic alphabets and should not be used to represent the number "0")? ▶ ☐ ☐

19. Are the basic characters upright, i.e. not slanted? ▶ ☐ ☐

		YES	NO

20. Are cursive characters, e.g. italic, available for special coding purposes? ☐ ☐

21. Is it possible to adjust the orientation of the screen or the VDT about its vertical axis? ▶☐ ☐

22. Is it possible to adjust the screen about its horizontal axis? (screen angle) ▶☐ ☐

23. If the screen is fixed, is it approximately vertical? ☐ ☐

24. Is the upper edge of the screen at or below eye height? ▶☐ ☐

25. Where appropriate, does the visual display format correspond to the format which is used on documents, e.g. order forms? ▶☐ ☐

Coding, Format

		YES	NO

1. Is colour available as a means of coding in the display? ☐ ☐

2. How many colours is it necessary to distinguish between

    ▶ 1 - 5? ☐ ☐

    ▶ 5 - 10? ☐ ☐

    ▶ > 10? ☐ ☐

3. Is luminance, i.e. selective brightening used as a means of coding in the display? ☐ ☐

4. How many luminance levels it is necessary to distinguish between

    ▶ 2? ☐ ☐

    ▶ 3? ☐ ☐

    ▶ ≥ 3? ☐ ☐

5. Is it possible to clearly distinguish between the different luminance levels at maximum setting? ▶☐ ☐

6. Is a cursor provided? ▶☐ ☐

7. Is it possible to clearly distinguish the cursor from other symbols on the display? ▶☐ ☐

8. Is it possible to generate graphic symbols via the keyboard? ☐ ☐

		YES	NO
9.	Is it possible to blink selected parts of the display?	☐	☐
10.	Is the blink rate between 2 and 4 Hz?	▶☐	☐
11.	Is it possible to suppress the repeated blink action of the cursor?	▶☐	☐
12.	Is it possible to display characters of differing size?	☐	☐
13.	Is it possible to display characters of differing style?	☐	☐
14.	Are all displayed symbols unambiguous?	▶☐	☐
15.	If filters are used, are the characters in the display sharply defined?	▶☐	☐
16.	Is it possible to adjust the orientation of the screen or the VDT about its vertical axis?	▶☐	☐
17.	Is it possible to adjust the screen about its horizontal axis? (screen angle)	▶☐	☐
18.	If the screen is fixed, is it approximately vertical?	▶☐	☐
19.	Is the upper edge of the screen at or below eye height?	▶☐	☐
20.	Where appropriate, does the visual display format correspond to the format which is used on documents, e.g. order forms?	▶☐	☐
21.	Can forms be generated with protected fields?	☐	☐

The display screen and luminance

		YES	NO
1.	Is the character luminance		
	▶ greater than 45 cd/m^2? (minimum)	☐	☐
	▶ between 80 and 160 cd/m^2? (preferred)	▶☐	☐
2.	Is the character luminance adjustable?	▶☐	☐
3.	Do the character images remain sharply defined at maximum character luminance?	▶☐	☐
4.	Is the background luminance between 15 and 20 cd/m^2 under the appropriate office lighting conditions?	▶☐	☐
5.	Is the background luminance adjustable?	▶☐	☐

6. Is the contrast between the character and background

    ▶ 3 : 1? (minimum) ☐ ☐

    ▶ 5 : 1? (better) ☐ ☐

    ▶ 8 : 1 - 10 : 1? (optimal) ▶☐ ☐

7. Is the contrast between the screen background and other items in the working field, e.g. documents, better than

    ▶ 1 : 10? (acceptable) ☐ ☐

    ▶ 1 : 3 - 1 : 5? (preferred) ▶☐ ☐

8. Are the displayed character images stable? ▶☐ ☐

The Keyboard

General criteria

YES   NO

1. Is the keyboard detached from the display screen console, i.e joined by a cable? ▶☐ ☐

2. Is the weight of the keyboard sufficient to ensure stability against unintentional movement? ▶☐ ☐

3. Is the thickness of the keyboard, i.e. base to the home row of keys

    ▶ less than 50 mm? (acceptable) ☐ ☐

    ▶ 30 mm? (preferred) ▶☐ ☐

4. Is the distance between the underside of the desk frame and the home row of keys on the keyboard less than 60 mm? ▶☐ ☐

5. Is the profile of the keyboard

    ▶ stepped? ☐ ☐

    ▶ sloped? ☐ ☐

    ▶ dished? ☐ ☐

6. Is the angle of the keyboard in the range 5-15°? ▶☐ ☐

7. Is the surface of the keyboard surround matt finished? ▶☐ ☐

8. Is the reflectance of the keyboard surface (not single keys) between 0,40 and 0,60? ▶☐ ☐

	YES	NO

9. Is the luminance ratio between the keyboard, screen and documents less than 1:3 or 3:1? ▶☐ ☐

10. Is there at least a 50 mm deep space provided for resting the palms of the hands? ▶☐ ☐

Key characteristics

	YES	NO

1. Is the key pressure between 0,25 and 1,5 N? ▶☐ ☐

2. Is the key travel between 0,8 and 4,8 mm? ▶☐ ☐

3. For square keytops is the keytop size between ⌀ 12 and ⌀ 15 mm? ▶☐ ☐

4. Is the centre spacing between adjacent keys between 18 and 20 mm? ▶☐ ☐

5. Are the key legends resistant to wear and abrasion, i.e. are the legends moulded into the keytop? ▶☐ ☐

6. Are the keytop surfaces concave so as to improve keyboarding accuracy? ▶☐ ☐

7. Are the keytop surfaces such that specular reflections are kept to a minimum? ▶☐ ☐

8. Is the activation of each key accompanied by a feedback signal such as an
   - ▶ audible click? ☐ ☐
   - ▶ tactile click? ☐ ☐
   - ▶ or snap action? ☐ ☐

9. Do the keys have a low failure rate? ▶☐ ☐

10. What type of errors might occur as the result of a key failure
    - ▶ keystroke not registered (contact error)? ☐ ☐
    - ▶ keystroke is repeated (jammed key)? ☐ ☐

11. If two keys are activated simultaneously, is a warning signal given? ▶☐ ☐

12. Is the keyboard provided with a roll-over facility
    - ▶ 2-key roll-over? ☐ ☐
    - ▶ n-key roll-over? ▶☐ ☐

Keyboard layout

		YES	NO
1.	Does the layout of the alpha keys correspond to the conventional typewriter keyboard layout?	▶□	□
2.	Does the layout of the numeric keys - above the alpha keys - correspond to the conventional typewriter keyboard layout?	▶□	□
3.	Are the numeric keys grouped in a separate block:		
	▶ as the only numeric keyset?	□	□
	▶ or as an auxilliary keyset in addition	□	□
	▶ to the keyset referred to under 2?	□	□
4.	If an auxilliary numeric keyset is provided, are the keys arranged:		
	▶ as in the calculator layout i.e. 7, 8, 9, along the top row?	□	□
	▶ as in the telephone layout i.e. 1, 2, 3 along the top row?	□	□
5.	Is the space bar at the bottom of the keyboard?	▶□	□
6.	Does the number and type of function keys correspond to the requirements of the task?	▶□	□
7.	Does the arrangement of the function keys correspond to the sequences with which the task is carried out?	▶□	□
8.	Are keying errors critical as regards the success of the task in question, i.e. rather than merely inconvenient?	□	□
9.	Is the colour of the alphanumeric keys neutral, e.g. beige, grey, rather than black or white or one of the spectral colours red, yellow, green or blue?	▶□	□
10.	Are the different function key blocks distinct from the other keys by		
	▶ colour?	□	□
	▶ shape?	□	□
	▶ position?	□	□
	▶ distance (spacing)?	□	□
11.	Are the most important function keys colour-coded?	□	□
12.	Are all keys for which unintentional or accidental operation may have serious consequences especially secure by		
	▶ their position?	□	□
	▶ higher required key pressure?	□	□
	▶ key lock?	□	□
	▶ two handed (two key) chord operation?	□	□

13. Do the function key labels and symbols correspond to the same functions on other keyboards used e.g. typewriters or other VDTs at the same workplace? ☐ ☐

14. Are user-programmable function keys provided? ☐ ☐

Additional VDT and System Characteristics

YES   NO

1. Is the power dissipation from the VDT as low as possible? ▶☐ ☐

2. Is the VDT resistant to knocks and vibration? ▶☐ ☐

3. Is the operator secure against electrical accident even when tampering with the VDT? ▶☐ ☐

4. Does the VDT satisfy the requirements of all national and local safety standards? ▶☐ ☐

5. Are the operators and cleaning staff aware of which cleaning materials may be used without causing damage to the screen, housing and other components of the VDT? ▶☐ ☐

6. Is there sufficient maintenance access to both the VDT and VDT workplace? ▶☐ ☐

7. Are there any user-serviceable repairs, e.g. fuse changes, that can be quickly and easily carried out by the operator? ☐ ☐

8. Are the electrical supply cables and other services to the VDT and workplace adequately secured and concealed? ▶☐ ☐

9. Has the voltage supply to the VDT system been stabilised against fluctuations in supply voltage, e.g. due to variations in mains voltage, peak loads etc? ▶☐ ☐

10. Is the operator provided with a warning signal in the event of system or VDT malfunction
    - ▶ audible alarm? ▶☐ ☐
    - ▶ visual alarm? ▶☐ ☐
    - ▶ other? ☐ ☐

11. Is the operator provided with a warning in the event that the VDT is no longer able to register keystrokes, e.g. when the VDT memory storage is filled? ▶☐ ☐

12. Will security procedures be necessary? ☐ ☐

13. How is the operational status of the VDT, e.g. if the terminal is in send, receive or queue mode, made known to the operator:
    - ▶ no indication? ☐ ☐
    - ▶ flashing light indicator? ☐ ☐
    - ▶ continuous light indicator? ▶☐ ☐

	YES	NO

14. Is the response time of the system sufficiently short during peak working times? ►☐ ☐

15. If the response time is likely to vary appreciably, is the operator given an indication of waiting times? ►☐ ☐

16. If several terminals share a common transmission line to the computer, can each terminal transmit and receive information independently of the status of the other terminals on the line? ►☐ ☐

17. Is it necessary to consider special precautions, e.g. special carpeting or a copper grid carpet underlay, to safeguard against the discharge of static electricity to the VDT chassis? ☐ ☐

Chapter 4

ERGONOMIC REQUIREMENTS

FOR VDT WORKPLACES

Foreword

In the previous sections, the main individual components of VDTs have been dealt with from the point of view of their design and operation. Particular emphasis was placed on the ergonomic criteria which should be observed in the design of VDTs. In this section, attention is turned to the configuration of VDT workplaces, and in particular to the anthropometric requirements that should be considered in the design and layout of the workplace.

The likelihood that the operator of a VDT may experience feelings of fatigue or stress at work is governed to a very large extent by his or her sitting position whilst operating the VDT. The design of the workplace must take account of the position and freedom of movement required by the hands, arms, legs and head, as well as the viewing distances involved whilst working with the VDT screen, keyboard and other job aids such as source documents, telephones etc. These considerations result in specific requirements as regards working level, desk and seating heights, arm reach and the provision of foot rests, document holders etc. These, then, are among the most important parameters of the VDT workplace.

It must always be borne in mind, however, that no matter how well the ergonomic criteria for VDT workplace design are satisfied in practice this, in itself, is no guarantee against postural discomfort. If the job itself requires the individual to maintain a static position or permits only a few essential movements, some degree of postural discomfort is still to be expected. In striving to achieve an optimal workplace, therefore, it should be remembered that the tasks which are to be performed at each workplace themselves impose certain constraints on the design of the workplace. These constraints should be very carefully considered in practice. In particular, the working method should, as far as possible, be designed so as to eliminate the need for a static working position or repetitive movements either by providing for greater freedom of body movement or for short pauses.

WORKPLACE ERGONOMICS

Introducing a computer system into an office environment inevitably raises a number of organisational and work design issues which must be considered and resolved if the system is to be successfully implemented. The decision to purchase or lease a computer system can seldom be approached as one would approach the decision to buy an 'off-the-peg' type of product. The financial investment involved is usually quite large and getting the best return on this investment in terms of efficiency and productivity requires a thorough and detailed understanding of what it is that the system must be designed to do. It also depends upon an appreciation of the fact that the system is to be used by *people* which, like computers, come in a variety of shapes and sizes and which, as individuals, will tend to view the idea of working with a computer system with varying degrees of enthusiasm and anxiety.

It should be the basic axiom of systems design that a computer system should be tailored to meet the needs of the job that it is intended for and the people who must use it and not *vice versa*. This is a basic human requirement and applies to both the functional design of the system and the physical design of the various items of hardware that, together, make up a system. No matter how well the facilities of a computer system match the needs of the job, if it does not live up to the needs and expectations of those actually doing the job, they will become dissatisfied and disillusioned.

The involvement of future users at each stage in the planning and selection of a system is, therefore, an important feature of successful system implementation. This applies as much to the concept and design of the system as it does to the physical installation of the system and its components in the office environment, and this section of the report deals with the practical considerations involved in the design of VDT workplaces and offices.

If the VDT supplier also offers complete workplaces, it is easier for the purchaser to judge the extent to which the ergonomic requirements on workplace design are satisfied. Most suppliers, however, offer only the VDTs themselves, in which case the design of the workplace and the selection of office furniture is left to the discretion of the purchaser. But without an appropriate set of guidelines, this might not be as successful as would be hoped for. Indeed, the design of the VDT itself may prohibit the realisation of an optimal workplace.

There are many examples of display units which, at first sight, appear suitably sized and angled to fit the needs of the user but which when used are found to press the legs, stretch the arms and body too much, present the display screen at a less than optimum viewing angle or are in other respects awkward to use. For reasons such as these, the selection of the VDTs and the design of the individual VDT workplaces should be considered together rather than separately.

Importance of the VDT task

As far as VDT workplace design is concerned, there cannot, of course, be one single solution which will suit all situations. It is strongly recommended, therefore, that all decisions regarding work station layout and location should be taken with the full collaboration and involvement of the potential users. If the users have been fully involved from an early stage, then by the time the work stations and their locations are being considered, they should have developed a sufficiently detailed appreciation of what using the system will involve to enable them to participate in a realistic and informed manner.

To ensure an adequate design for a single work station or for a standard version to suit a particular range of tasks, it is essential that a full and detailed analysis is first made of the tasks involved. It is essential that the development programme is as much oriented to the needs of the human tasks as to the needs of the computer and the system. This is easy and obvious to state, but it is not quite so easy to realise in practice. This is partly due to the fact that whilst computer and engineering considerations can usually be evaluated in tangible cost terms, human needs and benefits cannot be so easily quantified. Nevertheless, the importance of taking human needs into account is beginning to be realised from experience by system engineers and by those who have themselves faced the practical problems of implementing a VDT system.

Types of VDT working area

VDT tasks generally fall into one of three task categories: [1]

- data entry
- dialogue-type tasks and
- data enquiry

Data entry workplaces

When the VDT is used primarily for text or data entry, the principal activities which are performed by the operator involve (a) reading information from a source document of one kind or another and (b) entering this information into the computer via the keyboard. In most data entry tasks, the source information is, for the most part, non-redundant, i.e. lacking in any form of predictable sequence, requiring frequent visual reference to the source document. Operators engaged in tasks of this kind are usually highly-skilled in keyboarding so that the speed with which the data is keyed is relatively high.

Field studies have shown that in tasks such as these, even the most difficult types of numerical data are usually touch-typed into the computer. Head movements are fairly frequent and usually occur at intervals of between one and four seconds. When entering alphanumeric information, on the other hand, more frequent visual reference is made to the keyboard. Head and eye movements therefore occur more frequently, and the keyboard is the main visual object for about half of the time.

Dialogue task workplaces

This type of activity is characterised by the flow of information from a document or person as the data source to the computer store and *vice versa*. Persons engaged in these types of activity seldom command the same level of typing skills as data entry personnel.

During the time in which the operator is in dialogue with the computer via the terminal, the principal activities involve looking at whatever documents may be necessary, and at the keyboard and the screen.

---

1. Not all types of VDT task can be exactly classified into one of these three categories. The borderlines between them are not very precise, and neither would it be difficult to introduce further categories. Nevertheless this sub-division does help to illustrate some essential features of the task-workplace relationship.

Data enquiry workplaces

The principal task at this kind of VDT workplace involves requesting information from the computer store. Once again, persons engaged in tasks of this kind rarely command the same keyboarding skills as those involved in purely data entry tasks and the frequency and duration of visual contact with the keyboard is usually very much greater.

Studies which have been made to date concerning the nature of VDT tasks have shown that the visual focus of the data entry task is that of reading information from a source document. In dialogue tasks, the source documents, the keyboard and the screen are of equal importance whilst at a data enquiry station, working with the VDT itself is the single most important visual aspect of the task.

At all three types of VDT workplace it is the keyboard which has the greatest influence on working method. In addition to the alphanumeric keys there are many function and command keys to be operated. Apart from VDT tasks which are solely or mainly concerned with numerical data entry, VDT operators spend quite a high proportion of the time looking at the keyboard. Even those with a high level of typing skill spend more time looking at the VDT keyboard than is commonly realised. VDT operators who do not command the skills of a typist - and this is true of the majority of VDT operators - necessarily spend most of their time looking at the keyboard whilst using the VDT.

General workplace considerations

There are a number of dimensions and clearances which, at a given work station, may need to be adjusted to suit the different sizes and shapes of the potential users. Generally speaking, there are three basic areas in which the match between the user and the VDT work station should be checked.

Can the user reach and operate the controls? The different controls which a user may need to operate should all be easily and safely accessible. The major controls on the VDT itself are the keyboard, power on/off and other controls e.g. brightness, contrast, modems, etc. There are also likely to be other items of equipment and controls which the user may have to operate in conjunction with the use of the VDT, e.g. typewriter, lighting, telephones, calculators, line printers, heating, etc.

Can the user see and read the displays? The different displays which the user may need to read or use whilst working at the VDT workplace, e.g. the keyboard, display screen, documents etc, should be favourably placed, i.e. at a suitable distance and location, in relation to the operator's working position. None of the displays should be concealed by other objects, particularly if the operator needs to change position whilst working, e.g when working alternately with the VDT and, say, a typewriter.

Can the user work in a comfortable position and get in and out of the work place easily? There are a number of basic clearances which are needed to safeguard against the user having to adopt an uncomfortable or potentially harmful posture, either when using the work station or when getting in or out. For example, short VDT operators may require a footrest, but adequate knee clearance between the underside of the desk and the seat of the chair is still required. The display screen should always be at a comfortable viewing distance and the keyboard should always be in such a position that it is easy to operate without awkward hand, arm and body positions.

Suitably sized equipment and office furniture is not only necessary for comfort, essential though this is for efficient work; it is also a matter of health and safety. Back problems account for a substantial proportion of industrial ailments and incorrect work place design is a major contributor to poor posture and the incidence of backstrain. It is an unfortunate, costly, but nevertheless quite common, misconception that workplace design and the selection of office furniture are secondary considerations in systems design and utilisation!

Desk space or additional work surfaces may be required in order to lay out, read and write on documents, printouts etc. The work surfaces should, therefore, be appropriate for such needs in terms of size, position and accessibility. A lectern placed between a detachable keyboard and the VDT screen can be useful for supporting source documents at an appropriate reading distance.

Another storage need which is often overlooked is that for a short term *buffer area* where incoming or outgoing documents or work can be batched or sorted. Items such as calculators, pencils, etc., also need to be stored. So too do personal belongings. Tripping over a handbag or briefcase is as inexcusable - and probably as painful - as tripping over an exposed cable!

The type of *seating* required depends on the length of time the user is likely to spend at the VDT and how frequently he or she will need to move away from it whilst working. A swivel chair, with a stable base but without arms, can be used to provide mobility if a fixed chair is not appropriate.

If more than one user or group of users is to share the VDT, there may be difficulties in locating the terminal in a mutually convenient place.

Terminal work stations often require a considerable quantity of equipment and materials to be accessible to the user. Unless adequate provision is made for unnecessary items such as waste paper, cables from VDTs, and for items such as modems, typewriter etc., the result is clutter. This is not only aesthetically unpleasant but can also present a real hazard to working posture.

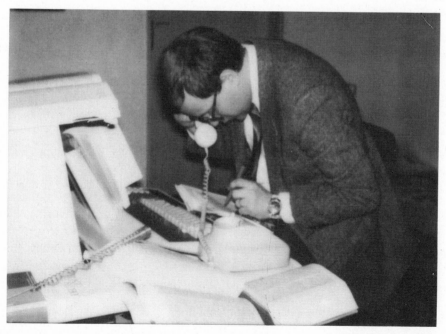

Figure 4.1 A cluttered VDT workplace is both unpleasant and can represent a real hazard to working posture.

Even with the best equipment, access will be required for routine servicing and *maintenance*. When designing the work station it is also worthwhile giving some thought to what access might be needed for non-routine repairs and servicing, e.g. repairs in the cable ducts under the floor.

There are also a number of different *physical environments* which should be considered, e.g. lighting, the thermal environment, noise, etc., in each of which the VDT can itself create a problem or be threatened. In deciding the best location of the VDTs in the office, careful account should be taken of these factors in order that a suitable environment can be created.

One of the most difficult compromises which must be made is that of providing enough *lighting* to adequately illuminate source documents or other printed or written materials, without illuminating the VDT screen and reducing the contrast of the display. Providing individual directional lighting for the reading of documents and a more diffuse and lower level of illumination for viewing the screen and other activities is not an entirely satisfactory solution to the problem. The human eye has then to continually adjust from light to dark when shifting vision from screen to paper. The greater the difference, the greater the amount of adjustment effort and hence fatigue.

The VDT screen should neither be completely black nor completely shaded since this increases the amount of visual adaptation required in looking from the display screen to the source documents and *vice versa*. By fitting baffles and diffusers to overhead lighting, and by appropriate positioning of the luminaires, a satisfactory compromise can usually be achieved. In addition, it is often possible to tilt the screen a few degrees away from the vertical to provide a suitable viewing angle and degree of illumination while at the same time avoiding unnecessary and distracting reflections on the screen.

There are also a number of features of VDTs which lead to potential *safety problems* for users. In addition to the electrical hazards which are common to many other items of office equipment, several components of VDTs operate with high voltages although these are normally well protected. It is important that objects such as paperclips should not be able to fall into the VDT through ventilation grilles or slots. Neither is the top of a VDT a suitable place to rest a cup of coffee!

VDTs are vulnerable to a number of hazards ranging from vibrations or knocks to fluctuations in the power supply which can cause the screen to clear and data to be corrupted. Even if these effects are only temporary, they can be extremely disruptive and frustrating to the user.

Chemical hazards might arise if plastic components are attacked by wrongly-chosen cleaning solvents, or if inflammable liquids are ignited by sparking contacts.

The use of model work-stations

One of the best ways to consider the arrangement of VDT work stations is for the computer personnel and the users to work together through some of the possible work station arrangements using either paper and pencil sketches, scale or full-size mock-ups. Mock-ups of this kind do not need to involve the real computer equipment; large cardboard boxes of the appropriate dimensions can be moved and experimented with quite easily.

Once satisfactory arrangements have been produced it is a simple matter to photograph or draw the layout, and any structural or other alterations can be completed before the proper equipment is installed. When properly conducted, mock-up trials of this kind can be useful in involving junior levels of personnel who might not have had the opportunity to be involved in the earlier stages of the computer project.

Anthropometric aspects of VDT workplaces

The efficiency of a posture is determined by the degree to which it loads the skeleton and the skeletal and postural muscles of the body. The effects of faulty sitting postures reveal themselves through spinal disorders and fatigue of the back muscles. In considering the working posture at a VDT workplace, therefore, special attention is paid to the arms, spine, pelvis and legs as the most affected skeletal parts of the body, and the neck, back, abdomen, arms and legs as the musculature involved.

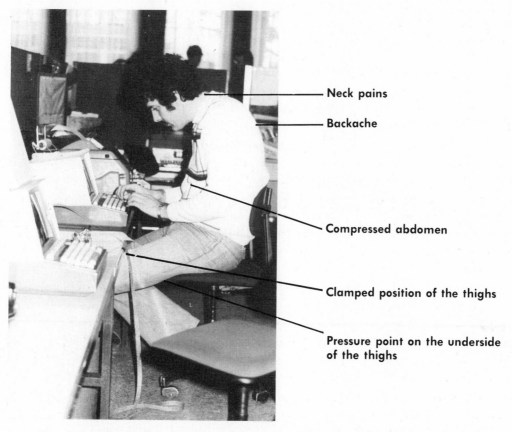

Neck pains

Backache

Compressed abdomen

Clamped position of the thighs

Pressure point on the underside of the thighs

Figure 4.2 The VDT workplace should be designed to match the physical characteristics of the individual. If not, the VDT operator may suffer a variety of physical discomforts. Ref. C.2

It should be remembered however, that any posture is bad if it has to be fixed or maintained for too long a period: muscular loading in a static position is more tiring than the loading induced by movement. With any posture, static loads are always present in one or other group of muscles. The effort required to maintain a fixed posture increases with time and eventually reaches such a fatiguing level, particularly in those parts of the musculature that are most heavily loaded, that the individual necessarily feels the urge to change position. So it is that even the 'most desirable' posture becomes tiring after a while.

The freedom and ability to change posture at frequent intervals contributes greatly towards delaying subjective feelings of fatigue. This is so for basically two reasons. Firstly, changes in posture and the engagement of different parts of the musculature helps to decrease the static work expended in any one particular group of muscles. Secondly, the mechanical work that is expended in changing posture tends to provide relief from purely static muscular loading.

With regard to the anthropometric matching of the workplace to the VDT operator, the following results have been determined from investigations which were carried out taking into account the factors shown in Figure 4.3.

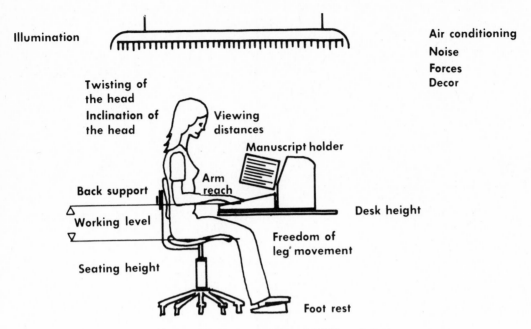

Figure 4.3 The most important aspects in the design of VDT workplaces

Working level

The working level is defined as the distance between the underside of the thighs and the palms of the hand, and is one of the most important characteristics of working posture in the sitting position. The working level should be determined with the individual sitting in a nearly upright position with the hands and forearms horizontal. According to one national standard (DIN 33402) the working level should fall in the range 220 to 250 mm corresponding to the lower 5% percentile limit for the female population and the upper 95% percentile limit for the male population.

The working level at a VDT workplace includes the distance between the seat of the chair and the upper surface of the thighs, the distance between the upper surface of the thighs and the underside of the desk, the thickness of the desk and the height of the keyboard measured between the desktop and the home row of keys.

The practical importance of the working level is best appreciated by considering the need (a) to provide sufficient knee clearance and (b) to provide for a working posture in which the position of the hands and arms is the most favourable when using the keyboard. Generally speaking, the knee clearance should be between 170 and 200 mm. Since desk thicknesses are typically of the order 20 to 40 mm for the desk top with an additional 20 mm allowing for the thickness of the desk frame, both requirements are satisfied only when the height of the keyboard is of the order 30 mm. Bearing in mind that on most existing types of VDT, the height of the keyboard is usually between 50 and 120 mm, it is clear that very seldom can both requirements be fully satisfied.

The desk top, desk frame and keyboard should be as thin as possible in order to ensure a working level between 220 and 250 mm. Detached keyboards with a height of more than 30 mm should be set into the desktop. Keyboards which are an integral part of the VDT chassis should not be built into the desk top since the screen is then usually placed in too low a position to permit comfortable viewing. The position of the keyboard should always be adjustable and adequate knee clearance must also be maintained.

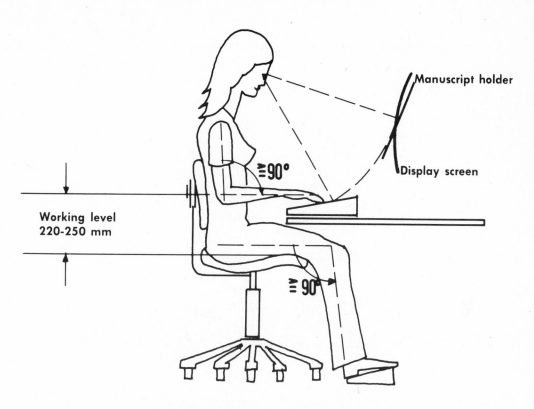

Figure 4.4 *The working level is defined as the distance between the underside of the thighs and the palms of the hands when operating the keyboard with the hands and forearms in an approximately horizontal position.*

Figure 4.5 *In this posture, the forearms are in the correct position, but the hands are inclined about the wrists at an unfavourable angle.*

Desk height

When working with a typewriter or a VDT, the operator supports himself in three positions:

- with the seat and underthighs on the chair,
- with the feet on .the ground or on a footrest, and
- with the back on the backrest of the chair

Figure 4.6 In this posture, comfortable viewing of the screen has resulted in too low a seating position. This gives more than adqeaute leg room but only at the expense of a very unfavourable position of the hands and arms when using the keyboard.

Having fixed any one of the three variables desk height, seating height and height of the foot rest, both of the remaining two variables must be adjustable. For the following reasons, however, it is more sensible to adjust the seating and foot support heights in relation to a *fixed desk height*.

An adjustable desk height cannot compensate for the effects of too great a keyboard height. In striving to achieve the correct working height, there is no substitute for a thin keyboard.

Many people in office environments are either unaware of the possibility of adjusting the height of their seat or choose not to make use of this facility. One might suppose, therefore, that individual VDT operators might be even less inclined to make use of desk height adjustment.

A partially adjustable desk top, i.e. one that permits adjustment of either the keyboard or screen height is more favourable, however, since this allows the operator to adjust the position of his or her head to one which minimises the strain in the neck and shoulders. Such a facility might also be used to help eliminate reflections from windows and lamps.

Desks for VDT workplaces should have a desktop height of
720 - 750 mm with a minimum free height of 650 - 690 mm. In
the case of keyboards which are detached from the display
screen, the keyboard height, i.e. the height of the home row of
keys above floor level, should be between 720 and 750 mm.

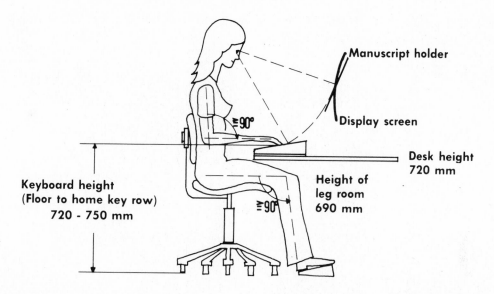

Figure 4.7 Recommended desk heights for VDT workplaces.

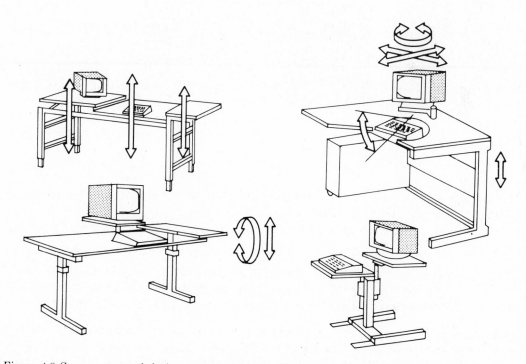

Figure 4.8 Some suggested designs to permit desk adjustment for VDT workplaces. Ref. O.9

Chair, seating height and back support

To obtain a good working posture, the chair height should be adjusted so as to enable
keyboarding in a position with the forearms approximately horizontal. The feet should

rest comfortably on the floor with the feet flat on the floor and with the thighs horizontal. In this position, the stabilising work required to maintain the sitting position is kept to a minimum and so too is the static stress in the back and leg muscles. If the user is unable to adopt such a position without stretching, a footrest should be provided for added support.

Figure 4.9 Two examples of poor VDT operating posture caused by too high keyboard height and too little leg room.

Most types of office chair are suitable for terminal workplaces provided that they are of the type with *back rests* for pelvic and lumbar support. The lumbar region is usually the most highly-strained part of the spine and the provision of a back-rest helps to minimise the static muscular work that is necessary to stabilise the trunk of the body in the sitting position. The back-rest serves as a 'lumbar pad', helping to maintain the correct curvature of the lumbar part of the spine and at the same time preventing rotation of the pelvis. The position of the back-rest, should be adjustable both in height and angle. The surfaces of the back-rest should curve smoothly outwards so that they do not cut into the body surface.

The pressure distribution between the body and the seat surface and the stability of the sitting position are both affected by the properties and design of the *seat coverings*. In both respects, rough textured and flexible materials are more suitable than shiny and hard materials. A textured material surface provides greater friction to help stabilise the sitting position; flexibility helps to evenly distribute the pressure and avoid pressure spots. The seat coverings should also permit air circulation over the surface of the skin.

Seats made of hard materials, even when contoured, should not be used when prolonged sitting is required. Curving down the front edge of the seat prevents it from cutting into the thighs in the sitting position.

> Chairs for VDT workplaces should be adjustable in height between 450 and 520 mm. The optimum height is attained with the feet flat on the floor and the thighs in a horizontal position.

> Chairs should be provided with adjustable backrests to provide pelvic and lumbar support in the seated position.

> Individual operators should be informed - and if necessary constantly reminded - of the possibility to adjust the height of the chair and the position of the backrest. In many instances, it has been found that postural discomfort among office personnel could have been avoided if those concerned had thought to adjust their seating position.

Work-place type	Desk height		Seating height		Foot height		Comment
	Fixed	Variable	Fixed	Variable	Fixed	Variable	
1	▓			▓	▓		Physiologically unsatisfactory
2	▓		▓			▓	Physiologically satisfactory and most economical
3	▓		▓		▓		The most unsatisfactory solution since the user must adjust himself completely to the features of the workplace
4	▓		▓			▓	See 3
5		▓		▓	▓		Physiologically very good but uneconomical
6		▓		▓		▓	Physiologically the best version but very costly
7		▓	▓		▓		Theoretical solution, uneconomical
8		▓	▓			▓	See 7

Figure 4.10 An economic and physiological appraisal of the adjustability of desk height, seating height and footrest height.

Foot rests

With a fixed desk height and variable seating height, the correct leg posture for smaller persons can only be achieved with the aid of a footrest. In this position, the thighs should be horizontal with the feet resting on the footrest so as to give a 90° or slightly greater bend angle at the knee.

> Footrests should be adjustable both in height, in the range 0 to 50 mm, and inclination, 10° to 15°, and should be large enough to cover the entire usable leg area. Ideally, footrests should be secured to the floor or to the desk in order to prevent sliding. Moveable footrests are less desirable but can be better than nothing.

Document holders

In order to avoid an unfavourable inclination of the head or even a complete sideways body movement when shifting vision between documents and the screen, document holders should be provided and used. In deciding the most suitable position of the document holder, the following considerations should be taken into account.

The most highly stressed part of the body is the neck, and more effort is expended when the head is moved in the vertical plane, e.g. when nodding the head, than when the head is rotated from side to side. In order to check the accurary of data which has been read from a document and displayed on the screen, the operator makes a series of rapid eye movements between the screen and the document. In order to relieve the neck of unnecessary strain, these eye movements should require only a horizontal movement of the head.

Figure 4.11 The copy holder should be positioned behind the keyboard. But when the keyboard is an integral part of the VDT chassis, the manuscript is then often too high. In this example, the problem is not too bad since the screen itself is not very high, in fact, it is too low to be read comfortably. Ref. K.26

If the user finds it difficult to read the text on the document, he or she will usually try to reduce the visual distance between the eyes and the document. This means that if the document is lying on the desk, additional strain is imposed on the neck or the back. If the document is placed next to and in the same plane as the display screen, the viewing distance can be reduced by moving the entire upper part of the body forward. This imposes much less strain on the neck and back. It is sensible, therefore, to place the document on the same level as the display screen. If it is also assumed that the document will be read with the head inclined forward at an angle of about 20°, it is also sensible to incline the document holder at an angle of 20° to the vertical so that the line of sight is at right angles to the plane of the paper.

These precautions are also advantageous from the point of view of the visual process. VDT workplaces are usually illuminated from above which means that the luminance of a source document is greatest when it is lying flat on the desk. By inclining the plane of the document, the illuminance is reduced until, with the copy inclined at 20° to the vertical, the luminance is approximately halved. For example, if the luminance ratio between the display screen and a document lying next to the keyboard is 1:6, the luminance ratio is reduced to 1:3 with the same ambient lighting and with the document inclined at 20°.

In practice, however, some flexibility must be maintained as to how these recommendations are implemented. Individual user needs may give preference to other solutions. For example, if the user needs to make additions or corrections to the text

Figure 4.12 A VDT with detachable keyboard. In this example the operator has the keyboard and manuscript in their most favourable positions, i.e. directly in front of him. Ref. K.26

Figure 4.13 The manuscript holder shown in this example is transparent, unstable and can give rise to troublesome reflections. Ref. K.26

shown on the document, a shallower angle may be preferred. Likewise, if the copy is secured onto the holder using a magnetic or other type of clip, individual users may again prefer a shallower angle. Preference might also be given to document holders with a bottom lip to secure the position of the document without the need for clips.

Figure 4.14 This type of manuscript holder is more satisfactory. Note the use of a magnet to retain the manuscript on the holder. Ref. K.26

Depending upon the way in which source documents are used, requirements as regards the type and position of the holder vary as shown in the following table.

Task	Frequency of manuscript change	Type and position of manuscript holder
Pure copy entry, no manipulation	Seldom	Size according to type of document Row marker: yes Position: to the left of the display screen, 20° angle
Copy entry with some manipulation,e.g. occassional notes	Seldom	Size: as above row marker: as above Position: to the right of the display screen
Pure copy entry, no manipulation	Frequent	Size: as above Row marker: preferably Position: to the left of the display screen, or between the keyboard and screen
Copy entry with some manipulation	Frequent	Size: as above Row marker: as above Position: to the right of the display screen
Pure copy entry, no manipulation (mostly numerical data)	Very frequent	Size: as above Row marker: no Position: to the left of the keyboard

Figure 4.15 Manuscript holder recommendations according to the type of VDT task and use of a manuscript.

If a dynamic copy feed and holder is used, this too should permit adjustment of height, reading distance and inclination.

Body movements which occur when reading source documents can often be unfavourable, but they cannot be entirely avoided. By providing a copy holder of an appropriate design, however, some of these movements can be reduced or transferred to less highly loaded parts of the body, e.g. as arm movement instead of neck movement or rotation of the body about the pelvis rather than bending of the neck.

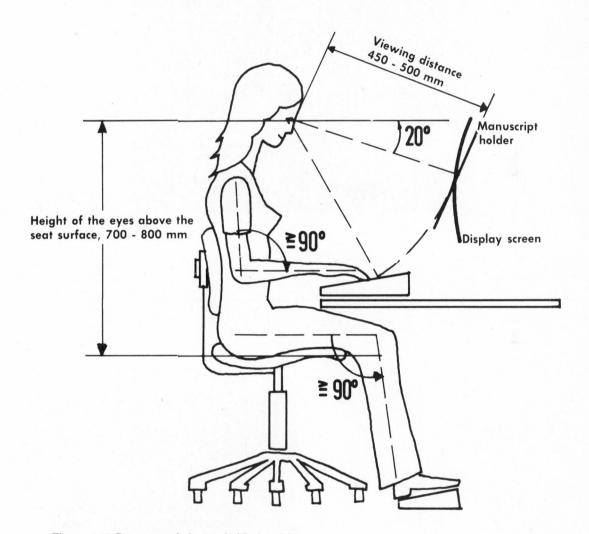

Figure 4.16 Recommended copy-holder position.

Arm reach and working level

Besides ensuring the correct working level, the desk upon which the VDT is placed should have a large enough area to accommodate all other necessary working aids. The keyboard should be within the arm reach of the operator, i.e. the back row of keys should be located at a distance of no more than 400 mm from the front edge of the desk. A free area of approximately 60 mm depth in front of the keyboard has been found to be useful as a resting place for the hands and to safeguard against the 'cutting' action between the edge of the keyboard and the operator's wrist.

Figure 4.17 When using the keyboard, the hands and forearms should be in such a position that there is no cutting action between the wrists and the edge of the desk.

A common fault at some VDT workplaces is inadequate provision for the use of documents; in some cases so little space is provided that the operator is required to rest documents on his or her knees!

Figure 4.18 Plenty of space should be provided for documents! Ref. G.20

Position and movement of the head

When seated and engaged in an activity such as reading, the most comfortable position of the head is such that the viewing angle is between 32° and 44° below the horizontal plane. This angle includes both the inclination of the head and the line of sight in approximately equal measure. In this position, therefore, the head is inclined forward at an angle of about 20° to the vertical.

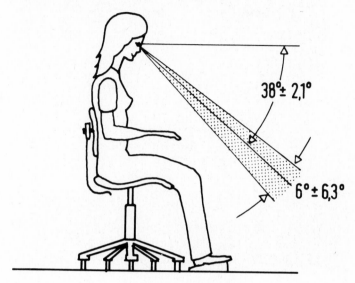

Figure 4.19 The normal viewing inclination for seated tasks.

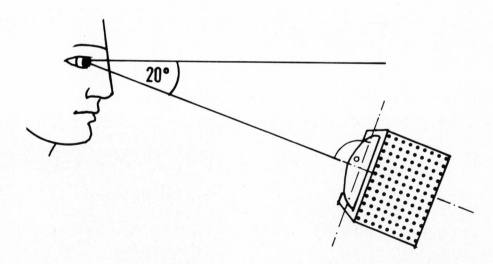

Figure 4.20 The display screen can be read comfortably with the eyes directed at an angle of about 20° below horizontal.

As far as reading the display screen and documents is concerned, this viewing angle can be achieved by placing the screen and the document holder in their most appropriate positions. In the case of the keyboard, however, this is no longer possible. In spite of the fact that most VDT operators spend a lot of time looking at the keyboard, the keyboard is first and foremost a manual operating field which should be positioned in such a way that the hands and arms are held in an optimal position whilst keyboarding. In this position, however, the viewing angle is much greater than that

171

which is necessary to minimise the strain in the neck and back. The keyboard viewing angle is usually about 60°. It is not possible, therefore, to simultaneously ensure the optimum positions of the head and the arms. For this reason, even persons who only occasionaly need to use the VDT should be well trained in using the keyboard so that as little time as possible is spent looking down at the keys. This, however, is seldom the case in practice!

Figure 4.21 A VDT with integral keyboard recessed into the desk top to provide an optimum keyboard position. Unfortunately, the screen is now too low for comfortable viewing. Note the inclination of the neck. Ref. K.26

Twisting of the head

Twisting the head sideways and down is usually caused by having to read a document that is placed on the desktop and to one side of the keyboard. In extreme cases, the head

(a)   (b)

Figure 4.22 Examples of poor workstation layout. (a) By having placed the manuscript on the desk top next to the keyboard, the operator is forced to turn her head down and to one side. (b) This operator, in using the low desk as an elbow support, has to bend her back. She will also be affected by glare from the white desk top. Ref. C.2

172

can be turned through an angle of 45° to 75° with the upper part of the body also in a twisted position. This type of very unfavourable movement can be reduced by the appropriate use of a document holder.

Viewing distance

The choice of viewing distances at the VDT workplace is important for several reasons:

- as a rule, three different objects - a document, the screen and the keyboard - are looked at in quick succession,
- the text which is presented on the documents is usually written or typed with small characters, typically less than 3 mm high,
- the characters on the display screen are also small in size.

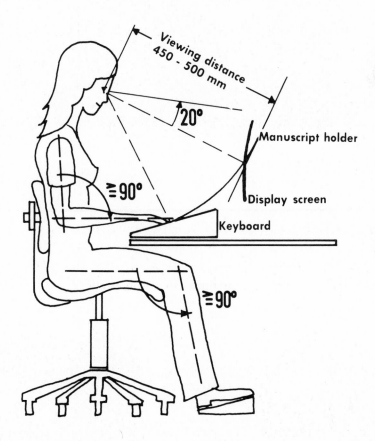

Figure 4.23 Recommended viewing distance.

In most office tasks, the speed of visual accommodation[1] is not especially important since, as a rule, the luminance is more or less uniform at each work station and the visual distances involved in most office tasks are much the same. But since it is often recommended that the viewing distance to the VDT screen should not exceed about 700 mm and since the keyboard is usually situated at a viewing distance of 450 to 500 mm, the speed and frequency of accommodation become very much more important.

1. The term *accommodation* is used to describe the adjustment of the eyes to accommodate changes in focal distance.

For physiological reasons, it is necessary to keep changes in viewing distance to a minimum in order to reduce accommodation time. The reason for this lies less in the actual saving of accommodation time but more to protect the individual from reading with non-optimally accommodated eyes.

In addition, because the screen and the keyboard cannot be located on the same visual plane, i.e. at desk level, there follows a change of focal point between these elements in the vertical plane. These changes in focal point stress the eyes and neck muscles more than would corresponding changes in the horizontal plane and should, therefore, be kept to a minimum.

WORKING ENVIRONMENT

Of the classical features of the working environment - lighting, temperature and noise - lighting is undoubtedly of the greatest importance as regards VDT workplaces. Nevertheless, temperature and air conditioning have also to be carefully considered since VDTs produce appreciable quantities of heat which should be compensated for by adequate air conditioning.

Noise problems at VDT workplaces usually stem from other items of equipment in the room and not from the VDTs themselves. However, in some VDTs, the noise which is emitted from the cooling fan and even the power supply can be irritating or distracting, especially for younger operators with a greater sensitivity to high frequency noise.

Lighting

Presuming normal vision, the quality of the lighting and the difficulty of the visual task together determine the ease with which a visual object can be recognised. Since the importance of viewing angle, luminance and screen contrasts, and the characteristics of the keyboard and source documents have been dealt with more fully in other sections, the following notes are intended only to serve as a guide to achieving optimum lighting conditions at VDT workplaces.

Illumination level

The illumination required for a particular task is determined by the complexity and visual difficulty of the task, the average standard of eyesight of those concerned, and the level of visual performance expected, i.e. the speed and accuracy of recognition.

Typical relationships between visual performance and illuminance for tasks of different size and contrast are illustrated in Figure 4.24. The size or contrast, or both, of some tasks may be great enough to ensure the required level of visual performance at a comparatively low illuminance, e.g. 50 Lux. The appearance of many working interiors, however, is gloomy at illuminances less than about 200 Lux For this reason, the minimum illuminance that is recommended for normal working spaces is 200 Lux, irrespective of the visual ease of the task.

In prescribing the levels of artificial illumination for VDT workplaces, various suggestions have been made, ranging from 100 Lux to 1000 Lux. The first value stems from a recommendation which is based on the argument that reflections on the screen can be avoided by maintaining the illumination level at such a low value. The IES Lux table, on the other hand, recommends a level of 1000 Lux for large offices.

In practice, however, neither of these two extreme values are suitable for VDT workplaces. Maintaining a uniform level of artificial illumination as low as 100 Lux would require at least a partial darkening of the room and the shielding of natural light sources, e.g. windows, to safeguard against the VDT operators from becoming dazzled by the greater luminance of the exterior. Darkening or partial darkening of the room can only be recommended if the work being carried out requires such an environment. This is most certainly not the case as far as the use of VDTs in offices is concerned.

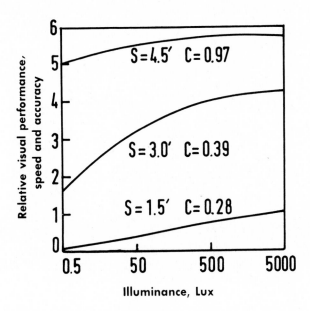

Figure 4.24 Relationship between visual performance and illuminance for different values of apparent size(S) and contrast(C). Ref. I.3

In any case, screen reflections cannot be satisfactorily eliminated by reducing the level of illumination; they can be controlled much more easily and effectively by appropriately positioning the VDT or by means of a suitable screen surface treatment.

All suggestions which aim to establish a lower limit on room illumination tend to overlook the fact that a major part of the information which is required when working with VDTs is contained in documents of one type or another. These too, and not only the display screen, must be capable of being read clearly and easily. It has been found that VDT operators, in general, judge the readability of their source documents to be more critical than the readability of the display screen.

From a physiological point of view, the readability of a document with 500 Lux illumination does not differ greatly from its readability with 100 Lux illumination. Although at least one investigation showed that reading performance was improved after having increased the level of illumination to 2000 Lux in an office environment, the same effect has not been demonstrated in connection with working with VDTs. On the contrary, it has been found that the reduction in critical fusion frequency as an indication of fatigue between morning and evening in a room with 1000 Lux illumination was greater than with 500 Lux. This was so because attempting to reduce the glare in the room had resulted in a less favourable luminance ratio between the documents and the display screen.

A quite detailed investigation was carried out in order to evaluate the subjective reaction of a group of VDT operators to the level of illumination as regards visual effort and agreeableness of the lighting. This investigation took place on the premises of a company in which VDTs of the same kind were installed in three offices in which the same type of work was carried out on a two-shift basis. The results showed that the VDT operators in two identical rooms, each with 500 Lux, judged both the degree of visual effort and agreeableness of the lighting to be similar. In the third room, with 1000 Lux, the operators rated the visual effort to be significantly higher. In each of the three rooms, the agreeableness of the lighting was judged to be better in the evenings than during the day.

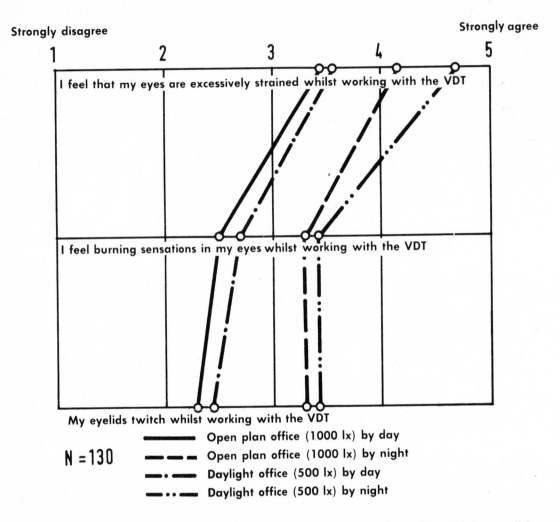

Figure 4.25 Subjective evaluation of visual discomfort under various office lighting conditions using the same types of VDT for the same tasks.

Field studies have also repeatedly shown that VDT operators, where it is possible for them to do so, turn down the lighting to levels corresponding to the range 300 to 500 Lux. The only relevant argument in favour of 1000 Lux is the ability to better match the illuminance indoors with that outdoors. But this is only justified on the basis of qualitative reasoning and not by quantitative measurement. In practice, the provision of partitions and similar fitments means that most people working in large offices are seldom able to look from the inside to the outside of the room. In any event, the illuminance of a VDT workroom can never be entirely matched with that of the outside world. For this reason it is recommended that:

> VDT working areas should be illuminated with 300 to 500 Lux illuminance with the best possible glare shielding to safeguard against both direct and reflection glare.

Luminance ratio relationships

Whenever we change our line of sight to view different objects, transient adaptive changes in visual sensitivity occur unless the luminance of every visible point in the environment is equal to the luminance of the central field of vision, i.e. the field that is occupied by the object that we are looking at. Generally speaking, the duration of these transient effects is quite brief, but their magnitude, and hence the visual effort involved, depends very much on the spatial distribution of luminances to which the eyes must adapt and re-adapt. In order to safeguard against the problems of visual fatigue that may occur as the result of these re-adaptation stresses it is usually recommended that the luminance ratio in the central field of vision should not exceed 1:3 and that the luminance ratio in the peripheral field of vision should not exceed 1:10.

It has been found that the luminance ratio between paper and the display screen at many VDT workplaces is usually about 1:6 with normal CRT displays and without screen filters. By using micromesh filters or polarisation discs, however, the luminance ratio is made very much worse - up to 100:1 and more - so that in spite of good character formation on the display screen, visual discomfort cannot be totally avoided.

> The luminance ratios in the field of vision comprising the keyboard and screen, the desk and the room should, if possible, not exceed 1:3:10.

These observations can also be related to the optical characteristics of the keyboard which, being one of the most important visual objects at the VDT workplace, should have a reflectance which, as far as possible, matches that of the display screen and paper. For this and other reasons, black is not a suitable colour for the keys.

The keyboard should be designed in such a way that the luminance ratios between the keyboard and screen, and between the keyboard and paper do not exceed 1:3. A ratio of 1:1 would be the theoretical ideal but this cannot be achieved in practice and neither is such a condition desirable in practice since an environment of uniform brightness is psychologically very unattractive.

Glare and reflection level

Glare is a gross disturbance of the adaptation process of the eyes caused by large differences in luminance, both spatially and in time.

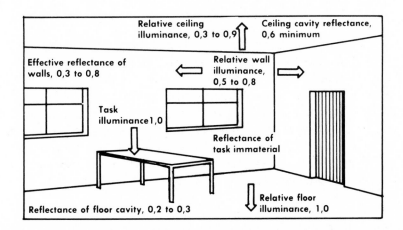

Figure 4.26 Recommended ranges of reflectance and relative illuminance for room surfaces. Ref. I.3

Direct glare can be satisfactorily avoided by the appropriate positioning of the luminaires. This is considered in more detail in a later section. But in addition to direct glare, neither should the problems of *indirect glare* be underestimated. This type of glare is caused by specular reflections from glossy surfaces and from too high luminance differences.

It is recommended that the reflectance of the surface of the work desk should be of the order of magnitude 0,4 to 0,6 and preferably towards the lower value. This helps to ensure a favourable similarity between the luminance of the desk top and that of the display screen. Within this range, the colour of the desk surface can be chosen freely although the surface should have a matt finish.

A bright floor covering with a reflectance of about 0,3 is also of some advantage since this helps to increase the diffuse components of the illumination.

Lighting installation

The principles which govern the choice of lighting system, i.e. quantity and distribution of luminaires, colour temperature, etc., for VDT working areas are precisely the same as for conventional office environments. The main requirement is that the quality of illumination is compatible with the requirements of a permanent supplementary artificial lighting installation or *PSALI*.

Colour temperature

Generally speaking, subjective preference is usually given to warmer light colours rather than to cooler colours. However, fluorescent lamps with the colour 'neutral white' are those which are most compatible with daylight and may be generally recommended.

Lighting installations with light sources of differing colour temperature can produce an irritating 'twilight' effect which should be avoided. For this reason, all lamps should have the same colour temperature.

Glare shielding

Investigations have repeatedly demonstrated that there is a strong correlation between the type of lighting equipment that is used at the VDT working area and complaints of visual discomfort. Together with illumination level and the colour temperature of the lights, glare shielding is an extremely important consideration in the illumination of VDT rooms. Increased perception of glare leads to greater psychological stress and thence to more rapid feelings of fatigue. Burning sensations in the eyes and the tendency to screw up the eyes are not only related to the type of lighting that is used, but also to the visual exactitude of the task.

Glare shielding of the lamps can be achieved by installing appropriate covers or *glare shields*. In order to find the optimal type of glare shielding for VDT workplaces, a field investigation was carried out to determine subjective reactions to direct and reflection glare and to investigate the psychological stress in relation to the type of glare shielding. On the basis of these investigations, it was possible to rank the order of subjective preference for the three most common types of glare shield pattern as follows:

1. prismatic pattern shielding
2. grid or louvre pattern shielding
3. smoked glass shielding

Qualitatively, then, the prismatic pattern and grid types of glare shielding are more generally preferred because of their ability to create a more favourable light distribution. The lights which are used to illuminate VDT working areas should, therefore, be shielded using either the prismatic or grid pattern types of glare shield. But when grid type shields are used, it should be borne in mind that the luminance directly beneath the lamps is not significantly reduced by the shield. In working positions such as these, an attempt must be made to reduce the risk of reflections from other objects e.g. the desk, keyboard etc. Alternatively, a combination of a coarse grid pattern with an additional smoked glass shield may be used to simultaneously reduce the glare and the luminance in positions directly below the luminaire. In spite of their disadvantages, however, a grid pattern type of shield should be preferred to a smoked glass shield.

Unshielded fluorescent lamps i.e. those in which the tubes are visible with a viewing angle of $45°$ or less are in all cases to be avoided.

The placing of the luminaires in the room

In order to minimise the perception of glare, the luminaires should be installed in a direction which is parallel to both the viewing direction of the VDT operators and to the windows. From a physiological point of view, these two requirements are quite correct, but implementing them may, in practice, result in too uniform a structure in the layout of the workroom. So, provided that the arrangement of the luminaires is such as to minimise the risk of glare, these recommendations need not be rigidly adhered to. This would apply, for example, to lighting installations in which the lamps cannot be seen directly when viewed from the side, e.g. when the lamps are recessed into the ceiling, with deep grid type installations etc.

The question as to whether or not the luminaires should be recessed into the ceiling depends, among other things, on the likelihood of problems caused by glare. When the lamps are recessed into the ceiling, the luminance of the ceiling is less than when the luminaires protrude or are suspended below ceiling level thus permitting illumination of the ceiling itself.

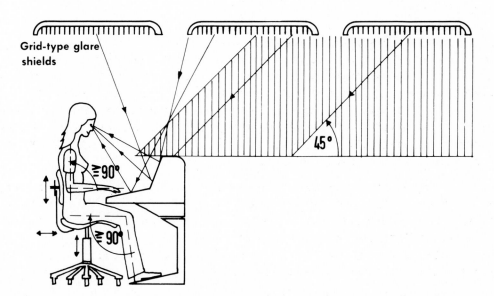

Figure 4.27 Direct and reflected glare at a VDT work station. A standard office lighting system with grid type glare shields to prevent direct illumination (non-hatched area). The operator is will nevertheless be subjected to some degree of reflected glare from the screen, the keyboard and the desk.

Architecturally extravagant solutions in the form of continuous lines of fluorescent lamps or lamps installed along the lower surfaces of a cassette-type ceiling structure can too easily lead to the type of 'screen contents' shown below. Installations of this kind should, therefore, be avoided.

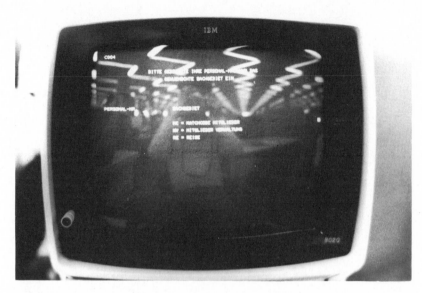

Figure 4.28 A continuous line of luminaires reflected in a VDT screen and obliterating the image.

If the luminance of the luminaires is of the order 500 cd/m^2 or more, the luminance of the ceiling should fall ideally in the range 150 to 200 cd/m^2. In fact, it has been found that ceiling luminances can be as low as 15 to 35 cd/m^2. For this reason, direct glare cannot be completely eliminated, but neither can ceiling luminances of the order 150 to 200 cd/m^2 be realised without directly illuminating the ceiling.

Lighting circuit arrangements

In order to avoid stroboscopic effects between the display screen and the fluorescent lamps and between the lamps themselves, the use of a 'duo-circuit arrangement' is recommended, particularly in smaller work rooms. In this type of circuit, a phase difference is introduced in the voltage supply to each lamp so that the maxima and minima of the light flux from the lamps no longer coincide. In larger work rooms it is sensible to couple neighbouring lamps with different phases of the three-phase mains supply. This has the effect of trebling the effective flicker frequency and a much lower fluctuation in lighting level is achieved.

In order to avoid flickering of the lamps towards the end of their life, DEOS or similar types of starters should be used since these prevent the illumination of defective tubes.

Windows and curtains

We are not concerned here with the necessity or otherwise of providing windows in work room but more with the requirements concerning their furnishing with cur blinds etc.

Curtains provide a necessary, but often insufficient degree of protection aga

SUMMARY OF RECOMMENDATIONS

Desks, Footrests

		YES	NO
1.	Are a sufficient number of work surfaces provided?	▶ ☐	☐
2.	Are the working surfaces of sufficient size?	▶ ☐	☐
3.	Are all items of equipment and job aids which must often be manually manipulated within the normal arm reach of the operator, i.e. within reach without requiring movement of the body?	▶ ☐	☐
4.	Is the desk height between 720 and 750 mm?	▶ ☐	☐
5.	Is the height of the keyboard above floor level between 720 and 750 mm?	▶ ☐	☐
6.	Is the surface of the desk matt finished?	▶ ☐	☐
7.	Is the reflectance of the desk surface:		
	▶ 0,4? (optimum)	▶ ☐	☐
	▶ 0,5? (acceptable)	☐	☐
	▶ 0,6? (maximum)	☐	☐
8.	Is the height of the leg area sufficient?	▶ ☐	☐
9.	Is the underside of the desk free of obstructions?	▶ ☐	☐
10.	Is the leg area at least 800 mm wide to permit unobstructed turning?	▶ ☐	☐
11.	Is the leg area at least 700 mm deep?	▶ ☐	☐
12.	Is the leg area shielded against heat from the VDT and other items of equipment?	▶ ☐	☐
13.	Is adequate space provided for storage of copies, handbooks, documents, personal belongings etc.?	▶ ☐	☐
14.	Is the leg area free from obstructions such as desk frame spars?	▶ ☐	☐
15.	Is it possible for the operator to easily re-arrange the workplace, e.g. by changing the positions of the VDT and other items of equipment?	▶ ☐	☐
16.	Is a footrest provided which covers the entire leg area?	☐	☐
17.	If footrests are used are they adjustable		
	▶ in height?	▶ ☐	☐
	▶ in inclination?	▶ ☐	☐
18.	Can the footrest be quickly and easily adjusted to cater for the different body sizes of the operators?	▶ ☐	☐

19. Is the surface of the footrest such as to enable comfortable movement of the feet without slipping? ▶☐ ☐

Chair

1. Does the design of the chair satisfy the requirements of the national standards? ▶☐ ☐

2. Is the chair stable i.e. safe from tipping over? (fivepoint base) ▶☐ ☐

3. If the chair is provided with castors are they self-locking? ▶☐ ☐

4. Is the seating height easily adjustable? ▶☐ ☐

5. Is the seat angle adjustable? ▶☐ ☐

6. Is the front edge of the seat rounded to avoid cutting into the thighs? ▶☐ ☐

7. Is the seat surface padded? ▶☐ ☐

8. Is the height of the backrest adjustable? ▶☐ ☐

9. Can the backrest be adjusted forwards and backwards? ▶☐ ☐

10. Can adjustments be made easily and safely from the seated position? ▶☐ ☐

11. Are the adjustment mechanisms safe against self- or unintentional release? ▶☐ ☐

12. Is there guidance available to the individual operators to help them achieve an optimum adjustment of their chair? ▶☐ ☐

Job Aids, Other Items of Equipment

Documents

YES NO

1. Do the documents that are necessary to the task satisfy the requirements of section I as far as
   - ▶ character formation? ▶☐ ☐
   - ▶ contrast between characters ▶☐ ☐
   - ▶ and background? ▶☐ ☐

		YES	NO

2. Are all paper surfaces matt? ▶☐ ☐

3. Can all of the information which is relevant to the task be easily read? ▶☐ ☐

4. Where appropriate, does the format used on documents such as order, billing forms etc., correspond to the display screen format? ▶☐ ☐

Siting of the VDT, job aids and other items of equipment

YES   NO

1. Are all job aids and items of equipment so positioned that - apart from short-term considerations - the operator may assume an optimum working posture according to the following criteria:
    - ▶ head inclined forward at an angle of ca 20°   ▶☐ ☐
    - ▶ spine slightly arched and forward leaning when seen from the side   ▶☐ ☐
    - ▶ upper arms vertical   ▶☐ ☐
    - ▶ no twisting of the head and trunk   ▶☐ ☐
    - ▶ thighs approximately horizontal   ▶☐ ☐
    - ▶ lower part of the leg approximately vertical   ▶☐ ☐
    - ▶ sufficient leg room both in height and depth   ▶☐ ☐
    - ▶ frequent changes of visual object accommodated within an angle of 15-30° relative to the normal viewing direction   ▶☐ ☐

2. Are all job aids and items of equipment in the visual and working field situated according to frequency of use?
    - ▶ their frequency of use?   ☐ ☐
    - ▶ their relation to the way the task is performed?   ☐ ☐
    - ▶ their importance?   ☐ ☐

ENVIRONMENTAL CONSIDERATIONS

Lighting

YES   NO

1. Is the illuminance between 300 and 500 lux? ▶☐ ☐

2. Is the operator's field of vision free of direct reflections from the display screen, keyboard, desk, papers etc? ▶☐ ☐

		YES	NO

3. Are there glare sources in the operators field of vision, lights, windows etc? ▶ ☐ ☐

4. Are the luminaires equipped with prismatic or grid-type glare shields? ▶ ☐ ☐

5. Is the lighting system equipped with duo- or three-phase switching? ▶ ☐ ☐

6. Are the VDT workplaces positioned such that the operators line of vision is
   - ▶ parallel to luminaires? ▶ ☐ ☐
   - ▶ parallel to windows? ▶ ☐ ☐

7. Are the windows fitted with external blinds? ☐ ☐

8. Are the windows fitted with internal blinds? ☐ ☐

9. Are the windows fitted with curtains with a reflectance in the range 0,5 to 0,7? ▶ ☐ ☐

10. Is the average reflectance of the ceiling greater than 0,7? ▶ ☐ ☐

11. Is the reflectance of the walls between 0,5 and 0,7? ▶ ☐ ☐

12. Is the reflectance of the floor about 0,3? ▶ ☐ ☐

13. Are the lamps fitted with starters to prevent flashing at the end of their useful life? ▶ ☐ ☐

14. Has the regular cleaning and maintenance of the luminaires been properly considered? ▶ ☐ ☐

Room Climate

		YES	NO

1. Is the work room air conditioned? ▶ ☐ ☐

2. Can the room temperature be maintained between 21 and 23°C? ▶ ☐ ☐

3. Can the relative humidity be maintained between 45 and 55%? ▶ ☐ ☐

4. Is the speed of air movement less than 0,1m/s
   - ▶ at neck height? ▶ ☐ ☐
   - ▶ at waist height? ▶ ☐ ☐
   - ▶ at ankle height? ▶ ☐ ☐

5. Are the individual operators and their neighbours protected against thermal loading from the equipment by

    ▶ thermal radiation?   ▶ ☐   ☐

    ▶ warm air flow?   ▶ ☐   ☐

6. Have steps been taken to avoid local hot spots, e.g. under desks, in corners etc?   ▶ ☐   ☐

Noise

YES   NO

1. Is the noise level:

    ▶ less than 55 dB(A) in task areas requiring a high level of concentration?   ▶ ☐   ☐

    ▶ less than 65 dB(A) in routine task areas?   ▶ ☐   ☐

2. Are the equipment noise levels no more than 5 dB(A) greater than the background noise level?

    ▶ VDT, e.g. fans, power supply but not the auditory feedback and signals from the keyboard?   ▶ ☐   ☐

    ▶ other items of equipment?   ▶ ☐   ☐

3. Is the noise environment free from high frequency tones?   ▶ ☐   ☐

4. Is the noise in the VDT room affected by external noise sources, e.g. neighbouring rooms, the outside world?   ☐   ☐

5. Are there other items of equipment in the workroom, e.g. printers, teletypes, which generate high or distracting levels of noise?   ☐   ☐

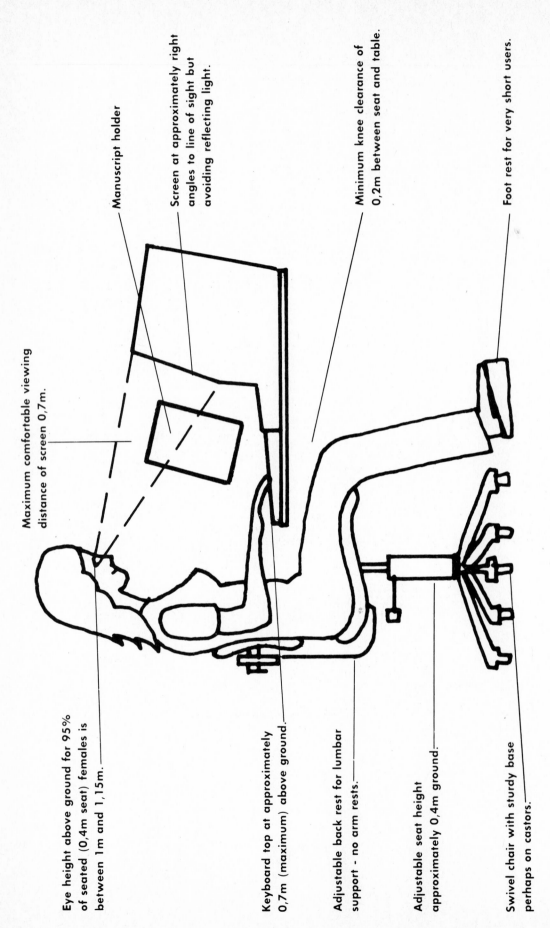

Maximum comfortable viewing distance of screen 0,7m.

Manuscript holder

Screen at approximately right angles to line of sight but avoiding reflecting light.

Minimum knee clearance of 0,2m between seat and table.

Foot rest for very short users.

Eye height above ground for 95% of seated (0,4m seat) females is between 1m and 1,15m.

Keyboard top at approximately 0,7m (maximum) above ground.

Adjustable back rest for lumbar support - no arm rests.

Adjustable seat height approximately 0,4m ground.

Swivel chair with sturdy base perhaps on castors.

Fig. 4.29 Typical dimensions for a VDT workstation.

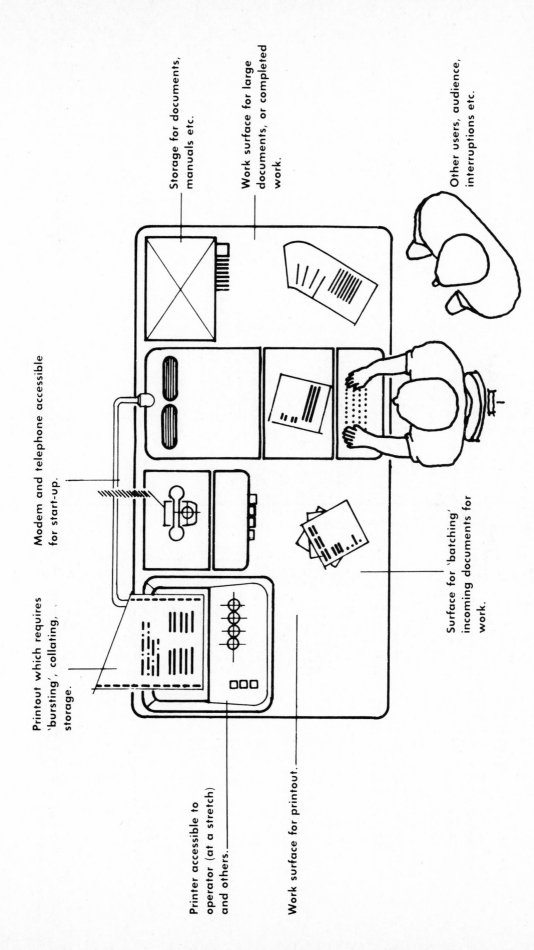

Storage for documents, manuals etc.

Work surface for large documents, or completed work.

Other users, audience, interruptions etc.

Modem and telephone accessible for start-up.

Printout which requires 'bursting', collating, storage.

Printer accessible to operator (at a stretch) and others.

Work surface for printout.

Surface for 'batching' incoming documents for work.

Fig. 4.30 VDT-printer workstation with work surfaces and storage facilities.

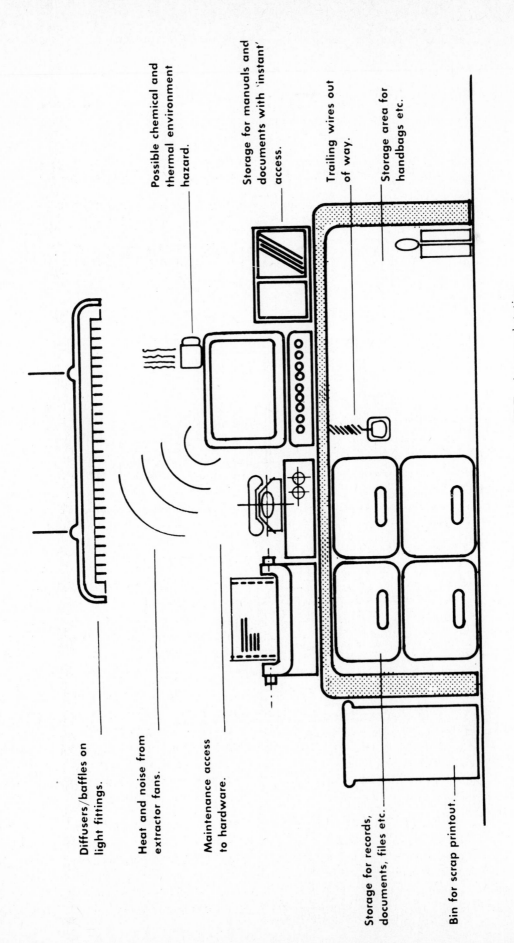

Diffusers/baffles on
light fittings.

Heat and noise from
extractor fans.

Maintenance access
to hardware.

Possible chemical and
thermal environment
hazard.

Storage for manuals and
documents with 'instant'
access.

Trailing wires out
of way.

Storage area for
handbags etc.

Storage for records,
documents, files etc.

Bin for scrap printout.

Fig. 4.31 Other points to note in a VDT-printer-workstation.

Chapter 5

THE HEALTH, SAFETY AND ORGANISATIONAL ASPECTS OF WORKING WITH VDTs

Foreword

The VDT is a relative newcomer to the office environment. Compared with more conventional types of office equipment, working with a VDT introduces a number of additional visual demands and with them, certain requirements as regards the design, implementation and use of VDTs. In the foregoing sections, these requirements have been looked at in some detail. It has been shown that, whilst there is nothing intrinsically harmful about working with a VDT, where these requirements are not correctly satisfied, working with a VDT can result in fatigue. The problems of fatigue among VDT operators are not inevitable, however, and in many cases, neither are they unique to occupation with VDTs.

This fatigue can arise from postural problems due to inadequate workplace design or from many other factors including, of course, the visual aspects of the task and the visual disabilities of those concerned. Fatigue may be experienced as various symptoms of discomfort or strain in the eyes, neck, back and other parts of the body. However, visual fatigue is not necessarily an indication that the source of the problem is actually visual. The eyes may even act as an 'early warning system' for the rest of the body.

This chapter deals with the types of postural and visual discomfort that can occur when working with a VDT. The possibility of irreversible, long-term effects on vision is also considered although this question is confounded by the fact that a high proportion of the working population, typically 20% to 30%, have uncorrected or inadequately corrected visual defects. The development of an appropriate set of eye tests for VDT operators has, therefore, been emphasised by many user organisations and occupational health authorities. This, too, has been one of the focal issues in this investigation and is considered in this chapter and later, but in more detail, in Appendix II.

Fatigue among VDT operators also depends to a large extent on the nature and organisation of the task. Complaints of physiological discomfort among VDT operators often cannot be entirely dissociated from the psychological reactions of the individual to his role, and the professional and organisational aspects of the task in relation to the introduction of a computer system. Among some professional categories this has highlighted some important features of the relationship between man and task. These too are considered in this chapter.

POSTURAL DISCOMFORT

The problems of working posture, i.e. the positions and movements of the body whilst performing a given task, depend on the nature of the task in question, the physiological structure and function of the body, and also on the psychological attitude and loading of the individual at work. It is essential, therefore, that when complaints of postural discomfort occur, the working situation should be investigated in its entirety in order to trace the most likely causes of the problem. In many cases, the problems will be found to lie in the poor design of the work place or working environment in which case they can usually be put right without too much difficulty. In others, complaints of discomfort might be the result of a more basic dissatisfaction at work, finding the solution to which might require a reappraisal of the organisation of the task in question.

The human body is designed for movement. Static loads induced by keeping the body, or parts of it, in a fixed position, are very much more tiring than the loads induced by movement. This is easily appreciated by considering the differences between standing and walking. Standing still, even for just a few minutes, can be very tiring, but a healthy person can walk for a much longer period of time without experiencing similar feelings of fatigue. At work, therefore, the most important work place design requirements follow as a direct result of the skeletal and muscular structure of the body and its affinity for movement and the need to minimise static strain. Based on the same reasoning, a workplace which requires the individual to maintain a single so-called 'optimum' posture, cannot in fact, be regarded as an 'optimum' workplace.

Working procedure

The criteria which have been considered in earlier sections concerning the optimal configuration of a workplace are a necessary but not, in themselves, a sufficient set of conditions to ensure freedom from postural discomfort at work. If the task is such as to require or permit only a minimum of body movements, the 'optimal' arrangement of the workplace may be of relatively little help.

Under some circumstances, however, the body movements associated with a particular task may themselves be a source of loading. This is particularly true if the nature and organisation of the task require the frequently-repeated movement of certain parts of the body during relatively long and uninterrupted periods of time. Since every workplace represents a compromise between a great many factors, not all of which can be optimised or assigned their most favourable value, the effects of postural and other forms of loading at work can often be reduced only by suitably organising the nature of the task in question.

Posture and individual behaviour

In practice, the success of any attempt to encourage a favourable working posture when working with VDTs depends very much on the attitudes of those concerned. It would be wrong to presume that the behaviour of the individual can be suitably altered simply by making available an appropriate series of recommendations as to what *should* be done. Experience alone tells us human behaviour is very difficult to change; old habits, particularly the bad ones, die hard! In reality, human nature is such that even when potential risks are well-known, individual behaviour can usually be changed to only a small extent and then very slowly. Good examples of this are the reluctance of many cigarette smokers to stop smoking in spite of the known health risks involved, and the frequent failure of many people working in noisy environments to use ear defenders.

The reason for this type of behaviour usually rests in the fact that we tend to behave in a way that maximises short term pleasure or comfort, pushing the thought of longer term consequences to the back of our minds even though we are conscious of them.

What then are the most important behavioural characteristics at work using VDTs, and what does the operator of a VDT himself try to optimise and why?

The most important aspects of most VDT task activities are:

- the visual process, i.e. looking at source documents, the display screen, keyboard etc.,
- operating the keyboard and
- working with a source document of some kind.

In general, the individual at work tends to assume a posture which is suited to the short term optimisation of the way the work is performed with little or no thought to the possibility of longer term effects such as fatigue. This is by no means a casual tendency but is due to the fact that we very quickly become aware of the short term difficulties in performing a task and it is these that we first seek to overcome. In working with a VDT, for example, one is immediately aware of whether or not it is possible to read the visual display easily. If the position of the keyboard is incorrect in relation to the position of the body, e.g. too high, too low or too far away, this is soon felt by feelings of tiredness in the arms or by the difficulty of working with the keyboard. If it is difficult or uncomfortable to refer to and manipulate, e.g. turn the pages of or make entries on a document, this too is very quickly appreciated. So, even if the individual appreciates the fact that a poor working posture may quickly lead to feelings of fatigue, he or she will usually chose to adopt such a posture if it is felt that by doing so, the job is made easier.

The use of source documents when working with a VDT illustrates this type of behaviour very well. If the task requires frequent reference to a document, e.g. in transcribing the information on a document into the computer system via the keyboard, the user may be reluctant to use a manuscript holder which is designed to permit reading in an optimum position. This is especially true if it is also necessary to make frequent written entries or notes on the document. In task situations such as these, the source document will more usually be placed at an optimal distance in relation to the arm reach of the operator and in a position which permits writing in a comfortable position. In other words, the document will usually be placed flat on the desk and either to the right or left of the keyboard in which position it is usually necessary to bend or twist the back and neck whilst reading or otherwise working with the document.

In a case such as this, it might be possible to improve the situation by dividing the working process into two successive stages, e.g. working with and making entries on the documents as the first stage before entering the data into the terminal as the second stage, with the workplace designed accordingly. By structuring the work in this way, the task is sub-divided into two activities which are carried out sequentially rather than in parallel, the emphasis being on relatively short periods engaged in each activity so as to permit frequent changes of posture. Apart from the organisational difficulties that may be involved, from an ergonomic point of view it would be to no advantage to sub-divide the work into long periods in each activity because feelings of fatigue might occur more rapidly as the result of the prolonged static posture in each activity.

The long term consequences of poor posture, especially the possibility of irreversible postural damage, are very seldom considered by the individual at work. This can readily be seen in all workplaces where the various stages or requirements of the task impose conflicting demands as regards posture. If it is not possible to satisfy all of the requirements associated with a particular type of work, it might also be possible to tackle the problem by providing for alternative tasks to provide a break from the primary task or by providing periodic rest pauses.

It should be noted, however, that these comments do not only apply to working with VDTs. They are equally true of all types of job and human activity at work.

Matching posture with the visual task

Figure 5.1 illustrates what, in the view of many ergonomists, is a favourable sitting posture whilst working with a VDT. But holding such a posture for a long period would eventually lead to such a high level of static muscular loading that a VDT operator would seldom be able to maintain such a posture for very long. Instead, he or she would usually adopt a posture which was found to be the most economical in the short term. Economic in this sense means that the actual posture is such as to minimise the loading in the back muscles, on the one hand, but which optimises the ability to perform the visual task in question on the other. An extreme example of this type of posture is illustrated in Figure 5.2, but it should be noted that this particular example has been selected to demonstrate as clearly as possible how the layout of the workplace *can* adversely affect working posture.

A posture such as this may well be economic in the short term, but the longer the time such a posture is maintained, the greater is the likelihood of more permanent strain the back muscles. This type of *muscle overloading syndrome* not only affects those parts of the body which are directly affected but can also lead to problems in other parts of the body. It is by no means unusual that the causes of some industrial ailments, for example spinal disc ailments, are wrongly diagnosed for this reason.

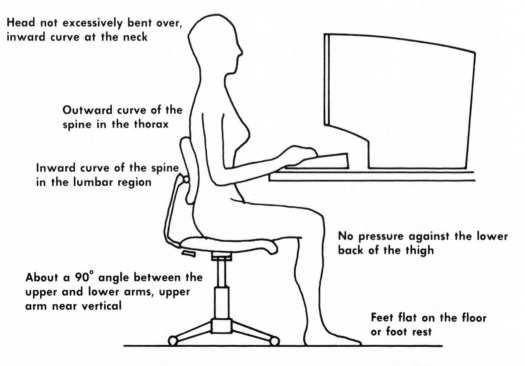

Figure 5.1 The main characteristics of a favourable sitting posture when working with a VDT. Although this posture may be considered correct in the ergonomic sense, it should be borne in mind that the human body is better adapted to movement than the maintaining of static positions. Any static posture, even the 'ideal', soon becomes fatiguing if is has to be maintained for too long a period.

One of the most important points to note in the posture shown in Figure 5.2 is the hanging position of the head. The head is supported with the least muscular effort only when the cervical vertebrae are erect. But with the head bent forward as in this example, the position of the head is supported by the muscles of the neck and shoulders.

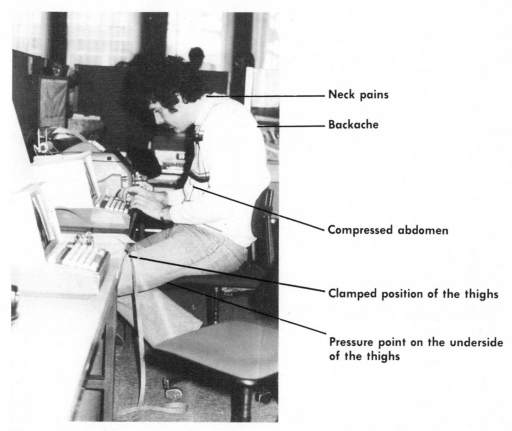

Neck pains

Backache

Compressed abdomen

Clamped position of the thighs

Pressure point on the underside of the thighs

Figure 5.2 A poorly designed workplace can easily result in a posture such as that shown in this example. It is essential that the design of the workplace and office furniture is tailored to the task needs and physical characteristics of the individual operator. Good workplace design is not a luxury; it is a necessary safeguard against discomfort and ill-health, and is conducive to increased job satisfaction and performance!

As mentioned earlier, most VDT operators position their source documents, not where there can be most easily read but more usually where they can be most easily manipulated. As a rule, this is somewhere on the left of the keyboard with the result that the entire upper part of the body must be twisted in order to read and work with the document.

Figure 5.3 summarises the main types of loading on different parts of the spinal column due to the following types of movement:

- bending the head and upper part of the body to view the screen, keyboard and source documents,
- sideways movement and twisting in looking from the screen or keyboard towards the document, and
- bending and stretching when alternately viewing the screen and keyboard.

In an investigation of the incidence of postural discomfort among office staff, it was found that 57% of a sample comprising 261 male and 117 female employees complained of problems in various parts of the back. 24% of the sample complained of problems in the neck and shoulders.[1]

Type of loading	Cervix	Thorax	Lumbar
Bending, stretching	+++	+	+++
Leaning sideways	++	+	++
Twisting	++	+	++
Leaning sideways and twisting	+++	+	+++
Strength	+	+++	++

Figure 5.3 The static and dynamic loading in various parts of the spinal column due to the positions and movements of the body when working with a VDT. (+= weak loading, ++= medium loading, +++= heavy loading).

By way of comparison, Figure 5.4 summarises the results of an investigation of the frequency of postural complaints among VDT operators engaged in data entry and other types of clerical work involving the use of VDTs.

	Copy typists			Clerical workers		
Type of discomfort	Agree %	Strongly agree %	Σ %	Agree %	Strongly agree %	Σ %
Lumbar	8	16	24	5	5	10
Thorax	24	36	60	19	25	44
Cervix	19	51	70	17	28	45

Figure 5.4 The frequency of complaints of discomfort in the neck and in the upper and lower regions of the back among a large sample of VDT operators engaged (a) in data entry tasks and (b) in other types of clerical and administrative tasks using VDTs.

These results show that complaints of discomfort in the back and neck are by no means uncommon among VDT operators but, notwithstanding the variation in tasks included in this survey, appear to occur to about the same extent as among other categories of office staff not using VDTs.

	Neckaches			Backaches			Headaches		
Type of task	4 %	5 %	Σ %	4 %	5 %	Σ %	4 %	5 %	Σ %
Copy typists	19	51	70	23	36	59	23	22	45
Info. typists	21	19	40	16	30	46	9	14	23
Clerical workers	17	28	45	19	25	44	18	12	30
Programmers	3	19	22	25	13	38	3	3	6
Editors	21	18	39	16	13	29	8	0	8

4 = Agree   5 = Strongly agree

Figure 5.5 The frequency of neck, back and head aches among VDT operators engaged in different types of VDT task.

1. Ref. P.3

It has been found that complaints of postural discomfort and visual fatigue due to working with VDTs do not occur independently but are correlated to a very significant degree. In addition, both types of symptom are highly correlated with the incidence of headaches. It has also been found that with increasing repetitiveness in the work, the frequency of all types of complaints increases markedly.

A rather more detailed analysis of the frequency of postural complaints among various professional groups is shown in Figure 5.5, and these results clearly indicate that:

- the physiological demands on VDT operators are highly dependent on the nature of the job that they are doing,
- the same demands tend to diminish when the work is of a less repetitive nature, and
- those categories of VDT operator with the least likelihood of postural discomfort are those whose jobs are of a varied nature and who are not bound to remain at their work place, e.g. programmers, editors etc.

A point that emerges very clearly from these observations is that, when considering the susceptibility of VDT operators to postural discomfort whilst using a VDT, one cannot lump all task categories together and speak of 'VDT operators' in general. Each type of VDT activity imposes its own professional, physical and psychological constraints on the people involved. Extrapolating the results of studies which are made within specific occupational groups to other groups with very different types of activity can be very misleading. It also brings us again to the dangers in placing too much faith in recommendations which refer, in effect, to an 'average VDT operator'; it is the comfort and well-being of the real person, and not that of a hypothetical average, that should be uppermost in our minds.

Nevertheless, based on these observations, there are two guiding principles that should be adopted when considering the general characteristics of VDT workplaces:

- the design of the workplace and the organisation of the task should encourage a less static working posture, i.e. by permitting as many changes in position as possible
- the design of VDT workplaces should permit the individual adjustment of reading distance, viewing angle etc.

Equipment design and the reduction of postural loading

In the previous section, the main effects of poor working posture were considered and so too was the possibility that part of the problem, and perhaps a large part, can be relieved by paying closer attention to the organisation of the job and its task components. Another way of helping to reduce the likelihood of postural discomfort among VDT operators lies in the appropriate design of the equipment itself. In this respect, it is necessary to consider which of the problems related to posture are related to each specific characteristic of the VDT and the use of job aids such as documents.

The display screen

Given that the position and the physical and optical properties of the display screen should be optimised from the visual point of view, it is necessary to consider the effect which these parameters have on the working posture of a VDT operator.

In practice, the display screen may give rise to a number of problems if

- the display is difficult to read, e.g. if the characters are too small, the contrast too low etc.,

- the screen is improperly sited, e.g. too high, too low or too much to one side, in relation to the position of the operator, or
- if the surface of the screen is highly reflective.

Each of these characteristics tends to encourage a poor working posture.

Figure 5.6 shows two spatial distributions of character brightness. On both screens, the incident light is diffusely reflected and the luminance of the screen is 10 cd/m^2 in every viewing direction. The characters in this display emit their light in a well-defined direction, and the optimum position for the viewing eye is, in this case, at point 1. Even very close to this point, say at point 2, the apparent contrast is greatly reduced. This means that the viewer would try to move his or her head in order to locate the viewing position giving maximum contrast. By comparison, the character luminance is more broadly distributed on the second screen, Screen 2, and the viewer is presented with a more or less uniform contrast over a broad range of viewing angles with the result that the viewer's freedom of movement is increased.

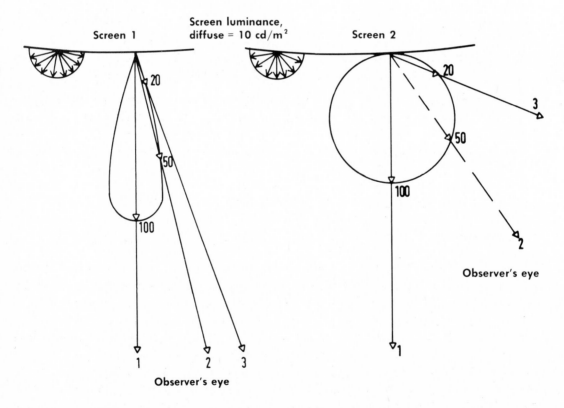

Figure 5.6 The effect of the spatial distribution of character luminance on the position of the head when reading a VDT screen. It is assumed that the diffuse background luminance of the two screens depicted in this example is 10 cd/m^2. In both cases, the perceived contrast is 1:10 when viewing the screen from point 1. When viewing the screen from point 2, the contrast is reduced to 1:5, and from point 3, to 1:2. In viewing screen 1, however, even slight changes in viewing direction about point 1 results in a marked loss of contrast. In other words, to ensure maximum contrast, the operator would find it necessary to view the screen from a particular angle and hold his or head in an essentially fixed position. When viewing screen 2, on the other hand, the operator can adopt a much wider range of viewing angles and head positions without incurring a significant reduction in contrast.

The practical importance of this type of effect is perhaps best appreciated by considering the problems experienced by those working with optical microscopes. The conditions under which a microscopist works is very close to that illustrated above as Screen 1. In order to attain the optimum viewing position, the microscopist must hold his or her head in a fixed position and always focus the eyes on the same point. This leads to a variety of back and eye problems, the cause of which, i.e. the lack of freedom of movement, is not easy to remedy.

When the characters in the display are difficult to read, the operator would be inclined to lean forward, i.e. to bend the upper part of the body towards the display screen. If the screen is positioned at a distance of, say, 500 mm, and even if, for a normally sighted person with good vision, the display is easy to read at this distance, many people with less good vision would try to reduce the viewing distance by bending forwards. But if the characters are such as to be easily readable by persons with average visual acuity at, say, 700 mm, and the screen is again positioned at a distance of 500mm, sufficient freedom of movement is provided for. In this case, the operator would not find it necessary to move his head as close as possible to the screen.

The possible effects of an incorrectly positioned display screen really require little explanation. Even so, it should be pointed out that the exact meaning of 'incorrectly positioned' in this sense varies from one type of work to another. If the task is such that text or data entry via the keyboard is secondary to reading text on the display screen, e.g. proof reading and correction, the optimum position of the display screen is that at which the text on the screen can be read as clearly as possible. But if, on the other hand, the task mainly involves text entry via the keyboard and only casual checking of the text in the display, it may be better to position the display screen at a somewhat smaller distance, and one which better corresponds to the viewing distance to the keyboard.

When the screen exhibits specular reflections, the operator would normally try to move his head into such a position that the reflections are no longer visible. This can, among other things, result in an inclined and awkward position of the neck. These types of problem can most easily and effectively be remedied by providing for moveability of the display screen about its vertical axis. This is one of the main reasons why it is generally considered to be less favourable to use display screens which are either in a fixed position at the work place or which are directly joined to the keyboard.

The keyboard

In contrast to handwriting, a VDT or typewriter keyboard is usually operated with the hands and arms in an unsupported position. Most of the common occupationally-induced ailments among skilled typing staff tend, therefore, to occur in the shoulder/arm region and in the tendons and tendon sheaths. Tenosinovitis, for example, was a common and well-known ailment among typists in the days of mechanical typewriters which required considerable force to operate the keys. By comparison, modern electric keyboards are less high and require much less key pressure, typically only about 5% of the pressure required to operate a mechanical keyboard. It might be suspected, therefore, that the incidence of tenosinovitis today would be less frequent, and this is indeed the case.

In spite of the advantages of electric keyboards in comparison to their mechanical predecessors, however, symptoms of fatigue in the shoulders and arms are still not uncommon among keyboard operators. The results from an investigation among a large number of typists, for example, revealed that 20% complained of tenosinovitis. More detailed examination showed, however, that not one did in fact suffer this ailment. Several authorities have attributed this to the fact that the general symptoms of tenosinovitis can also be caused as the result of a poor posture when operating the keyboard rather than by any form of mechanical over-exertion. In this sense, therefore, complaints such as these represent a syndrome, the *shoulder-arm syndrome*.

This syndrome can occur quite frequently when working with VDTs and even persons who operate the keyboard relatively infrequently have been found to experience this type of problem. At this point, the results from a recent survey among a large number of VDT operators are quite illustrative. In response to the question:

"Since I have been working at this workplace, I have suffered from tenosinovitis"

the following answers were given:

Task	Average work Time at the VDT	'Yes' %
Data input	7,5 h	17-22
Clerical tasks	4 h	10
Programmers, editors	3,5 h	0
Tasks involving work with two VDTs, constant visual alternation [1]	5 h	20

1. This is based on the results of a survey carried out in three organisations in which a high proportion of the VDT operators were required to work with two visual display units.

Figure 5.7 The frequency of complaints of tenosinovitis among VDT operators engaged in different types of VDT task. Complaints of this kind are symptomatic of a fatigue syndrome in the arms and shoulders caused by static loads in the arms which, during keyboarding, are held in an angled and unsupported position.

These figures show very clearly that with repetitive and concentrated types of VDT task such as data entry, about 20% of the employees surveyed were affected by this syndrome. Even among clerical staff, about 10% complained of having suffered tenosinovitis.

Symptoms such as these are, nevertheless, not a necessary result of introducing VDT equipment; they can be very effectively combatted by paying heed to the configuration of the working place and to the organisation of the working procedure. These symptoms are caused by a static loading of the arms which, during keyboarding, are held in an angled and unsupported position. It is essential, therefore, that this type of posture is avoided as far as possible. In other words, the distance between the thighs and the palms of the hands, i.e. the working level, must be as small as possible.

In the past, when the problem of reducing the thickness of keyboards had yet to be resolved, keeping the working level to a minimum was partly achieved by reducing the desk height. Nowadays, however, there is no reason why the desk height should be reduced for VDT operators. It can be successfully argued, in fact, that it is the thickness of the keyboard, and not the height of the desk that must be reduced. And since some modern keyboards are no more than 30mm thick, in comparison to the 80 to 100 mm thick keyboards of only a few years ago, it is clear that the technical problems involved in reducing keyboard thickness can indeed be resolved.

The reduction in stress in the arm muscles is not the only argument in favour of reducing keyboard height; there is an additional point, and one which concerns overall posture. This is illustrated in Figure 5.9.

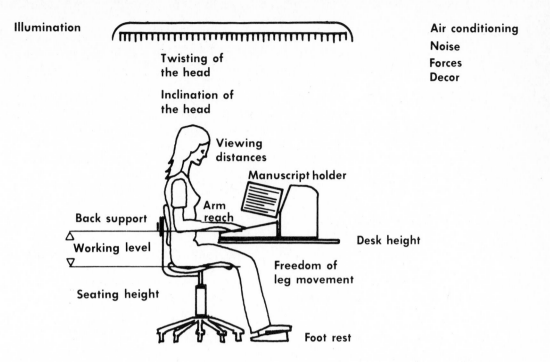

Illumination

Air conditioning
Noise
Forces
Decor

Twisting of
the head

Inclination of
the head

Viewing
distances

Manuscript holder

Back support

Arm
reach

Working level

Desk height

Freedom of
leg movement

Seating height

Foot rest

Figure 5.8 The main characteristics of a VDT workplace. Each of these characteristics must be carefully considered in matching the design of the workplace to the task needs and physical characteristics of the individual VDT operator.

*Figure 5.9 In striving to minimise the loading in the neck, back and arms, there is no substitute for a thin keyboard. This example shows the effect of working with a keyboard at the incorrect height whilst making visual reference to a source document placed to one side of the keyboard. Only by making use of a manuscript holder and a thin keyboard can the positions of the head and arms **both** be comfortably ensured.*

In order to be able to read the source document, this woman must bend forward. If, in a case such as this, the seating height were to be kept at the same level but the desk top were to be lowered, she would find it necessary to bend still further forward, thus increasing the risk of strain in the neck and back. Although one might be tempted to think that the problem could be avoided by lowering the seating height this is not, in fact, the case. By lowering the seating height, this operator would find it necessary to hold her arms in a more elevated, and hence more tiring, position whilst using the keyboard. In other words, she herself would have to make the choice between an uncomfortable position of the hands and arms whilst using the keyboard but less strain in the neck and back, and vice versa. It would not be possible to juggle the seating and desk top heights to avoid both types of discomfort simultaneously. A much better solution would be to reduce the thickness of the keyboard and not the height of the desk in order to minimise the need to bend the head forward whilst maintaining a comfortable position of the hands and arms when keyboarding.

Even so, it has sometimes been argued that because most users of VDTs are not skilled typists, one need not attach so much importance to this kind of workplace consideration, but in fact, a keyboard which is to be used by an unskilled typist must satisfy even more stringent requirements.

At this point we should consider what other keyboard characteristics, besides height, should be controlled so as to help to reduce the loading on the user? To begin with, we must presume that even the most skilled typist must make occasional visual reference to the keyboard. A VDT keyboard is a complex instrument, and very few VDT operators can get by without the need for some visual contact with the keyboard. Of course, the frequency and duration of visual contact differs from person to person and from task to task. The longer it takes to assimilate the information on the keys and the more unfamiliar the user is with the keyboard, the longer is the duration of visual contact with the keyboard.

It has already been stated that if an object is such as to require both visual and manual contact it is seldom possible to place the object in a position that is optimal with regard to both the eyes and the hands. In the case of working with a keyboard, the user would normally chose to adjust the seating height in order to be able to use the keyboard with the arms in their most comfortable position.

The relationship between keyboard characteristics and postural discomfort among VDT operators is also clearly demonstrated by considering the colour and reflection characteristics of VDT keyboards.

Consider firstly, those occasions when a VDT operator would normally find it necessary to make visual reference to the keyboard. When data is being entered from a source document, visual reference to the keyboard is first made after having looked at the document. If both objects - the paper and the keyboard - have very different average luminances, then in looking from the paper to the keyboard and vice versa, the durations of accommodation and pupil adjustment are longer than would have been the case if both objects had the same luminance. In theory, it would take rather longer for the subject to locate a particular target key. More importantly, however, these characteristics can have a material influence on the posture of the VDT operator and the possibility of a variety of forms of postural and visual discomfort.

The practical significance of the keyboard colour and reflection characteristics is illustrated in Figures 5.10 to 5.13. The survey on which these results are based involved more than 800 VDT operators working in different companies in widely differing room conditions and involved in a wide variety of tasks. In spite of these differences, however, these diagrams show very clearly the importance of keyboard colour. The results shown in Figure 5.10, for example, shows how working posture could be much improved and the frequency of complaints of postural discomfort reduced by chosing a light colour rather than black as the keyboard colour.

Keyboard colour is not only important as regards working posture. It was stated earlier that the incidence of visual discomfort among VDT operators cannot be treated separately from the question of posture. This is illustrated in Figure 5.11 which shows that working with a black keyboard also leads to a significantly greater frequency of complaints concerning burning sensations in the eyes. In analysing the data shown in Figures 5.10 and 5.11, it was confirmed that the complaints of postural and visual discomfort were very highly correlated.

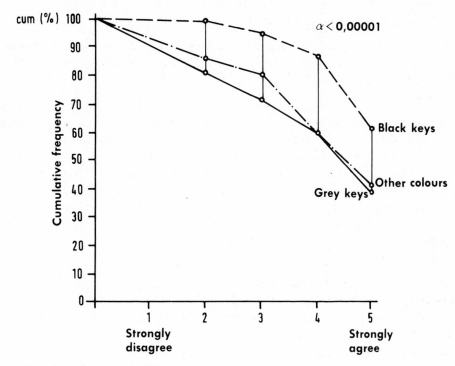

Figure 5.10 Subjective ratings of the incidence of discomfort in the back in relation to the colour of the keyboard.

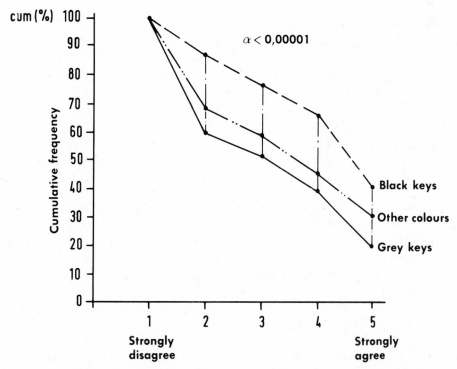

Figure 5.11 Subjective ratings of the incidence of visual fatigue in relation to the colour of the keyboard.

The results shown in these two diagrams demonstrate that it is possible to reduce the incidence of problems of visual fatigue among VDT operators by relatively simple means, in this case by chosing an appropriate keyboard colour. In addition to colour, however, the surfaces of the keyboard also have a certain reflectance, and in Chapter 2, it was shown that with the same direct reflectance, darker coloured surfaces are more glossy than light colours.

In the development of future generations of VDTs and electronic typewriters, the designers should not rely on earlier and even many of the current recommendations concerning typewriter desk heights. Of much greater importance is the height of the keyboard surface above floor level.

The problem of reflected glare during keyboarding is something that anyone who has at any time worked with a typewriter or VDT keyboard is quite familiar with. Reflections on the keytops obscure the key legends, an effect which one tries to avoid by moving the head to a position in which the reflections are no longer visible. But in doing so, the neck is exposed to still greater strain, see Figure 5.12. This also restricts the freedom of head movement; the key legends can only be clearly identified when viewing from a direction in which the glare image is no longer visible.

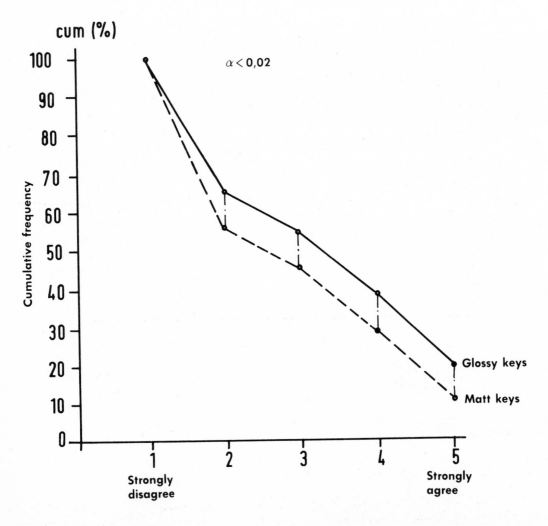

Figure 5.12 *Subjective ratings of the incidence of neck pains in relation to the reflection characteristics of the keyboard.*

That the results shown in the preceding diagrams do not merely reflect a casual tendency, Figure 5.13 shows quite impressively that complaints of fatigue among the operators of VDTs with black and glossy keyboards are twice as frequent as similar complaints among the users of lighter coloured and less reflective keyboards.

To summarise then, the incorrect choice of keyboard characteristics can result in unfavourable types of loading on the individual. It is no coincidence or fault of planning, therefore, that so much time has been devoted in this report to the subject of 'keyboards'. The VDT keyboard is a vital aid to communication between the user and the computer. Compared with typewriter keyboards, however, a VDT keyboard is a still more critical instrument as far as operator comfort is concerned since most VDT keyboards are, and must be capable of being, operated by untrained or unskilled persons.

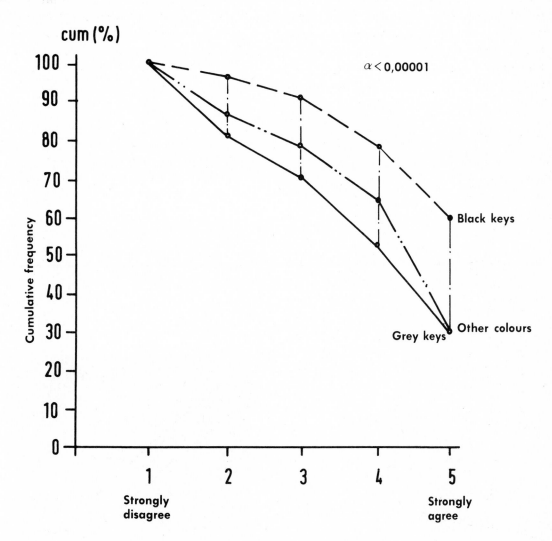

Figure 5.13 *Subjective ratings of the incidence of tiredness and fatigue in relation to the colour of the keyboard.*

The use of documents

The importance of documents in most VDT tasks is clearly shown by the fact that about 80% of VDT operators also work with hardcopy. For the most part, this concerns paper copy of one type or another, but due to the varying properties of paper, different problems may be caused depending upon the task in question.

In using documents at a VDT workplace, there are four activities that might be involved, i.e. reading (basic task), turning over pages (aid function), manipulation, e.g. making notes (basic function) and copying (after reading).

Three of these functions require working with the hands in addition to visual work, and even the task of reading may not necessarily be a purely visual task since the fingers of the hand are often used to trace the lines of text. It is quite understandable then that the user will usually place his documents in a position where they can be most easily manipulated. When a document holder is not provided - and this is unfortunately very often the case in practice - documents will be positioned most favourably as regards touch, and in this position they are no longer favourably placed as visual objects. This is a very common and important fault at all workplaces involving working procedures of this kind.

Whether or not it is possible for a VDT operator to change posture without making the visual task more difficult depends on the optical properties of the visual object. But how much freedom of movement *is* there when reading from a document?

Consider firstly the range of viewing angles between the eye and the paper within which unfavourable postural effects can occur. The desirability of a posture such as that shown in Figure 5.14 has been considered in the previous section. At this point, we are concerned mainly with the relationship between the readability of a document and working posture as such. Figure 5.15 shows the results of an investigation made to determine the frequency of viewing angle whilst reading, and the corresponding difficulty of reading pencil handwriting. It should be noted that in the posture shown in Figure 5.14, the viewing angle is greater than in these tests because the manuscript is positioned even more to one side than was considered usual during this investigation. It can be seen that the slope of the curve showing relative task difficulty becomes very steep for viewing angles greater than about 30°. When this angle approaches 40°, the difficulty of reading is so apparent to the reader himself that he tries continually to find a reading position in which reading ability is improved. It is this activity that then determines the posture of the remainder of the body. Very often, the user will find it necessary to bend over the document, sometimes with the head twisted to one side.

Figure 5.14 The principal activity in data entry tasks is that of reading the information contained in a source document. If a manuscript holder is not provided (or used), the document is placed to one side of the keyboard with the result that the operator finds it necessary to twist the head sideways through quite a large angle and to bend the head forward in order to reduce the viewing distance. Many people engaged in this type of VDT task find it necessary to work in this position for very long periods, sometimes all day. Closer attention to workplace design and the use of a manuscript holder can greatly help to reduce the likelihood of fatigue in this type of VDT task. Ref. C.2

The extent to which this is necessary also depends upon the physical characteristics of the document in question and the prevailing lighting conditions. In this example, the text is hand-written using a lead pencil which tends to become unreadable at large viewing angles due to glare. If one reads hand written pencil text on glossy paper, there are very few angles which permit optimum reading ability. In the case of matt text printed or written on matt paper, the range of viewing angles and the corresponding freedom of movement is much greater.

The quality of the documents itself constitutes something of a problem at most workplaces. In general, and usually for organisational reasons, most VDT operators work with carbon or photocopies rather than originals. In many cases, even the quality of the originals leaves something to be desired as far as readability is concerned.

Copies and carbon duplicates are the most common types of document at most workplaces. So too is hand-written copy. The use of documents such as these has always been one of the causes of poor posture among typing staff. Whilst other employees find documents of this kind easier to read because they can pick them up and hold them, this is no longer possible when working with a keyboard. Instead of taking the document in the hand and directing the position of the document to suit the eyes, the eyes have

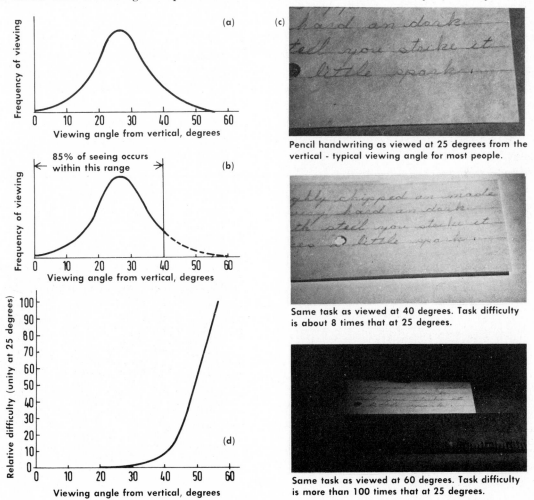

Pencil handwriting as viewed at 25 degrees from the vertical - typical viewing angle for most people.

Same task as viewed at 40 degrees. Task difficulty is about 8 times that at 25 degrees.

Same task as viewed at 60 degrees. Task difficulty is more than 100 times that at 25 degrees.

Figure 5.15 Task viewing angles. (a) People use a range of viewing angles in their work but the peak is about 25° (b) 85% of seeing occurs within a range of 0 to 40″, with seeing at larger angles limited to occasional glances due to foreshortening and increased viewing distance. (c) Photographs of actual pencil handwriting sample (handwriting used in the original research to determine levels of illumination) as seen at viewing angles of 25, 40 and 60″. (d) Curve showing the relative difficulty of the pencil handwriting shown in (c) as measured with the Visual Task Evaluator. Ref. I.2

instead to be directed towards the document, and the position of the head and body adjusted accordingly.

In practice, very little can be done to change this particular characteristic of working with a keyboard and a document, but the effects can be lessened by:

- reducing the quantity of handwritten text, particularly using lead pencil,
- when the work requires the reading of large quantities of written or printed matter, the lighting should be sufficient to permit good readability but without impairing the readability of the screen, and
- placing the documents, as far as possible, on document holders.

By following these simple rules, most of the negative effects of having to work with documents at a VDT workplace can be reduced, but they cannot be totally avoided.

VISUAL DISCOMFORT

Visual discomfort and fatigue are often presumed to be basically visual problems. To some extent this is true; visual fatigue occurs due to the *effort* of trying to see, but the need to expend more or less effort in trying to see is not entirely a question of visual ability. It has been shown in the foregoing sections that many of the symptoms of visual discomfort among VDT operators are so closely related to, and in many cases a direct consequence of, poor working posture that the two types of problem cannot be dealt with separately. In some cases, however, the cause of poor posture can be traced to certain types of defective vision among those concerned.

Where VDT operators have complained of visual discomfort, most of these complaints have referred to what is commonly, although often rather loosely, described as 'eye-strain'. More specifically, such complaints have referred to symptoms such as burning sensations in the eyes, twitching of the eye muscles, headaches etc. It cannot be emphasised too strongly however, that *visual symptoms such as these do not necessarily imply a purely visual problem.*

The causes of visual discomfort

The symptoms of visual fatigue are manyfold and so too are the factors which can give rise to or accelerate visual fatigue at work. But not all of these factors are directly related to the visual task itself, and it is necessary to distinguish between what might be termed the personal and occupational sources of visual discomfort.

The most important *personal factors* which can determine the likelihood of visual fatigue at work are:

- incidence of uncorrected eye sight defects, e.g. short- or long-sightedness, fault of accommodation, astigmatism, etc.,

- poor working posture

- constitutional factors such as tiredness, poor health, the effects of smoking, drinking etc.

- age

The *occupational factors* which might be expected to affect the incidence of visual fatigue relate to the design characteristics of the terminals, to the type and mode of working with the VDT and to the workplace environment:

- factors related to the keyboard and display unit, e.g. character size, spacing and focus (legibility), the optical characteristics of the keyboard and display screen, etc.

- factors related to the type and mode of working, e.g. duration of uninterrupted working periods, degree of concentration required, freedom to pause at will, the use of documents and other job aids,

- factors related to the office environment, e.g. level of illumination, availability of daylight and artificial light, the effects of reflecting surfaces such as windows, desks, paintwork etc.

The importance of most of these factors has already been considered in some detail but, in this section, we shall look at some of the visual problems which can arise when working with VDTs but which are not necessarily posture or even task related.

Defective vision

Very few people possess what might be called perfect vision. In fact, since visual performance steadily deteriorates throughout adult life, 'perfect vision' is, at best, a relative concept. The decrease in visual performance is especially marked between the ages of about 30 and 50 years, and this, and the effects of other common disorders of the visual system must be taken into account when considering the visual aspects of working tasks.

Most people try to compensate for minor visual defects by adjusting visual distance, e.g. by tilting the head, leaning closer to or farther away from the visual object. Certain types of deficiency can also be overcome by increasing the level of illumination. However, if it is necessary to maintain an awkward position to ensure ease of reading this, in itself, may lead to postural discomfort and it may also cause or aggravate existing visual defects.

In this section, therefore, the most common types of visual disorder are reviewed before considering the types of spectacle correction which are normally prescribed to compensate for these disorders and their suitability in connection with VDT tasks.

Visual disorders and their correction

Hyperopia or 'long sight' occurs when the refractive power of the eye is insufficient to bring the image on the retina into the correct focus. The focal plane of the image, in this case, is behind the retina and only objects situated a long way from the eyes, i.e. those requiring less refractive power, appear in focus.

If this condition is uncorrected, the person concerned may chose to move away from near visual objects thus reducing the amount of refractive power needed to bring the object into clear focus. Persons with uncorrected hyperopia tend, therefore, to sit further away from the visual information surfaces of the workplace, e.g. the display screen. But if, as the result of moving away from the visual object of the task, other aspects of the task are made more difficult, e.g. using the keyboard or writing on a document, the mildly hyperopic person may chose to increase visual distance by tilting the head backwards rather than by moving away from the task.

Hyperopia does not necessarily imply a reduction in accommodation range. Especially among younger people, the condition of hyperopia may be partially compensated for by accommodation, i.e. the ability of the eye to increase the refractive power of the lenses. This condition is known as *latent hyperopia*, and in cases such as this, the muscular action controlling accommodation is increased with the result that visual discomfort may occur with prolonged visual effort.

Hyperopia can be corrected for by means of spectacle lenses which supplement the refractive power of the lenses of the eyes. The accommodation range, however, remains the same.

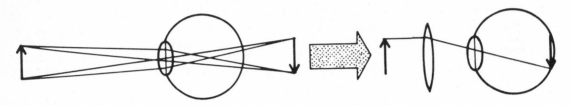

Figure 5.16 Hyperopia or 'long sight' and its refractive correction.

The condition of *myopia* or 'short sight' occurs when the refractive power of the eyes is too strong, with the result that the focal plane of the image is in front of the retina. In order to bring an object into clear focus, persons with uncorrected myopia will usually try to reduce the viewing distance, either by sitting or bending the head closer to the visual object.

The need for close viewing distances, even for mildly myopic individuals, may require frequent movement of the head and upper part of the body in attending to different visual tasks, e.g. reading the display, documents etc. Whilst the frequency of movement is not, in itself, disadvantageous, the positions of the head, neck and other parts of the body may easily lead to strain and fatigue in the neck and back.

Myopia can be corrected by means of spectacle lenses which reduce the effective refractive power of the eye.

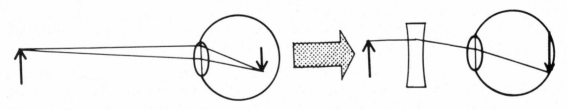

Figure 5.17 Myopia or 'short sight' and its refractive correction.

In the normal eye, the cornea, lens and ball of the eye are spherically symmetrical so that the light entering the eye is refracted uniformly with respect to the meridians of each of the light refracting parts of the eye. In this case, the image that is projected onto the retina is an undistorted replica of the visual object. In the astigmatic eye, however, one of the light refracting parts of the eye, usually the cornea, is spherically asymmetric with the result that light is refracted unequally in different meridians. This condition is known as *astigmatism*.

Depending on the degree of refractive error, the visual acuity of both far and near objects is reduced, and they may also appear to be distorted. People suffering mild astigmatism are often inclined to tilt the head to one side in order to reduce the amount of distortion.

The term *phoria* is used to describe an imbalance of the muscles which control the orbital position and movement of the eyeballs. The result of such an imbalance is the projection of different images of a given object on the retina in each eyeball. One of the principal effects of phoria is the greater effort required to converge the eyes, and to adjust convergence e.g. when looking from a remote object to a closer one.

Provided that the muscular imbalance is only slight, a single clear image can be perceived by increasing this muscular effort although this may result in rather rapid symptoms of fatigue depending upon the actual degree of phoria. Furthermore, this type of self-correction may only be possible within a certain range of viewing distances.

Almost every second person suffers from a *latent phoria* in the sense that some degree of phoria occurs at one or other visual distance albeit that the effects are usually not troublesome.

Due to aging of the visual system, the accommodation power of the eyes decreases as we get older. This means that, for a normally sighted person i.e. one with a far point of vision at infinity, the near point of vision moves progressively farther and farther away. This condition, called *presbyopia*, is caused by a progressive inability of the lens to change its shape thus limiting the range of visual distances over which objects can be brought into focus.

The use of glasses

Most common disorders of the visual system can be compensated for by the use of spectacles or corneal contact lenses. Needless to say, defective vision should be corrected for as effectively as possible but it is worthwhile giving a little thought to what this means in practice.

From an occupational point of view, the correction of visual defects should permit the carrying out of the task or tasks in question with optimum visual ability. If the job with which an individual is engaged comprises several tasks, each with differing visual requirements, spectacle correction which is designed to compensate for a specific deficiency, e.g. short or long sight, may be sufficient for only one task. This might also be true if the job comprises a single task but one which involves the use of several items of equipment and job aids, each with differing visual requirements.

The most common form of spectacle correction involves the use of spectacles with monofocal lenses to permit focussing at a predetermined near distance. Spectacles such as these are usually called "reading glasses", and would normally be prescribed in cases where the individual is engaged in tasks requiring clear near vision for long periods of time and where a large field of view is helpful. The main disadvantage in using reading glasses is that they improve clarity of near vision at the expense of far vision. If the task in question requires the clear vision of both near and far objects, therefore, they must be removed and, if necessary, replaced by another pair of glasses.

The use of spectacles with monofocal lenses poses few problems in using VDTs provided that accommodation ability is sufficient. This is usually the case for younger persons but due to the reduction in accommodation with age, may still result in some problems among older persons.

Differences in lens prescription cause significant changes in the range of comfortable viewing distance and it is important that the lenses are not too strong for the visual task in question. The ranges of acceptable focus to within $\pm\,0.5$ diopter for various strengths of near point lenses are shown in the following table:

Lens strength (diopters)	Range of focus (image within $\pm\,1/2$ diopter)
1	670 mm - 2000 mm
1,5	500 mm - 1000 mm
2,0	400 mm - 670 mm
2,5	330 mm - 500 mm
3,0	280 mm - 400 mm

Figure 5.18 The ranges of acceptable focus for various strengths of near point spectacle lenses.

Consider the case of a 50 year old person (accommodation range 2 diopters) who wears spectacles to correct for near sight, the spectacles giving a near point of 300 mm (near point distance 3,33 diopters). The far point in this case is located at 750 mm (1,33 diopters). In practice, the display screen of a VDT is located at a distance of about 700 mm whilst the viewing distance of the keyboard is more usually about 450 - 500 mm.

Looking alternately to the screen and the keyboard requires almost continual accommodation and, at this age, the process of accommodation requires a period of more than one second, and this is a very long time. For this reason, this person would normally try to overcome the problem by trying to reduce the visual distance involved by changing posture but then, only at the expense of increased strain in other parts of the body and particularly in the back and neck.

The spectacle wearer whose glasses are corrected for a near point of 250 mm is in a still less fortunate position since only images within a range of 500 mm can be seen sharply.

The range of focus is decreased from 1330 mm at 1 diopter to 120 mm at 3.0 diopters. This is an important factor because without a sufficient range of focus, it may be necessary to resort to changes in posture in order to ensure the most comfortable viewing distance. Most office tasks involve viewing distances between 400 mm and 700 mm and not all relevant visual tasks can be placed at the same visual distance. It is essential, therefore, that if a VDT operator is required to wear glasses, lenses are chosen which provide a sufficient *range* of focus.

Another difficulty which can arise when wearing spectacles or contact lenses of which the strength of one lens differs significantly from that of the other, is that the image of a given object on the retina of one eye may be larger than that on the other. This condition is called *aniseikonia*, the effects of which are much stronger when wearing spectacles because the plane of the lenses is farther away from the principal plane of the eye than contact lenses are. The change in retinal image size caused by wearing spectacles and contact lenses of various strengths is shown in Figure 5.19.

In order to provide clear focus at different distances one can use *multifocal lenses*, some varieties of which are illustrated in Figure 5.20.

Many people with long-sight use so-called bifocal glasses with two lens segments, the lower of which is intended for near vision and the upper part for far vision, e.g. for 300 mm and for 700 mm upwards. If a VDT operator wears bifocals, the keyboard can be viewed through the lower part of the lens although the user may bend forward a little in order to see the keyboard as clearly as possible. The display screen may then be viewed either through the lower part or through the upper part of the glass lenses. In the former case, the visual distance might be about 500 mm and the viewing posture is likely to result in pains in the neck. When looking through the upper part of the glasses, on the other hand, the user would usually prefer to position the screen as far away as possible, but since the apparent sizes of character images in the display remain the same, the visual task is made more difficult by doing so. The visual angle for 3 mm high characters at 500 mm is 20,6′ and at 700 mm only 14,7′.

If the task involves different viewing distances, the use of multifocal lenses to improve the visual ease of the task may lead to discomfort of the back and neck due to poor posture. This is true for all kinds of visual task which require different viewing distances and the maintaining of a particular posture for long periods.

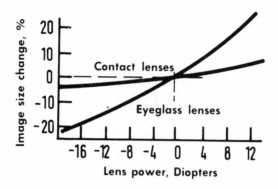

Figure 5.19 The change in retinal image size caused by wearing spectacles and contact lenses of various strengths. Ref. R.18

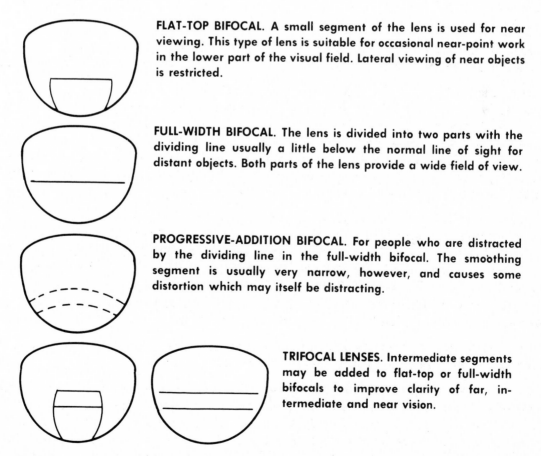

FLAT-TOP BIFOCAL. A small segment of the lens is used for near viewing. This type of lens is suitable for occasional near-point work in the lower part of the visual field. Lateral viewing of near objects is restricted.

FULL-WIDTH BIFOCAL. The lens is divided into two parts with the dividing line usually a little below the normal line of sight for distant objects. Both parts of the lens provide a wide field of view.

PROGRESSIVE-ADDITION BIFOCAL. For people who are distracted by the dividing line in the full-width bifocal. The smoothing segment is usually very narrow, however, and causes some distortion which may itself be distracting.

TRIFOCAL LENSES. Intermediate segments may be added to flat-top or full-width bifocals to improve clarity of far, intermediate and near vision.

Figure 5.20 Some examples of multifocal spectacle lenses. Ref. R.18

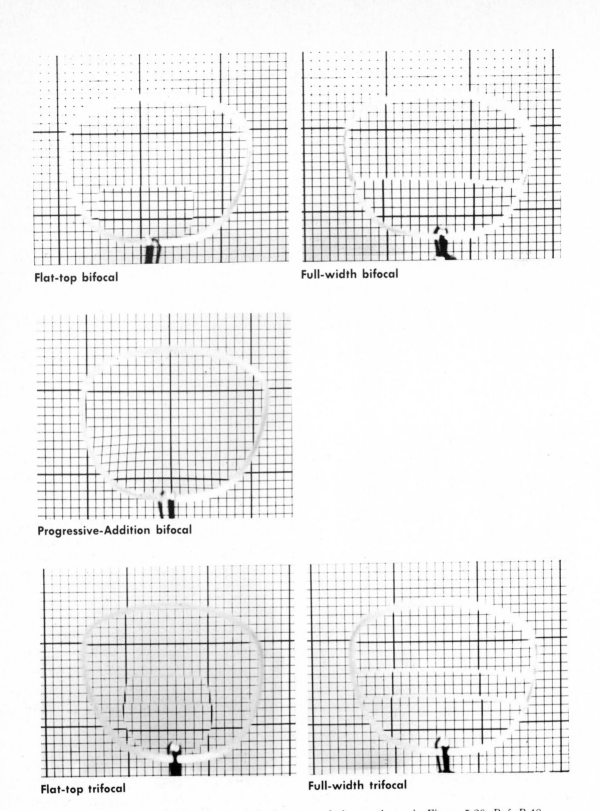

Flat-top bifocal

Full-width bifocal

Progressive-Addition bifocal

Flat-top trifocal

Full-width trifocal

Figure 5.21 Photographs taken through the spectacle lenses shown in Figure 5.20. Ref. R.18

On the question of visual 'damage'

A question which many VDT operators themselves ask is whether or not it is possible that the eyes may become 'damaged' as a result of working with VDTs. In spite of a great deal of research, however, there is no evidence at present to suggest that using a VDT is likely to damage the eyes or eyesight.

214

The use of VDTs in office environments has introduced a number of new visual demands on those that work with them. This, in turn, has meant that certain requirements as regards the design, implementation and the use of VDTs should be satisfied in order to keep the risk of postural and visual discomfort whilst working with a VDT to a minimum. In the foregoing sections, these requirements have been looked at in some detail. It has been shown that where these requirements are not correctly satisfied, working with a VDT can result in unnecessary fatigue. This fatigue can arise from postural problems due to inadequate workplace design, or from a host of other factors including, of course, the visual aspects of the task and the visual abilities of the persons concerned.

Fatigue among VDT operators may be experienced as various symptoms of discomfort or strain in the eyes, regardless of whether or not the source of the problem is actually visual. The eyes may even act as an 'early warning system' for the rest of the body and may feel tired or sore even though the cause of the fatigue lies elsewhere.

Throughout this report it has been shown that symptoms of postural and visual fatigue are not uncommon among VDT operators, particularly in certain task categories. These problems are not inevitable, however, and neither, in many cases, are they uniquely associated with working with VDTs. The fact that they occur is merely an indication that the constraints on working method and posture which are introduced by the use of VDTs are often not sufficiently well-understood and catered for.

Visual fatigue occurs as the result of the effort of trying to see. This effort may require an unfavourable posture. Poor lighting may be the cause of or at least aggravate the problem. Prolonged visual concentration on objects which are not clearly in focus or prolonged concentration on a single point can very quickly lead to symptoms of visual fatigue.

The main symptoms of fatigue, e.g. burning sensations in the eyes, tiredness, headaches etc, are *reversible*. After a short period of rest, the symptoms recede and a normal feeling of well-being is restored. The possibility that *irreversible* effects might accrue from working with VDTs cannot be supported on the basis of current medical experience. This is not to say, however, that such a possibility and, perhaps more importantly, individual anxieties concerning such a possibility should not be taken seriously.

There are, and will continue to be, less than ideal VDTs and VDT workplaces in many organisations for some time to come. These may well cause unnecessary or excessive fatigue which will be experienced day after day by some operators. Although there is no evidence to suggest that this fatigue will cause irreversible damage to the eyes or visual system, the possibility that prolonged fatigue from using VDTs might have some long term effects cannot be entirely precluded.

The problem is further compounded by the fact that a high proportion of the working population have uncorrected or inadequately corrected visual defects. Estimates of the exact proportion vary but it is likely to be between 20% and 30%. The result has been that many VDT operators who have experienced symptoms of discomfort or fatigue in their eyes have been told, when they consulted their optician, that they needed glasses. Inevitably, the need for glasses is then connected with the use of VDTs.

Eyesight defects and other conditions which can result in excessive loading of the eye muscles can aggravate visual discomfort in all types of close visual work. Unfortunately, defective vision is common, even among young adults, and tends to become the rule rather than the exception after the age of 40 years. Neither does the use of spectacles necessarily guarantee that the defect has been satisfactorily cured. This was clearly demonstrated by the results of an investigation among a sample of 500 clerical and administrative workers, 50% of whom were found to have defective vision and in which 37% of the spectacle wearers required re-prescription. 69% of the non-spectacle wearers in this sample required positive correction. The results from a similar investigation conducted in Scandinavia also showed that up to one third of employees exhibited uncorrected or insufficiently well corrected sight defects. In a recent investigation among the 300 employees of a leading news agency in the United Kingdom it was found that two thirds had adequate eye sight, and of the remaining one third 20 definitely required correction, and 4 were declared unsuitable for working with VDTs.

The reassurance that is needed to overcome the anxiety that working with a VDT may result in damaged eyes or impaired vision can only come from the results of valid, long-term observations. Whilst it is not the object of this report to state the need or otherwise for such an investigation, it is nevertheless necessary to draw attention to some of the conditions that must be satisfied in order that an investigation of this kind may yield valid and reliable results.

The procedures with which an occupationally-related study such as this is designed and carried out must be well defined and controlled. In principle, investigations of this kind are relatively straightforward but the practical difficulties involved in selecting the members of the sample and control groups, establishing the appropriate test procedures, collecting and analysing the results etc, should not be underestimated. Ergonomics research has shown that the nature of the task has a major effect on fatigue. In the case of working with VDTs, this and the duration of working with the VDT are factors to be carefully considered. The number of individuals involved must necessarily be large and representative of the variety of tasks and working conditions in question. In the case of working with VDTs, this is very large indeed. Account must also be taken of the fact that quite a high proportion of the original control and subject groups are likely to change profession or in some other way become ineligible to continue participation within the study at some stage. The number of subjects must, therefore, be high enough to ensure that the anticipated final number is sufficiently large to draw meaningful conclusions.

Ergonomics research has shown that the nature of the task has a major effect on fatigue. In the case of working with VDTs, this and the duration of working with the VDT are factors to be carefully considered.

Eye tests for VDT operators

A second difficulty arises in respect of the measurements or tests that must be carried out on each member of the subject and control group in collecting the data.

A number of authorities have considered the need for a relevant set of procedures with which to test the eyesight of VDT operators. This, too, has been a focal theme in the course of the present investigation. It would be unfortunate, however, if inappropriate tests were used and it would be wasteful if the resultant data could not be coordinated in some way so that any trends which might otherwise remain concealed in a number of small groups could be detected.

In order to develop a series of eyesight testing procedures therefore, a special VDU Eye Test (VET) Advisory Group was established in the United Kingdom, and the eye test procedures that have been recommended by this group are described in Appendix II.

In formulating the test procedures for screening the eyesight of potential VDT operators and for permitting an on-going investigation, the following criteria were observed:

- the test procedures should be both relevant and sufficiently straightforward as to be able to be administered by suitably qualified local authorities rather than by a centralised authority. For this reason, no tests have been considered which depend upon highly specialised equipment or which can only be conducted in research laboratories,

- neither the tests themselves nor the way the tests are conducted should unduly inconvenience the subject, place him under unnecessary strain nor be likely to introduce bias in the results. In addition, it was considered desirable that the tests should take no longer than one half-hour to administer in order to minimise the cost of the investigation and the inconvenience to the individual,

- the data which is gathered from the tests should be reported in such a way as to permit centralised analysis.

Based on these requirements, a package of tests has been agreed and it is felt that, when suitably administered, this procedure will be sufficiently comprehensive to allow for the early detection of abnormalities without being unduly complex.

The emphasis in the test package is on those aspects of the image forming apparatus, of binocular vision and of the oculo-motor system which promote the formation of a sharply outlined single perception when both eyes are used. This is the process in reading characters on a VDT screen or a source document and is, therefore, the area of most concern. It is also the area where the individual is most likely to be able to detect a defect such as blurred or double vision.

The following tests are recommended:

1. Unaided Visual Acuity
2. Refractive Findings
3. Corrected Visual Acuity
4. Amplitude of Accommodation
5. Suppression
6. Distant Muscle Balance (Maddox rod)
7. 1 metre Muscle Balance (Maddox rod)
8. Near Muscle Balance (Maddox wing)

It should be pointed out that the procedures recommended here are not a substitute for normal health care. Indeed, one of the consequences of instituting this test procedure will be that a number of the people screened, whether they are VDT operators or not, will be found to require glasses or a change of lenses. Such people should be advised to consult their own opticians in the normal way. However, if they require special prescriptions specifically for VDT work then it seems reasonable that they should be provided by the employer. Indeed the viewing distance for VDTs usually falls in between the near point and distant vision for which spectacles are normally prescribed.

The tests themselves are only part of the data necessary to effectively monitor the effects of prolonged VDT use. For example, it will be important to know how long the individual uses a VDT each day. It will also be necessary to record, in general terms, the type of work involved since for some tasks, e.g. data entry, the display screen is looked at far less than for others e.g. text editing. The tester should therefore complete a record sheet for each subject in order to provide the additional information about their work and use of the VDT that is necessary to make the results statistically meangingful.

Cataracts

The question as to whether or not a cataract condition can be caused as the result of working with VDTs has become a controversial issue, not least within the medical community itself. This controversy centres around the likelihood that exposure to certain forms of non-ionising radiant energy, and microwave radiation in particular, may induce cataracts in the eyes, this condition having been termed *radiant energy* or *capsular cataract*. The common feature of this form of cataract is that the cataract is initiated at the surface of the lens. Most other types of cataract occur mainly as opacification of the substance of the lens.

The link between the occurrence of such a condition and the use of VDTs can only be established when sufficient clinical evidence exists with which to positively demonstrate the existence of such a condition, and then only if it can be shown that VDTs are emitters of the offending form of radiant energy.

As to whether exposure to microwave radiation, in itself, may cause a cataract condition, there is some evidence to suggest that this may be so, but the evidence is both sparse and disputed. The most convincing evidence for the existence of the condition derives from certain sectors of the avionics industry and particularly among those working with radar installations which are potentially high emitters of microwave radiation. Cases of capsular cataract have been reported and clinically confirmed among these occupational groups in several countries but the etiology of the condition has seldom been sufficiently well established so as to conclusively indict microwave radiation as being the cause of the condition. It is also worth noting that the results of an ocular examination among 1300 U.S. servicemen who had worked with radar and a control group who had not, lead to the conclusion that there was no evidence to suggest that people had suffered cataracts as a result of exposure to microwave not just to small amounts but even large amounts.

Neither is it well-established that VDTs are capable of emitting radiation in the microwave region of the spectrum. Several types of electromagnetic radiation are produced in a VDT. Ultraviolet, visible and infra-red radiation are emitted by the phosphor material when stimulated by the electron beam within the CRT. X-rays may also be generated within the CRT. Radio frequency (RF) radiation is also produced by some of the electronic components and circuits. But in a correctly functioning VDT, there is no part of the equipment which would normally be considered capable of emitting radiation in the microwave band. Of course, the possibility might exist that otherwise non-emitting components may emit this form of radiation when malfunctioning, and this should, perhaps, be the subject of further investigation. Whether or not this might be of practical significance, however, would depend upon which components were affected and by what type of malfunction. In most cases, malfunction in the electronic circuitry of a VDT leads to either malfunction of the entire VDT or to a display condition that is apparent to the operator and which would presumably be corrected because of the practical difficulty of working with the VDT.

To summarise, the evidence relating the incidence of capsular cataract and occupation with VDTs is at present little more than conjectural, but the evidence linking this condition and exposure to non-ionising radiation is perhaps less so. It remains, therefore, to be demonstrated whether or not VDTs are capable of emitting this type of radiation during normal operation and during malfunction. Although this hardly seems likely, the possibility should nevertheless be properly investigated.

Visually precipitated epilepsy

Epilepsy is believed to occur in about 0,5% of the population and may be as high as 0,8% among children between the ages of 5 and 14 years. It has been estimated that probably between 1 and 3% of the epileptic population is subject to visual reflex epilepsy, i.e. epileptic seizures induced by visual stimulation, the condition being much more common among children than in the adult population. The incidence of photosensitive epilepsy, i.e. epileptic sensitivity to flickering lights, is probably between 1:2 500 and 1:10 000. The condition is more common in females than in males, and most commonly occurs between the ages of 6 and 12 years, the incidence dropping off quite steeply after the age of 16-18 years. It has been suggested that puberty may play some part in the genesis of this type of epilepsy and there is also some evidence of a genetic factor.

Quite a high proportion of photosensitive epileptics, possibly as high as 50%, are prone to suffer seizures whilst watching television. This condition is known as *television epilepsy*. There is a further group of people, whom it is probably better not to regard as epileptic, who are prone to seizures only when exposed to provocative visual stimulation. Television epilepsy is a form of visual reflex epilepsy caused by a sensitivity to flickering light and most likely also to pattern.

The optimum flash rates to induce convulsions in photosensitive epileptics has been found to be between 10 and 25 Hz with a peak of sensitivity between 15 and 20 Hz. Most flicker sensitive epileptics respond to stroboscopic stimulation at frequencies near 16 Hz. There is a good deal of evidence to suggest that the combined presence of pattern and flicker may extend the sensitivity range. The results from one investigation, for example, showed that whilst the mean sensitivity range for diffuse stimulation was 11-32 Hz, the range was increased to 10-43 Hz with patterned stimulation. This difference confirms a conclusion which has been drawn by most researchers in this field, namely that patterned stimulation is more epileptogenic than diffuse stimulation. It has also been found that many photosensitive epileptics are not only sensitive to flicker but also to stationary striped patterns, and that by vibrating the patterns, the incidence of pattern sensitivity is doubled. There is also some evidence to suggest that TV-epileptic seizures are more frequent when viewing black-and-white receivers than when viewing colour receivers.

The epileptogenic effects of working with VDTs has not been studied, but it seems reasonable to presume that same principles should apply.In fact, it may well be so that the more marked linear pattern of text on a visual display screen and the jitter and other types of image instability that frequently occur on VDTs may lead to a somewhat greater sensitivity to seizures among those prone to this condition. VDTs which use storage CRTs should present no problem but VDTs which use the refreshed, TV-type of CRT may be expected to induce seizures in the same type of people as are adversely affected by watching domestic TV.

The effect of pattern is likely to be particularly important when considering the epileptogenic effects of viewing an alphanumeric display screen. In addition to the lines of text on the display screen, the television raster presents an array of stripes, which, if the signal strength is low, also undergoes small oscillations known as line jitter. In addition, the stripe pattern is refreshed at 50 Hz, and the lines may be interlaced to give an effective image on the retina similar to that produced by horizontal lines vibrating at 25 Hz with a superimposed jitter.

It might also be suspected that a visual display screen could represent a more provocative stimulus compared with a TV screen because of the closer viewing distance.

The optimum spatial frequency for pattern sensitivity has been found to be 2 cycles per degree of visual angle with a range of about 0,5 to 8 cycles per degree. It has also been found that striped patterns cease to result in sensitivity when only one cycle of the pattern substands an arc of 3,75' or less. With the 625 line system in which 287 lines are visible at any one time, this corresponds to a viewing distance of 1,91 times the diagonal size of the screen. With the appropriate combination of screen size and viewing distance this condition can certainly be achieved when working with a VDT.

The epileptogenic effects of flicker and pattern can be reduced by reducing the size, luminance and contrast of the visual stimulus and by monocoluar viewing. All of these conditions can be satisfied when viewing a TV or VDT screen but the price may well be a greater likelihood of eye strain.

Pattern and the stroboscopic fluctuation of luminance are essential ingredients to the inducement of this type of seizure. It is possible, however, that the stimulus in many TV-induced seizures is not the line and frame scanning frequencies of the set, and not the types of malfunction which can cause fluctuations at lower frequencies, but minor instabilities in the system producing a low frequency flicker which is not immediately obvious to the viewer. This might occur, for example, due to hunting in the automatic gain control circuit, with poor resolution and stability of the image close to the edges of the screen and with minor faults in line synchronisation. Sensitivity to frequencies below about 8 Hz is uncommon, so that in connection with the use of VDTs, a 5 Hz or less blinking cursor is unlikely to prove epileptogenic.

It seems reasonable to presume, therefore, that persons who are subject to TV or other forms of visual reflex epilepsy may be prone to seizures when working with or in the vicinity of a VDT. Albeit that this condition affects only a small proportion of the population and one which is in any case unlikely to be occupationally exposed to VDTs, it would seem a wise precaution, in the event that a potential user of a VDT who is known to have a history of photosensitive epilepsy, should undergo an appropriate medical examination before using the equipment. If the individual concerned was shown to be likely to suffer seizures or other forms of discomfort due to this type of sensitivity, some other form of employment should be considered.

PROBLEMS RELATED TO AIR CONDITIONING

Complaints of physical discomfort among office workers can often be traced to the effects of air conditioning. In the course of the present investigations too, it was found that complaints of discomfort among VDT operators were, in many cases, due to or aggravated by poor air conditioning. It was also shown that the causes of complaints of this kind are tangible and can be quantitatively examined with the help of physical measurements. But the fact that both the charactersitics and effects of poor air conditioning can be identified, and to some extent even measured, this does not mean that the problems are always quite so easy to remedy in practice. This is partly due to the technical difficulties involved in designing and controlling air conditioning systems. But a part of the problem also lies in the very nature of human physiology.

Even in these investigations, it has been found that there are certain types of problem which neither are, nor can be, resolved at the technical level due to the fact that human physiology is as it is. This applies particularly to one of the basic questions of air conditioning, namely the problem of holding all of the relevant climatic components at a constant level.

In order that the human body can adjust its rhythm to a 24-hour cycle, some external stimuli are needed. Nature provides these stimuli, for example, as the cycles of light and temperature throughout the day. In contrast, however, air conditioning systems are constructed in such a way as to maintain or try to maintain a constant set of conditions. For this reason, the basic principle on which air conditioning systems are construed is a false one. But aside from the technical difficulties that may be involved in seeking to overcome this problem, we run into another, basically psychological problem: people react to natural and artificial environments in very different ways.

For example, an outdoor illumination of 5000 Lux would normally be judged to be rather subdued but indoors, such a level of illumination would be described as very bright. Neither do we necessarily consider all changes in natural temperature to be acceptable simply because they are part of nature's rhythm. It is human nature to widthdraw from or avoid any condition of climate which we find to be unacceptable, provided, of course, that we have the freedom to do so. And outside of our working lives, we do indeed have a certain degree of freedom to chose or modify the climate that we live in or are exposed to. At work, however, one is subjected to a particular set of environmental conditions which, as individuals, we usually have little possibility to modify or influence. For this reason, when considering the climatisation of any form of working environment, it is necessary to find that set of conditions which is acceptable to the majority of the people concerned and then try to hold these conditions at a constant level.

Temperature

It has been found that both too high and too low temperature has an adverse effect on well-being and performance at work. Too high a temperature induces feelings of tiredness. Too low a temperature, on the other hand, induces the need for movement and also leads to a reduction in attentiveness. As one author put it: "The guarantee of a comfortable room climate is a necessary requirement to maintain the feeling of well-being and full performance ability."[1]

What is understood to be a 'comfortable temperature', however, is usually a matter of personal preference. It has also been found that, on average, women feel most comfortable with a room temperature that is about $2°$ higher than that which is usually preferred by men. But it is also true that our opinion as to what constitutes a comfortable temperature changes from time to time. It is virtually impossible, therefore, to generate a room temperature in which all employees are equally well satisfied, and the results from several investigations have shown that it is very seldom that more than 95% of employees in a given working environment describe the room temperature as comfortable. More recent investigations have shown that even this figure may be too optimistic. In many office rooms, it has been found that no more than 50% of those employed considered the room temperature to be comfortable.

At least part of the problem is caused by the effects of sitting close to a window. Many office employees prefer to sit by a window, the view to the outside world providing visual relaxation from the office interior. Very often, however, those sitting close to a window experience the temperature there as being too low because on cooler days, the body gives off more heat to the window area than it receives from it.

As a general rule, it is recommended that the temperature in office rooms should be maintained in the range 21 - 23° C and between 26 - 28° C on hot summer days. By keeping the inner temperature within these ranges, the difference between inside and outside temperature is kept as small as possible.

1. Ref. P.3

Relative humidity

Relative humidity is another important component of room climate, and one which has a strong influence on comfort and well-being. Too dry air leads to a drying out of the mucous membranes of the eyes and nose. This inhibits the self-cleaning of the breathing system thus increasing the risk of infection, and increases the sensitivity of the eyes to various forms of discomfort.

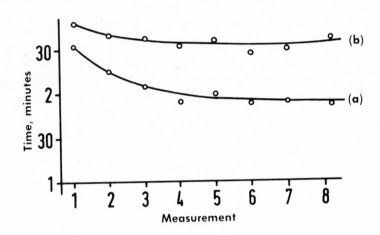

Figure 5.22 The effect of (a) a normal and (b) a 'close' room climate on the time required to perform a given task. Ref. P.3

Relative humidity may also have an effect on working performance. The results from a series of tests with persons in two room climates, one a normal office climate with temperature 20 - 22° C and 40-50% R.H., and the other a 'close' atmosphere with temperature 22 - 24° C and 60-80% R.H. showed that, in the close environment, there was a certain 'working in' effect and a significantly longer time was required to carry out individual tasks. Although relative humidity is usually related to temperature sensitivity, it is now well established that both characteristics should be treated independently. In this particular investigation, it was not possible to determine if these effects were due to the difference in temperature or to the difference in relative humidity, but the results clearly indicated the negative effects of a too moist air.

In most offices, however, the air is too dry rather than too moist, and between 70% and 95% of those interviewed in a recent investigation judged the air in the working room to be 'too dry'. Physical measurements which were made during this investigation confirmed that this was a quite justified opinion.

As a general rule, it is recommended that the relative humidity in office environments should be between 50 and 55%.

Air circulation

Air circulation, particularly in closed rooms such as offices, has a significant effect on comfort, but precisely how pleasant or unpleasant this is experienced to be depends on the prevailing room temperature and on a number of other factors e.g. whether or not the individual is perspiring, moving about etc. Generally speaking, a draught is felt to be more unpleasant when the temperature is low.

Experiments have shown that people are more sensitive to air movements than is commonly supposed. 23% of those questioned in a particular investigation of office working conditions experienced an air current of 0,1m/sec to be an uncomfortable draught.

The parts of the body that are most sensitive to draughts are the head, neck, shoulders and arms. Some types of visual discomfort, e.g. dryness and burning sensations in the eyes, can also be partly attributed to the effects of air movements in drying out the mucous membranes of the eyes.

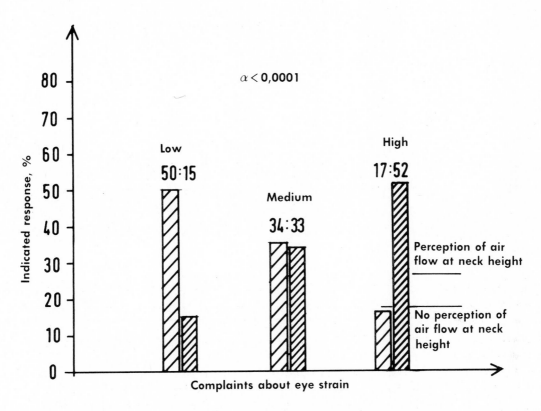

Figure 5.23 The effects of draughts in the region of the neck and throat on the sensitivity of VDT operators to eye strain. This diagram shows the correlation between the responses of VDT operators to the questions 'I experience a draught around my neck' and a group of questions concerning the incidence of visual discomfort e.g. burning sensations in the eyes, twitching of the eye-lids, itching of the eyes and a subjective feeling of intense eye strain when working with the VDT". [1]

Due to the circulation of air, dry air is felt to be even more dry. To ensure the comfort of those who work in offices, therefore, it is necessary to avoid even very small air currents in the room at head and neck height.

1. The use of the terms 'Low', 'Medium' and 'High' along the horizontal axes in Figures 5.23, 5.25 and 5.26 is based on the reactions of more than 800 VDT operators to the questions shown in the legends to these diagrams. Of those surveyed, 69% worked in climatised rooms, and 31% in non-climatised rooms. In answering the question, each operator was requested to indicate which number in the range 1 to 5, best described his or her feeling as to the relevance of the question. In this scale, '1' corresponded to the feeling that, to the person concerned, the question was 'completely irrelevant' and '5' corresponded to the feeling that the question was 'completely relevant'. In other words, this scale of numbers provides a measure of the intensity of the individual operators reaction to the question. In these diagrams, the responses are lumped into three categories where 'Low' refers to the group that had few complaints or gave a negative response to the question, 'Medium' refers to the group that had some complaints or gave an essentially non-committal response to the question, and 'High' refers to the group that complained most or gave a positive response to the question concerned.

Other factors which help to determine the quality of the air in a work room are the oxygen content, odour and the presence of pollutants in the air. In order to ensure a pleasant and fresh quality of the air, sufficient ventilation is essential.

In smaller offices, window ventilation may be sufficient but in larger offices some form of air conditioning system would normally be necessary. In this case a minimum free ventilation rate of 30 to 50 cubic metres of air per person and per hour is required. However, such a large quantity of air cannot be introduced into a room without creating some form of draught. This being the case, one should then ensure that the currents of air are directed away from the most cold and draught sensitive parts of the body.

Air conditioning of VDT workrooms

The cooling load in a modern office building is distributed among several different factors, see Figure 5.24. These calculations do not include the effects of office equipment, however, because, at the time these calculations were made, this was not a significant factor. But the situation in rooms which are equipped with VDTs is a different matter.

(a)

Heat source	Exterior offices[1]				Interior offices
	North	East	South	West	
Glass	27%	56%	51%	56%	-
Lighting	61%	37%	41%	36%	84%
Occupants	12%	7%	8%	8%	16%
	100%	100%	100%	100%	100%

1. Per cent at time of maximum load in each office

(b)

Heat source	Office building A	Loan office B	Chain store C	Clinic D
Glass	11,8%	27,0%[2]	5,7%	14,8%
Lighting	42,3%	12,9%	23,3%	16,9%[3]
Roof and walls	0,7%	16,8%	12,0%	33,4%
Occupants	15,4%	12,2%	33,4%	15,5%
Ventilation	26,6%	31,1%	21,4%	19,4%
System power	3,2%	-	4,2%	-
	100,0%	100,0%	100,0%	100,0%
Glass + lighting	54,1%	39,9%	29,0%	31,7%

2. Large expanse of window exposed west. 3. Assumes 50% of lighting in use.

Figure 5.24 Examples of the cooling load distribution (a) in a modern office building and (b) for several types of office installation.

In a survey in which a sample of 1021 VDT operators were asked if they felt that the air temperature in the VDT room was pleasant or otherwise, only 14% described the temperature as 'pleasant'. A further 10% replied that the temperature was more or less satisfactory. In other words, less than 25% of this group found the air temperature to be satisfactory or better!

A VDT emits quite a lot of heat. In most installations, the combined thermal emission from the VDTs is sufficient to raise the average temperature in the room, often in spite of ventilation. The change in temperature has been measured in several VDT workrooms, and on the basis of these experiments, a cooling load calculation has been made which showed that with $7 m^3$ per person and a power consumption of 350 watts per working place, about 50% of the cooling load was attributable to the VDTs. With a loading of 100 watts/unit and 400 watts/unit respectively, and $10m^3$/per person, the cooling load increased by 30% and 120% respectively. These differences are very great indeed.

In order to determine whether or not these quantities of heat can be removed without disturbing the people working with the VDTs, the reaction of people working in climatised and non-climatised VDT working rooms has been compared. As expected, there were fewer people in the climatised type of working room who described their working place as being too warm, 30% as opposed to 45% respectively. In both cases, however, the temperature was described as being pleasant just as infrequently. In a climatised room, the optimum temperature can be maintained by increasing the amount of ventilation, but this means that, in many cases, it is not possible to remove the heat which is emitted from the VDTs without a greater circulation of air in the room.

There is no doubt that the well-being and performance of the individual at work is affected by room temperature and the effects of draughts. More than half of those questioned complained about the effects of draughts around their legs and neck, and complaints about draughts and pains in the neck are very closely correlated.

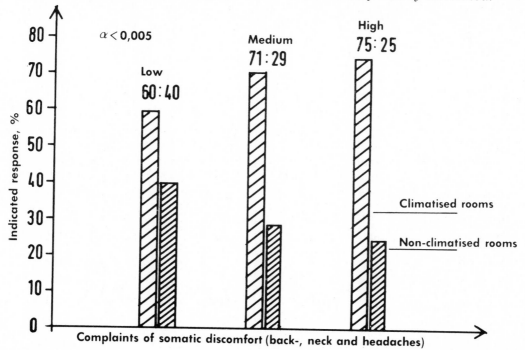

Figure 5.25 The frequency of complaints of somatic discomfort, e.g. back-, neck- and headaches among VDT operators working in climatised and non-climatised workrooms. This diagram compares the responses of VDT operators working in climatised and non-climatised rooms to the questions 'I suffer (a) back, (b) neck and (c) headaches whilst working with the VDT.

In those rooms where fewer complaints about draughts were recorded, there were significantly less frequent complaints about pains in the neck. To resolve the problem, therefore, one should not strive to increase the cooling load but rather to select VDTs with a lower heat output and to arrange the equipment more favourably in the room.

The problem of dry air in VDT work rooms can also be assessed in terms of the subjective reaction of VDT operators to the dryness of the air. In the course of the survey referred to earlier and in answer to the question: "do you think that the air is too dry"?, 72% of those in rooms with air-conditioning and 68% of those in rooms without air-conditioning answered: "yes". It should be noted, however, that the air in the climatised rooms was, in fact, measured to be more moist. The fact that a roughly equal proportion of those working in air conditioned rooms described the air as being too dry can be explained by the draughtier conditions in the climatised rooms.

It is clear, then, that the climatisation of rooms with VDTs poses a number of problems in that air-conditioning may disturb those employed in the room in several different ways.

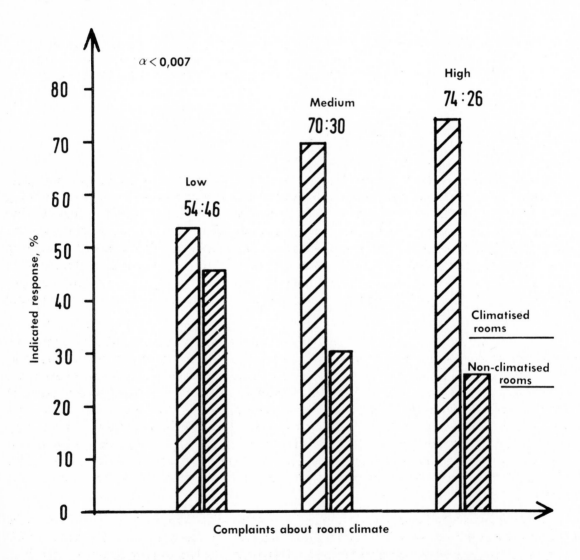

Figure 5.26 Subjective ratings of complaints about room climate among VDT operators in climatised and non-climatised work rooms. This diagram compares the responses of VDT operators working in climatised and non-climatised work rooms to the question 'I have problems with the room climate'. Even though many of those working in non-climatised rooms felt the temperature to be too high, there were on the whole fewer complaints than among those working in climatised rooms.

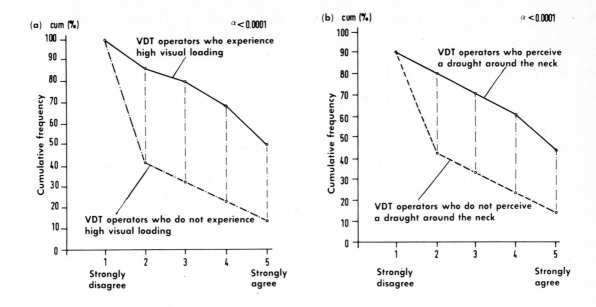

Figure 5.27 Subjective ratings of complaints about (a) draughts around the neck and throat and (b) burning sensations in the eyes, showing the correlation between the incidence of a draught in the region of the head among VDT operators in climatised work rooms and the incidence of visual discomfort.

PSYCHOLOGICAL ASPECTS

How to measure mental work load? This is a problem that industrial psychologists have wrestled with for many years in order to provide a quantitative way of describing the sensitivity of the individual to the various factors which constitute the situation 'man at work'. At present, there is no dearth of theoretical descriptions of the psychological aspects of man's relationships and reactions to work and his working environment. Some are able to satisfactorily explain certain practical observations of fatigue and individual behaviour, but none has yet been able to produce convincing or reliable correlation with all aspects of psychological behaviour in the everyday working environment.

Most techniques of work structure and response analysis approach the problem from two directions, namely by studying the *objective* and *subjective* reactions to given task and occupational situations. In taking the objective approach, the task is analysed into its structural components and the human demands of the task are described in terms of the individual requirements associated with each phase or component of the task. This approach to 'measuring' the mental work load on the individual at work is satisfactory provided that the components of 'mental work load' are well enough defined and that there is some yardstick by which the intensity of this type of load can be measured. This is one of the drawbacks in attempting to define levels of mental work load, as it were, from the outside.

It might be argued that since the individual himself is in the best position to describe the nature and intensity of this type of work load, the problem is best examined from *his* point of view, i.e. from the inside. In subjective approaches to task analysis, therefore, the individual himself is requested to describe his working situation in the light of his own experience. On the face of things, this would seem a logical way of approaching the problem but the technique is not without some drawbacks. The first problem is that of 'asking the right questions'. As with the analysis of more objectively definable types of reaction, it is also necessary to begin an investigation of this kind with a clear understanding and definition of the components of mental work load. A sufficiently detailed understanding of the nature of the task in question is also necessary if the questions are to be meaningful and expressed in the right way. The success of an investigation of this kind depends as much on the *way* a subject is questionned as on the subject and scope of the questions themselves. Most people have considerable difficulty in describing their reactions to a particular situation. In formulating a survey of this kind, therefore, the questions must be as explicit, unambiguous and as relevant as possible, and the way in which the response is invited should be similarly unambiguous and should aid the subject in his or her ability to express a reliable opinion.

Techniques of subjective or experience analysis of man at work have been undertaken many times and in a wide variety of industrial environments. But for the time being, there is still a lack of any standardised procedure with which to make reliable comparisons between the levels of mental work load associated with different types of task. Neither is it usually possible to compare levels of mental work load associated with a particular task but one which is performed in different ways, e.g. as the result of changes in task organisation or production machinery due, say, to technological innovation.

The study of mental work load

As individuals, and depending upon our physical and psychological make-up, each of us has certain possibilities and limitations as regards what we can accomplish at work. If the organisational and technical aspects of our work and the environment in which we work fail to take these possibilities and limitations into account, we will experience some form of 'overloading' which might be physical, psychological or both. As individuals, we also tend to respond differently to changes in the organisational and technical structure of our work. A change in procedure that might prove to be a stimulus to one may well prove to be a burden or source of pressure to another. Much depends on the relationship we have to our work and to attitudes which stem from a sense of identity and involvement, personal motivation, etc.

In most traditional approaches to analysing fatigue at work, the human body was itself likened to a machine among the positive characteristics of which are the ability to perform a given task under a variety of conditions and to derive satisfaction from so doing. Among the negative characteristics of the human 'machine' are tendency to fatigue, the reduction in performance in the short term and, depending upon the task in question, the possibility of health damage in the longer term. In the early days of fatigue reseach, attention was mainly focussed on muscular fatigue. In heavy, manual types of work, i.e. those types of occupation that were most extensively studied, bodily damage could easily occur due to overexertion and to the onesidedness of physical loading at work. But this approach has since changed. Many of the leading authorities in this field have not been able to find any tangible distinction between physical and mental fatigue since mental fatigue, like physical fatigue, is also closely linked to the change in function of the human organism.

In analysing the mental work load on an individual at work, therefore, the main objective is to determine which personal, occupational and environmental factors are responsible for the loading and to what extent. Only then is it possible to make meaningful suggestions as to how the psychological demands on the individual at work can be reduced and by what means. A prime goal in this type of investigation is to determine the types of fatigue to which the subject is prone, the degree of fatigue, its effects on the person concerned and the circumstances which are more or less conducive to the progression of fatigue. It is also important that the disposition and personality of the person concerned is examined since this too can have a significant influence on his or her relationships within and outside of the working environment.

It was mentioned earlier that the problem of studying fatigue and the psychological aspects of man at work is usually approached from two directions, i.e. by studying the objective and subjective reactions of an individual to his work and working environment. These types of reaction can be investigated in terms of:

- individual *experience*, e.g. personal opinion, subjective response,
- the levels and changes in levels of *performance* or *productivity*, e.g. by measuring error rates, changes in mean levels and fluctuations of output, etc., and
- *physiological reaction*, e.g. EEG activity, breathing rate, pulse rate, etc.

Since the beginning of the century, there have been many attempts to define the characteristics of physical and mental fatigue on the basis of these three types of reaction. From a practical point of view, however, the basic problem lies in the fact that, when considered individually, none provides a sufficiently reliable and quantitative way of describing all of the relevant aspects of the response of a given individual to physical and psychological activity. In order that the results from such an investigation can be considered meaningful and trustworthy, therefore, studies of this kind must necessarily be broad in scope. Even so, the measurement and analysis of fatigue and mental work load in an industrial environment is a very difficult and complex undertaking. Nevertheless, the need for investigations of this kind has continued to grow with the realisation that, in many occupational environments, the problems of physiological discomfort and disorder cannot be separated from the psychological aspects of the task.

In spite of the fact that fatigue is still largely an undefined concept, the symptoms of fatigue are manyfold. Some of them can only be described in subjective terms, i.e. on the basis of the experience of the individual and his or her ability to describe the experience. Others can be examined in more objective terms.

The objective symptoms of fatigue depend, but to varying extents, on disturbances of the following types of process:

- reception and perception of information,
- coordination,
- attention and concentration,
- thought,
- motor and control functions, and
- social relationships.

Subjective methods of investigation

There are basically two ways of inviting an individual to describe his reaction to a particular factor or condition related to his job, a particular aspect of his job or the conditions under which he works. Both types of investigation involve the use of questionnaires and interviews, the main function of which is to elicit information about the main components of fatigue and individual reaction and to do so in a way that maximises the ability of the individual to express his experience as accurately and reliably as possible. By providing some form of scale to help the subject express his response to a particular question, the analysis of this type of investigation is also made very much easier. With the appropriate choice of questions, this type of analysis can also aid in the analysis of the more objective symptoms of fatigue and psychological loading.

The first type of approach involves asking the subject to describe his reaction to a particular question at that particular point in time, i.e. to invite an immediately applicable response. In a survey of this kind, a number of key questions are formulated and the 'answer' is expressed in the form of one number selected from a given scale of numbers which describes the intensity of the subject's reaction at that time. Taking the second approach, the subject is invited to respond to the question in the light of his previous experience, i.e. to comment retrospectively. This is a well-proven and quite reliable approach to this type of subjective investigation and one which lends itself quite readily to the kind of multifactor analysis that is necessary in order to identify the probable causes of the subject's responses.

Insofar that certain forms of physical and mental fatigue and the way that a subject might describe problems of this kind may be quite strongly influenced by particular aspects of the subject's personality and attitude, this type of survey must also seek to establish a profile in respect of self factors such as these, e.g. emotional stability, introversion/extroversion etc. It is is also necessary to investigate the factors which lead to a greater or lesser degree of motivation on the part of the subject, e.g. greater financial reward, the desire for more responsibility,praise, recognition, success etc.

Performance methods of investigation

In studying fatigue and psychological behaviour at work on the basis of performance, it is presumed that the degree of fatigue can be measured in terms of the change in performance or output during the period of the investigation. In analysing fatigue in relation to VDT tasks, the following three measures of performance have been considered:

- reduced vigilance for visual stimuli, reduced speed of perception, and misinterpretation,
- reduced eye and hand coordination, and
- reduced attentiveness and concentration, increased frequency of errors, reduced general level of performance, increase in performance fluctuation.

The main drawback in attempting to measure the degree of fatigue in terms of changes in productivity, error rate etc., is that the subject is often found not to suffer a reduction in performance capability in spite of the fact he or she is clearly aware of sensations of fatigue. Neither is it uncommon for the subject to show a measurable increase in the mean level of performance, e.g. by making fewer mistakes. Although this might, at first sight, seem paradoxical, this type of behaviour corresponds very well with the theories of activation and compensation.

In spite of the fact that one may be well aware of certain symptoms of fatigue, it is possible to compensate for the tendency to lose concentration, to slow down or stop working, or to become less attentive by means of increased activation. In this way, the subject may even be able to cope with a higher work load in spite of the sensations of fatigue. In the course of the present investigations it has also been found that with more demanding types of task, i.e. tasks carrying a high level of responsibility, requirements as regards accuracy etc, tend to encourage higher levels of activation in order to compensate for the effects of fatigue. But this is probably not without its price. The physical loading, e.g. higher heart beat rate, which is associated with higher levels of activation is also an important human factor since this may have a direct bearing on the effect of physical and mental fatigue on the private life of the individual.

Even though changes in the level of performance may not necessarily provide a reliable measure of fatigue at the end of a working day, the time needed to run down the high level of activation is also an important human factor since this may have a direct bearing on the effect of physical and mental fatigue on the private life of the individual.

Physiological methods of investigation

On the face of things, physiological examination appears to offer a useful way of investigating fatigue at work. This is certainly true to some extent, but investigations of this kind are usually very time consuming and often require sophisticated types of instrumentation and expertise which may not be suited to 'on-the-spot' types of investigation. Furthermore, if the test instrumentation is such that the behaviour of the subject is affected, e.g. by restricted freedom of movement or other types of inconvenience or discomfort, this type of investigation may result in a quite uncharacteristic type of behaviour on the part of the subject thereby introducing bias in the results. In addition, to draw meaningful conclusions, the number of subjects must necessarily be very large, and the costs of undertaking this type of investigation on a industrial scale may be and often are prohibitive.

Part of the difficulty can be overcome by making use of only a limited number of subjects, but only when the risk that the results might be unrepresentative, unreliable or difficult to interpret is fully appreciated. In addition, if the subject is aware that he is one of a select group of subjects, he may, in the beginning at least, react quite uncharacteristically. A feature of all investigations of this kind, therefore, is the need to provide a 'working in' period during which the subject can get accustomed to being the subject of an investigation.

Alienation

The term *alienation* is used by social scientists to characterise the difference between the condition of an individual that would exist by virtue of his own 'nature', and the state that is compelled by virtue of the culture in which he exists. This enforced adjustment on the part of an individual can be a major source of inner conflict, sometimes to the extent that the individual may temporarily or even permanently question his own identity.

Although this type of conflict is a source of pressure, this is not to say that the complete absense of this type of pressure represents some kind of ideal situation. The history of social and cultural development provides ample evidence to show that pressure is an essential ingredient of progress. Societies develop, not when the external pressures on them are minimal, but rather when they are optimal. And precisely the same is true of the development of an individual: the ideal situation is that with the optimum level of demand or challenge.

Alienation is an extremely important aspect of mans behaviour in his working environment. This is particularly true in respect of the reaction of an individual or a professional group to changes in the technical or organisational aspects of their work or particular phases of it.

There are many forms of pressure and demand to which we might be subjected as work, and we tend to view these pressures differently according to whether or not we consider that they constitute a positive or negative aspect of the job. To illustrate this effect, we might consider the case of a newspaper editor. Newspaper journalists and editors are highly motivated and regard their work as being mentally creative. Tenacity and the ability to work creatively under pressure are among the hallmarks of a good journalist. Provided that the pressures to which the journalist feels himself subject are, so to speak, of a 'professional' nature, i.e. concerned with the act of journalism, the pressures are accepted as part of the job and may even be considered to be a source of stimulation rather than alienation. But if he is subjected to other sources of frustration on a level other than the professional level, e.g. concerned with the 'mechanics' of being a journalist, these frustrations may contribute to a certain degree of dissatisfaction and alienation. Although, in this example, we have taken the situation of a journalist, precisely the same is true of any professional category, where certain types of pressure are considered 'all part of the job' - and sometimes among the more stimulating parts - whilst other types of pressure, often seemingly trivial in relation to professional pressures, may be considered intolerable and may actually become a hindrance to the work.

Although factory workers are often regarded to be alienated in their working environment, many authorities in this field believe that, in modern times, many categories of office worker can experience still higher levels of alienation. In any professional group, this may come about for a variety of reasons some of which may lie within the working environment and others in the general social environment. The phrase 'the job isn't what it used to be' is a symptom of alienation and reflects a sudden or progressive loss of identity with the job, perhaps as the result of some degree of de-skilling caused by higher levels of automation.

The use of the term 'alienation' is often rather diffuse and imprecise, but alienation can be viewed on at least two levels, i.e. the social level and the psychological level.There can be no doubt that there is a very close relationship between these types of alienation and the optimal fulfillment of the function of working, i.e. individual, economic and social goals. The social level of alienation is characterised by the situation in which the the individual's job in the overall production process, the work and the results of his work have become independent of him as an individual. In other words, he no longer feels master of his job but feels mastered by his job. This type of alienation is not linked to a particular technology but does reflect what, in many occupational groups, appears to be a growing social-political phenomenon.

Of more immediate concern to the individual however, is the psychological level of alienation. He may feel powerless, 'just a number' or a 'cog in the machinery of a large organisation', as someone doing a job that he does not see the sense of, as stressed but nevertheless isolated within the working environment, self-alienated due to the inability to reach the goals and satisfy the expectations that he has set for himself.

Modern computer and office business systems are highly sophisticated tools, the correct application of which can take away the drudgery and tedium of many types of hitherto labour and time intensive clerical and administrative tasks, e.g. cost and wage accounting, bookkeeping, etc. It may seem strange, therefore, that the use of computers in the office environment is often referred to in terms of 'machine control'. One reason, perhaps, is the fact that clerical staff are very often willing to make use of and accept computer systems as an auxilliary aid but may resent the use of a computer in performing tasks which detracts from the individual's sense of authority and value. In addition, prior to the introduction of computer systems into the office environment, office personnel worked with paper 'storage'. Albeit that this way of handling information is usually rather cumbersome, information processing and storage on paper is a tangible and visible activity. In a computer system, on the other hand, information processing is an abstract operation and one which requires that those making use of the computer comply with the mechanical and operational constraints of the computer. In many modern office environments, large numbers of personnel work with a computer system using a VDT as an input and control device. Whilst doing the job, the VDT provides the operator with the sole means of 'seeing' what the computer is actually doing. In order to be able to work with the system and the VDT, the operator must learn at least:

- how to operate the alphanumeric keyboard,
- how to operate a function keyboard in the most appropriate way,
- the main computer commands and coding instructions, and
- the facilities of the programmes that are available to him and how they can be accessed and used.

In order to use the system most effectively, he must also learn at what times he can work most effectively with the computer, how long each of the main processes lasts etc. The user of a computer system must also learn that the output of the desired information is only possible:

- if the correct input has been made,
- when the computer is ready and available to process the information and send it back.

The latter point is particularly important in many practical situations. A newspaper editor, for example, places great store on the speed with which he receives the processed text from the computer; he wants it as quickly as possible. But depending upon the design of the system, he may have to wait an indefinite period while the computer processes the input of another editor who works with the same system and enjoys higher priority or calculates wages and salaries if the system is so designed.

In the course of these investigations, it has been found that journalists tend to view their job as being:

- interesting, demanding and of a variable nature,
- such to provide a high level of personal responsibility and autonomy,
- such as to give the individual journalist the feeling that he is his own master,
- stimulating and motivating to such an extent that the high work loading is not felt to constitute a correspondingly high pressure,
- of a value that the journalist is aware of and can himself appreciate.

The journalist works under the pressure of time. The quantity of his work is not usually calculable in advance, and the quality of his effort cannot be measured in terms of quantity. The product of his labours has a high social relevance and is constantly open to scrutiny and criticism. In journalism, therefore, as in most other professional groups, the individual tends to react with more sensitivity to the idea that his job may be constrained or controlled by a machine. In being aware of his social role, the journalist may even react with more suspicion than other groups to this idea. Because the work of a journalist is of a creative nature, it is the creative, and not the mechanical processes of the work that is of greatest concern to the journalist. To most journalists, replacing the traditional tools of journalism, i.e. pen, paper and typewriter, by a computer system using VDTs as the input device, is acceptable provided that the use of this type of tool does not restrict his editorial independence or inhibit the creative aspects of his work.

Generally speaking, the risk of frustration and alienation increases if the individual feels inhibited or constrained by the 'mechanics' of his profession. This may also reduce the identity of a person with the product of his work, and since this is one of the most important components of job satisfaction, the effects of technological innovation should be carefully considered from this point of view.

Alienation and machine control

In most work processes and organisations, there is an unmistakable structure of authority. Due to the hierarchical nature of any enterprise or the multimomemt nature of a given type of occupation, one man controls another. Within to certain limitations, this is a situation that we are used to and prepared to accept. But generally speaking, man is not prepared to accept that his work is controlled by a machine. Whilst the control of one man over another is an attribute of social existence, the control of man by a machine can be regarded as a deficiency in the concept and use of the machine and one which should be put right.

The classical example of the control of human work by a machine is conveyer belt types of work. The pace and rhythm of the belt dictates when and where the individual must execute his task. Another example is the older type of telex machine with mechanically reduced typing speed.

In the modern industrial environment, there are many examples of production machinery, and the computer is certainly one of these examples, which have altered the balance of control between man and machine. Computers are ideally suited to performing the repetitive and tedious types of job that, when manually performed, result in a monotonous type of task activity. But removing some of the burden is not without its price. A computer does only what it is instructed to do. In human relationships, we are tolerant of error and even semantic mistakes. In man-computer relationships, however, there is no margin for error. The computer is only able to act on such commands as are issued in its own and very precise language. Unlike the human being, a computer has no ability to *induce*; it can only *deduce*.

There are some occupational groups whose task is it to live with these peculiarities of computer systems, e.g. programmers, systems engineers. During the past few years, their efforts have had a rich reward. Today we speak in terms of 'software packages' in contrast to the tightly restricted programming capacity of the earlier types of computer. The VDT has added a new dimension to the accessing of the data storage and programming capacity of computers. The cost of data storage has shown a steady decline thanks to the birth of the 'chip' and the growth of microprocessor technology.

Control of performance by the computer

The use of the computer to control individual levels of performance, e.g. by counting input or production rates for piece-work rate assessment, can constitute a significant source of mental work loading. Part of the reason for this lies in the fact that the employee fears or resents an anonymous type of control over his job. If the quality of the work being performed cannot be measured in the more quantitative terms of productivity, the idea that the computer may be used in this way tends, in any case, to be viewed with great suspicion. In the present investigations, it was found that people have strong feelings that their work is the subject of control if the job is of a more routine nature, e.g. data entry, and all the more so if they are performing piece work.

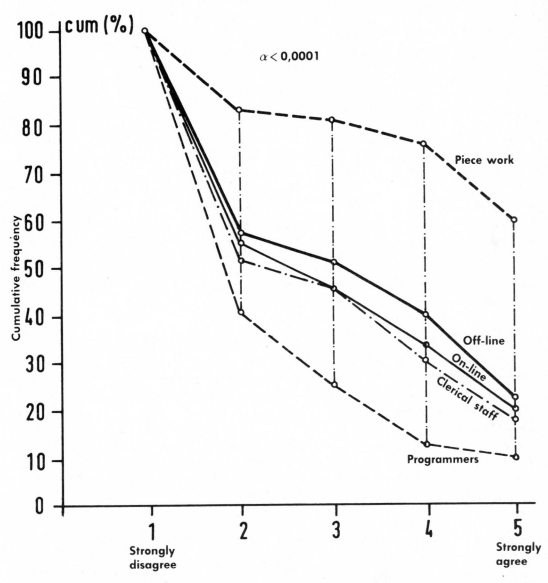

Figure 5.28 The proportion of VDT operators performing piece work with performance control by the computer who complain of being 'strongly controlled at work' is more than six times higher than the group experiencing the least control, i.e. computer programmers.

This and other characteristics of routine work can lead to a higher degree of fatigue depending upon the organisation of the job. To test this idea, a sample of 50 VDT input typists performing piece work and 130 VDT input typists doing the same kind of work but not on piece rates were questionned before and after work in order to investigate their personal conditions. In the second of the two groups, performance was controlled only on the basis of group performance. The results from this investigation showed that the changes in factors such as sociability, frame of mind, state of stress, fatigue and inner security, were much greater among the computer controlled typists than in the other group.

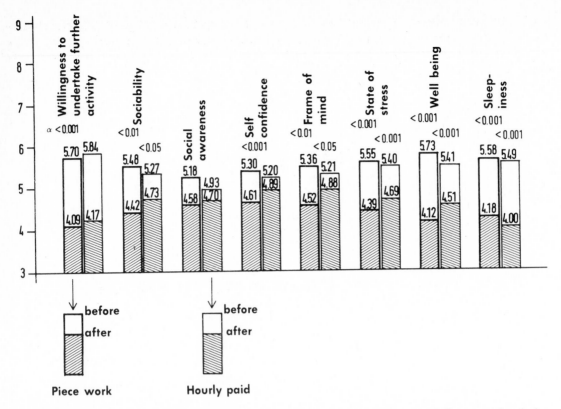

Figure 5.29 *There are large differences in the way piece work and hourly paid VDT copy typists feel before and after work. After work, both groups are reluctant to undertake further activities involving effort, and both suffer a decrease in the desire for social contact but more so in the case of piece workers. Among both groups, tension builds up during the day but piece workers experience a greater level of fatigue and decrease in general feeling of well-being.*

Fatigue and monotony

It is a well established fact that monotonous types of work lead more rapidly to feelings of fatigue. To investigate the relationship between monotony and fatigue in connection with VDT tasks, more than 1000 VDT operators in different jobs were surveyed. The results showed that those with the most onesided types of activity, i.e. input copy typists doing piece work, find it necessary to summon up the greatest level of will-power in order to continue working. Among professional groups such as programmers and editors, hardly anyone gave a positive response to this question. The response to the question concerning the exertion of will-power correlates very well with complaints about fatigue. For example, only 10% of the programmers gave the strongest response to questions concerning fatigue, compared with 55% of the input and copy typists.

Fatigue/monotony relation and loss of qualification

If the introduction of a computer system changes a more challenging job into a more routine one, the response of the subjects to monotony is significantly increased.

The results from this investigation showed that about 20 to 30% of input typists and about 10% of other categories of clerical worker complained of monotony. But in surveying VDT operators who were employed in more routine types of task than was the case prior to the introduction of a VDT system, it was found that 60% complained of monotony although the nature of the job was very similar to that being performed by other typist groups with a much lower frequency of complaints concerning monotony. This group also experiences a level of fatigue which is much higher even than among typists engaged in piece work.

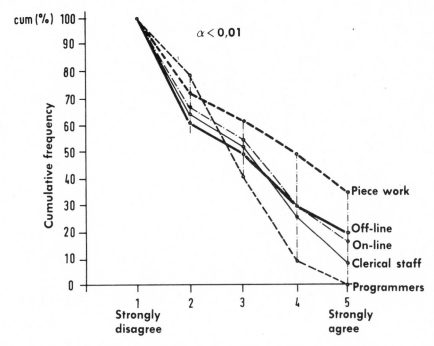

Figure 5.30 If a person does not like his job, he must summon up more will-power to go to work. The percentage of each sample group who experienced this effect was 0% in the case of computer programmers and 37% among piece rate copy typists using VDTs. The more routine the job, the higher is the percentage of those employed who are conscious of this effort of will power.

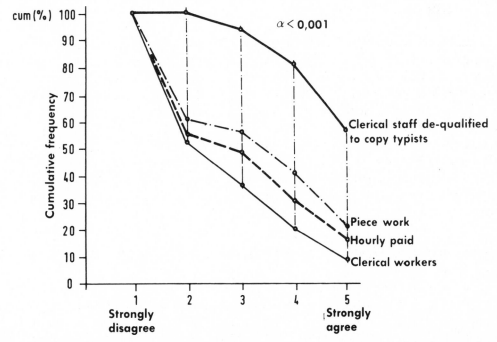

Figure 5.31 The feeling of monotony correlates strongly with the quality of the job. Copy typists experience a greater degree of monotony than other groups of clerical worker using VDTs. It was found that clerical staff whose work had been de-qualified to that of copy typist experienced the highest degree of monotony, 60% compared with 10% for normal clerical type work.

This kind of fatigue is not caused as the result of a high level of performance required by the job, but by a feeling of alienation. This is also reflected in the response of those surveyed as to whether or not they found their job to be meaningful.

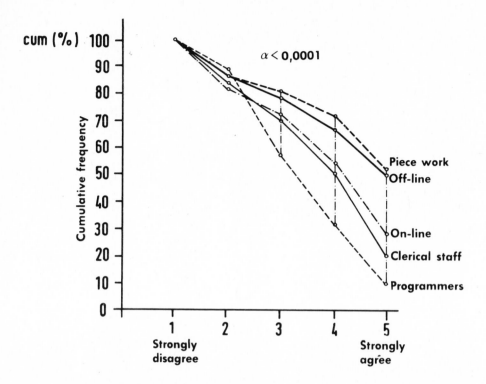

Figure 5.32 *More routine jobs are more likely to induce feelings of extreme fatigue. In responding to the question 'my work is very fatiguing', only 10% of computer programmers but more than 50% of copy typists would strongly agree with the statement.*

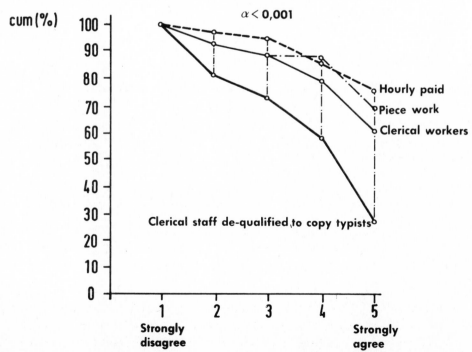

Figure 5.33 *The problem of alienation among clerical staff showing the effects of de-qualification. Only 28% of de-qualified clerical workers could strongly agree that their job had 'meaning'.*

Only 28% of those engaged in tasks with a lower level of qualification than earlier found their job 'meaningful'. This is a clear sign of alienation. So, when introducing a computer system and restructuring the work procedures accordingly, very careful attention should be paid to this type of problem. New computer systems are expected to be 'interactive' but neither they, nor the people who use them can function to the best advantage if the human interface does not work properly. This will always be the case if challenge is replaced by routine.

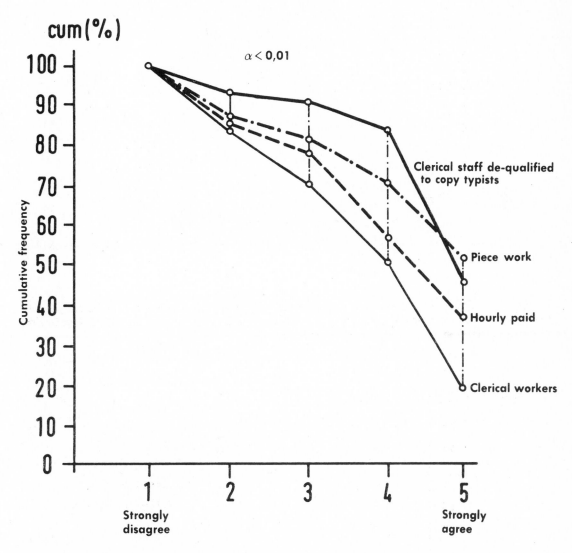

Figure 5.34 The experience of extreme fatigue among clerical workers using VDTs. The dequalified clerical workers experienced higher levels of fatigue than piece work copy typists in spite of less performance.

Job satisfaction

Although there is no precise definition of 'job satisfaction', one can say that it is an attitude, the components of which are borne of feelings of satisfaction and dissatisfaction in all aspects of the relationships of man at work. It is a concept that is very closely linked to motivation, the influencing factors of which can be divided into two categories, i.e. *motivators* or factors creating satisfaction, and *hygiene factors* or factors creating dissatisfaction.

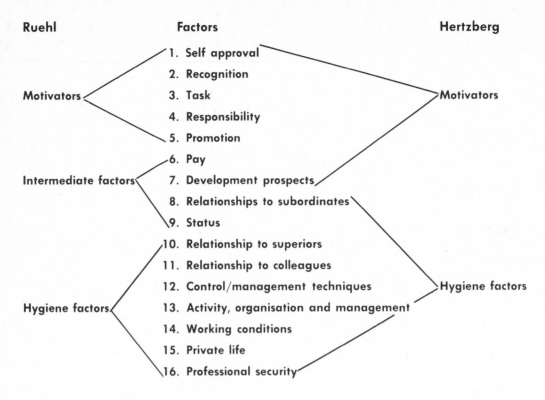

Ruehl	Factors	Hertzberg
Motivators	1. Self approval 2. Recognition 3. Task 4. Responsibility 5. Promotion	Motivators
Intermediate factors	6. Pay 7. Development prospects 8. Relationships to subordinates 9. Status	
Hygiene factors	10. Relationship to superiors 11. Relationship to colleagues 12. Control/management techniques 13. Activity, organisation and management 14. Working conditions 15. Private life 16. Professional security	Hygiene factors

Figure 5.35 The motivator and hygiene factors of job satisfaction according to RUEHL and HERZBERG. See Ref. C.2

In taking this approach to describing job satisfaction, it is quite clear that job satisfaction and its opposite are best viewed as two separate dimensions and not as two poles of a scale in a single dimension.

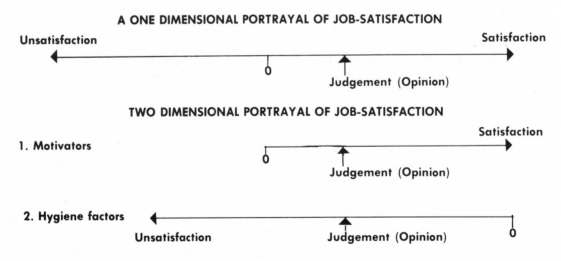

Figure 5.36 The scale of job satisfaction.

A lack of motivators, in itself, does not result in job dissatisfaction. By a similar token, when an individual positively judges the hygiene factors which he considers most relevant to his working situation, e.g. pleasant working conditions, this does not necessarily indicate job satisfaction. Only when the individual senses a lack of motivators and at the same time adversely judges the hygiene factors does the slide towards job dissatisfaction begin.

In addition to the groups of factors that fall into the 'motivator' and 'hygiene factor' categories, there is a group of intermediate factors which, if they are positively judged, act as motivators and if they are negatively judged, act as hygiene factors. This group includes pay, relationships with subordinates, development prospects, status etc.

The results from a recent U.S. government survey have shown that there is a very close relationship between job satisfaction and the 'quality' of life, including physical and psychological health. This survey has shown that job satisfaction and life expectancy, heart diseases, stomach ulcers, arthritis and epileptic seizure are mutually related to a very significant degree. Aggression and frustration at work is often reflected in family relationships and can also lead to aggressive attitudes in social and political life.

To some extent, the results of this survey conflict with the theory of 'compensation' according to which restrictions which are experienced during working time are compensated for in private life through a less restricted way of life. As this survey has shown, in fact, negative factors in one's working life similarly affect one's private and social relationships.

At this point, we might consider which of the motivator and hygiene factors of job satisfaction can directly or indirectly be affected by the introduction of a new technology at work and how they may be affected.

Factor	Effect	Comment
16. Professional security	Yes, direct	If former qualifications or skills are made redundant
15. Private life	(?) indirect	Depending on job satisfaction
14. Working conditions	Yes, direct	No explanation needed
13. Organisation	Yes, direct/indirect	If the work organisation is altered
12. Management technique	(?) indirect	If the work organisation is altered
11. Relationships with colleagues	Yes, indirect	E.g. if a working group is disbanded
10. Realtionships with superiors	(?)	If the work organisation is altered
9. Status	Yes, direct	See 16
8. Relationships with subordinates	Yes, direct/indirect	If the work organisation is altered see also 11
7. Development prospects	Yes, direct/indirect	Higher value tasks may go to specialists, Qualifications may be less necessary
6. Pay	Yes, direct	See 7 and 9
5. Promotion	Yes, direct	See 7 and 9
4. Responsibility	Yes, direct	E.g. different division of responsibility, see also 3
3. Task	Yes, direct	E.g. different task structure and allocation
2. Recognition	(?)	If the work organisation is altered
1. Self approval	Yes, direct/indirect	See 'Alienation and machine control'

Figure 5.37 The direct and indirect influence of the introduction of a new technology on job satisfaction.

It can be seen, therefore, that nearly all of the factors that contribute to job satisfaction can be affected by the introduction of modern technology and, using this table, each person can construct an impression of how his own situation may be likely to change.

This table also illustrates the criteria that must be satisfied if a new technology, e.g. VDT and computer technology, is to be introduced in a way that does not conflict with the main functions of work, i.e. economic, social and individual goals. It should also be noted that the improvement of working conditions as part of social development is an irreversible cultural process.

Work allocation and job satisfaction

Work and task allocation and the division of responsibility are basic factors as far as job satisfaction is concerned. Generally speaking, satisfaction with the job itself is very much more important to us than satisfaction with workplace conditions and circumstances. In the course of the present investigations, it was found that some professional groups are quite unaware of poor workplace conditions provided that the quality of their work is not affected. In some other groups, the main contributing factors were feelings of a lack of significance and a lack of meaning in the work.It was also found that, among many groups of clerical worker, the lack of demand on their mental abilities was a major contributor to job dissatisfaction. This is by no means a new observation but is one which reflects an important feature of job satisfaction, namely that job satisfaction arises from the complexity of the duties performed.

Nevertheless, many workers themselves express a desire for more routine in their work, and even among those who look for greater complexity or challenge, the job obviously cannot be complicated indefinitely. If this were the case, work allocation and the delegation of responsibility would become senseless. Individual expectations as regards work and task content vary according to the principles by which they, as individuals, judge the motivators and hygiene factors that apply to their job. For example, in a survey among a large number of VDT operators engaged in a very repetitive type of task, it was found that 30% would be prepared to take on greater responsibility for the same wage whilst a further 50% would take on greater responsibility for a higher wage. In other words, the desire for greater responsibility with less routine was a common desire but payment was ranked quite differently as one of the motivating factors.

Clearly there is an optimal complexity associated with a particular type of job, the level of which varies from one person to another. Work allocation is, therefore, an important factor as far as the effectiveness of the job is concerned. It is also an important consideration in reducing work load, and most critics of work allocation tend not to disagree as far as the principle is concerned but more in respect of its degree in particular job environments.

The degree of work allocation

One of the main goals of social and work scientists is to find ways of matching the activity of working to man's abilities in the most favourable or optimum way. This was as much the goal of the so-called 'psychotechnologists' of the 1920's as it is today, but in our times, we have more ways and means at our disposal to help make this possible.

The computer, if used effectively, could be one of these means.

A worthwhile goal in any work context is that of freeing the job from its more repetitive elements in order to make more time available for the more creative or challenging parts of the job. Take the case of the sports editor of a newspaper as an example. With the aid of a computer system, there would no longer be any necessity to draw up the football league tables by hand; the names of the clubs can be very easily stored within the computer. This leaves him more time to write his commentaries and check those of the other sports writers. In researching an article, say on the history of the Derby, he can draw the names and data of the Derby winners from the data store, provided of course that this store exists in his system, without having to spend perhaps several hours in background research.

Enlarging the work field can be accomplished in several ways. *Job enlargement* describes an increase in the content of the work by allocating new operations thus giving a quantitative increase in the size of the work field. Taking the example of the sports writer, this would be the case if he were made responsible for, say, tennis as well as football. *Job enrichment* implies a qualitative change in the work field. For example, in the previous example, the work field would have become enriched if the sports writer himself considered it to be more satisfying that the scope of his job had been enlarged in this way. *Job rotation* implies some variety in the way a job with a number of repetitive elements is tackled. Our sports writer, for example, does not work with figures and numbers on one day and with commentaries on another. He himself has a certain degree of freedom to structure his approach to the more routine and the more creative parts of his job. The work field can also be enlarged by *creating group autonomy* by appropriately planning and sharing the work load.

The creation of autonomous work groups is one of the most progressive ways of qualitatively enlarging the work field. The editorial department of a newspaper provides a good example of this type of division of work and responsibility. Each editorial group is responsible for its own field of activity, the division of task responsibility within its own field and for the quality of its work whilst maintaining close coordination with the other editorial groups.

This brief description of some of the ways in which human fields of working may be developed helps to illustrate the trend to find better ways of improving the quality of work. As such, they have no special correlation with working with VDTs but in some cases they may have.

Job quality and job satisfaction

Job enlargement is a quantitative increase of the workfield that does not necessarily lead to greater job satisfaction. If the job, in its initial form, is sufficiently large in scope to be satisfying, the introduction of additional job elements would lead to a decrease of job satisfaction rather than to a further increase. If the increase in the number of job elements requires more and difficult learning and a new and permanent form of adaptation to the new elements, job enlargement may prove to be a burden rather than a source of enrichment.

Job enrichment on the other hand can be seen as a positive effort to improve job satisfaction, particularly if the creative elements of the job can be increased at the expense of more repetitive and monotonous elements.

Job rotation helps to minimise onesidedness in the work loading on an individual. If job rotation is accompanied by the introduction of new elements into the job, this may require more learning, more adaptation and perhaps also to the need for greater effort, with the result that his workload may be increased rather than decreased. Job rotation does not necessarily mean a qualitatively more rewarding or satisfying task but in many working situations can be an effective way of combatting monotony.

The concept of *autonomous work groups* has been ranked among the most progressive approaches to improving the situation of man at work. But the approach is not without some attendant problems. In some industrial environments, and particularly in production environments, pressures for higher performance can come from within the group and from neighbouring groups as well as 'from the top'. In many cases, the 'group' can more effectively control the individual performance of its members than a manager would find it possible to do. Other problems can arise among management staff who might possibly have some difficulty in adapting their own working style and relationships at work in accordance with the changed conditions.

The introduction of new work structures is essentially a social problem. The costs of poorly designed work procedures are eventually paid by the community as a whole. Here, only the problems of work load and job satisfaction have been considered, and then only briefly. But one cannot separate the various aspects of job quality, work load and pay from each other. Every change in these conditions is the subject of negotiation between the social partners concerned, i.e. trade unions and employers. It should not be forgotten, therefore, that job satisfaction is only one problem, although a very important one, in a much larger complex.

Workload and time pressure

One of the distinguishing features of work planning in some industries is that it is not always possible. To some extent, this is true of the press. News comes unplanned so that the workload is unpredictable. This means that both man and machine must be flexible in being able to adapt to changing pressures of work. Every period of calm is followed by a period of hectic activity.

Another feature of the press is that a job, e.g. writing a story, is never really finished. To the journalist, the story can always be altered and improved and this is one of the reasons why a newspaper journalist and editor works under time pressure. News also loses its topicality after a short period of time. Old news is no news! The journalist also works to a deadline, when everything must be ready, but to the editorial staff of a newspaper, what this 'everything' includes is not exactly known until the closing minutes.

When a computer system is installed in an environment such as this, it is essential that the various parts of the system do what they are intended to do and do so with the maximum reliability if those using the system are to have confidence in this way of doing the job. The meaning of 'reliability' in this sense varies according to the function of the individual and his level of responsibility. To illustrate this, 49 editors and 62 input typists in a leading European news agency which handles as many as 4000 lines of text on VDTs per hour were asked:

> a) if technical disturbances were a rare occurrence at their workplace, and
> b) if they found these types of technical breakdown and failure to be a major source of annoyance.

All of those questionned were working with the same system and with identical equipment, and the results were as follows. 62% of the editors and 30% of the input typists said that technical disturbances were not a rare occurrence. 62% of the editors and 37% of the input typists felt that breakdowns of this kind were a major source of annoyance. Since both groups worked with the same system, the different responses were not caused by the characteristics of the system. Since the technical disturbances were not caused by the individual VDTs but by the system, both groups were also judging the same level of unreliability. The main reason for the difference in response lies in the different function and level of responsibility of the two groups. The input typists do not edit. The text which they enter into the system is first edited by the editor who is responsible for the content and style of each story that he releases.

As far as the relationship between the requirements of each type of job and the reliability of the system is concerned, it should be noted that 62% and 37% of the subject groups were annoyed by technical disturbances which occurred just as often for both groups and then relatively infrequently. Had breakdowns occurred more often, they would probably have tried to find some way of making up for lost time and this would have involved a change in the basic procedure associated with each task.

Systems response times can also be a cause of mental loading and the results from the same survey showed that the editors experienced a response time of 6 seconds to be too long and frustrating. In making simple editing changes to text using a VDT, one needs response times of no more than about 2 seconds. This does not apply to complex functions such as hyphenation and justification. In an environment such as this, therefore, the reaction of the individual editors to indefinite response times between seconds and minutes as is the case in some systems might well be imagined.

The time pressure in jobs such as these can be reduced, but not totally avoided, if the system is reliable, flexible and fast. An attempt to do away with the time pressure factor altogether would, in the newspaper industry for example, bring the whole job into question since journalists understand their function to be that of supplying information in the shortest possible time. It is the technical causes of delays that is the main source of annoyance, not the self-imposed time pressure.

Job organisation and physical demand

The results from these investigations have also demonstrated how the loading associated with more routine types of VDT task can lead to physiological problems. It was found, for example, that off-line input typists seek orthopedic treatment for backaches more frequently than any other category of clerical worker using VDTs. This underlines the need to put computer technology to work in order to create less routine work and not to do the reverse.

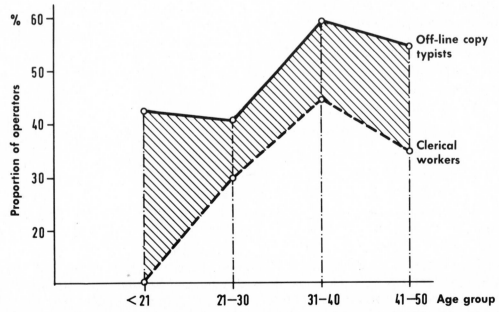

Figure 5.38 The effect of job routine on the incidence of backaches in clerical staff. The first group, off-line copy typists, experience more frequent pains in the back and a higher percentage of this category seeks treatment. The percentage is significantly lower among other clerical staff.

Ergonomic requirements of VDTs and activation

A higher degree of activation indicates a higher degree of work loading. By measuring the levels of activation in different professional groups using VDTs, it was found that the highest level of activation is experienced by flight plan controllers with high levels of individual responsibility. Certain categories of clerical staff, particularly those with difficult visual tasks, e.g. using other types of display in addition to the VDT, were found to rank next, and these were followed by off-line input typists and other groups of clerical worker. Computer programmers belong to the group with the lowest degree of activation. Compared with other occupational groups, VDT users are placed in the medium range of the activation range.

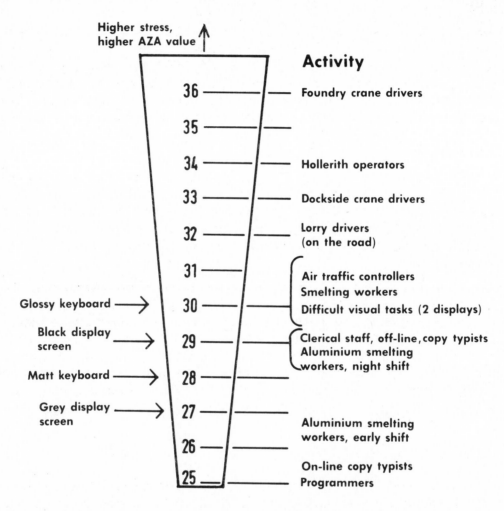

Figure 5.39 A comparison between the activation of VDT operators and other professional groups, using the AZA scale of general central activation proposed by BARTENWERFER, Ref.B.7. This diagram also illustrates the differences in activation caused by certain positive and negative ergonomic aspects of VDT design. The higher the position in this scale, the higher the degree of activation.

It is also possible to relate the ergonomic characteristics of the VDT to the level of activation. The results from these investigations showed, for example, that there is a two-point difference in activation level between the users of grey displays and the users of black displays. This difference can be compared with the response of workers in an aluminium smelting plant who work a day and night shift. A slightly greater difference in activation was observed in the response of users of matt and glossy keyboards.

This approach to relating the level of demand on a VDT user to the ergonomic features of the equipment is both useful and illustrative. There is a very clear difference between the increase in activation as the result of a challenging job and increases caused by ergonomic deficiencies in the design of the equipment. Differences due to the nature of the job can be more easily accepted because they reflect the different levels of skill, responsibility and autonomy among different professional groups. But differences in activation caused by ergonomic deficiency in the design of the equipment are less easy to accept. Thus it is that the ergonomic criteria for VDT and workplace design have come to assume such importance.

On the subject of rest pauses

There is no definition of a 'pause' that is universally accepted by all partners in industry, i.e. employers, employees and their trade unions. A rest pause may be interpreted as an interruption from work, as a specific rest period, as a period of inactivity, as an interruption from specific phases of a task etc. Some authors also include periods of inactivity that arise due to the nature and organisation of the task, e.g. data entry and response waiting times in computer dialogue tasks, as pauses. Others include periods of inactivity such as these as among the more burdening parts of the working procedure.

In conjunction with most VDT and computer tasks, waiting times such as these can be taken to constitute a pause in the sense that the body is provided with a period of rest, but against this, the overall stress on the individual is not necessarily reduced. This is particularly true if waiting times, especially if they are of unpredictable duration and if they occur at critical stages in the performance of the task, represent a source of psychological stress.

As far as working with VDTs is concerned, the term 'pause' should be used to describe a period of recovery from the physiological and psychological stresses induced during the preceding working period. The nature of these stresses and the relative importance of the physiological and psychological components of fatigue vary according to the specific nature of the task in question. Nevertheless, a period of time during which the individual is inactive, or apparently so, but is not free to become disengaged from the task, does not, by this definition, constitute a pause. *It is the recovery value of a rest pause that is important and not the duration of periods of real or apparent inactivity.*

Fatigue and pauses

Fatigue is also a very broad concept for which there exists no unequivocal definition. Generally speaking, however, fatigue can be considered as a reaction to any form of physiological-psychological loading which leads to a reversible reduction in the efficiency of the human body and its organs.

The causes and effects of fatigue can be described in terms of three basic characteristics:

> • stress; fatigue occurs as the result of one or more types of physiological or psychological stress or both,
> • insufficiency; fatigue leads to reduced physical or mental efficiency or both, and
> • reversibility; fatigue is reversible in the sense that the effects of fatigue can be overcome.

Fatigue can also take a variety of forms, and in considering the provision of rest pauses in connection with a particular type of work, the types of fatigue to which an employee may be prone and the rate at which symptoms of fatigue can occur should be considered very carefully. This is essential if the rest pauses are to serve their real purpose, i.e. to permit recovery.

It is possible to distinguish between the following types and causes of fatigue:

- *visual fatigue* caused by stress in the visual system,
- *muscular fatigue* caused by static, dynamic or repeated muscular stress,
- *general body fatigue* caused by physical stress in the entire body,
- *mental* or *psychological fatigue* caused by mental or spiritual overexertion or both,
- *dexterity* or *nervous fatigue* caused by stress in the psychomotor system,
- *chronic fatigue* caused by the combined effects of different types of prolonged fatigue, and
- *sensations of fatigue* caused as a result of prolonged monotony at work or elsewhere.

Whilst it would not be difficult to sub-divide the various types of fatigue in a different way or even to introduce other ways of referring to the types of fatigue, this list nevertheless provides a useful guide in judging the causes and symptoms of fatigue in relation to specific types of work and task.

The measurement of fatigue

The provision of rest pauses should always be set in relation to the frequency with which the symptoms of fatigue manifest themselves and the period required for recuperation. Ideally, these should be investigated by measuring fatigue at work but, in practice, this is very difficult, and in many cases, impossible to do.

Of the three characteristics of fatigue that were referred to earlier, it is the difficulty of finding a way to accurately and reliably measure the reduction in efficiency due to fatigue that makes the observation of fatigue very difficult in practice. The results from a large number of investigations of VDT tasks have shown that the efficiency of a VDT operator at work, when measured using a variety of tests that were conducted before and after work, did not necessarily reveal any reduction in performance or efficiency, whilst other tests showed that subjective feelings of fatigue did indeed occur. It is not possible to reliably investigate the characteristics of fatigue at work by relating fatigue to working efficiency, i.e. to some measure of performance or productivity, alone. This is because many people, when they become aware of the fact that are getting tired, tend to compensate by exerting more effort, concentration or will-power in order to carry on with the job, in some cases to such an extent that performance actually increases.

Even the question as to what constitutes 'stress at work' causes certain problems in measuring fatigue and this is especially true when there is some uncertainty as to the extent to which periods of inactivity may or may not be sources of stress. For the reasons given earlier, this is particularly true in the case of many job categories involving the use of computer systems.

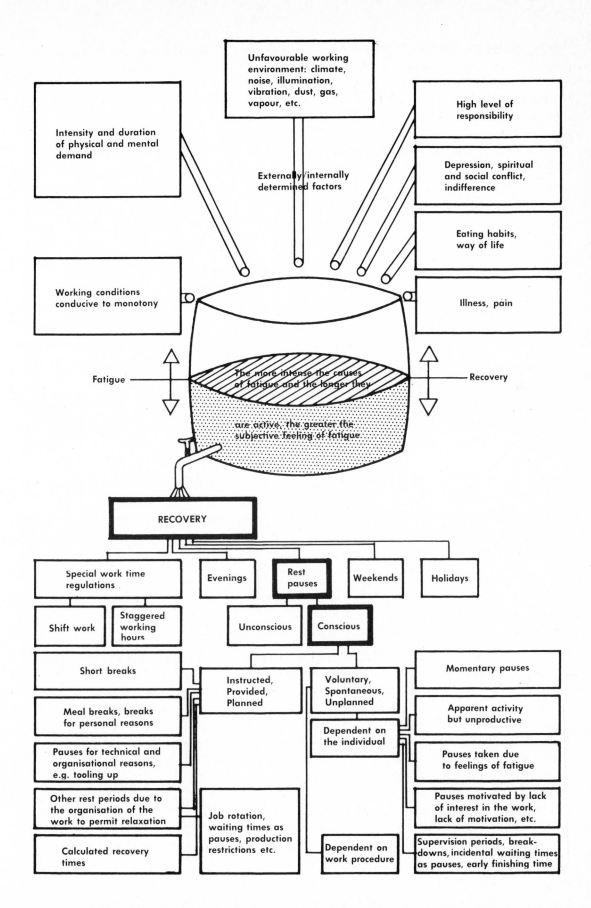

Figure 5.40 Schematic representation of the combined effects of different factors leading to fatigue and the way in which these factors are affected by different types of recuperation. Ref. G.10

Additional problems arise when the organs prone to fatigue are themselves so robust that they exhibit no or very few observable symptoms of fatigue. This is so, for example, in the case of the eyes which are among the most efficient and robust systems in the human body. The light-sensitive part of the eye, the retina, exhibits no characteristics of fatigue. The muscles of the eye do, however, exhibit observable symptoms of fatigue but these can be caused by other forms of stress and not only to visual fatigue, for which reason the measurement of these symptoms as an indicator of visual fatigue is not very reliable.

In practice, therefore, neither the causes nor the effects of fatigue at work can usually be measured reliably and expressed in quantitative terms. So, whilst all theories of fatigue may be able to explain and in some cases provide a means for observing certain aspects of the fatigue process, none is yet able to describe and permit the measurement of the overall organic process of fatigue.

The provision of rest pauses

A rest pause is a means of overcoming or avoiding the condition of occupationally induced fatigue and it is worth re-stating that it is the recovery value and not the nominal duration of a rest pause that is important.

It is a popular misconception that the recovery value of a rest pause depends entirely upon its length. In practice, however, it is not only the length of a rest pause that is important, it is also a question of when the pause is taken. In order to maximise the recovery value of rest pauses, their timing and duration cannot be considered separately, and this can be illustrated by observing the reaction of people at work in jobs requiring physical effort, see Figure 5.41.

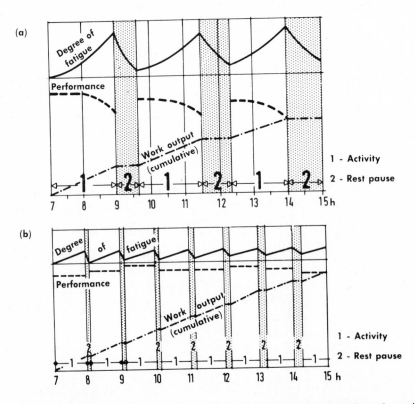

Figure 5.41 Performance and cumulative productivity during a single shift of moderately heavy manual work when rest pauses are first taken (a) after and (b) before the degree of fatigue has progressed to a high level. Ref. B.18

As these diagrams clearly show, frequent pauses which are taken before the onset of a high level of fatigue are very much more effective than longer but less frequent rest pauses which are taken after an appreciable reduction in the level of performance has occurred, i.e. after longer periods of continuous working. Depending upon the nature of the job, the cumulative level of fatigue can be markedly reduced and overall performance improved in spite of the reduction in overall working time in having provided for frequent, but short duration, rest pauses, see Figure 5.42.

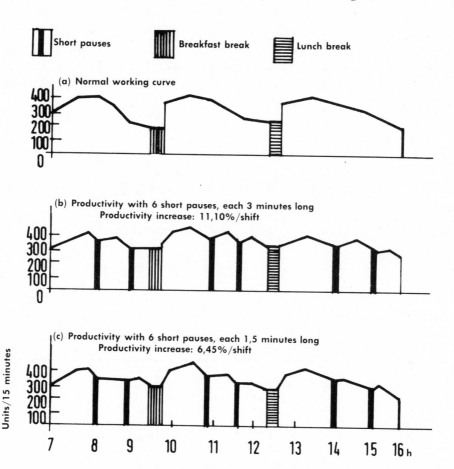

Figure 5.42 The effect of different pause structures on performance. Ref. H.5

That the same basic principle is true in connection with tasks involving mental effort can be seen in Figure 5.43. The results from this investigation showed that:

- the most favourable regulation of rest pauses is such that pauses are taken prior to the onset of a noticeable degree of fatigue, and
- pause times of between 5 and 10% of the total working time are compensated by the recuperating effects of the pauses.

Pauses and the nature of the activity

The need to rest is as important to human well-being and satisfaction as the need to work. But not all types of occupation are equally demanding from the point of view of the provision of rest periods. In some types of activity, particularly those involving prolonged physical or mental effort and in industries in which individual incomes are productivity related, the provision of specified rest periods during the working day is a necessary safeguard to the well-being of those thus employed. In many other types of activity, on the other hand, and particularly those in which the nature of the job provides the individual with the freedom to pause at his own discretion, the provision of specified rest pauses may often be judged to be superfluous.

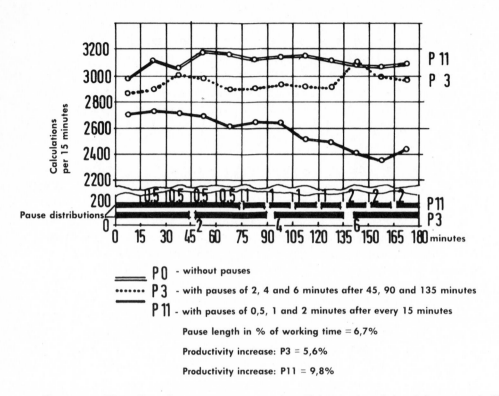

Figure 5.43 *The effect of pause structure on the efficiency of work involving mental effort during a three hour working period with a combined rest period of 12 minutes. Ref. G.8*

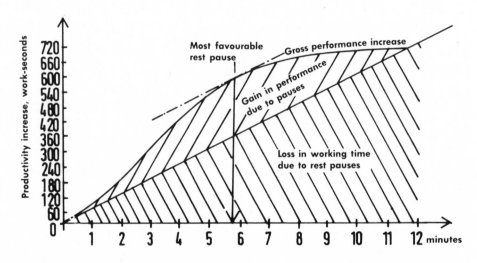

Figure 5.44 *The effect of different pause lengths after two-thirds of a two hour working period involving concentrated mental effort on the marginal increase of performance. Ref. G.7*

When considering the provision of rest pauses in connection with a specific type of job, therefore, the results of investigations made in connection with other types of activity must be interpreted with some caution. Most investigations concerning the recovery value of rest pauses have been undertaken in connection with heavy, manual types of work but clearly, regulations based on these types of activity cannot, *per se* be applied in judging the pause requirements in, say, administrative or similar types of office working situation.

In many industries, and the printing and publishing industry is a good example, production calls for a wide variety of skills and professions, each with its own characteristic professional requirements and working conditions. In an industry such as this, the rhythm of work may vary from one department to another. Even within a given department, the pace and rhythm of activity may vary considerably throughout the duration of the working day. Furthermore, the different levels of creative and other skills in the various editorial and production departments in, say, newspaper production, serves well to highlight the fact that the provision of rest pauses must be considered in relation to the nature of the task, and this is true with respect to both the frequency and duration of rest pauses.

In most production environments, the provision of fixed rest pauses for production staff can be accommodated in such a way that the employee can recover from the effects of the preceding working period without adversely affecting the production schedule. Among many categories of administrative staff, on the other hand, the similar provision of fixed rest pauses might, in itself, constitute a source of pressure and may in any case be superfluous due to the lack of a fixed structure or procedure in the way the work is carried out. This is very much the case, for example, among journalists and most of the editorial staff of a newspaper.

The discussion of rest pause provisions is by no means a closed question but these few comments are intended to serve as a guide as to how the question might be approached. Most important is the need to consider rest pauses in relation to the task and to bear in mind that rest pauses shall not themselves be a source of inconvenience or stress to the individual at work.

APPENDIX I

ERGONOMIC CHECKLIST

FOR VDTs

AND VDT WORKPLACES

APPENDIX I

Ergonomic Checklist for VDTs and VDT Workplaces

Foreword

The following checklist summarises the recommendations contained in the report concerning:

- the design and operating characteristics of VDTs
- the design of VDT workplaces
- the design of the VDT workroom
- environmental considerations

In order to make the checklist easy to use and apply in practice, each item is covered by one or more questions, the answers to which may be either YES or NO. In those cases where a general recommendation can be made, the preferred answer is appropriately indicated. For example:

	YES	NO
Is the character height greater than or equal to 3,0 mm?	►☐	☐

In some cases, however, the importance that is attached to a particular requirement cannot be assigned in general terms. The wide range of tasks that are being performed using VDTs makes this to some extent inevitable. In cases such as these, therefore, no indication is given of a generally preferred answer, this being left to the discretion of the user in relation to the specific requirements of the task in question.

In using this checklist, the user should guard against drawing the conclusion that provided every item has been answered with the appropriate YES or NO, the VDT, workplace etc., may be expected to be totally favourable from the ergonomic point of view. Checklists of this kind provide a useful means of drawing the attention of equipment manufacturers and users to some of the important relationships between the characteristics of the individual at work, the job that he or she is doing and the characteristics of the equipment and working environment with and within which the job is to be carried out. Each of these "elements" represents a basic component of the situation "man at work" and each - not least the physical attributes of the individuals themselves - varies between wide limits.

In having established a series of guidelines such as those contained in the checklist, their application should be approached with a certain degree of caution. In every real working situation, it is the comfort and well-being of the *real individual* that should be secured. It is this individual and his job that are the centrepieces of the working situation.

In applying the recommendations contained in this checklist, therefore, there must remain a certain degree of flexibility. Any solution must necessarily be a compromise. A too rigid and implicit adherence to recommendations such as these without some understanding of how they have been arrived at and, at the same time, some measure of common sense, is certainly no guarantee of success in striving to achieve a favourable and conducive working environment.

THE DESIGN AND OPERATING CHARACTERISTICS OF VDTs

The Display Screen

Character formation

	YES	NO
1. Does the screen have a display capacity, i.e. number of available character spaces, that is sufficient for the task?	▶ ☐	☐
2. If the display capacity is less than the maximum capacity required by the task, is there sufficient display memory?	▶ ☐	☐
3. Is the display memory accessed by		
▶ roll scrolling?	☐	☐
▶ page scrolling?	☐	☐
▶ pan scrolling?	☐	☐
4. Is scrolling under keyboard control?	▶ ☐	☐
5. Is the character set sufficient for the task?	▶ ☐	☐
6. Is the colour of the characters in the display		
▶ white?	☐	☐
▶ yellow?	☐	☐
▶ green?	☐	☐
▶ other?	☐	☐
7. Is the character height greater than or equal to 3 mm?	▶ ☐	☐
8. Do the character height and viewing distance ensure a visual angle of at least 16°, preferably 20°?	▶ ☐	☐
9. If the characters are generated by dot matrix, do the individual dots merge sufficiently well so as to produce a sharp and well defined image?	▶ ☐	☐
10. Is the resolution of the dot matrix		
▶ 5 x 7? (acceptable)	☐	☐
▶ 7 x 9 or greater? (preferred)	▶ ☐	☐
11. Is the character width 70-80% of the upper case character height?	▶ ☐	☐
12. Is the stroke width between 12% and 17% of the character height?	▶ ☐	☐

13. Is the space between the characters between 20% and 50% of the character height?   ►☐   ☐

14. Is the row spacing between 100% and 150% of the character height?   ►☐   ☐

15. Does the VDT permit the display of both upper and lower case characters?   ►☐   ☐

16. In displaying lower case characters do descenders project below the base line of the matrix?   ►☐   ☐

17. Is it possible to clearly distinguish between the following characters

     X and K?   ►☐   ☐

     O and Q?   ►☐   ☐

     T and Y?   ►☐   ☐

     S and 5?   ►☐   ☐

     I and L?   ►☐   ☐

     U and V?   ►☐   ☐

     I and 1?   ►☐   ☐

18. Is it possible to clearly distinguish between the number "0" and the letter "O" (it should be noted that the letter Ø is included in several Nordic alphabets and should not be used to represent the number "0")?   ►☐   ☐

19. Are the basic characters upright, i.e. not slanted?   ►☐   ☐

20. Are cursive characters, e.g. italic, available for special coding purposes?   ☐   ☐

21. Is it possible to adjust the orientation of the screen or the VDT about its vertical axis?   ►☐   ☐

22. Is it possible to adjust the screen about its horizontal axis? (screen angle)   ►☐   ☐

23. If the screen is fixed, is it approximately vertical?   ☐   ☐

24. Is the upper edge of the screen at or below eye height?   ►☐   ☐

25. Where appropriate, does the visual display format correspond to the format which is used on documents, e.g. order forms?   ►☐   ☐

Coding, Format

		YES	NO
1.	Is colour available as a means of coding in the display?	☐	☐
2.	How many colours is it necessary to distinguish between		
	▶ 1 - 5?	☐	☐
	▶ 5 - 10?	☐	☐
	▶ ≥ 10?	☐	☐
3.	Is luminance, i.e. selective brightening used as a means of coding in the display?	☐	☐
4.	How many luminance levels it is necessary to distinguish between		
	▶ 2?	☐	☐
	▶ 3?	☐	☐
	▶ ≥ 3?	☐	☐
5.	Is it possible to clearly distinguish between the different luminance levels at maximum setting?	▶ ☐	☐
6.	Is a cursor provided?	▶ ☐	☐
7.	Is it possible to clearly distinguish the cursor from other symbols on the display?	▶ ☐	☐
8.	Is it possible to generate graphic symbols via the keyboard?	☐	☐
9.	Is it possible to blink selected parts of the display?	☐	☐
10.	Is the blink rate between 2 and 4 Hz?	▶ ☐	☐
11.	Is it possible to suppress the repeated blink action of the cursor?	▶ ☐	☐
12.	Is it possible to display characters of differing size?	☐	☐
13.	Is it possible to display characters of differing style?	☐	☐
14.	Are all displayed symbols unambiguous?	▶ ☐	☐
15.	If filters are used, are the characters in the display sharply defined?	▶ ☐	☐

	YES	NO

16. Is it possible to adjust the orientation of the screen or the VDT about its vertical axis? ▶☐ ☐

17. Is it possible to adjust the screen about its horizontal axis? (screen angle) ▶☐ ☐

18. If the screen is fixed, is it approximately vertical? ▶☐ ☐

19. Is the upper edge of the screen at or below eye height? ▶☐ ☐

20. Where appropriate, does the visual display format correspond to the format which is used on documents, e.g. order forms? ▶☐ ☐

21. Can forms be generated with protected fields? ☐ ☐

The display screen and luminance

	YES	NO

1. Is the character luminance
   ▶ greater than 45 cd/m^2? (minimum) ☐ ☐
   ▶ between 80 and 160 cd/m^2? (preferred) ▶☐ ☐

2. Is the character luminance adjustable? ▶☐ ☐

3. Do the character images remain sharply defined at maximum character luminance? ▶☐ ☐

4. Is the background luminance between 15 and 20 cd/m^2 under the appropriate office lighting conditions? ▶☐ ☐

5. Is the background luminance adjustable? ▶☐ ☐

6. Is the contrast between the character and background
   ▶ 3 : 1? (minimum) ☐ ☐
   ▶ 5 : 1? (better) ☐ ☐
   ▶ 8 : 1 - 10 : 1? (optimal) ▶☐ ☐

7. Is the contrast between the screen background and other items in the working field, e.g. documents, better than
   ▶ 1 : 10? (acceptable) ☐ ☐
   ▶ 1 : 3 - 1 : 5? (preferred) ▶☐ ☐

8. Are the displayed character images stable? ▶☐ ☐

The Keyboard

General criteria

		YES	NO
1.	Is the keyboard detached from the display screen console, i.e joined by a cable?	▶ ☐	☐
2.	Is the weight of the keyboard sufficient to ensure stability against unintentional movement?	▶ ☐	☐
3.	Is the thickness of the keyboard, i.e. base to the home row of keys		
	▶ less than 50 mm? (acceptable)	☐	☐
	▶ 30 mm? (preferred)	▶ ☐	☐
4.	Is the distance between the underside of the desk frame and the home row of keys on the keyboard less than 60 mm?	▶ ☐	☐
5.	Is the profile of the keyboard		
	▶ stepped?	☐	☐
	▶ sloped?	☐	☐
	▶ dished?	☐	☐
6.	Is the angle of the keyboard in the range 5-15°?	▶ ☐	☐
7.	Is the surface of the keyboard surround matt finished?	▶ ☐	☐
8.	Is the reflectance of the keyboard surface (not single keys) between 0,40 and 0,60?	▶ ☐	☐
9.	Is the luminance ratio between the keyboard, screen and documents less than 1:3 or 3:1?	▶ ☐	☐
10.	Is there at least a 50 mm deep space provided for resting the palms of the hands?	▶ ☐	☐

Key characteristics

		YES	NO
1.	Is the key pressure between 0,25 and 1,5 N?	▶ ☐	☐
2.	Is the key travel between 0,8 and 4,8 mm?	▶ ☐	☐
3.	For square keytops is the keytop size between ⌀ 12 and ⌀ 15 mm?	▶ ☐	☐

| | | YES | NO |

4. Is the centre spacing between adjacent keys between 18 and 20 mm? ▶□ □

5. Are the key legends resistant to wear and abrasion, i.e. are the legends moulded into the keytop? ▶□ □

6. Are the keytop surfaces concave so as to improve keyboarding accuracy? ▶□ □

7. Are the keytop surfaces such that specular reflections are kept to a minimum? ▶□ □

8. Is the activation of each key accompanied by a feedback signal such as an

  ▶ audible click? □ □

  ▶ tactile click? □ □

  ▶ or snap action? □ □

9. Do the keys have a low failure rate? ▶□ □

10. What type of errors might occur as the result of a key failure

  ▶ keystroke not registered
  (contact error)? □ □

  ▶ keystroke is repeated
  (jammed key)? □ □

11. If two keys are activated simultaneously, is a warning signal given? ▶□ □

12. Is the keyboard provided with a roll-over facility

  ▶ 2-key roll-over? □ □

  ▶ n-key roll-over? ▶□ □

Keyboard layout

| | | YES | NO |

1. Does the layout of the alpha keys correspond to the conventional typewriter keyboard layout? ▶□ □

2. Does the layout of the numeric keys - above the alpha keys - correspond to the conventional typewriter keyboard layout? ▶□ □

3. Are the numeric keys grouped in a separate block:

    ▶ as the only numeric keyset? ☐ ☐

    ▶ or as an auxilliary keyset in addition ☐ ☐

    ▶ to the keyset referred to under 2? ☐ ☐

4. If an auxilliary numeric keyset is provided, are the keys arranged:

    ▶ as in the calculator layout i.e. 7, 8, 9, along the top row? ☐ ☐

    ▶ as in the telephone layout i.e. 1, 2, 3 along the top row? ☐ ☐

5. Is the space bar at the bottom of the keyboard? ▶ ☐ ☐

6. Does the number and type of function keys correspond to the requirements of the task? ▶ ☐ ☐

7. Does the arrangement of the function keys correspond to the sequences with which the task is carried out? ▶ ☐ ☐

8. Are keying errors critical as regards the success of the task in question, i.e. rather than merely inconvenient? ☐ ☐

9. Is the colour of the alphanumeric keys neutral, e.g. beige, grey, rather than black or white or one of the spectral colours red, yellow, green or blue? ▶ ☐ ☐

10. Are the different function key blocks distinct from the other keys by

    ▶ colour? ☐ ☐

    ▶ shape? ☐ ☐

    ▶ position? ☐ ☐

    ▶ distance (spacing)? ☐ ☐

11. Are the most important function keys colour-coded? ☐ ☐

12. Are all keys for which unintentional or accidental operation may have serious consequences especially secure by

    ▶ their position? ☐ ☐

    ▶ higher required key pressure? ☐ ☐

    ▶ key lock? ☐ ☐

    ▶ two handed (two key) chord operation? ☐ ☐

13. Do the function key labels and symbols correspond to the same functions on other keyboards used e.g. typewriters or other VDTs at the same workplace? ☐ ☐

14. Are user-programmable function keys provided? ☐ ☐

Additional VDT and System Characteristics

		YES	NO
1.	Is the power dissipation from the VDT as low as possible?	▶ ☐	☐
2.	Is the VDT resistant to knocks and vibration?	▶ ☐	☐
3.	Is the operator secure against electrical accident even when tampering with the VDT?	▶ ☐	☐
4.	Does the VDT satisfy the requirements of all national and local safety standards?	▶ ☐	☐
5.	Are the operators and cleaning staff aware of which cleaning materials may be used without causing damage to the screen, housing and other components of the VDT?	▶ ☐	☐
6.	Is there sufficient maintenance access to both the VDT and VDT workplace?	▶ ☐	☐
7.	Are there any user-serviceable repairs, e.g. fuse changes, that can be quickly and easily carried out by the operator?	☐	☐
8.	Are the electrical supply cables and other services to the VDT and workplace adequately secured and concealed?	▶ ☐	☐
9.	Has the voltage supply to the VDT system been stabilised against fluctuations in supply voltage, e.g. due to variations in mains voltage, peak loads etc?	▶ ☐	☐
10.	Is the operator provided with a warning signal in the event of system or VDT malfunction		
	▶ audible alarm?	▶ ☐	☐
	▶ visual alarm?	▶ ☐	☐
	▶ other?	☐	☐
11.	Is the operator provided with a warning in the event that the VDT is no longer able to register keystrokes, e.g. when the VDT memory storage is filled?	▶ ☐	☐
12.	Will security procedures be necessary?	☐	☐
13.	How is the operational status of the VDT, e.g. if the terminal is in send, receive or queue mode, made known to the operator:		
	▶ no indication?	☐	☐
	▶ flashing light indicator?	☐	☐
	▶ continuous light indicator?	▶ ☐	☐
14.	Is the response time of the system sufficiently short during peak working times?	▶ ☐	☐
15.	If the response time is likely to vary appreciably, is the operator given an indication of waiting times?	▶ ☐	☐

16. If several terminals share a common transmission line to the computer, can each terminal transmit and receive information independently of the status of the other terminals on the line? ▶ ☐   ☐

17. Is it necessary to consider special precautions, e.g. special carpeting or a copper grid carpet underlay, to safeguard against the discharge of static electricity to the VDT chassis? ☐   ☐

DESIGN OF WORKPLACES

Desks, Footrests

YES   NO

1. Are a sufficient number of work surfaces provided? ▶ ☐   ☐

2. Are the working surfaces of sufficient size? ▶ ☐   ☐

3. Are all items of equipment and job aids which must often be manually manipulated within the normal arm reach of the operator, i.e. within reach without requiring movement of the body? ▶ ☐   ☐

4. Is the desk height between 720 and 750 mm? ▶ ☐   ☐

5. Is the height of the keyboard above floor level between 720 and 750 mm? ▶ ☐   ☐

6. Is the surface of the desk matt finished? ▶ ☐   ☐

7. Is the reflectance of the desk surface:

    ▶ 0,4? (optimum) ▶ ☐   ☐
    ▶ 0,5? (acceptable) ☐   ☐
    ▶ 0,6? (maximum) ☐   ☐

8. Is the height of the leg area sufficient? ▶ ☐   ☐

9. Is the underside of the desk free of obstructions? ▶ ☐   ☐

10. Is the leg area at least 800 mm wide to permit unobstructed turning? ▶ ☐   ☐

11. Is the leg area at least 700 mm deep? ▶ ☐   ☐

12. Is the leg area shielded against heat from the VDT and other items of equipment? ▶ ☐   ☐

13. Is adequate space provided for storage of copies, handbooks, documents, personal belongings etc.? ▶ ☐   ☐

14. Is the leg area free from obstructions such as desk frame spars? ▶ ☐   ☐

YES   NO

15. Is it possible for the operator to easily re-arrange the workplace, e.g. by changing the positions of the VDT and other items of equipment? ▶☐ ☐

16. Is a footrest provided which covers the entire leg area? ☐ ☐

17. If footrests are used are they adjustable

 ▶ in height? ▶☐ ☐

 ▶ in inclination? ▶☐ ☐

18. Can the footrest be quickly and easily adjusted to cater for the different body sizes of the operators? ▶☐ ☐

19. Is the surface of the footrest such as to enable comfortable movement of the feet without slipping? ▶☐ ☐

Chair

1. Does the design of the chair satisfy the requirements of the national standards? ▶☐ ☐

2. Is the chair stable i.e. safe from tipping over? (fivepoint base) ▶☐ ☐

3. If the chair is provided with castors are they self-locking? ▶☐ ☐

4. Is the seating height easily adjustable? ▶☐ ☐

5. Is the seat angle adjustable? ▶☐ ☐

6. Is the front edge of the seat rounded to avoid cutting into the thighs? ▶☐ ☐

7. Is the seat surface padded? ▶☐ ☐

8. Is the height of the backrest adjustable? ▶☐ ☐

9. Can the backrest be adjusted forwards and backwards? ▶☐ ☐

10. Can adjustments be made easily and safely from the seated position? ▶☐ ☐

11. Are the adjustment mechanisms safe against self- or unintentional release? ▶☐ ☐

12. Is there guidance available to the individual operators to help them achieve an optimum adjustment of their chair? ▶☐ ☐

I.11

Job Aids, Other Items of Equipment

Documents

                                                            YES   NO

1. Do the documents that are necessary to the task satisfy the requirements of section I as far as

   ▶ character formation?   ▶☐   ☐

   ▶ contrast between characters   ▶☐   ☐

   ▶ and background?   ▶☐   ☐

2. Are all paper surfaces matt?   ▶☐   ☐

3. Can all of the information which is relevant to the task be easily read?   ▶☐   ☐

4. Where appropriate, does the format used on documents such as order, billing forms etc., correspond to the display screen format?   ▶☐   ☐

Siting of the VDT, job aids and other items of equipment

                                                            YES   NO

1. Are all job aids and items of equipment so positioned that - apart from short-term considerations - the operator may assume an optimum working posture according to the following criteria:

   ▶ head inclined forward at an angle of ca 20°   ▶☐   ☐

   ▶ spine slightly arched and forward leaning when seen from the side   ▶☐   ☐

   ▶ upper arms vertical   ▶☐   ☐

   ▶ no twisting of the head and trunk   ▶☐   ☐

   ▶ thighs approximately horizontal   ▶☐   ☐

   ▶ lower part of the leg approximately vertical   ▶☐   ☐

   ▶ sufficient leg room both in height and depth   ▶☐   ☐

   ▶ frequent changes of visual object accommodated within an angle of 15-30° relative to the normal viewing direction   ▶☐   ☐

2. Are all job aids and items of equipment in the visual and working field situated according to frequency of use?

   ▶ their frequency of use?   ☐   ☐

   ▶ their relation to the way the task is performed?   ☐   ☐

   ▶ their importance?   ☐   ☐

ENVIRONMENTAL CONSIDERATIONS

Lighting

		YES	NO
1.	Is the illuminance between 300 and 500 lux?	▶ ☐	☐
2.	Is the operator's field of vision free of direct reflections from the display screen, keyboard, desk, papers etc?	▶ ☐	☐
3.	Are there glare sources in the operators field of vision, lights, windows etc?	▶ ☐	☐
4.	Are the luminaires equipped with prismatic or grid-type glare shields?	▶ ☐	☐
5.	Is the lighting system equipped with duo- or three-phase switching?	▶ ☐	☐
6.	Are the VDT workplaces positioned such that the operators line of vision is		
	▶ parallel to luminaires?	▶ ☐	☐
	▶ parallel to windows?	▶ ☐	☐
7.	Are the windows fitted with external blinds?	☐	☐
8.	Are the windows fitted with internal blinds?	☐	☐
9.	Are the windows fitted with curtains with a reflectance in the range 0,5 to 0,7?	▶ ☐	☐
10.	Is the average reflectance of the ceiling greater than 0,7?	▶ ☐	☐
11.	Is the reflectance of the walls between 0,5 and 0,7?	▶ ☐	☐
12.	Is the reflectance of the floor about 0,3?	▶ ☐	☐
13.	Are the lamps fitted with starters to prevent flashing at the end of their useful life?	▶ ☐	☐
14.	Has the regular cleaning and maintenance of the luminaires been properly considered?	▶ ☐	☐

Room Climate

		YES	NO
1.	Is the work room air conditioned?	▶ ☐	☐
2.	Can the room temperature be maintained between 21 and 23°C?	▶ ☐	☐
3.	Can the relative humidity be maintained between 45 and 55%?	▶ ☐	☐
4.	Is the speed of air movement less than 0,1m/s	▶ ☐	☐
	▶ at neck height?	▶ ☐	☐
	▶ at waist height?	▶ ☐	☐
	▶ at ankle height?	▶ ☐	☐
5.	Are the individual operators and their neighbours protected against thermal loading from the equipment by		
	▶ thermal radiation?	▶ ☐	☐
	▶ warm air flow?	▶ ☐	☐
6.	Have steps been taken to avoid local hot spots, e.g. under desks, in corners etc?	▶ ☐	☐

Noise

		YES	NO
1.	Is the noise level:		
	▶ less than 55 dB(A) in task areas requiring a high level of concentration?	▶ ☐	☐
	▶ less than 65 dB(A) in routine task areas?	▶ ☐	☐
2.	Are the equipment noise levels no more than 5 dB(A) greater than the background noise level?		
	▶ VDT, e.g. fans, power supply but not the auditory feedback and signals from the keyboard?	▶ ☐	☐
	▶ other items of equipment?	▶ ☐	☐
3.	Is the noise environment free from high frequency tones?	▶ ☐	☐
4.	Is the noise in the VDT room affected by external noise sources, e.g. neighbouring rooms, the outside world?	☐	☐
5.	Are there other items of equipment in the workroom, e.g. printers, teletypes, which generate high or distracting levels of noise?	☐	☐

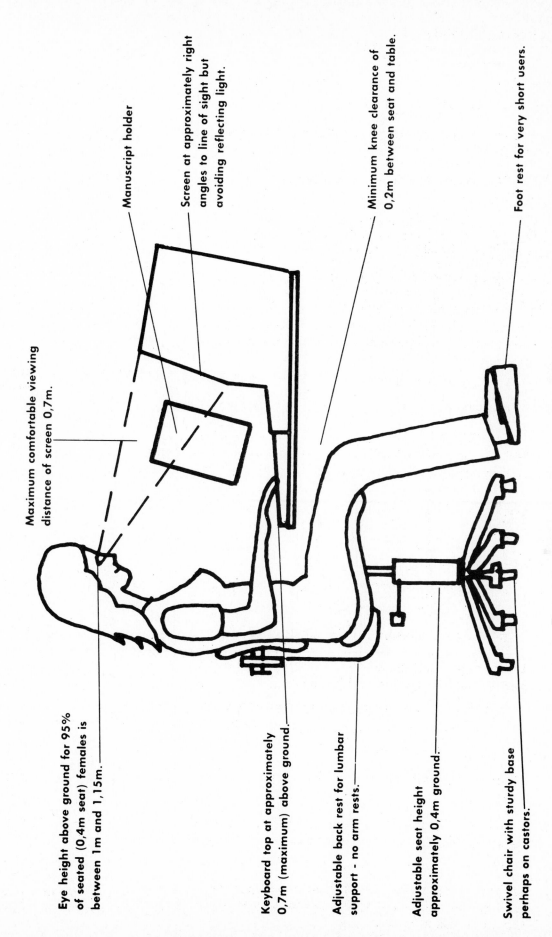

Manuscript holder

Screen at approximately right angles to line of sight but avoiding reflecting light.

Minimum knee clearance of 0,2m between seat and table.

Foot rest for very short users.

Maximum comfortable viewing distance of screen 0,7m.

Eye height above ground for 95% of seated (0,4m seat) females is between 1m and 1,15m.

Keyboard top at approximately 0,7m (maximum) above ground.

Adjustable back rest for lumbar support - no arm rests.

Adjustable seat height approximately 0,4m ground.

Swivel chair with sturdy base perhaps on castors.

Typical dimensions for a VDT workstation.

I. 15

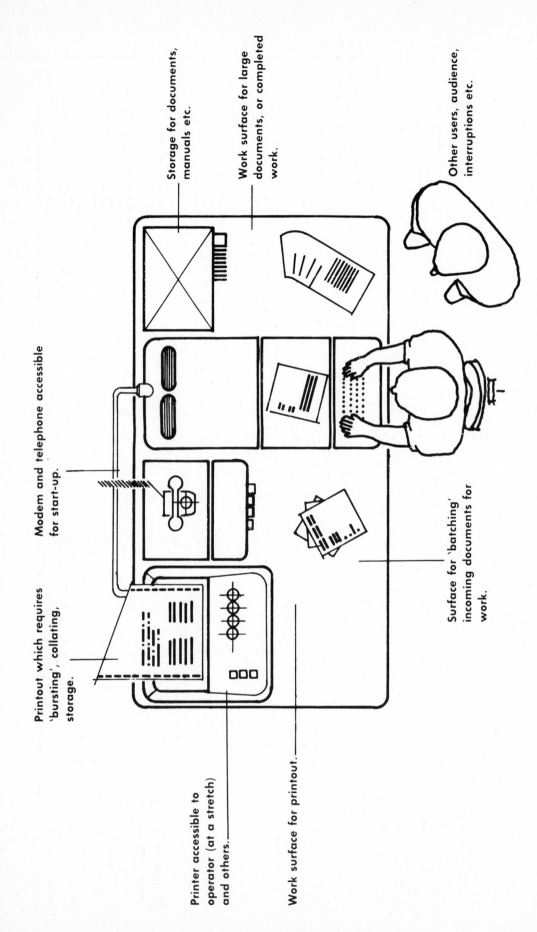

Storage for documents, manuals etc.

Work surface for large documents, or completed work.

Other users, audience, interruptions etc.

Modem and telephone accessible for start-up.

Printout which requires 'bursting', collating, storage.

Printer accessible to operator (at a stretch) and others.

Work surface for printout.

Surface for 'batching' incoming documents for work.

VDT-printer workstation with work surfaces and storage facilities.

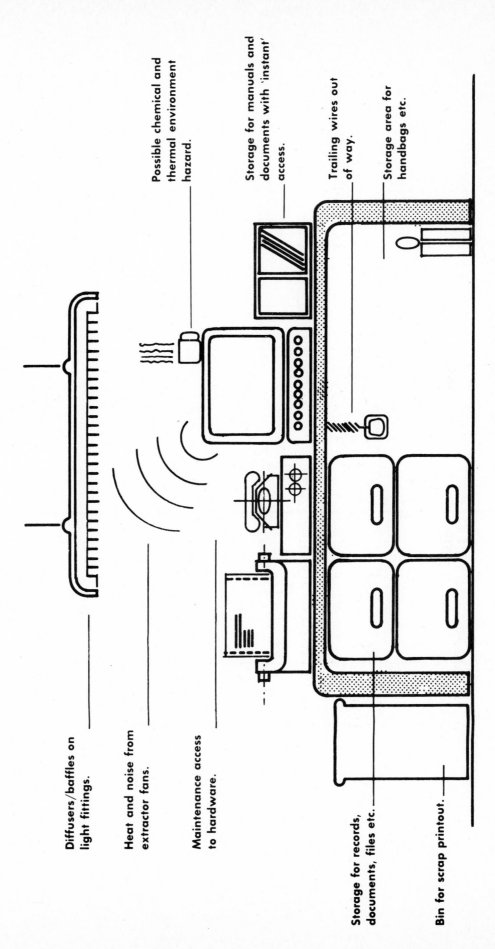

Diffusers/baffles on light fittings.

Heat and noise from extractor fans.

Maintenance access to hardware.

Possible chemical and thermal environment hazard.

Storage for manuals and documents with 'instant' access.

Trailing wires out of way.

Storage area for handbags etc.

Storage for records, documents, files etc.

Bin for scrap printout.

Other points to note in a VDT-printer-workstation.

APPENDIX II

EYE TESTS FOR VDU OPERATORS

- A Discussion Document -

APPENDIX II

Eye Tests For VDU Operators

A Discussion Document

Summary of Conclusions

In view of the widespread concern about any possible effects on eyesight of prolonged VDU use, and in view of the piecemeal testing planned and already taking place, a set of eyesight tests for VDU operators is recommended. These tests should be widely available in a standardised and reliable form. They represent a compromise but should be adequate for the present situation.

It is not recommended that all VDU operators should be required to undergo such tests. In general, people should have their sight tested more frequently than they usually do. However, that is outside the scope of this particular document. What is being recommended is that where the use of VDUs is particularly intensive or prolonged, or where there is real concern over fatigue caused by inadequate attention to ergonomics, then a long term check should be kept on the operators' eyesight using the tests described here.

It must be emphasised that the VET Advisory Group does not have evidence that health is at risk but feel that the further studies being undertaken will help in time to allay any anxiety. In the meantime the real problem with VDUs is more concerned with ensuring adequate attention to ergonomics in their design, implementation and use.

This document is being distributed for comment to the various parties concerned in this debate. There will be difficulties in establishing this procedure and there will be practical problems which will need to be debated very fully in many organisations. Management and unions will need to agree on what should happen if someone were found with an existing visual problem of such magnitude that they should not start using VDUs, for example, alternative employment. There will still be problems in interpreting individual test results since defects do occur normally. It may even be argued that the publicity generated by introducing an eye testing scheme causes more problems and worry than the effect it is there to detect.

These and other issues have yet to be resolved. It is hoped that informed discussion will allow a fuller and more detailed document to be produced and a carefully considered scheme to be implemented.

Comments and contributions are welcome and should be sent initially to VET Advisory Group, c/o D.J. Hart, IFRA, Washingtonplatz 1, D-6100 Darmstadt, F.R.G.

Preamble

Visual Display Units (VDUs) are becoming increasingly common in a wide range of office and other working environments. Not only are they being used regularly by more people than a few years ago, they are also being used more intensively. Indeed, in a number of industries using VDUs is a full time job. In many cases, the introduction of VDUs is associated with major changes in the work organisation, which can result in jobs being radically altered or even replaced. In such a rapidly changing environment, managements are frequently unwilling or even unable to make public the longer term employment implications of computerisation projects. As a result, considerable uncertainty surrounds many computerisation projects. When this is coupled with the reluctance most people feel for major changes, there is ample opportunity for fears and worries about computers to flourish.

In certain industries, fears about the lack of future job opportunities may be entirely realistic and well founded. This clearly is a problem which society as a whole must solve if we are to benefit from the tremendous potential of micro-chip technology. However, there is a very real danger that less realistic and unfounded fears may also thrive, which is to no-one's advantage. One area where fears abound and facts are scarce concerns the possible health hazards of using VDUs. In particular, the fear that continued or prolonged use of a VDU may cause irreparable damage to eyes or vision has been given considerable exposure in the media.

This problem has been confounded by the fact that a substantial proportion of the working population typically have uncorrected or inadequately corrected visual defects. Estimates of the exact proportion vary but it is likely to be between 20% and 30%. The result has been that a number of VDU operators, who have experienced various symptoms of discomfort or fatigue in their eyes, have been told, when they consulted their optician, that they needed glasses. Inevitably, they connected the need for glasses with VDU use. Support for regular eye tests for VDU operators has therefore come both from those concerned with industrial safety and from those concerned with possible compensation claims.

Despite a considerable amount of research, there is at this time no evidence to suggest that using a VDU is likely to damage eyes or eyesight. What the research does show is that failure to apply ergonomic knowledge to the design, implementation or use of VDUs, frequently results in unnecessary fatigue among the operators. This fatigue can arise from postural problems due to inadequate workplace design, or from a host of other factors, including of course the visual aspects of the task. The fatigue may well be experienced as various symptoms of discomfort or strain in the eyes whether or not the source of the problem is visual. The eyes may even act as an early warning system for the rest of the body and may feel tired or sore even though the cause of the fatigue lies elsewhere.

None of the above problems is inevitable. Ergonomics knowledge already exists to permit VDUs to be designed, implemented and used in a way which does not result in undue fatigue. This information is presented in the main body of this report which has been produced jointly with the Universities of Berlin and Loughborough and brings together the latest evidence from these and other research centres.

Nonetheless there are, and will be, less than ideal VDUs and VDU workplaces in many organisations for some time to come. These may well cause unnecessary or excessive fatigue which will be experienced day after day by some operators. Although there is no evidence that this fatigue will cause damage to the eyes or the visual system, it is of course possible that prolonged fatigue from using VDUs could have some long term effects. However it is extremely unlikely that such changes would be detected by a test of visual acuity (the ability to distinguish fine detail).

Ergonomics research has shown that the nature of the user's task has a major effect on fatigue. TV viewing, and the use of radar, for example, are sufficiently different from current VDU use that experience in these areas may not be relevant to the present problem.

A number of organisations are testing or are planning to test their VDU operators' eyesight. It would be unfortunate if inappropriate tests were used and it would be wasteful if the resultant data could not be co-ordinated in some way so that any trends could be detected which might otherwise remain concealed in a number of small groups.

Furthermore, the reassurance necessary to overcome the fears and worries discussed earlier in this document will only come from evidence that is generally regarded as valid. Long term effects can only validly be established by long term studies since the types of VDU and types of intensitve use have only been around for a relatively short period.

VET Advisory Group

In recognition of the above facts, it was decided that a VDU Eye Test (VET) Advisory group should be formed with the primary objective of establishing a set of tests suitable for monitoring VDU operators' eyesight over a period of some years.

The advisory group first met formally in July 1978. Some of the initiative for the group came from an initial one day meeting in Loughborough in April 1978 attended by representatives of 25 interested organisations. The participants in the advisory group have considerable experience relevant to the testing of VDU operators' eyesight and in addition represent or are in close contact with the main interested parties. The members of the advisory group are as follows:

Dr. R. Owen	Medical Adviser - Trades Union Congress
P.T. Stone	Head of the Vision and Lighting Research Group, Loughborough University
Prof. R.A. Weale	Director of the Department of Visual Science, Institute of Opthalmology, University of London
Dr. E.H. Burgess Chairman	Medical Adviser's Office, Civil Service Department
T.F.M. Stewart Secretary	IFRA Project Leader, Loughborough University
Dr. B. Malde	IFRA Project Member, Loughborough University

In addition, help has been received from the British Optical Association, The Health and Safety Executive and various other bodies.

Before describing the test package which is being proposed in this discussion document, it is necessary to review the various constraints recognised by the advisory group. In view of the urgency of the need for suitable tests, it was clear that all the tests recommended should be currently available throughout Britain in a standardised and reliable form. For this reason, no tests have been considered which depend on highly specialised equipment or which can only be conducted in research laboratories. A further constraint was that the tests should not take more than one half hour to administer in order to minimise the cost and inconvenience to the individuals involved.

A package of tests has been agreed and it is felt that, suitably administered, this procedure will be sufficiently comprehensive to allow for the early detection of abnormalities without being unduly complex.

Eye Test for VDU Operators

The emphasis in the test package is on those aspects of the image forming apparatus, of binocular vision and of the oculo-motor system which promotes the formation of a sharply outlined single perception when both eyes are used. This is the process involved in reading characters on a VDU screen or indeed a source document and is therefore the area of most concern. It is also the area where the individual is most likely to be able to detect a defect such as blurred or double vision. The tests recommended are as follows:

1. Unaided Visual Acuity
2. Refractive Findings
3. Corrected Visual Acuity
4. Amplitude of Accommodation
5. Suppression
6. Distant Muscle Balance (Maddox rod)
7. 1 metre Muscle Balance (Maddox rod)
8. Near Muscle Balance (Maddox wing)

Unaided Visual Acuity is established conventionally with a letter test (Snellen chart) or, better, with a Landolt C or E. It is defined as normal, when, at a viewing distance of 6 metres, the patient resolves a target with maximum contrast and detail, subtending at the eye 1' of arc.

If unaided vision is not normal, this **may** be due to malfunction in the image-forming mechanism. This consists of the cornea, pupil, and crystalline lens. Malfunction can usually be remedied with suitable glasses, made up essentially of **spherical** and, sometimes, **cylindrical** refracting surfaces. If the latter are used, as happens in the correction of astigmatism, the direction of the **axis** of the cylindrical surface has to be specified. Once refraction has been optimised, 'corrected' vision or **corrected visual acuity** can be determined.

Contrary to popular belief, the crystalline lens plays a secondary role in image formation: it is the cornea that is the principal image-forming device. The lens controls fine focus, a faculty known as **accommodation**. Like refraction, it is measured in dioptres (d), but actually expresses a change in focus, and therefore a dioptric variation. In children it is some 12D, and drops progressively through adult life, reaching zero at about the end of the sixth decade. This is known as presbyopia.

When both eyes can see but do not contribute to a binocular perception, the inactive percipient is said to be **suppressed**. This results often from amblyopia, squint, etc.

Muscle balance is also important. Eyes looking at a target have to turn in such a way as to direct the visual axes at the target, and the amount of turning (convergence) has to be consonant with the amount of focusing for that distance. This consonance may be correct for some viewing distances rather than others. **Maddox instruments** present a separate image to each eye, and enable one to assess whether or not both eyes are aiming at the same point. Older eyes have fewer problems as the distance increases: their phoria (discrepancy between focusing and convergence distances) diminishes as the viewing distance increases.

Test Administration

If the tests are conducted by an optician then various pathological conditions such as cataracts or glaucoma can also be detected at an early stage. However the majority of the tests can be conducted using proprietary vision testers such as the Keystone Telebinoccular, Mavis Tester or the Orthorater by trained lay personnel.

It should also be pointed out that the procedures recommended here are not a substitute for normal health care. Indeed, one of the consequences of instituting this test procedure will be that a number of the people screened, be they VDU operators or not, will be found to require glasses or a change of lenses. Such people should be advised to consult their own opticians in the normal way. However, if they require special prescriptions specifically for VDU work, then it seems reasonable that these should be provided by the employer. Indeed the viewing distance for VDUs usually falls in between near point and distant vision for which spectacles are normally prescribed.

The tests themselves are only part of the data necessary to monitor effectively the effects of prolonged VDU use. For example, it will be important to know how long the individual uses a VDU for each day. It will also be necessary to record in general terms the type of work involved, since for some tasks, for example, data entry, the display is looked at far less than for others e.g. text editing. The tester should therefore complete a record sheet for each subject, which will provide the additional information about their work and use of VDU, which is necessary to make the results statistically meaningful. A sample record sheet is attached at the end of this document. This raises two problems which have yet to be overcome.

First, there is the question of how the data base of test data will be managed and maintained. The second problem is closely related to this and concerns the confidentiality of what may effectively be medical records. Part of the reason for issuing this as a discussion document is so that these issues can be discussed widely by the parties concerned. However, it is hoped that some suitable means will be found for ensuring that central records can be kept since this is the only way that trends can be detected. Eyesight does deteriorate with age and so it is important that a large enough sample of subjects is tested to ensure that any deviation from the normal incidence of defects can be detected. In some industries it may be possible to keep records from non-VDU users as a control group (e.g. this is currently being done in the U.K. Post Office using these tests) but there will be many situations where this is just not possible.

It need not be expensive to maintain such a data base since the participating organisations will be bearing the most direct costs of sight testing. However, it will be important that the co-ordinating body is seen to be responsible and independent. In the United Kingdom, for example, the Employment Medical Advisory Service of The Health and Safety Executive could well be such a body.

Conclusions

In view of the widespread concern about any possible effects on eyesight of prolonged VDU use, and in view of the piecemeal testing planned and already taking place, a set of eyesight tests for VDU operators is recommended. These tests should be widely available in a standardised and reliable form. They represent a compromise but should be adequate for the present situation.

It is not recommended that all VDU operators should be required to undergo such tests. In general, people should have their sight tested more frequently than they usually do. However, that is outside the scope of this particular document. What is being recommended is that where the use of VDUs is particularly intensive or prolonged, or where there is real concern over fatigue caused by inadequate attention to ergonomics, then a long term check should be kept on the operators' eyesight using the tests described here.

It must be emphasised that the VET Advisory Group does not have evidence that health is at risk but feel that the further studies being undertaken will help in time to allay any anxiety.

allay any anxiety. In the meantime the real problem with VDUs is more concerned with ensuring adequate attention to ergonomics in their design, implementation and use.

This document is being distributed for comment to the various parties concerned in this debate. There will be difficulties in establishing this procedure and there will be practical problems which will need to be debated very fully in many organisations. Management and unions will need to agree on what should happen if someone were found with an existing visual problem of such magnitude that they should not start using VDUs, for example, alternative employment. There will still be problems in interpreting individual test results since defects do occur normally. It may even be argued that the publicity generated by introducing an eye testing scheme causes more problems and worry than the effect it is there to detect.

These and other issues have yet to be resolved. It is hoped that informed discussion will allow a fuller and more detailed document to be produced and a carefully considered scheme to be implemented.

Comments and contributions are welcome and should be sent initially to VET Advisory Group, c/o D.J. Hart, IFRA, Washingtonplatz 1, D-6100 Darmstadt, F.R.G.

VET VDU EYE TEST RECORD SHEET

To be completed by subject:

Name..Date of Birth......................

Organisation..Sex...................

Job..

Have you had a VDU Eye test before?..............................If yes, when was it?..................

How long have you used a VDU?...

Make and model of VDU used:...

On average, how many hours per day do you use a VDU?...

Is this all at one time?..............................If not, how long is a typical session?..................

Tick the category that best describes your **own** use of a VDU.   Do you work mainly with

..... Input Only   ..... Text
..... Mainly input but reading some output also   ..... Data
..... A mixture of inputting and reading output   ..... Program instructions
..... Mainly reading output but some input also
..... Reading output only

On average how many hours per day do you watch television?...

At what distance...feet/metres (delete as appropriate)

To be completed by tester

TEST	RIGHT EYE	LEFT EYE
Unaided Visual Acuity		
Refractive Findings	SPH CYL AXIS	SPH CYL AXIS
Corrected Visual Acuity		
Amplitute of Accomodation (Dioptres)	Corrected for near =	Corrected for near =
Suppression	YES/NO	YES/NO
Muscle Balance (Dist.) Maddox Rod	H. V.	H. V.
Muscle Balance (1 Metre) Maddox Rod	H. V.	H. V.
Muscle Balance Near (33 cm) Maddox Wing	H. V.	H. V.

Spectacles currently used:...............................Distance........Close........Work Only.......Remarks:........

New Spectacles required:...............................Distance........Close........Work Only........Remarks:........

Optician's Signature:..

Date:...Address: ....

APPENDIX III

BIBLIOGRAPHY

APPENDIX III

Bibliography

In the course of the present investigation, a great many references have been noted which are relevant to the theme of the investigation. Some of these references are listed in the following bibliography.

Bearing in mind the number of disciplines involved, and the number of industrial, academic and medical groups within which this subject has been considered, it cannot be claimed that this bibliography is complete. Nevertheless, those sources are listed which the authors know of and have found to be useful in providing background material for the investigation.

A

1. ADAMS H.L., The comparative effectiveness of electric and manual typewriters in the acquisition of typing skill in a Navy radioman school. Journal of Applied Psychology, 1957, 41, 227-230.

2. ADAMS J.A., Response feedback and learning, Psychological Bulletin, 1968, 70, 486-504.

3. ADRIAN W., Physiologische und psychologische Blendung, Sueddeutsche Optikerzeitung, 21, 1966, 3-10.

4. ALDEN D.G., DANIELS R.W., KANARICK A.F., Human factors principles for keyboard design and operation: a survey review. Honeywell Micro Switch, PPBS 70-90, March 1970.

5. ALDEN D.G., DANIELS R.W., KANARICK A.F., Keyboard design and operation - a review of the major issues, Human Factors, 1972, 14, 275-293.

6. ALEXANDER S.N., Comments on standard versus Dvorak keyboards, Unpublished Memo March 9, 1965 to A.V. Austin, Direction National Bureau Standards. (Reported by Siebel 1972)

7. ALLEN S., Nusvensk frekvensordbok, del 1, Almqvist & Wiksell, Stockholm, 1970, 1, 1053.

8. ANDREW I.D.C., ANDERSON D.M., McKERRAL J.D., Ergonomics study for a naval console design, EMI Electronics Report No. DMP2895, 1967.

9. AUSTRALIAN POST OFFICE, Dvorak keyboard experiment - follow-up investigation, Australian Post Office, Melbourne, 1953.

10. A unified framework of methods for evaluating visual performance aspects of lighting. Commission de l'Eclairage, CIE No. 19 TC-3.1, 1972.

11. AYOUB M.M, Work place design and posture, Human Factors, 1973, 15, 3, 265-268.

B

1. BAINBRIDGE E.A., Human factors in the design of consoles, 1962, RAE Inst. of Aviation Medicine FPRC MEMO 179.

2. BAINBRIDGE L., The influence of display type on decision making, 1971, IEE Conference on Displays, Loughborough.

3. BALDWIN T.S., BAILEY L.J., Readability of technical training materials presented on microfiche versus offset copy, Journal of Applied Psychology, 1971, 55, 37-41.

4. BARMACK J.E., SINAIKO H.W., Human factors problems in computer generated graphic displays. Inst. for Defence Analysis AD.636.170 Arlington, Va.

6. BARTLEY S.H., Fatigue: Mechanism and Management, Springfield, CC. Thomas, 1965.

5. BARRETT W.J., The evaluation of microfilm readers, Journal of Micrographics, 1972, 6(2), 51-63.

7. BARTENWERFER H., Ueber Beanspruchung und Ermuedung bei psychischer Aktivitaet, Habil. Schrift, Marburg, 1965.

8. BARTENWERFER H., Psychische Beanspruchung und Ermuedung, in 'Handbuch der Psychologie', Band 9, A.Mayer, B.Herwig, Gottingen, 1970.

9. BEDWELL C.H., The problems associated with fine and other visually difficult concentrated tasks in industry, Ann. Occup. Hygiene, 1961, 3, 84-93.

10. BEDWELL C.H., The eye, vision and visual discomfort. Lighting Research and Technology, 1972, 4, 151-158.

11. BERTELSON P., DE CAE A., Experimental comparison of two types of numerical keyboard, Bulletin du CERP, 1961, 10, 131-144.

12. BESSEY E.G., MACHEN G.S., An operational test of laboratory determined optima of screen brightness and ambient illumination for radar viewing rooms, Journal of Applied Psychology, 1957, 41, 51-52.

13. BEYER P., SCHENK H.D., ZIELTOW E., Wirksamkeitsuntersuchungen zur Leuchtdichte- und Farbcodierung von Anzeigenelementen. Forschungsbericht 71-57, Deutsche Forschungs- und Versuchsanstalt fur Luft- und Raumfahrt, Braunschweig, 1971.

14. BINNIE C.D., DARBY C.E., HINDLEY A.Y., Electroencephalographic changes in epileptics while viewing television, British Medical Journal, 4, 1975, 378-379.

15. BLACKWELL H.R., Development and use of a quantitative method for specification of interior illumination levels. Illuminating Engineering 54 (1959).

16. BLACKWELL H.R., Development of visual task evaluations for use in specifying recommended illumination levels. Illuminating Engineering vol. 56, 1961, 543-544.

17. BODENSEHER H., A console keyboard for improved man-machine interaction, IEE Conference on MCI, Teddington, 1970.

18. BOHRS H., Angewandte Arbeitswissenschaft, 75, June 1978.

19. BOISSIN J.P., Aspect actuel de problemes poses par les terminaux d'ordinateurs, Air France document, 1976.

20. BORSCHKE A., Ueber die Ursachen der Herabsetzung der Sehleistung durch Blendung, Zeitschrift fur Psychologie und Physiologie der Sinnesorgane, 1904, 35, 161-194.

21. BOWEN H.M. GRADIJAN J.M., Graphical display of multiparametric information. USAF Reports AMRL-TDR-62-115 (Parts 1 & 2) Wright-Patterson Air Force Base, 1963.

22. BOWEN H.M., GUINESS G.B., Preliminary experiments on keyboard design for semi-automatic mail sorting, Journal of Applied Psychology, 1965, 49, 194-198.

23. BOYCE P.R., Current knowledge of visual performance, Lighting Research and Technology, 1973, 5, 204-211.

24. BRADLEY J.V., WALLIS R.A., Spacing of push-button on-off controls, Engineering and Industrial Psychology, 1959, 1, 107-119.

25. BRAUNSTEIN M., ANDERSON N.S., A comparison of reading digits aloud and keypunching, IBM Research Centre Memo RC-185, 1959.

26. BROOKS R., Search time and color coding, Psychonomic Science, 2, 1965, 281-282.

27. BROWN L.D., Measurement of fatigue in abnormal physical environments. In the effect of abnormal physical conditions at work, edited by C.N. Davis, P.R. Davies and F.H. Tyrer, Livingstone, Edinburgh 1967.

28. BRUTON D.M., Medical aspects of cathode ray rube display systems, Trans. Soc. Occup. Med., 22, 1972, 56-57.

29. BRYDEN M.P., Symmetry of letters as a factor in tachistoscopic recognition. J. Exp. Psychol. 80, 1967, 513-524.

30. BURGER C.E., DE JONG J.R., Aspects of ergonomic job analysis, Ergonomics, 1962, 5, 185.

31. BUSCH G.K., Probleme der Ergonomie bei der Anwendung von Sichtgeraeteanzeigen im Bank- und Versicherungswesen. Internationaler Bund der Privatangestellten, Fiet, Genf 1977.

C

1. CAKIR A., Die Gestaltung von Datenarbeitsplaetzen, Die Berufsgenossenschaft, Feb. 1978, 83-86.

2. CAKIR A., REUTER H.J., VON SCHMUDE L., ARMBRUSTER A., Anpassung von Bildschirmarbeitsplaetzen an die physische und psychische Funktionsweise des Menschen, Forschungsbericht April 1978, Der Bundesminister fuer Arbeit und Sozialordnung, Bonn, F.R.G.

3. CAMERON C., Fatigue problems in modern industry, Ergonomics, 1971, 14, 713-720.

4. CAMERON C., A theory of fatigue, Ergonomics, 1973, 16, 633-648.

5. CAMPBELL F.W., GREEN D.G., Optical and retinal factors affecting visual resolution, J. Physiol., 181, 1965, 576-593.

6. CARLSON B.O., STRABY A., Occupational health aspects of work with copying paper (Swedish), Reports of the CO-OPs Ergonomics Laboratory No. 1, 1974, Stockholm.

7. CARLSOO S., People with stiff back should not perform keying tasks (Swedish), Arbetsmiljoe, 1976(7), 23-25.

8. CARMICHAEL L., DEARBORN W.F., Reading and Visual Fatigue, Houghton Mifflin Co. Cambridge Mass. 1947 (483 pp).

9. CARMICHAEL L., Reading and visual work: A contribution to the technique of experimentation on human fatigue, Trans. New York Acad. Sciences, 1951, 14, 94-96.

10. CHAMBERS J.B., STOCKBRIDGE H.C.W., Comparison of indicator components and push-button recommendations, Ergonomics, 1970, 13, 4, 401-420.

11. CHRIST R.E., Review and analysis of colour coding research for visual displays, Human Factors, 17, 542-570, 1975.

12. CLAUER C.K., NEAL A.S., ERDMAN R.L., Evaluation of some display parameters with human performance measures, Proceedings of the 7th National Symposium of the Society for Information Display, 1966, 15-23.

13. COCKING R.W., In place of QWERTY, Daily Telegraph Supplement, No.301, 24.7.1970.

14. COFFEY J.L., A comparison of vertical and horizontal arrangements of alphanumeric material, Human Factors, 1961, 3, 93-98.

15. COLLINS B.L., Review of psychological reaction to windows, Lighting Research and Technology, 1976, 8, 80-88.

16. COLLINS J.B., PRUEN B., Perception time and visual fatigue, Ergonomics 1962 5, 5.

17. CONNELL B., JOLLEY D.J., LOCKWOOD P., MERCER S., Activation of photosensitive epileptics whilst watching television; observations on line frequency, colour and picture content, Journal of Electrophysiological Technology, 1975, 1, 281-283.

18. CONRAD R., HULL A.J., The preferred layout for numeral data entry keysets, Ergonomics, 1968, 11, 165-173.

19. CONRAD R., LONGMAN D.J.A., Standard typewriter versus chord keyboard - an experimental study, Ergonomics, 1965, 8, 71-88.

20. CORKINDALE K.G.G., The evaluation of visual display, IEE Conference on Displays, Loughborough, 1971.

21. CORNOG D.Y., ROSE F.C., WALKOWICZ J.L., Legibility of alphanumeric characters and other symbols, National Bureau of Standards, Misc. Publications No 262-1, Washington 1964.

22. CORNOG J.R., ROSE F.C., Legibility of alphanumeric characters and other symbols, National Bureau of Standards, Misc. Publications No 262-2, Washington 1967.

23. CROUCH C.L., BUTTOLPH L.J., Visual relationships in office tasks, Lighting Design and Application, May 1973, 23-25.

D

1. DANIELS R.W., GRAF G.P., The influence of keyset interlocks on operator performance, Honeywell Micro Switch PO 08132, 1970.

2. DEININGER R.L., Desirable push-button characteristics, IEEETransactions Human Factors in Electronics, HFE-1, 24-30, 1960.

3. DEININGER R.L., Human factors studies of the design and use of push-button telephone keysets, Bell Telephone System Monograph 3643, Bell System Technical Journal 39, 995-1012, 1966.

4. DEININGER R.L., BILLINGTON M.J., RIESZ R.R., The display mode and the combination of sequence length and alphabet size as factors in keying speed and accuracy, IEEE Transactions Human Factors in Electronics HFE-7, 110-111, 1966.

5. DEININGER R.L., BILLINGTON M.J., MICHAELS S.E., Operator speed and accuracy with literal and combination codes for processor input, IEEE Transactions Man-Machine Systems, MMS-9, 10-14, 1968.

6. DESROSIERS E.V., The effect of image/surround brightness contrast ratios on student preference, attention, visual comfort and visual fatigue. Dissertation, Boston University School of Education, Boston, 1976.

7. DEVOS-PERTIPEZ C.A., A propos des facteurs d'ambiance au poste de terminal d'ordinateur, Dissertation, University of Lille, Department of Occupational Medicine, 1973.

8. DICKERSON E., Visual criteria aid job placement, International Journal of Occupational Health and Safety, May/June 1976, 39-41.

9. DIEHL M.J., SEIBEL R., The relative importance of visual and auditory feedback in speed typewriting, Journal of Applied Psychology, 1962, 46, 365-369.

10. DIETRISCH E., HILBERT D., Arbeitswissenschaftliche Aspekte bei der Gestaltung eines Mikrofilm-Lesearbeitsplatzes, Informatik, 1975, 22, 40-43.

11. DILL A.B., GOULD J.D., Flicklerless regeneration rates for CRT displays as a function of scan order and phosphor persistence, Human Factors, 1970, 12, 5, 465-471.

12. DIN 66234 Teil 1, Characteritics for adapting display work places to man: character shapes, Feb. 1978.

13. DOLATTA T.A., SELFRIDGE O.G., Functional specifications for typewriter-like time sharing terminals, Princeton University Computer Centre, April 1968.

14. DUDEK R.A., COLTON G.M., Effects of lighting and background with common signal lights on human peripheral vision, Human Factors, 1970, 12, 4, 401-407.

15. DUNCAN J., FERGUSON D., Keyboard operating posture and symptoms in operating, Ergonomics, 1974, 17, 651-662.

16. DUNN R.F.H., Lighting in radar rooms, Light and Lighting, 1972, 65, 6-9.

17. DURAFFOURG J., JANKOVSKY F., LANTIN G., LAVILLE A., PINSKY L., TEIGER C., Le travail de correction sur ecran cathodique, Laboratoire de Physiologie du Travail et d'Ergonomie, CNAM, Paris, 1978.

18. DYSTER-AAS K., FRISTEDT B., Sight and lighting in industry, National Board of Occupational Safety and Health, AI-Rapport Nr.12, 1969, Stockholm.

19. DYSTER-AAS K., FRISTEDT B., Eye check-ups in occupational medicine, Ibid.

E

1. EARL W.K.N., GOFF J.D., Comparison of two data entry methods, Perceptual and Motor Skills, 1965, 20, 369-384.

2. EDWARDS E., LEES F., Information display in process control IEE Conference on Displays, Loughborough, 1972.

3. ELLIS K., Methods of scanning a large visual display, Occupational Psychology, 1968, 42, 181-188.

4. EMANUEL J.T., GLONEK R.J., Microscope operations, recommendations for workplace layout and fatigue reduction. Motorola Semiconductor Product Division, Phoenix, August 1974.

5. EVANS R.A., MARTIN W.K., A proposal for simple conversion of QWERTY keyboard typewriters into SI units, CEGB Generation Development and Construction Division, Southern Project Group, SPG TR8 1970, 1971.

F

1. FELL J.C., LAUGHERY K.R., STM-mode of presentation for alphanumeric information, Human Factors, 1969, 11, 4, 401-406.

2. FERGUSON D., An Australian study of telegraphists cramp, British Journal of Industrial Medicine, 1971, 28, 280-285.

3. FERGUSON D., Shiftwork and health, Pers. Pract. Bulletin, 1971, 27, 113-122.

4. FERGUSON D., DUNCAN J., A study of the effect of equipment design on posture, Proc. Australian and New Zealand Society of Occupational Medicine, 1972, 56-60.

5. FERGUSON D., DUNCAN J., Keyboard design and operating posture, Ergonomics 1974, 6, 731-744.

6. FERGUSON D.A., MAJOR G., KELDOULIS T., Vision at work, visual defect and the visual demand of tasks, Applied Ergonomics, 1974, 5, 2, 84-93.

7. FITTS P.M., Cognitive aspects of information processing 111 Set for speed versus accuracy, Journal of Experimental Psychology, 1966, 71, 849-857.

8. FOURCADE J., MARTIN J.P., DEFAYOLLE M., Attention visuelle - posture, Le Travail Humain, 1975, 38, 119-132.

9. Foerdergemeinschaft Gutes Licht, (FGL), Lichtanwendung, Richard Pflaum Verlag, 1976.

10. FORTUIN G.J., Visual Power and visibility, Dissertation Rijks Universiteit Groningen, 1951.

11. FREMMER H., Erfassung von Beanspruchung des Menschen und Ermittlung notwendiger Erholungszeiten, Angewandte Arbeitswissenschaft, Mitteilung des IfaA, Koln, 57, Aug. 1975.

12. FRY G.A., The relation of blur and grain to the upper limit of useful magnification, In E. Bennet et al, Human Factors in Technology, McGraw-Hill, New York 1963.

G

1. GEACINTOV T., PEAVLER W.S., Pupillography in industrial fatigue assessment, Journal of Applied Psychology, 1974, 59, 213-216.

2. GIBSON E.I., Principles of perceptual learning and development. Appleton, New York 1969.

3. GIDDINGS R.J., Contrast enhancement with CRT and other self-luminous display devices, IEE Conference on Displays, Loughborough, 1971.

4. GIDDINGS R.J., Alphanumerics for raster displays, Paper presented to 1970 ERS Conference, Elliot Flight Automation, 1970.

5. GOULD J.D., Visual factors in the design of computer controlled CRT displays, Human Factors, 1968, 10, 4, 359-376.

6. GOULD J.D., SCHAFFER A., Visual monitoring of multi-channel displays, IEE Transactions on Human Factors in Electronics, HFE-7, N2, 69-76, 1966.

7. GRAF O., Ueberlohnendste Arbeitspausen bei geistiger Arbeit, in 'Physiologische Arbeiten', E. Kraepelin, 1922.

8. GRAF O., Arbeitsphysiologie, Wiesbaden, 1960.

9. GRALL T.B., An experimental investigation of the quantitative effects of postural support on man's systemic stress mechanism, University of Loughborough, Department of Human Sciences, Dissertation, 1974.

10. GRANDJEAN E., Physiologische Arbeitsgestaltung; Leitfaden der Ergonomie, Thun/Munchen, 1967, 111.

11. GRANDJEAN E., Physiologische Untersuchung ueber die nervoese Ermuedungen bei Tele-fonistinnen und Bueroangestellten, Int. Zeitschrift fur angewandte Physiologie einschliesslich Arbeitsphysiologie, 1958, 17, 400-418.

12. GRANDJEAN E.P., WOTZKA G., SCHAAD R., GILGEN A., Fatigue and stress in air traffic controllers, Ergonomics 1971, 14, 159-165.

13. GREEN B.F., The time required to search for numbers on large visual displays, MIT Lincoln Laboratory Report 36, 1953.

14. GREEN D.G., CAMPBELL F.W., Effect of focus on the visual response to a sinusoidally modulated spatial stimulus, Journal of the Optical Society of America, 1965, 55, 1154-1157.

15. GREGORY M., POULTON E.C., Even versus uneven right hand margin and the rate of comprehension in reading, Ergonomics, 13, 4, 427-434, 1970.

16. GREGORY R.L., Eye and Brain - the psychology of seeing, World University Library, 1973.

17. GRIFFITH R.T., The mini-motion typewriter keyboard, Journal of the Franklin Institute 246.5, 1949, 399-425.

18. GRIND W.A., VAN DE BOUMANN A.M., A model of a retinal sampling united based on a fluctuation theory. Kybernitik 4, 1968, 136-141.

19. GROVER D., (ed), Visual display units and their application, IPC Science and Technology Press Ltd., London, 1976.

20. GUNNARSSON E., OSTBERG O., Fysisk och psykisk arbetsmiljo i ett terminalbaserat datasystem. Arbetarskyddsstyrelsen Undersokningsrapport 1977:35.

H

1. HAIDER M., SLEZAK H., Arbeitsbeanspruchung und Augenbelastung an Bildschirmgeraeten, Wien 1975.

2. HANES L.F., Human factors considerations in international keyboard arrangement, NCR Human Factors Report 72-55, 1972.

3. HANES L.F., KINKEAD R.D., Research in manual data entry, NCR Human Factors Report AT 47-18, 1971.

4. HANEY R.W., The effect of instructional format on a functional testing performance, Human Factors, 1969, 11, 2, 181-188.

5. HANHART A., Die Arbeitspause im Betrieb, Thalwil/Zurich, 1954.

6. HARING D.R., Computer driven display facilities for an experimental computer based library, AFIPS Proceedings 33, 1, 255-265, 1968.

7. HARMON G.H., User problems with micrographic imagery, Proc. National Micrographics Assoc. Ann. Conference 1975, 24, 69-72.

8. HARRIET J., QWERTY lives another day, Office Equipment News, 15, 16, 57, 1972.

9. HARRIS W.P., GREEN B.F., WILSON E.A., LIAUDANSKY L.H., The design of characters for the Charactron, MIT Lincoln Laboratory Tech. Report 117, 1956.

10. HART D.J., The human aspects of working with visual display terminals, IFRA Research Report 76/02, Feb. 1976.

11. HARTMANN E., Beleuchtung und Sehen am Arbeitsplatz, Muenchen 1970.

12. HARTRIDGE H., The visual perception of fine detail, Philosphical Transactions of the Royal Society of London, 1947, 232.B, 519-671.

13. HAUGWITZ T., Opthalmologische Probleme am Arbeitsplatz, Klinische Monatsblaetter fuer Augenheilkunde, 1967, 151, 101-108.

14. HAYMAN E., Design criteria for CRT alphanumeric displays, IEE Symposium on MMS, Cambridge 1969.

15. HECHT E. ZAJAC A., Optics, Addison-Wesley Publishing Company, 1974.

16. HEMINGWAY J.C., ERICKSON R.A., Relative effects of raster scan-lines and image subtense on symbol legibility on TV, Human Factors, 1969, 11, 4, 331-338.

17. HILLIX W.A., COBURN R., Human factors in keyset design, U.S. Navy Electronics Laboratory NEL Report 1023, 1961.

18. HIRSCH R.S., Effects of standard versus alphabetical keyboard formats on typing performance. Journal of Applied Psychology, 1970, 54, 6, 484-490.

19. HEMINGWAY J.C., ERICKSON R.A., Relative effects of raster scan-lines and image subtense on symbol legibility on TV, Human Factors, 1969, 11, 4, 331-338.

20. HITT W.D., SCHUTZ H.G., CHRISTNER C.A., RAY H.W., COFFEY L.J., Development of design criteria for intelligence display formats, Human Factors, 1961, 3, 86-92.

21. HOFLING G., Kopfschmerzen durch Leuchtstofflampen? Herne, Schilling Verlag, 1973.

22. HOISMAN A.J., HANNAH L.D., SCHARF E.S., An experimental investigation of intelligence information display parameters, American Institute for Research, AIR-C86-5/63, Pittsburgh, 1963.

23. HOLLER H., KUNDI M., SCHMID H., STIDL H.G., THALER A., WINTER N., Arbeitsbeanspruchung und Augenbelastung an Bildschirmgeraeten, Wien, Automationsausschuss der Gewerkschaft der Privatangestellten, 1975.

24. HOLLWICH F., DIECKHAUS B., MEINERS C.O., Die physiologische Bedeutung des Lichtes fur den Menschen, Lichttechnik, 1975, 27, 388-394.

25. HOLLWICH F., Leuchtroehrenlicht - Ist "Neonlicht" fuer die Augen schaedlich? Deutsche Medizinische Wochenschrift, 1976, 17, 678-679.

26. HOPKIN V.D., Some neglected psychological problems in man machine systems. 8th Conference of WEAAP, Zurich, Sept. 1969, 140-154.

27. HOPKINSON R.G., Magnitude of discomfort caused by high brightness, Nature, 1958, 181, 1076.

28. HOPKINSON R.G., COLLINS J.B., The ergonomics of lighting, Macdonald Technical and Scientific Press, London, 1970.

29. HOSOKAWA M., HIGASHIDA T., Studies on the fatigue of operators in telegraph and telephone services, Japanese Journal of Industrial Health, 1968, 10, 395-409.

30. HOWELL W.C., KRAFT C.K., Size, blur and contrast as variables affecting the legibility of alphanumeric symbols on radar type displays, WADC TR 59-536, 1959.

31. HUDDLESTON H.F., Evaluation of alphanumerics for a 5x7 matrix display, IEE Conference on Displays, Loughborough, 1971.

32. HULTGREN G.V., Work places for CRT terminals, STANSAAB Documentation Service, 1974.

33. HULTGREN G.V., KNAVE B., Discomfort glare and disturbances from light reflections in an office landscape with CRT display terminals, Applied Ergonomics, 1974, 5, 2-8.

34. HULTGREN G.V., KNAVE B., WERNER M., Eye discomfort when reading microfilm in different enlargers, Applied Ergonomics, 1974, 5, 194-200.

I

1. IBM 3270 Human Factors Study, File 5360/5370/53-09, IBM Systems Development Division, New York, 1972.

2. IES Lighting Handbook, Illuminating Engineering Society, 5th edition, Ed. J.E. Kaufman, 1972.

3. The Illuminating Engineering Society, IES Code for Interior Lighting, London, 1973.

4. IFRA Symposium proceedings, Editorial use of electronics, Paris, March 5/6 1974.

5. IFRA Symposium proceedings, The electronic ad department, Zurich, April 15/16 1975.

6. IFRA Symposium proceedings, Planning a newspaper system, Munich, February 12/13 1976.

7. IFRA Symposium proceedings, Electronic editing - nice or necessary? Amsterdam, March 9/10 1976.

8. IFRA Symposium proceedings, Electronic advertising systems, Munich, March 1/2 1977.

9. IFRA Symposium proceedings, Electronic editorial systems, London, May 3/4 1977.

10. ISO 2126, Alphanumeric keyboard operated with both hands, ISO, Geneva, 1971.

J

1. JANSEN J., Techniques de l'Eclairage, Philips Technical Library, 1956.

2. JEAVONS P.M., HARDING G.F.A., Photosensitive epilepsy, Clinics in Developmental Medicine No.56, Spastics International Medical Publications, London, 1975.

3. JEDEC Electron Tube Council, Considerations used in establishing the x-radiation ratings of monochrome and colour picture tubes, JEDEC publication No. 94, Washington D.C., June 1975.

4. JOHNSON E.W., WOLFE V.V., Bifocal spectacles in the etiology of cervical radiculopathy, Archives of Physical Medicine and Rehabilitation, 1972, 53, 201-205.

5.   JONES J.C., Anthropometric data and fitting trials, The Architects Journal, 1963, 6, 317-325.

6.   JONES M.R., Colour coding, Human Factors, 1962, 4, 355-365.

7.   JONES C.H., HUGHES J.L., ENGVOLD K.J., A comparitive study of management decision making from computer terminals, AFIPS, 1970, 36.

8.   JUDICH J.M., The effect of positive-negative microforms and front-rear projection on reading speed and comprehension, National Micrographics Association Journal, 1968, 2, 58-61.

K

1.   KANARICK A.F., PETERSON R.C., Effects of value on the monitoring of multi-channel displays, Human Factors, 1969, 11, 4, 313-320.

2.   KANNER, W., SOMMER J., WITTGENS H., Arbeitsbedingungen und psychosomatische Befindlichkeit des Maschinenpersonals in einem Rechenzentrum, in: Der aertzliche Dienst, amtliches Fortbildungs- und Mitteilungsorgan fur die Aerzte und die Psychologen der Deutschen Bundesbahn, Heft 11/12, Darmstadt 1975.

3.   KAVALENKO I.G., Hygienic requirements in working with microfilms, Hygiene and Sanitation, 1970, 35, 344-348.

4.   KERN J.L., The computer operator interface, Control Engineering, 1966, 13, 9, 114-118.

5.   KINKEAD R.D., GONZALEZ B.K., Human factors design recommendation for touch operated keyboards, Honeywell Microswitch, March 1969.

6.   KINNEY G.C., SHOWMAN D.J., The relative legibility of upper case and lower case typewritten words, Information Display, 1967, 4, 34-39.

7.   KLEMMER E.T., A ten-key typewriter, IBM Research Memo RC-65, 1958.

8.   KLEMMER E.T., Numerical error checking, Journal of Applied Psychology, 1959, 43, 316-320.

9.   KLEMMER E.T., Communication and human performance, Human Factors, 1962, 4, 75-79.

10. KLEMMER E.T., Grouping of printed digits for manual entry, Human Factors, 1969, 11, 4, 397-400.

11. KLEMMER E.T., Keyboard entry, Applied Ergonomics, 1971, 2, 1, 2-6.

12. KLEMMER E.T., LOCKHEAD G.R., Further data on card punch operation performance, IBM Research Note NC39, 1961.

13. KLEMMER E.T., LOCKHEAD G.R., Productivity and erros in two keying tasks: a field study, Journal of Applied Psychology, 1962, 46, 401-408.

14. KOMOIKE Y., HORIGUCHI S., Fatigue assessment on key punch operators, typists and others, Ergonomics, 1971, 41, 1, 101-109.

15. KRAFT W.P., Job enrichment for production typists - a case study, in 'New perspectives in job enrichment', ed. J.R. Maher, New York, 1971.

16. KRIVOLAHVY J., KODAT V., CIZEK P., Visual efficiency and fatigue during the afternoon shift, Ergonomics, 1969, 12, 735-740.

17. KROCHMANN J., BEYER A., Untersuchungen ueber eine das Flimmern kennzeichnende Formel, Lichttechnik 14, 1962, 446-451.

18. KROEMER K.H.E., Ergonomics aspects of keyboard arrangement, Wright patterson AFB, 1972.

19. KROEMER K.H.E., Ueber den Einfluss der raeumlichen Lage von Tastenfeldern auf die Leistung an Schreibmaschinen, Int. Zeitung f. angew. Physiol. 1964, 20, 240-251.

20. KROEMER K.H.E., Vergleich einer normalen Schreibmaschinen-Tastatur mit einer "K-Tastatur", Int. Zeitung f. angew. Physiol. 1965, 20, 453-464.

21. KROEMER K.H.E., Zur Verbesserung der Schreibmaschinen-Tastatur, Arbeitswissenschaft, 1965, 4, 11-16.

22. KROEMER K.H.E., Ueber die Hoehe von Schreibtischen, Arbeitswissenschaft, 1963, 4, 132-140.

23. KROEMER K.H.E., ROBINETTE J., Ergonomics in the design of office furniture: a review of European literature, Int. Journal of Industrial Medicine and Surgery, 1969, 38, 115-125.

24. KROEMER K.H.E., Human engineering the keyboard, Human Factors, 1972, 14, 1, 51-63.

25. KRUGER H., Arbeitsphysiologische Beurteilung visueller Informationsuebermittlung, Arbeitsmedizin, Sozialmedizin, Praeventivmedizin I, 1977, 4-6.

26. KULLBERG J., Arbete vid bildskaermsterminaler ur ergonomisk synvinkel, Grafiska Forskningslaboratoriet, Stockholm, 1976.

L

1. LAKOWSKI R., Theory and practice of colour vision testing, A review, British Journal of Industrial Medicine, 1969, 26, 173-189, 265-288.

2. LANDIS D., SILVER C.A., JONES J.M., MESSICK S., Levels of proficiency and multidimensional viewpoints about problem similarity, Journal of Applied Psychology, 1967, 51, 3, 216-222.

3. LANYON R.I., GIDDINGS J.W., Psychological approaches to myopia; a review, American Journal of Optometry and Physiological Optics, 1974, 51, 271-281.

4. LEE D.R., BUCK J.R., The effect of screen angle and luminance on microfilm reading, Human Factors, 1975, 17, 461-469.

5. LICKLIDER J.C.R., Man-computer partnership, International Science and Technology, 1965, 18-26.

6. LOCKHEAD G.R., KLEMMER E.T., An evaluation of an 8-key word writing typewriter, IBM Research Report RC150, 1959.

7. LONGMORE J., Lighting of workplaces, Applied Ergonomics, 1970, 1, 5, 277-288.

8. LOVIE A.D., LOVIE P., The effects of mixed visual contrast schedules on detection times for both free and horizontally structured visual search, Ergonomics, 1970, 13, 6, 735-741.

9. LOWE R.T., Display systems design, in J.H. Howard, Electronic Information Display Systems, Spartan Books, Washington 1963.

10. LUCKETT L.W., CASE L.M., RACKLIN J.A., Radiation exposure from a cathode ray tube display device, 20th Annual Meeting Health Physics Society, Buffalo N.Y., July 1975.

11. LUCKIESH M., MOSS F.K., Muscular tension resulting from glare, Journal of General Psychology, 1933, 8, 455-460.

12. LUCKIESH M., MOSS F.K., Fatigue of convergence induced by reading as a function of illumination intensity, American Journal of Opthalmology, 1935, 18, 319-323.

13. LUNDERVOLD A.J.S., Electromyographic investigations of position and manner of working in typewriting, Acta. Physiolog. Scandinavia, 1951, Supplement No. 84.

14. LUTZ M.C., CHAPANIS A., Expected locations of digits and letters on ten-button keysets, Journal of Applied Psychology, 1955, 29, 314-317.

15. LUXEMBERG H.R., KUHN R.K., Display Systems Engineering, McGraw-Hill, New York, 1968.

M

1. MAAS J.B., JAYSON J.K., KLEIBER D.A., Effects of spectral difference in illumination on fatigue, Journal of Applied Psychology, 1974, 59, 524-526.

2. MATHO R.S., Eye strain from convergence insufficiency, British Medical Journal, 1972, 2, 564-565.

3. MAIRE F., Ergonomie, La Bacomiere, Boudry-Neuchatel, Suisse, 1965.

4. MAJEWSKI T.R., Factors affecting the punching speeds of Hollerith operators, mechanical factors outside the control of the operators, Cranfield Note No. 6, 1954.

5. MARTIN A., A new keyboard layout, Applied Ergonomics, 1972, 3, 1, 48-51.

6. MARTIN J., Design and man-computer dialogues, Englewood-Cliffs, N.J., Prentice-Hall, 1973.

7. MAUDERLI W., Report of radiation survey on a Harris 1100 editing and proofing terminal, Radiation Data Systems, Gainesville Fla., April 1972.

8. MAUDERLI W., Report of radiation suvey on a Harris 1500 video typewriter, Radiation Data Systems, Gainesville Fla., Sept, 1973.

9. MAUDERLI W., Report of radiation survey on the Harris 1600 terminal, Radiation Data Systems, Gainesville, Fla., Dec. 1974.

10. MAYFIELD C.E., A comparison of three arrangements of alphanumeric data for air traffic control displays, Franklin Institute Research Lab. Interim Report, Project B1860, Contract FAA/BRD 423, Federal Aviation Agency, Washington DC 20025, 1964.

11. MAYZNER M.S., Factors affecting information storage and retrieval in man, Report AD 486382, Department of Industrial Engineering, New York University, 1966.

12. MAYZNER M.S., GABRIEL R.F., The effect of spatial organisation of the stimulus on short-term retention, Journal of Psychology, 1964, 58, 17-21.

13. MAYZNER M.S., ADLER S., COHEN A., SCHOHBERG K.M., A study of the effects of irrelevant information, Journal of Psychology, 1965, 61, 257-262.

14. McLEAN M.V., Brightness contrast, colour contrast and legibility, Human Factors, 1965, 7, 521-526.

15. McCLEOD D., BANNON R.E., Microscopes and eye fatigue, Industrial Medicine and Surgery, 1973, 42, 2, 7-9.

16. McCORMICK E.J., Human Factors Engineering 1964, Second Edition, McGraw-Hill, New York.

17. MEIER H., Deutsche Sprachstatistik, Georg Olms Verlagsbuchhandlung, Hildesheim, 1967.

18. MENZEL W., Menschliche Tag-Nacht Rhytmik und Schichtarbeit, Benno Schwabe Verlag und Co., Basel/Stuttgart, 1962.

19. MICHAELS S.E., Qwerty versus alphabetic keyboard for operators of various skills, Bell Telephone Laboratory Report HF 13, 5, 1971.

20. MICHAL V., Visual fatigue, Ceskoslovenska Oftalmologie 1954, 10, 362-367. See also Building Research Station Library No. 76553.

21. MILLER R.B., Archetypes in man-computer problem solving, Ergonomics, 1969, 12, 4, 559-581.

22. MILLER R.B., Response time in man-computer conversational transactions, AFIPS Conference Proceedings, 1968, 33(1) 267-277, Washington, Thompson.

23. MINOR F.J., Experimental comparison of two keyboard interlock systems, Journal of Engineering Psychology, 1946, 3, 9-15.

24. MINOR F.J., REVESMAN S.K., Evaluation of input devices for a data setting job, Journal of Applied Psychology, 1962, 46, 332-336.

25. MONETA K.B., Optimum physical design of an alphabetical keyboard, Part 1 - survey of the literature, Post Office Engineering Department (U.K.), Research Report No. 20412, 1960.

26. MOOG P., Codierung von Informationen auf Sichtgeraeten, PDV-Berichte Nr. KFK-PDV 61, Gesellschaft fur Kernforschung, Karlsruhe, 1975.

27. MOON P., SPENCER D.E., The visual effect of non-uniform surrounds. JOSA 35, 1945, 233-248.

28. MOORE T.G., The design of tactile coding for machine control buttons, University of Loughborough, LUTERG 39, 1972.

29. MORFIELD M.A., WIESEN R.A., GROSSBERG M., YNTEMA D.B., Initial experiments on the effects of system delay on on-line problem solving, MIT Lincoln Lab. Tech. Note 1959, 5, 1969.

30. MORGAN C.T., COOK J.S., CHAPANIS A., LUND M.W., Human engineering guide to equipment design, McGraw-Hill, New York, 1963.

31. MOSS C.E., MURRAY W.E., PARR W.H., MESSITE J., KARCHES G.J., An electromagnetic radiation survey of selected video display terminals, DHEW/NIOSH, Cincinnatti, Ohio, 1977.

N

1. NEMITZ R., WALDHUBEL T., WENK S., OHM C., Forschung, Entwicklung und Einsatz neuer Technologien in der Text- und Datenerfassung und -Verarbeitung, Bielefeld, Feb. 1978.

2. NEWMAN K.M., DAVIS A.K., Relative merits of spatial and alphabetic encoding of information for a visual display, Journal of Engineering Psychology, 1962, 1, 102-126.

3. NEWMAN K.M., DAVIS A.K., Multidimensional non-redundant encoding of a visual symbolic display, U.S. Navy Electronics Lab. NEL Report 1048, 1961.

4. NICKERSON R.S., Man-computer interaction - a challenge for human factors research, Ergonomics, 1969, 12, 4, 501-517.

5. NICKERSON R.S., ELKIND J.I., CARBONELL J.R., Human factors and the design of time sharing computer systems, Human Factors, 1968, 10, 127-133.

6. NICKERSON R.S., PEW R.W., Oblique steps towards the human factors engineering of interactive computer systems, ARPA, AFOSRC, F44620-71-C-0065, 1971.

7. NITSCH J., Theorie und Skalierung der Ermuedung, Phil., Diss. TU Berlin 1971.

8. NOTTBOHM L., Arbeitsplatzgestaltung als Mittel zur Gesunderhaltung, Arbeitswissenschaft, 1967, 69-72.

9. NYGAARD K., BERGO O.T., The trade unions - new users of research, Proceedings of the ALTORG Conference on "The Impact of Computer and Automation on Management, Structure and Work Design", Berlin, International Institute of Management, 1974.

O

1. ONISHI N., NOMURA H., SAKAI K., Fatigue and strength of upper limb muscles of flight reservation operators, Journal of Human Ergology, 1973, 2, 133-141.

2. OSSANA J.F., SALZER J.H., Technical and human engineering problems in connecting terminals to a time sharing system, AFIPS Proceedings 1970, 37, 355-362.

3. OSTBERG O., CRTs pose health problems for operators, International Journal of Occupational Health and Safety, Nov/Dec 1975.

4. OESTBERG O., Office computerisation in Sweden; worker participation, workplace design considerations, and the reduction of visual strain. Proceedings of NATO Advanced Study Institute on Man-Computer Interaction, Athen, Sept. 5-18, 1976.

5. OSTBERG O., Review of visual strain with special reference to micro-image reading, Proceedings of the International Micrographics Congress, Stockholm Sept. 1976.

6. OSTBERG O., The physiology, psychology and measurement of glare, University of Lulea Technical Report 24T, 1977.

7. OSTBERG O., Terminals are not dangerous, Arbetsmiljoe, 1976, 1, 24-26.

8. OSTBERG O., Designing CRT workplaces. A handbook, Statskontoret, Stockholm, 1976.

9. OSTBERG O., HOLMGREN D., GUNNARSON E., Desks for CRT computer terminals - a review, Arbetarskyddsstyrelsen AMMF 101/76, Stockholm, 1976.

10. OSTBERG O., STONE P.T., Methods for evaluating discomfort glare aspects of lighting, Psychological Reports, Gothenborg, Sweden, 1974, 4, No. 4.

11. OSTBERG O., STONE P.T., BENSON R.A., Free magnitude estimation of discomfort glare and working task difficulty, Psychological Reports, Gothenborg, Sweden, 1975, 5, No. 15.

12. OSTBERG O., Interindividual differences in circadian fatigue patterns of shift workers, British Journal of Industrial Medicine, 1973, 30, 341-351.

13. OTTOSSON A., HOKFELT S., Belysning inom grafisk industri, Ljungforetagen, Orebro, 1975.

14. OWSOWITZ S. SWEETLAND A., Factors affecting coding errors, Rand Memo RM-4346-PR, AD 614415, Rand Corporation, Santa Monica, Cal.

P

1. PALME J., Interactive software for humans, FOA 1 Report 1975, Swedish National Defence Research Institute, C10029-M3(E5), Stockholm.

2. PAUL L.E., SARLANDIS K., BUCKLEY E.P., A human factors comparison of two data entry keyboards, 6th Annual Symposium of the IEEE Professional Group on Human Factors in Electronics, 1965.

3. PETERS T., Arbeitswissenschaft fuer die Bueropraxis, Kiehl Verlag, Ludwigshafen, 1973.

4. PETERS T., Datenterminalarbeitsplaezte aus arbeitsmedizinische-ergonomischer Sicht, Arbeitsmedizin, Sozialmedizin, Praeventivmedizin, Oktober 1975, 10, 193-196.

5. PETERS T., Was heisst eigentlich menschengerechter Arbeitsplatz und Bueroraumgestaltung? Fachtagung des AWV, Cologne,1976-10-19.

6. PETERS T., Arbeitsmedizinische Forderungen an die Bildschirmtextverarbeitung, 5th European Congress for Text Processing, INTERTEXT, Nov. 1977.

7. PETERS J.R., BRISBANE A.D., An alphanumeric word module using planar Ga (As P) arrays in a programmed function keyboard, IEE Conference on Displays, Loughborough, 1971.

8. PHILLIPS A., Computer peripherals and typesetting, HMSO, London, 1968.

9. PLATH D.W., The readability of segmented and conventional numerals, Human Factors, 1970, 12, 5, 493-497.

10. POLLOCK W.T., GILDNER G.G., Study of computer manual input devices, Tech. Doc. Report No. ESD-TDR-63-545, 1963.

11. POOCK G.K., Colour coding effects in compatible and non-compatible display control arrangements, Journal of Applied Psychology, 1969, 53, 4, 301-303.

12. POOLE H.H., Fundamentals of display systems, Spartan Books, Washington 1966.

13. POULTON E.C., The measurement of legibility, Printing Technology, 12, 1968, 72-76.

14. POULTON E.C., Searching for letters or closed shapes in simulated electronic displays, Journal of Applied Psychology, 1968, 52, 348-356.

15. POULTON E.C., Arousing stresses can improve performance whatever people say, Aviation, Space and Environmental Medicine, 1976, 47, 1193-1204.

16. POULTON E.C., BROWN H.C., Rate of comprehension of an existing teleprinter output and of possible alternatives, Journal of Applied Psychology, 1968, 52, 16-21.

17. PRICE D.G., Whither keypunch? Datamation, June 1967.

18. PROMISEL D.M., Visual target location as a function of number and kind of competing signals, Journal of Applied Psychology, 1961, 45, 420-427.

Q

R

1. RADL G., Bildschirme nicht gesundheitsschaedlich, Berufspraxis, VDI-Nachrichten 18, 1978-05-05, 22.

2. RADL W., BURGER H., KVASNCKA E., SCHAAF E., THAU G., Psychische Beanspruchung und Arbeitsunfall, Dortmund 1975.

3. RADL-KOETHE H., SCHUEBERT E., Comparative studies of the legibility of light emitting numerals, IEE Conference on Displays, Loughborough, 1971.

4. RAYNOR K., McCONKIE G.W., What guides a readers eye movements? Vision Research, Vol 16, 828-837, Pergammon Press, London, 1976.

5. REMINGTON R.J., ROGERS M., Keyboard literature survey; Phase 1, bibliography, IBM Corporation, Systems Development Division, Technical Report TR 29, 0042, 43, 1969.

6. RESCHKE B., Eine empirische Studie zur Erfassung der Beanspruchung an Arbeitsplaetzen mit Datensichtgeraeten. Unveroeff. Diplomarbeit, Institut fuer Psychologie/Institut fuer Arbeitswissenschaft TU Berlin 1976.

7. REY P., The interpretation of changes in critical fusion frequency, In W.T. Singleton et al, 'Measurement of Man at Work', London, Taylor & Francis, 1971.

8. REY P., Sichtprobleme an Bildschirmen, Seminar "Visual problems and visual displays", Geneva 1977-11-16.

9. RICHE C.V., KINNEY G.C., Studies in display legibility, NATO AGARD Conference Proceedings No. 23, 1969.

10. RINGEL S., Information transfer from command-control displays, NAT AGARD Conference Proceedings No. 23, 1969.

11. RINGEL S., HAMMER C., Information assimilation from alphanumeric displays; amount and density of information presented, U.S. Army Personnel Research Office Report TRN-141, AD 601973,1964.

12. RINGEL S., VICINO F.L., Information assimilation from alphanumeric displays; amount of information presented and removed, U.S. Army Personnel Research Office Report TRN-139, 1964.

13. ROEDLER F., Arbeiten aus dem Bundesgesundheitsamt zur Problematik fensterloser Raeume, Bundesgesundheitsblatt 13, 1970, 269-276.

14. ROHMERT W., Mechanisierung und Automatisierung aus Arbeitswissenschaftlicher Sicht, Arbeitsmedizin, Sozialmedizin, Arbeitshygiene, 1970, 12, 305-309.

15. ROHMERT W., Ermittlung von Erholungspausen fuer statische Arbeit des Menschen, Int. Zeitung f. angew. Physiolog. 1960, 18, 123-164.

16. ROHMERT W., LUCZAK H., Zur ergonomischen Beurteilung informatorischer Arbeit, Int. Zeitung f. angew. Physiolog. 1973, 31, 209-229.

17. RUBIN J., The viewing characteristics of negative vs positive microfilm images as they affect visual fatigue, National Micro News, 1957, No. 29.

18. RUPP B.A., HIRSCH R.S., Human factors of workstations with display terminals, IBM Document HFC-22, Nov. 1977.

S

1. SACKMAN H., Experimental analysis of man-computer problem solving, Human Factors, 1970, 12, 2, 187-201.

2. SCHMIDTKE H., SCHMALE H., Beziehungen zwischen Sehschaerfe und Arbeitserfolg, Arbeitsmedizinische Fragen in der Opthalmologie, Vol. 1, Symposium, Basel, Karger Verlag 1969.

3. SCHMIDTKE H., HOFFMANN E., SCHMIDTKE G., Die psychophysische Belastung an Ausgewaehlten Arbeitsplaetzen elektronischer Datenverarbeitungsanlagen. Siehe Soziale Probleme der Automation in Bayern. Bayerisches Staatsministerium fuer Arbeit und Soziale Fuersorge, 1969.

4. SCHOBER H.A.W., DEHLER H., KASSEL R., Accommodation during observation with optical instruments, Journal of the Optical Society of America, 1970, 60, 103-107.

5. SCHMIDTKE H., Die Ermuedung, Bern/Stuttgart 1965.

6. SCHULZ B., Arbeitswissenschaftliche Untersuchungen an Datensichtgeraeten, Unveroeff. Diplomarbeit TU Berlin 1976.

7. SCHULZE H.H., Organisation des Buero- und Verwaltungsbereiches. Stichwort in: Grochla E. (Hrsg.), Handwoerterbuch der Organisation, Stuttgart 1973.

8. SCHUTY H.G., An evaluation of formats for graphic trend displays, Human Factors, 1961, 3, 99-107.

9. SCHUTY H.G., An evaluation of methods for presentation of graphic multiple trends, Human Factors, 1961, 3, 108-119.

10. SEGAL J., Die physiologische Wirkung des Lichtes von Leuchtstoffroehren, Sowjetwissenschaft, Naturwissenschaftliche Beitraege (Berlin), 1961, 366-373.

11. SEPPAELAEA P., TURUNEN M., Ergonomics aspects of microfilm reading, Tyoeterveyslaitoksen Tutkimuksia, Helsinki, 1974, No. 87.

12. SHACKEL B., Ergonomics in the design of a large digital /computer console, Ergonomics, 1962, 5, 229-241.

13. SHACKEL B., SHIPLEY P., Man-computer interaction - a review of ergonomics literature and research, EMI Report DMP3472, 1970.

14. SHERMAN R.A., Eyes for the job, Industrial Medicine, 1970, 39, 60-63.

15. SHIFFRIN R.M., ATKINSON R.C., Storage and retrieval proceses in long-term memory. Psychol. rev. 76, 1969, 179-193.

16. SHURTLEFF D.A., OWEN D., Studies in display symbol legibility, Part IV: Leroy and courtney symbols. Mitre Corp. Bedford, Mass. 1966.

17. SIEGEL A.I., FISCHL M.A., Dimensions of visual information displays, Journal of Applied Psychology, 1971, 55, 470-476.

18. SILVER C.A., Decision quality as a means of visual display effectiveness, Journal of Applied Psychology, 1966, 50, 109-115.

19. SIMONS D.J., DAY E., GOODELL W., WOLFF H.G., Experimental studies of headache: Muscles of the scalp and neck as sources of pain, Research Publications of the Association of Research in Nervous and Mental Disease, 1942, 23, 228-244.

20. SIMPSON G.C., A comparison of the legibility of three types of electronic signal displays, Ergonomics, 1971, 14, 4, 497-507.

21. SMITH S.L., Colour coding and visual search, Journal of Experimental Psychology, 1962, 64, 434-440.

22. SMITH S.L., GOODWIN N.C., Blink coding for information display, Human Factors, 1971, 13, 3, 283-290.

23. SMITH W.A., Accuracy of manual entries in data collection devices, Journal of Applied Psychology, 1967, 51, 362-368.

24. SPENCER H., REYNOLDS L., Factors affecting the acceptability of microforms as a reading medium, Royal College of Art, London, Readability of Print Research Unit, 1976.

25. SOMMER J., Arbeitsleistung und Beleuchtung, Arbeit und Leistung, 1969, 23, 142-158.

26. SOMMER J., HERBST C.H., Einfluss der Beleuchtung auf die Arbeit and der Schreibmaschine, Lichttechnik, 1971, 23, 23-26.

27. STATSKONTORET Laegesrapport, Terminalfunktioner och terminalarbetsplats, Svenska Statskontoret, 1974-09-10.

28. STEFANSSON S.B., DARBY C.E., WILKINS A.J., BINNIE C.D., MARLTON A.P., SMITH A.T., STOCKLEY A.V., Television epilepsy and pattern sensitivity, British Medical Journal, 2, 1977, 88-90.

29. STENHOUSE STEWART D.D., Some observations on a tendency to near-point esophoria and possible contributory factors, British Journal of Ophthalmology, 1945, 24, 37-42.

30. STEWART T.F.M., OSTBERG O., MACKAY C.J., Computer terminal ergonomics, a review of recent human factors literature. University of Loughborough 1974.

31. STEWART T.F.M., Displays and the software interface, Applied Ergonomics, 7.3, 1976 137-146.

32. STEWART T.F.M., Designing systems for people, Advanced Data Entry Techniques Conference, London, Sept. 1978.

33. STEWART T.F.M., Human factors aspects of working with VDUs, in "Visual display units and their application", ed. D. Grover, IPC Science & Technology Press, London 1976.

34. STOCKBRIDGE H.C.W., Microshape-coded knobs or buttons for Post Office keys, CSEE, MOD Tech. Memo. 67, 1959.

35. STOCKBRIDGE H.C.W., Microshape-coded push buttons, CEPRE MOD Tech. Memo. 137, 1959.

36. STOCKER A.C., Display, paper and lighting: the visual system in command centres, Information Display, 1964, 1(1), 16-26.

37. STOCKER A.C., The size and contrast of hard-copy symbols, Information Display, 1966, 3(5), 36-42.

T

1. TAYLOR R.L., Reading spatially transformed digits. J. Exp. Psychol. 96, 1972, 396-399.

2. THOMAS M.P., Human coding performance; a review, University of Loughborough LUTERG 66, 1972.

3. THOMSON F.M., Polarity and projection mode effects on microform reading performance, Dissertation, Department of Industrial Engineering. Purdue University, 1974.

4. TIRRELL J.A., KLEMMER E.T., The effects of coding on keying rate, IBM Research Report RC-775, 1962.

5. TREIER P., Zur Ermuedungsproblematik und zur Pausengestaltung, Angewandte Arbeitswissenscahft, Mitteilung der IfaA, Koln, 75, June 1978.

U

1. UDRIS I., Beanspruchungsaspekte der Arbeitsorganisation im Dienstleistungssektor. Referat gehalten auf der 17. Arbeitstagung der Sektion Arbeits- und Betriebspsychologie des Berufsverbandes Deutscher Psychologen (BDP), Kiel, 1975.

2. UDRIS I., BARTH H., Mental load in clerical work, Proceedings of the 6th Congress of the International Ergonomics Association, 1976, 192-197, Santa Monica, Cal, Human Factors Society.

3. ULRICH E., Some experiments on the function of mental training in the acquisition of motor skills, Ergonomics, 1967, 10, 4, 411-419.

4. ULLRICH O.A., WALKUP L.E., Psychophysical aspects of micro-image reading, Battelle Technical Review 1966, 15, 10-14.

5. UNGAR P.E., Sight at work, Work study, March 1971, 46-48.

V

1. VAN COTT H.P., KINKADE R.G., Human engineering guide to equipment design, US Government Printing Office, Washington, 1972.

2. VAN GEFFEN L.J.H.J., A review of keyboarding skills, Advances in Computer Typesetting, 2-11, Proceedings of the International Typesetting Conference, IOP, London.

3. VARTABEDIAN A.G., Human factors evaluation of several cursor forms for use on alphanumeric CRT displays, IEEE Transaction on MMS 11, 2, 132-137, 1970.

4. VARTABEDIAN A.G., Legibility of symbols on CRT displays, Applied Ergonomics, 1971, 2, 3, 130-132.

5. VARTABEDIAN A.G., The effects of letter size, case and generation method on CRT display search time, Human Factors, 1971, 13, 4, 363-368.

W

1. WALLIS D., Human factors in the design and use of naval equipment, Royal Navy PRC Report RNP 60/962 1960.

2. WALTERS F., DC gas discharge matrix displays, IEE Conference on Displays, Loughborough, 1971.

3. WEALE R.A., Retinal illumination and age, Trans. IES, London, 1961, 26, 95.

4. WEAR L.K., DORF R.C., An interactive keyboard for man-computer communication, AFIPS Proceedings, 36, 1970.

5. WEICHARD H., Die Anpassung des Arbeitsplatzes an den Menschen aus arbeitsmedizinischer Sicht, Arbeitsmedizin, Sozialmedizin, Arbeitshygiene, 1966, 11, 393-397.

6. WEST L.J., Vision and kinesthesis in the acquisition of typewriting skill, Journal of Applied Psychology, 1967, 51, 161-166.

7. WESTON H.C., Visual fatigue, Illuminating Engineering, 1954, 49, 63-76.

8. WESTON H.C., Sight, Light and Work, Lewis, London, 1962 (2nd edition).

9. WESTON H.C., ADAMS S., Further experiments on the use of special spectacles in very fine processes, Reports of the Industrial Health Research Board, 1929, No. 57.

10. WHITFIELD D., Validating the application of ergonomics to equipment design - a case study, Ergonomics, 1964, 7, 165-174.

11. WOODSON W.E., CONOVER D.W., Human engineering guide for equipment design, Cambridge University Press, London 1964.

X

Y

1. YLLO A., The bio-technology of card punching, Ergonomics,1962, 5, 75-79.

Z

1. ZARAT M., Cataracts in avionic environments, British Journal of Ophthalmology, 61, 1978, 380.

APPENDIX IV

GLOSSARY OF TERMS

A

Absorptance -- That proportion of the quantity of light incident on an object which is absorbed within the object, the energy normally being converted into heat.

Acceleration potential -- The voltage between the cathode in a *cathode ray tube*, CRT, and the tube face which attracts the beam of focussed electrons causing them to impinge on the *phosphor*.

Access time -- The time interval between the instant at which data is called for and the instant at which delivery is completed. See also *response time*.

Accommodation -- The ability of the eyes to adjust to or "accommodate" different viewing distances.

Acoustic coupler -- A *modem* that enables a *remote terminal* to be connected with the central processor using a conventional telephone receiver and by dialling over a public or leased telephone line.

Adaptation -- The adjustment of the eyes and the sense of vision in relation to the amount of available light.

Alphanumeric -- Pertaining to a character set that contains both letters and numerals.

Aniseikonia -- A visual condition among spectacle wearers whereby the image of a given object on the retina of one eye may be larger than that of the other. This condition is caused by differences in lens strength.

Application package -- A programme or set of programmes designed to perform a given function or set of functions, e.g. typesetting, text editing.

Artificial click -- A type of *auditory feedback* in which the operator of a VDT hears an artificial click that replaces the real click from a typewriter mechanism.

Aspect ratio -- The ratio between the height and width of the viewing area of a VDT screen.

ASCII -- Pronounced "asky". Strictly USASCII, the USA standard data code; the U.S. version of the ISO 7-bit data code.

Associative coding -- A type of coding in which a unique code is associated with an item of data, e.g. telephone dialling codes.

Astigmatism -- A visual disorder caused by an uneven curvature of the cornea.

Asynchronous data channel -- A communication channel capable of transmitting data but not timing the information. Sometimes called an Anisochronous data channel.

Asynchronous modem -- A *modem* which cannot transmit timing information in addition to the data; a modem which does not require synchronisation with the associated terminal equipment. Sometimes called an "anisochronous" modem.

Asynchronous terminal -- A terminal using the start-stop transmission method.

Auditory feedback -- Indication that an action has been effected, e.g. the actioning of a keystroke by the detection of an audible signal, e.g. a click.

Auxilliary keyset -- A separate pad or block of keys, usually numeric, in addition to the main alphanumeric keyset on the terminal keyboard. Usually, but not necessarily, an integral part of the main keyboard.

Auxilliary storage -- Any peripheral device, e.g. tape, disc etc., upon which data may be stored. As opposed to the *internal storage* capacity of the central computer. See also *Backing store*.

B

Backing store -- An intermediate storage medium, e.g. paper tape, card, disc etc., onto which data is entered from an off line terminal for later processing by the central computer. Also any auxilliary storage medium.

Badge Reader -- A card, usually of plastic, containing a notched or magnetic stripe code for identifying the operator.

Bandwidth -- The range of signal frequencies that can be transmitted by a communication channel with defined maximum loss or signal distortion.

Barrel distortion -- See *Pin cushion distortion.*

Baud -- A measure of the transmission speed capability of a communications line or system. In a sequence of binary signals, 1 Baud=1 Bit/sec.

Bin -- Colloquial term sometimes used to describe *buffer* storage in a computer system.

Binary code -- A coding system employing the binary digits *ones and zeros* to represent a letter, digit or other character in a computer.

Binary digit, Bit -- The smallest unit of information and storage capacity in a computer system. Also a single pulse in a sequence or train of pulses.

Burn resistance -- The ability of a phosphor to withstand local overheating or "burn" due to the conversion into heat of the residual energy of the electron beam, i.e. that part of the electron beam energy that is not converted into visible light.

Bus -- A path over which information is transferred in a digital computer from any of several sources to any of several destinations. Also called a channel, line or trunk.

Byte -- A collection of 8 bits.

C

Cathode ray tube, CRT -- An electronic vacuum tube in which an electron beam is generated and used to energise a phosphor screen which thereby emits visible light.

Central processing unit, CPU -- The computer at the centre of an *on-line* system which performs the processing according to the *applications package*. Also called *host computer.*

Character -- The actual or coded representation of a digit, letter or special symbol but not a space.

Character generator -- An encoding device which converts a stored code into appropriate information in the correct order for writing on the *cathode ray tube* face so that the appropriate character image is formed and becomes visible to the VDT operator.

Character rounding (enhancement) -- The technique of improving the shape of a displayed character within its basic limitations by stretching or moving certain dots with respect to others.

Check bit -- A unit within a *byte* or *word* of data which is used to check the validity of the data.

Chord keying -- A keyboard safeguard in which two or more keys must be depressed simultaneously in order to action critical commands from the keyboard.

Clock -- Shorthand term for the source or sources of timing signals used in *isochronous data channels*.

Clock rate -- The speed or frequency at which the *clock* oscillator produces control pulses which schedule the operation of the computer.

Cluster -- A data network in which two or more terminals are connected to a line or data channel at a single point.

Code -- A system of symbols and rules for use in representing information.

Command -- A pulse, signal or set of signals that occur in a computer as the result of an instruction and which initiate one step in the process of executing the instruction.

Concentrator -- A device used to divide a data channel into two or more channels of lower average speed, dynamically allocating channel space according to demand in order to maximise data throughput at all times.

Contention -- A condition in a computer system when two or more terminals attempt to transmit data in a communication line at the same time.

Control character -- A character whose occurrence in a particular context initiates, modifies or stops a function. There are 32 such characters in the ASCII data code.

Control unit -- That part of a central or intermediate processor that directs the sequence of operations, interprets the coded instructions and initiates the proper signals to the computer circuits to execute the instructions.

Core (storage) -- The memory or *internal storage* capacity of a computer.

Critical fusion frequency (CFF) -- As the frequency of a flickering stimulus increases, a point is reached where the flicker ceases and the individual sensations are fused into a continuous, uniform sensation. This point is known as the 'critical fusion frequency'.

CRT -- *Cathode ray tube.*

Cursor -- A symbol or sign which acts as a flag to identify one and only one of the character spaces on the display screen of a VDT that will be affected by a command or action.

Cursor control keys -- Those keys which specifically control the movement of the cursor on a VDT; necessary for editing operations and for rapid access to any part of the display screen.

Cycle time -- The length of time used by a computer for one operation, usually measured in micro- or nanoseconds.

D

Data reduction -- The removal of superfluous information from a message.

Data store -- The part of a terminal in which received data is held during operation. A method of storing data, usually in binary coded form.

Data transmission -- The automatic transfer of data between two points, usually the computer and a terminal, in a computer system. The data are transferred via a telegraph, telephone or radio circuit.

Delete -- The ability to remove surplus material from text, simultaneously eliminating the gaps which would otherwise be formed.

Demodulation -- The process of retrieving an original signal from a modulated carrier wave. This technique is used in data sets to make communications signals compatible with business machine signals.

Directory -- A meaningful list of the contents of a system pertaining to a given parameter, e.g. user's name, subject head etc.

Disc drive -- The device which reads information from or writes information on a magnetic disc.

Display memory -- The internal storage capacity of a VDT to permit a greater character display capacity than the screen is able to accommodate. The display memory is accessed by means of a scrolling facility.

Downtime -- The time during which a computer system is not functioning properly.

Dot matrix characters -- Character images on a VDT display screen that are represented by an appropriate number and location of dots within a defined cell or "matrix" of dot positions.

Dot matrix memory -- Commercially available integrated circuits which produce defined dot sequences when driven by the code and timing of a character generator.

E

EBCDIC -- *E*xtended *B*inary *C*oded *D*ecimal *I*nterchange *C*ode; an 8-bit character code which can represent 256 characters and which is used primarily in IBM equipment.

Envelope -- The part of a total message which is concerned with the control and command of transmission to and from defined destinations of the data message contained within it.

F

Facsimile character generation -- The technique of writing characters on a display screen by copying those already written and stored in a master set.

File -- A collection of related records, usually, but not necessarily, arranged in sequence according to a *directory* key contained in each record.

Fixed data -- Data that is written on the display screen of a VDT but which cannot be altered by the operator.

Flicker -- A form of image instability caused by the perceived dimming and brightening of the character images as they are *refreshed* on the display screen. See also *Critical fusion frequency (C.F.F.)*.

Formatting -- The structuring of the display screen into protected and accessible areas within which various actions can be performed in fields.

Form filling -- The entering of information into pre-defined areas or fields in the display screen. Appropriate for buffered terminals only.

Full duplex -- Pertaining to the simultaneous, independent transmission of data in both directions over a communications line. Also called duplex; see also *half duplex* and *simplex*.

Full duplex channel -- A channel capable of transmitting data in both directions at the same time.

Function keyset -- A collection of keys, each of which is associated with a specific *command*.

G

Gas panel -- A display screen formed from an array of small tubes, e.g. neon tubes, the selective illumination of which is used to generate the desired character images.

Glare -- A visual condition caused by excessive luminance variations within the field of vision, e.g. when bright sources of light such as windows or lamps or their reflected images fall in the line of sight.

Grain -- The particle size of the phosphor coating on the interior surface of the CRT face.

H

Half duplex transmission -- The alternate and independent transmission of data in both directions, but in only one direction at a time, over a communication line. See also *full duplex, simplex*.

Half duplex channel -- A data channel capable of transmitting data in both directions but in only one direction at a time.

Half shift enhancement -- A method for improving the shape of dot matrix characters by selectively moving some of the horizontally disposed dots through a distance equal to one half of the dot spacing, to the right or left as required.

Hard copy unit -- A printer associated with a processing system which, on command from the operator or programme, can print out the information displayed on a VDT screen or contained in storage.

Hardware -- The physical equipment which makes up a computer system, e.g. CPU, terminals and other input/output (I/O) and storage devices. As opposed to the programming software.

Head -- A device that reads, writes or erases data on a storage medium, e.g. the fixed or moving electromagnetic heads used to read, write and erase data on magnetic discs or drums. Also the set of perforating and reading devices used for punching and reading paper tape.

Header -- A series of characters that precedes a message giving addressing, source and other information concerning the message to follow. The front part of the message *envelope* carrying the data necessary to allow the system to transmit the message to and from the correct destinations.

Holding time -- The time during which a communication line is in use for transmission.

Host computer -- The central computer on which the application programmes are run. The central computer in a centralised computer network, also called *CPU* and *Mainframe*.

Hyperopia -- A visual disorder caused by insufficient refractive power of the eye due to which only objects far from the eyes appear to be in focus. Also called 'long sight'.

I

Illuminance -- That part of the luminous flux that is incident on a unit area of a surface, i.e. a measure of the quantity of light with which a surface is illuminated. Measured in units of Lux (lx).

Image stability -- The perceived stability, i.e. freedom from flicker and movement, of the character images on the display screen. The main causes of image instability are fluctuations of the voltage supply, e.g. variations in mains voltage, voltage spikes etc. scan line *jitter* and *flicker*.

Implosion shield -- A protective perspex plate installed in front of the CRT tube face to protect the operator in the event of tube failure.

Intelligent terminal -- A terminal which incorporates a microprocessor capable of performing processing functions independently of the central processor.

Interface -- An electronic device which enables one piece of equipment to communicate with or control another.

Interlace -- A technique used in television receivers and some VDTs in which alternate frames are displayed so that their raster scans interlace. In this way, a basic rate of 25 frames/second, for example, is made to appear refreshed at 50 frames/second.

Internal storage -- The total memory or storage capacity within and controlled by a central processor.

Isochronous data channel -- A communication channel capable of transmitting timing information in addition to data. Also called a synchronous data channel.

J

Jitter -- A type of visual display image instability in which the individual lines appear to oscillate due to too low signal strength or poor synchronisation. Also called line jitter.

K

Key force -- The force required to depress the key so as to ensure positive contact and the actioning of the keystroke.

Key travel -- The displacement of the key from its static to fully depressed position; also called stroke.

Kill -- A commonly-used expression to denote the deletion of information from a data storage area.

Kill file -- A storage area to which all or selected items of deleted or "killed" information is committed enabling recall at a later stage if necessary. A useful attribute of systems handling information, the inadvertent deletion of which may have serious consequences.

Kinesthetic feedback -- Indication that an action has been effected, e.g. the actioning of a keystroke, by the sensation of touch, position or movement.

L

Latency -- The time required to locate the first character of a location in storage; calculated as access time minus work time.

Leased line -- A telephone or telegraph line leased from the postal authorities or their "carrier" and dedicated to use by the lessee.

Leased network -- A data network of telephone or telegraph lines or channels leased from the postal authority or their "carrier" and dedicated to use by the lessee.

Lens system -- An assembly of magnetic and/or electrostatic components which modifies the path of the electron beam emitted from the cathode of a *CRT*. The lens system is used to achieve a sharp focus of the beam at the tube face.

Limited distance modem -- A simplified *modem* designed for operation over distances up to about 35 miles, usually over privately owned wires where the bandwidth limitations of the telephone system do not apply. Sometimes called a "baseband" or "short-haul modem".

Line switching -- A method of establishing communication in a switched network, e.g. by dialling, whereby the channel so established remains dedicated to the user for the duration of his "call".

Line time -- The time that the transmission line is occupied in transmitting a message.

Local terminal -- A VDT that is linked directly to a computer or control unit.

M

Machine language -- A language that is used directly by a computer; a "machine language programme" is a set of instructions written using a code that the computer is able to identify.

Mainframe -- The central processing unit or *CPU* of a large computer system.

Menu -- A collection of items, e.g. a list or *directory* of the contents of a given *file*, from which the operator may select.

Merge -- To combine two or more sets of data into a single set.

Message format -- Rules for the placement of parts of a message, e.g. heading, address, text and end of message.

Message switching -- The switching technique of receiving a message or group of messages, storing until the proper outgoing circuit and station are available and then re-transmitting toward their destination.

Microcomputer -- An integrated circuit performing basic programme instructions.

Micromesh filter -- A fine mesh that is placed in front of or in contact with a VDT display screen in order to reduce the visibility of reflections on the screen.

Minicomputer -- A computer designed with integrated circuitry but with less storage capacity than large computers but usually able to perform the same or similar tasks.

Modem -- A contraction of the term "modulator-demodulator". A device used to convert serial digital data from a transmitting terminal to a signal that is suitable for transmission over a telephone channel, and to reconvert the signal to serial digital data for acceptance by a receiving terminal.

Multi-dropped line -- A single communication line to which terminals are attached at more than one point.

Multiplex -- To interleave or simultaneously transmit two or more messages on a single data channel.

Multiplexer -- A device used to divide a data channel into two or more independent fixed data channels of lower speed; see also *concentrator*.

Multi-point -- A line or data channel connecting terminals at more than one point. Sometimes called multi-drop; see also *Cluster*.

Multi-threading -- The apparent ability of a computer to handle more than one terminal user at any given time.

Myopia -- A visual disorder caused by excessive refractive power of the eyes with the result that only objects close to the eyes appear to be in focus. Also called 'short sight'.

N

Narrative format -- A basic, single column display format, i.e. a format lacking in tabular or any other specific type of formatting constraint.

N-key roll-over -- A keyboard characteristic in which the keyboard is able to generate all keystrokes in the correct sequence when two or more keys are depressed at the same time.

Non-erasable storage -- Storage media, e.g. punch cards, paper tape, the information on which cannot be erased to permit re-use.

Non-volatile storage -- Storage media that retain information in the absence of power, e.g. magnetic drums, tapes, discs etc.

O

Off-line system -- A systems configuration in which the input/output devices, e.g. the terminals, are not in direct communication with the central processor.

On-line system -- A systems configuration in which the input /output devices, e.g. the terminals, are in direct communication with the central processor.

P

Page scrolling -- A technique used in recalling information from the *display memory* in which, as the information is recalled, the entire screen content is renewed to make room for the new data. Analogous to the page-by-page presentation and indexing of printed information. See also *roll scrolling, pan scrolling*.

Pan scrolling -- A variation of *roll scrolling* in which the movement of the lines of data up and down the screen is smoother, i.e. less jerky, than the conventional roll scroll and more similar to the smooth panning of the credits following a TV programme. True pan scrolling cannot be achieved on a CRT display employing raster scanning but the effect can be approached by roll scrolling at slow speed.

Parity -- The condition of the number of items in a group, e.g. bits in a byte, being odd or even. Used as a basis for checking certain types of error in data transmission.

Parity bit -- A binary digit or *bit* appended to a group of bits to make their sum always odd or always even.

Parity check -- The automatic transmission of additional *parity bits* to enable the receiving device to check the accuracy of the transmitted data.

Password -- A word or code used to identify the operator of a VDT or computer system.

Peripheral equipment -- The input/output units and auxilliary storage of a computer system.

Persistence -- The ability of a screen *phosphor* to continue to emit light after the original stimulation has ceased.

Phoria -- A term used to describe an imbalance of the external muscles which control the orbital position and movement of the eyeballs.

Phosphor -- A coating of luminescent material which emits visible light when struck by a beam of electrons within an evacuated glass tube such as a *CRT*.

Phosphor efficiency -- The proportion of the energy of the electron beam that is converted to light energy by the phosphor.

Photopic vision -- A term used to describe vision and the spectral sensitivity of the human eyes when light-adapted, e.g. in daylight.

Pin cushion distortion -- A type of image distortion on the face of a CRT due to the different radii of curvature of the electron beam and the CRT screen. Without corrective circuitry, a line drawn across the screen would appear to bow in an arc, the effect being greatest along the edges of the screen. Also called 'barrel distortion'.

Plasma panel -- An assembly of small neon tubes arranged in matrix form to provide a display screen.

Point-to-point connection -- A communication line or channel that connects two and only two devices, e.g. a terminal and a central processor.

Polarisation filter -- A type of screen filter in which the intensity of the reflection of incident light is reduced through the polarising action of the filter. That is, only light waves in one plane are allowed to escape the field of the filter.

Polling -- The interrogation of each terminal in a multi-point or clustered network by the computer to determine whether it is ready to receive or transmit data. This is necessary if data transmission can only be initiated by the computer.

Polling overhead -- The time which is lost due to the computer having to make routine polling interrogations of all terminals in order to remain in control of the system.

Presbyopia -- The reduction of accommodation with age due to a progressive inability of the lens to change its shape thus limiting the range over which objects can be brought into focus.

Processor utilisation -- The amount of time, usually expressed as a percentage of total available time, during which the processor is engaged in performing necessary and useful tasks.

Protected field -- A designated field on a display screen within which no keyboard initiated action can make any change.

Protocol -- A set of rules governing the flow of information within a communication system.

Q

R

Random access -- A system of *file management*, usually on disc, in which data may be accessed independent of its file location or the location of the data previously accessed.

Raster -- The pattern of *scan lines* traced across the face of the *CRT* by the electron beam.

Raster scan -- A method of scanning a CRT display in a series of horizontal lines. The technique used in television receivers and most types of VDT incorporating refreshed CRTs.

Redundancy -- That part of the total information content of a message which can be eliminated without loss of essential information. Also a type of information, the full content of which may be predicted from a knowledge of only part of the total information. In this sense, human language is more redundant than most types of numerical data.

Redundancy checking -- A method of error detection involving the transmission of additional or redundant data together with the message data in such a way that, by comparing the two sets of data, the receiving terminal can determine to a certain level of probability whether or not an error has occurred in transmission.

Reflectance -- The ratio between the quantity of light that is reflected from a given surface and the total quantity of light that is incident on the same surface.

Reflected glare -- A *glare* condition caused by the reflection of bright sources of light, e.g. windows, luminaires etc., from illuminated surfaces within the field of vision.

Refresh -- A technique used to regularly energise the *phosphor* coating in the CRT in order to ensure an apparently continuous and stable, but in fact transient image.

Refreshed CRT -- A cathode ray tube in which the image must be continuously refreshed in order to remain visible.

Refresh rate -- The frequency with which the image on the face of *refreshed CRT* is refreshed.

Remote connection -- A connection in which one device, e.g. a VDT, is located remote from the computer system. This generally means that the data connection is via a leased or switched telephone line.

Remote terminal -- A VDT with its own refresh store, editing capability and a *modem* interface.

Response time -- The elapsed time between the generation of an enquiry at a data terminal and receipt of the response at the same terminal.

Rim guard CRT -- A CRT with a tension band clamped around the edges to prevent the flying out of fragments in the event of a tube failure. In practice, the tension band helps to guard against the electron gun bursting through the face plate.

Roll-over -- A keyboard characteristic that permits the correct interpretation of keystroke sequence when two or more keys are depressed at the same time; see also *Two-key roll-over, n-key roll-over*.

Roll scroll -- A technique used in recalling information from the *display memory* in which, as each line of text is recalled, all existing lines on the display screen move up or down by one line to make room for the new line. The movement of the lines of data is discontinuous and similar to the line feed movement of paper in a line printer.

S

Scotopic vision -- A term used to describe vision and the spectral sensitivity of the human eyes when dark-adapted, e.g. at night.

Screen Buffer -- The buffer from which the display on a VDT is refreshed.

Screen format -- The structure or layout of a visual display, e.g. column text format (narrative), tabular, division into protected and unprotected areas, etc.

Serial data transmission -- A method of data transmission whereby data characters or *bytes* are transmitted one *bit* at a time over a single path.

Single-line buffer -- A necessary part of a television raster generator, in which a whole line of information must be available sequentially up to ten times for horizontal slicing.

Site polling -- A technique in which all terminals at a given site are polled as a group, the local controller assuming the role of supervisor for this purpose. Site polling reduces the *polling overhead.*

Specific poll -- The process by which a particular terminal is invited to transmit or receive a message.

Spooling -- The writing onto a *backing store* of data which is normally sent directly to the central processor or to some other peripheral device. The data is usually stored temporarily on the backing store until it can be despooled, i.e. read from the backing store and sent to its eventual destination.

Stand-alone terminal -- A terminal which can be directly connected with a *modem*, i.e. not one of a terminal *cluster.*

Stand-alone processing system -- A processing system which does not depend on a host processing computer for normal operation.

Start-stop transmission -- A method of serial data transmission in which each character or *byte* is transmitted as a self-contained piece of information needing no additional synchronising or timing information to be transmitted.

Status poll -- A computer-initiated request for information about the present status of a terminal.

Storage tube -- A special purpose cathode ray tube with a wire mesh on which alphanumeric or graphical information is stored. The information is displayed on the screen without refreshing from a dynamic store.

Stored programme VDT -- A VDT whose principal external and internal characteristics are contained within a stored programme control section.

Stripping -- The process of removing the *head* and *tail* parts of a message *envelope*, leaving only the essential data for processing or display.

T

Tabulation markers -- Symbols used to designate *protected fields* in the visual display but may also be used as tabulation settings similar to the use of tab settings on a typewriter.

Tactile feedback -- Indication that an action has been effected, e.g. a keystroke, by the sense of touch.

Tail -- The series of codes that are transmitted with, but immediately after the message to denote end of message; the last part of the message *envelope*. See also *Header.*

Teletype-compatible terminal -- A hardcopy terminal or VDT which is compatible with a teletype either at the functional or software level.

Television (TV) scan -- A regular series of horizontal *scan lines* from the top to bottom of the CRT face. Both line scan and frame rates are defined by international standard, e.g. for a 625 line system.

Terminal -- An input-output (I-O) device for transmitting and-or receiving data on a communication line.

Thin-film layer filter -- A vapour deposited screen filter layer with a thickness equal to one quarter of the wavelength of light; also called a +-4 filter.

Transformational coding -- A method of data coding in which the data is transformed into coded form by the application of a strict set of transformational rules.

Transformational coding -- A method of data coding in which the data is transformed into coded form by the application of a strict set of transformational rules.

Transmittance -- The ratio between the quantity of light that is transmitted through a given surface and the quantity of light that is incident on the same surface.

Transposition error -- A keyboarding error in which characters are keyed in reverse order.

Tube shield -- A shield or shroud that is sometimes installed around the display screen of a VDT in order to reduce or avoid reflections.

Turn-round time -- The time taken to reverse the direction of data flow in a *half duplex channel*.

Two-key lock-out -- A keyboard characteristic that inhibits all further keyboard action when more than one key is depressed.

Two-key roll-over -- A keyboard characteristic that permits any two keystroke sequence to be correctly interpreted when the two keys are depressed at the same time.

Two-shot moulding -- A technique used in the manufacture of keys in which each key is moulded in a two-stage process. Keys manufactured in this way are durable and the key legends are moulded deeply into the surface.

Typamatic key -- A key which automatically repeats the character or function associated with it when the key is depressed for more than a short period of time, typically about half a second.

U

Unit buffer terminal -- A terminal which has no cummunication buffer, e.g. a teletype terminal.

Unprotected field -- Any part of a visual display, the structure or contents of which may be altered on command from the VDT operator.

UPS -- *U*ninterruptable *P*ower *S*upply. A voltage stabilised mains power supply to a computer system to safeguard against fluctuations of voltage caused by loading variations at the central power station, switching on and off of heavy items of equipment etc.

V

Variable data -- Data on a VDT screen that may be modified, e.g. added to or deleted, by the operator.

VDT -- *V*isual *D*isplay *T*erminal; a terminal which comprises a keyboard for data input and a display screen for control of the input.

Vector drawing -- A method of character generation in which the electron beam is steered so that the required character shape is 'written' on the face of the CRT. The beam brightness is also controlled so that only the required strokes are made visible.

Visual acuity -- The ability of the eye to discriminate or resolve fine detail. One of the best available measures of legibility.

Voice grade channel -- A communication channel which is suitable for the transmission of speech, digital or analogue data. The bandwidth of voice grade channels usually extends from about 300 to 3500 Hz.

Volatile memory -- A storage medium on which the information is lost when the power supply is turned off, e.g. delay-line storage.

W

Word -- A storage location usually comprising 8, 12, or 16 bits. Two characters, for example, may be stored in one word of a 16-bit computer. In some computers, the principle of chaining is used to achieve longer words.

Word length -- The number of bits or characters in a word.

Working level -- When operating the keyboard in the seating position, the working level is the distance between the underside of the thighs resting on the seat of the chair and the underside of the hands in the keyboarding posture.

X

Y

Z